Security

translation
TRANSNATION
SERIES EDITOR **EMILY APTER**

A list of titles in the series appears at the back of the book.

Security

POLITICS, HUMANITY, AND THE PHILOLOGY OF CARE

John T. Hamilton

PRINCETON UNIVERSITY PRESS

Princeton and Oxford

press.princeton.edu

Library of Congress Cataloging-in-Publication Data

Hamilton, John T.
    Security : politics, humanity, and the philology of care / John T.
    Hamilton.
        p. cm. — (Translation/transnation)
    Includes bibliographical references (p.) and index.
    ISBN 978-0-691-15752-8 (hardcover : alk. paper)   1. Caring—Religious
    aspects—Christianity.   2. Caring.   3. Security, International.   I Title.
    BV4647.S9H35 2013
    128—dc23   2012032275

British Library Cataloging-in-Publication Data is available

This book has been composed in Minion

Printed on acid-free paper. ∞

Printed in the United States of America

10 9 8 7 6 5 4 3 2 1

For my Father,
who always advised:
"Be good! And if you can't be good, be careful!"

In memoriam

Quel beau livre ne composerait-on pas en racontant la vie et les aventures d'un mot?

Balzac, *Louis Lambert*

Contents

ACKNOWLEDGMENTS   ix

PART ONE: *Preliminary Concerns*   1

  1. *Homo Curans*   3

  2. Security Studies and Philology   7

  3. Handle with Care   25

PART TWO: *Etymologies and Figures*   49

  4. A Brief Semantic History of *Securitas*   51

  5. The Pasture and the Garden   68

  6. Security on the Beach   83

  7. Tranquillity, Anger, and Caution   114

PART THREE: *Occupying Security*   135

  8. Fortitude and Maternal Care   137

  9. Embarkations   168

  10. *Lingua Homini Lupus*   182

  11. Repercussions   201

  12. Revolution's Chances   224

  13. Vital Instabilities   238

  14. The Sorrow of Thinking   262

  15. Surveillance, Conspiracy, and the Nanny State   284

ON THE MAIN   299

WORKS CITED   301

INDEX   317

Acknowledgments

WARMEST THANKS ARE DUE first of all to Emily Apter, who initially encouraged me to pursue this project. Her questions and interventions have been a source of inspiration throughout. I would also like to thank all the graduate students, at both Harvard University and New York University, who participated in my seminars on the topic of "security." Many of the arguments and formulations contained in this book directly stem from these wondrously fruitful conversations. I am also grateful for having had the privilege to present earlier versions of my chapters at various institutions: Princeton University, Oxford University, the Universiteit Leiden, the Freie Universität Berlin, and Berlin's Zentrum für Literatur und Kulturforschung. The project has benefited immensely from a conference on the topic, which I organized in 2008 at New York University's Humanities Initiative: many thanks to my colleagues Michèle Lowrie, Jacques Lezra, Anselm Haverkamp, Jane Tylus, and to all the participants in helping me to actualize this exciting event. I am, indeed, particularly grateful to Michèle Lowrie, with whom I first discussed the possibility of proposing "security" as the theme for NYU's Poetics and Theory Institute. We have since shared our manuscripts on the subject, and I have, as always, learned a great deal from her. An earlier version of chapter 15 appears in *Terror and the Roots of Poetics*, Jeffrey Champlin, ed. (New York and Dresden: Atropos, 2012), and I am grateful to the press for allowing its reprinting here. In 2009 I put together an especially engaging workshop on "Security" at Harvard's Radcliffe Institute together with Michèle Lowrie, Marc Shell, Kristin Ross, and Stefan Willer. Special thanks are due to them as well as to others who have read and commented on disparate parts of my work: Tamar Abramov, Homi Bhabha, David Damrosch, Beatrice de Graaf, Lauren Faraone, Paul Fleming, Maryam Monalisa Gharavi, Eckart Goebel, Martin Hägglund, Adriana Chimu Harley, Daniel Hoffman-Schwartz, Michael Levine, Richard Sieburth, Barbara Natalie Nagel, Eyal Peretz, Almut-Barbara Renger, Victoria Rimell, Avital Ronell, John Smith, Nikolaus Wegmann, Sigrid Weigel, Antje Wessels, and Cornel Zwierlein. Finally, loving thanks to my family—to Donna, Jasper, and Henry—who continue to support and sustain me with inspiring hope and thoughtful care.

PART ONE

Preliminary Concerns

Homo Curans

Dulcia sunt ficata avium sed cura gubernat.
Sweet are the livers of birds, but concern reigns.

Inscription from the Mithraeum beneath
the Church of Santa Prisca, Rome

AMONG THE HUNDREDS OF FABLES collected and revised by the Roman grammarian Hyginus (d. AD 17), one has proved to be particularly relevant among later poets and philosophers. The brief tale relates how Cura—a personification of "care," "concern," "anxiety," or "trouble"—formed the first human being. Although many of the narrative's details may be found in other mythic anthropogonies from a variety of cultures and traditions, Hyginus's account is the only extant version that ascribes the creative role to an allegory of Care. When crossing a shallow river, Cura spotted the bank's muddy clay, gathered it up, and molded it into a figure. She then asked Jupiter, who was presently passing by, to breathe spirit into her freshly crafted work. The god readily obliged, yet became angry when Cura expressed her desire to name the animated figure after herself. Jupiter felt instead that the honor should be his. The debate escalated when Tellus, Earth herself, emerged on the scene and insisted that the new creation bear her name. To resolve the issue, the three antagonists summoned Saturn, who immediately pronounced judgment:

> Jupiter, since you have given the spirit, take the soul after death; Tellus, since she provided the body, should receive the body. And since Cura first molded him, let Cura possess him as long as he is alive; but since there is a dispute over the name, let him be called *homo*, since he appears to have been made from *humus*. (*Fabulae* 220)

Thus the fable that began with creation ends with the designation of a name, with the determination of a species. The first phase concerns being, the second involves language. With this combination of ontology and semantics or nature and convention, we obtain not only an etiological explanation for one question (Why is the word for "human being" *homo* in Latin?) but also a philosophical anthropology that folds one question (What is mankind?) into another (What is mankind called?).

Although distinct, these two areas of concern are related insofar as both re-volve around the issue of gift. "Human being" (*homo*) is portrayed first and foremost as a recipient, as a creature endowed with multiple donations from the gods: a form, a body, a spirit, and a name. These provisions are not freely given but rather impose a series of obligations or debts. Divine expenditure in the past requires human compensation in the future; and in this myth the human is not lacking in benefactors to whom his very existence is bound by inevitable, fateful duty, if not guilt. For the most part, the terms of exchange established by Saturn are sufficiently clear: man will ultimately owe his body to Earth and his spirit to Jupiter of the sky. Death would appear to occasion the final reckoning and settle all accounts. Yet, unlike the first gift of creation, the second gift—the gift of a name—sparks a heated philological controversy among the gods, a dispute that is not as simple to reconcile. What obligation does a name incur? To whom or to what must man satisfy this debt? Can a designation, once as-cribed, be returned to its source? And is the source itself—in this particular case, the source of concern—even nameable?

In terms of structure, the story of corporeal fabrication and subsequent ani-mation is somehow deemed insufficient. The myth of mankind's physical and spiritual origin presents a whole that contains a lack, one that requires a further step, a narrative supplement that closes off but also opens up the story. Once body and spirit have been coupled, a single name must be found, one that would presumably secure the identity of the newly composed creature. Through name, the physiospiritual dichotomy that inheres in the galvanized corpus can be further reinforced as a recognized entity. Upon forming her creature, Cura does not fail to take care of this task. It is, indeed, unthinkable that Care would ever be so careless.

Yet, the gift of the name ultimately imposed by Saturn, by a law from with-out, gives the creature over to exteriority, to the improper outside that frames and also contaminates every proper name. The inner being, constituted by a split—the split between body and spirit—will henceforth be assigned fresh di-chotomies, unforeseeable divisions. For the name, which is always a name for others, draws mankind into history, into circulation. Once the creation story overflows into a story of nomination, humanity flows into an inscrutable, prop-erly improper future. At the behest of Saturn, or perhaps Time itself, the vivi-fied clay will be possessed by Cura—its being will be informed by Concern or Anxiety or Worry—but its name will be *homo*. In other words, its being will fail to coincide with its name. It may be that to live with Care is to suffer this non-coincidence wrought by the ongoing succession of time, which renders all iden-tity, all selfsameness over time, worrisome.

Cura's primary task is to unify. With muddied hands, she brings together the dual aspects, spirituality and materiality, that define the human condition. The conglomeration of Tellurian gravity and Jovian levity is indebted to the artistic and persuasive endeavors of divine maternal solicitude. Concerned worry or even careful vigilance would seem to result from the attempt to keep together what would otherwise be separate. Still, human existence is traversed by a fragile caesura. If it is argued that all anxiety (*cura*) is ultimately an anticipation of death, this emotion could be specified as the fear that the corporeal and spiritual components of life will one day be torn asunder. For death is here defined as being either an inanimate body or an incorporeal spirit, as the state of being either a corpse or a god. Cura's competence—the capacity of care—to maintain heterogeneous qualities is a way to stave off both versions of human lifelessness.

Cura's creature is not named after Tellus or after Jupiter, presumably because Tellurian or Jovian existence would be no existence at all. Indeed, it would be a nonexistence, when the cadaver is absorbed back into the earth and the spirit goes on to reside in the invisible heavens. Hyginus proposes instead that human life—mortal life, one that lives in time and in time will pass away—falls directly under the governance of Care. This time-bound life of mankind, subject to contingency and impermanence, is a life with Cura, *cum cura*, fraught with disquiet, apprehension, and concern. Only in the perfect repose of death will humanity be without the anxiety that haunts its place in the midst of historical flux. It is only after death—*posthumously*—or at the end of history when humanity will be removed from Cura, apart from Care, *se-cura*. That is to say, at least according to this myth, it is only when man is no longer alive that he will achieve *security*.

Although the word does not appear in Hyginus's text, *securitas* is nevertheless implicit, insofar as it denotes a state of being removed from care. The word is transparent enough, featuring three distinct components: the prefix *sē-* (apart, aside, away from); the noun *cura* (care, concern, attention, worry); and the suffix-*tas* (denoting a condition or state of being). *Securitas*, therefore, denotes a condition of being separated from care, a state wherein concerns and worries have been put off to the side. Man will be literally secure when he is removed from Cura's governance, when his unified being is split apart, back into its discrete elements. As the story suggests, *securitas* describes either the cadaveric or the discarnate repose that is achieved post-mortem. With death, the constitutive conjunction of body and soul disintegrates. At this point, the gifts that constitute life are paid back to their donors. The delicate seam that carefully holds life together is always but a reminder of debts to be settled.

Cura represents this presentiment. She appears as an allegory of concern for mankind's future, for the destination that may be specifically understood as a future of loss, ostensibly the loss of the object for which Care cares. "As long as he lives," man lives with concern, predicated by mortality and finitude. To be entirely secure or carefree would require the negation of time itself, for it is in time that threats emerge, giving rise to fresh concerns. As Saturn's pronouncement suggests, man's removal from care—his security—is purchased with devitalization. All the same, the extreme cases that this myth posits need not be understood in so stark a manner. Although *perfect* security—either the Tellurian security of perpetual peace or the Jovian security of eternal im-mortality—is mortally inaccessible, some measure of security is nonetheless possible in this life, if only by the fact that mankind is composed of earthly matter and heavenly spirit: gifts that grant a modicum of security, albeit provisional.

Hyginus's tale thus poses a series of crucial questions. Is the history of mankind's desire for security nothing other than the history of an ambition to evade time and its contingencies? Is the dream of being secure ultimately an expression of some death drive or nirvana principle, a wish to rejoin the silence of the tomb or the redemptive bliss of paradise? Must the will to security always imply a striving toward these modes of timelessness, a desire for refuge in the protected quarters of the grave or the impregnable fortress of the Empyrean, where, beyond the reach of time and its effects, one is at last safe from all harm, immune from every danger? Is the longing for security in fact a denial of our humanity, our *humility*? Or is it not rather informed by the recognition that any attainment of security in this life is necessarily limited, ephemeral, subject to change? If security promises to make us carefree, how can we avoid becoming careless? How could any measure of security be possible without vigilance, anticipation, and concern, without making calculations or weighing risks? How can one ever be without care without care?

2

Security Studies and Philology

THERE ARE FEW TERMS in today's political and cultural lexicon as severely over-worked, as multifunctional or potentially ambiguous as *security*. The word is vertiginously ubiquitous, serving a vast array of discourses from practically every area of human society. Articles, advertisements, and public announcements tirelessly feature this key term, which more and more appears to define our day-to-day lives, imposing itself wherever we turn, confronting or informing us, reassuring, upsetting, or intimidating us, influencing our decisions or governing our behavior. More indirectly, security alerts and concerns in the forms of cautionary notices, warning labels, and televised legal disclaimers reflect a general will to protect and safeguard against dangers large and small—a worry that is equally discernible in the countless safety measures that punctuate ordinary experience, from police patrols and home alarm systems to scanners, detectors, and surveillance cameras, from checked bags and walled borders to secured Web sites and personal identification numbers, from life insurance and pet insurance to safe sex and child-safety lids, sunscreen and insect repellent, guardrails and seatbelts.

How did we collectively arrive at such a state, on both local and global levels, where "security" needs to be addressed so habitually, so emphatically, so diversely? Why the countless statements, individual and collective, expressing a desire for safety, a need for protection, a concern for reassurance, an aspiration to know *for sure*? Is our age unique in this regard? Are we in fact living at a point in history that should distinguish itself specifically as an "age of security," which is tantamount to saying an "age of anxiety"? Have fundamental changes in mankind's relation to the world—changes attributable, say, to globalization, pluralization, privatization, deregulation, or technological advancement—left us radically *unsure*, no longer capable of applying traditional frames of reference for processing or understanding what is taking place all around us, for calculating what is yet in store? Is this the *terminus* toward which modernity had been leading us, and where postmodernity has dropped us off?

Clearly, the desire or need for certain kinds of security is no recent invention. What could be more basically human than the appeal for defense, certitude, and trust, whether in this world or the next? As beings living in and constituted by time, prone to encounter contingencies, surrounded by innumerable risks, have we not always been driven to save ourselves from peril, to arrive peacefully into safe harbor? Is it not human nature to seek a firm ground for our judgments and our actions? Has the compulsion to ward off potential harm ever been absent from the human mind? Some might speculate back to our collective archaic past, to our initial exit from the shaded protection of the forest or the cave into the exposed horizon of the savanna, where our bipedal stance afforded greater talents for anticipation but also more opportunities for anxiety, where a large portion of experience took place behind our backs, where our capacity to see further was purchased with the liability of being seen. In this sense, the longing for security would appear to be an anthropological given, a rudiment of our species as mortal organisms, no less ancient or hallowed or—in the end—that much different from the instinct of self-preservation.

Notwithstanding, if the desire for security is truly universal, why, then, are we today witnessing this inflated focus, this inexhaustible dissemination that in many ways resembles propaganda? Why are we faced with the term *security* in such a huge variety of contexts with such a bewildering scope of applications? Are we actually dealing with a universal good? Or should we not instead take security to be a component in strategies of power, a thoroughly historical tool for implementing control among the populace and among ourselves, a mechanism of governance, including self-discipline, which draws decisive lines and sanctions exclusionary practices, a formidable instrument of life management that derives its persuasiveness, undeniability, and legitimacy from this presumed universality? In this regard, the term's ambiguity might be said to increase its ideological efficacy. As Anthony Burke suggests, "Security's power lies in the very slipperiness of its significations, its ironic structure of meaning, its ability to have an almost universal appeal yet name very different arrangements of order and possibility for different groups of people."[1] By means of semantic malleability, "security" could name a desire that everyone admittedly shares, transhistorically and transculturally, even if there remains vast disagreement on what the word means, what it expresses, and how it performs, that is, even if we can never be sure what "security" is concretely doing for us or to us.

Consider the endless series of modifiers and determinants that are regularly employed to specify what ostensibly remains a very fluid and mutable notion: national security, social security, and home security; human, environmental, and energy security; airport and supply chain security; infrastructure and so-called cybersecurity. Projects, procedures, and technologies aim to provide physical and emotional security as well as economic and debt security. There are security deposits and equity securities, as well as the "security thread" woven into banknotes to prevent counterfeiting. There are security keys and security wings, security guards and security envelopes, convertible securities and fixed-income securities, not to mention the "security blanket"—by far the

[1] See Anthony Burke, *Beyond Security, Ethics and Violence: War against the Other*, 33.

best-known of Donald Winnicott's "transitional objects"—or, more recently, Bruce Schneier's "security theater," whose impressive display of technological gadgetry and uniformed personnel attempts to offer anxiety-ridden travelers but a palliative feeling of safety and confidence.[2] A truly all-purpose signifier, with ease and spectacular amenability, *security* floats from one region of interest to the next, invading conceptual neighborhoods, arousing field-specific suspicions, ever conjuring fresh scenarios of concern.

If the root sense of security names a state or condition where concern has been removed (*sē-cura*), then we must grapple with the consequence that discourses of security continue to generate more and more causes of worry, including concern over the meaning and function of "security" itself. This mechanism moves well beyond the fact that security for one party generally spells insecurity for another. On the purely synchronic level of today's usage, it readily becomes clear that security projects often exhibit a disjunction between intention and effects. This malfunction encompasses, for example, what international relations scholars term "the security paradox"—"a situation in which two or more actors, seeking only to improve their own security, provoke through their words or actions an increase in mutual tension, resulting in less security all around."[3] Yet, this effect, the result of stirring up the proverbial hornet's nest, does not exhaust the list of problems that security induces. Ambivalence is evident at every turn. For example, from the standpoint of individual psychology, we could say on the one hand that specific security issues convert vague anxiety into a determined source of fear. Here, security projects are appealing insofar as they help us focus and prepare. They work by isolating and identifying a real or imaginable threat, effectively stabilizing our worries by naming a particular source of potential instability. On the other hand, a security alert might conjure a fear that otherwise might have never cropped up. The publication of security measures can transform our everyday world into a perilous place, calling attention to dangers hitherto unsuspected, reminding us of our vulnerabilities, our fragility. From yet another perspective, in training our consciousness upon a recognized peril we may become blind to other unrecognized or unrecognizable dangers. In becoming free of care in one situation, we may become careless regarding another, lulled into a "false sense of security."

Although security projects allow us to act preventatively, to enjoy some conviction that we can control the future at least to a certain degree, insofar as they deal with imminence, with something that is still to come, security measures

---

[2] Donald Winnicott first proposes the psychoanalytic theory of "transitional objects" in 1951. For a full elaboration see his book-length study, *Playing and Reality*. The concept of "security theater" is introduced and discussed in Bruce Schneier, *Beyond Fear: Thinking Sensibly about Security in an Uncertain World*, 38–40.

[3] Ken Booth and Nicholas Wheeler, *The Security Dilemma: Fear, Cooperation and Trust in World Politics*, 9. The notion of the "security paradox" or "security dilemma" was first identified and developed by John Herz in "Idealist Internationalism and the Security Dilemma."

must always negotiate between knowability and ignorance. We may be partially relieved in circumscribing a known threat—a known unknown—yet this achievement does little to suppress anxiety before an entirely unknown danger—an unknown unknown.[4] Perhaps for this reason, we transfer our concerns to political and social institutions or even to refined technologies, which we believe are capable of accomplishing much more than any single individual. Shoving concerns to the side does not annihilate them altogether; they may go away, but that would only suggest that they are on their way to some other place. From social contract theory to security software, we are accustomed to leaving our personal cares to some external system designed to take care of everything. We allow our worries to be relocated; we watch them be sent off so that they may be domesticated elsewhere by powers that transcend our own, relatively feeble capacities. It is obvious that decisions of this nature retain the menacing consequence of personal impotence. By allowing an institution or a technology to remove my concern, I forfeit my own responsibility and relax my own agency—two choices that should be the cause for further alarm.

Security almost always works at cross-purposes because the concern for security is at bottom a concern to be without concern. In striving to eliminate apprehension, in turning the alleviation of worry into a pressing source of worry, security unworks itself. This fundamental problem has long been recognized. Indeed, when we turn to the diachronic axis, when we consider the history of usage, we discover that security has persistently been regarded with deep ambivalence. Simply put, the term's ambiguity stems from the varying values of *cura*, the "concern" that security appears to eliminate. Defining *securitas* as "the condition or state of being free from care" does little to conceal a host of complexities that in fact has driven centuries of denotative and connotative distinctions generating vacillating viewpoints and judgments. Far from designating a single notion, *cura* and therewith *securitas* branch off into different meanings with different values, wandering off into divergent semantic fields.

In Latin usage, the meaning of *cura* shifts according to *quality* and *value*. Regarding quality, *cura* can denote something either physical or mental—an object of concern or the concern for an object; and in terms of value, it can be marked either negatively or positively. In the negative sense, *cura* as a mental disposition may be translated as "anxiety," "nervous fear," or "burdensome solicitude"—a troubling of the mind or an internal unease that impedes action. As something physical, negatively valued *cura* could be understood as the "pain" or "danger" itself, anything that causes worry. In contrast, taken positively, mental *cura* may signify "attentiveness," "diligence," or "assiduous administration." It is the care one devotes to a project, the concern one exhibits for

---

[4] Cf. J. Peter Burgess, *The Ethical Subject of Security*, 3–4.

Table 2.1. Basic Semantic Field of cura

	Negative	Positive
Mental	"anxiety"	"attentiveness"
Physical	"pain"	"object of concern"

oneself and for others, or the consideration one bestows to a task or an office at hand. Finally, as something physical, positive *cura* is the work itself, an object of study, a work of art, or simply the beloved person for whom one cares.

Given the polysemy of *cura*, the meaning of *securitas* alters depending on the type of care or concern it strives to erase. Accordingly, *securitas* reverses the particular value of the "care" it sidelines:

Table 2.2. Corresponding Semantic Field of securitas

	Negative	Positive
Mental	"tranquillity"	"indifference"
Physical	"safety"	"negligence"

On the one hand, *securitas* may suggest either the privation of anxious concern ("tranquillity") or the removal of the very cause of fear ("safety, protection"). Insofar as fear itself possesses a privative force, we could say that, by negating anxiety, security negates the negation that prevents us from enjoying a prosperous life. Hence, *securitas* may be rendered as "confidence" or "serenity," a state whereby we are liberated from obstacles and limitations, free from the paralysis of worry, protected from invasive and detrimental violence. The privation of fear that this security provides restores us to the peace from which we would be otherwise deprived. On the other hand, *securitas* can just as well refer to "indifference" (the lack of interest) or "negligence" (the lack of concern for a person or object). By removing *cura* as commitment or concentrated effort, by ignoring the loved one or neglecting one's work, the elimination of care denotes "heedlessness," implying that one is no longer driven by the concerns that are believed to define and guide human existence, moral behavior, or practical action. Free from these kinds of concern, we are secure in the sense of being inattentive or indifferent, foolhardy or delinquent. In this case, the privation of devoted attention threatens to leave us deprived.

Whereas *securitas* is advantageous if it extirpates a troubling *cura* like fear, anger, or pain, it counts as a decided disadvantage when it abolishes the *cura* that motivates vigilance or dedicated engagement. Thus, *securitas* can name a *good* like assurance, certitude, safety, or prevention; or it can designate an *evil* like apathy, complacency, or recklessness. Again, by eradicating care, security leaves us either carefree or careless. All the same, reducing the meanings of *security* to the alternative of being either carefree or careless is only a first step that compels further elaboration. The shifting values and qualities ascribed to *cura* as well as the various ways its elimination can be understood have motivated long and complicated semantic careers in philosophy and literature, theology and law, ethics, psychology, and anthropology. Contributing to these histories is a rich assortment of analogous terms for worry, disquiet, and solicitude, for safety, serenity, and certitude, for negligence and indifference—each one acting as a portal into disparate discourses with particular contexts, concepts, and usages.

In addition to these Latinate legacies, there is the equally important cluster of Greek terms that count as master words of Hellenistic philosophy, terms that further shape and guide the potential senses of security as the alleviation of anxiety (Platonic *ameleia*), the elimination of disturbances (Epicurean *ataraxia*), the balancing of angry urges (Democritean *euthymia*), the suppression of strong emotions (Stoic *apatheia*), and the removal of the fear or the cause of stumbling (*asphaleia*). The expansive lexicon of Greek words for care and concern augments the nexus of affiliated ideas across history, for example: the moral-philosophical "care of the self" (*epimeleia heautou*) and the "exercises" (*meletai*) or the *askēsis* devoted to that end; the mythical river of "Insouciance" (*Amelēs*), which according to Plato, courses through the Underworld's "plain of Forgetfulness [*Lēthē*]" and whose waters "no vessel can hold" (*Rep.* 621a); and later the melancholic "torpor" (*acedia*, the privation of *kēdos*, "care"), which Christian theologians numbered among the seven mortal sins. Taken altogether, security's semantic field begins to resemble more a rhizomatic network producing nearly infinite opportunities for interpretation and instrumentalization, for metaphors and mythic recastings, each actualization remaining unable to control the latencies that underlie and often undercut every historical instance.

A main premise of the following study is that security is an urgent philological problem. It is *urgent* because concepts, claims, and procedures of security circulate, like never before, through almost every channel of our political, social, and individual existence, working as both a guarantor of safety and a source of instability. And what this ambiguity ultimately reveals is that the problem is also *philological*, if only because the word continues to be bandied all too casually—formulated, medialized, preached, and promoted despite, or rather perhaps precisely because of, its frustrating vagueness. A philological approach, which would consider usage in particular historical, linguistic, and cultural contexts, stands ready to counter trends that hollow out the term and turn it into a tool for supporting dominant powers and practices. Philology is arguably capable of accomplishing this task insofar as it slows us down. It slackens the pace that fuels ideological designs. As Friedrich Nietzsche remarked, philology is the "venerable art which demands of its votaries one thing above all: to go aside, to take time, to become still, to become slow."[5] In other words, philology works carefully, *cum cura*. In the case of security, it should put to the side the desire to sideline all concern. A method of resistance, philology patiently questions the historical amnesia that diminishes the word's semantic and conceptual range, thereby preventing an all-too-easy, all-too-quick—and perhaps, all-too-human—slippage into platitude.

Despite the term's broad applicability and staggeringly complex history, present academic engagement with security tends to restrict its analyses to topics dealing with international relations, political science, and law enforcement. Pressing debates concerning the significations, mechanisms, and effects of security formulate questions from the perspectives of national defense, diplomacy, governance, jurisprudence, surveillance, liberty, exceptionalism, and normativity.[6] This disciplinary focus is both insightful and blind. Realist recommendations for improving state security, liberal correctives for prioritizing human security, and even dissident protests against securitization *tout court*, explore security issues with much penetration and nuance, yet all presume knowledge of what "security" essentially is and thus exclude whatever else "security" may be. Instead, the term's astonishingly discursive versatility should give us pause.

That is not to suggest that issues of security should not constitute a principal area of inquiry for political and governmental scholars. On the contrary, security, along with sovereignty, freedom, justice, democracy, progress, and human rights, incontestably belongs to those cardinal concepts that have most prominently oriented and motivated the major questions, policies, and practices of the modern era.[7] However, when security is considered more broadly and historically, beyond the general senses of defense, containment, and civil order, we then arrive at a semantic cluster whose internal complexities and multiple directions would overwhelm any single, disciplinary point of view. On the basis of present usage alone, it does not take long to see that the term "security" refers to a widely disparate and hence confusing range of actions and concepts: safety and salvation; calculability and probability, certification and validation, fixing and binding, privacy and confidentiality.[8] Such hyperutility arguably comes at a cost. Belonging everywhere, "security" seems to belong nowhere precisely. While granting that political theory has been fruitful for understanding how specific security projects are proffered, maintained, and abused, it is less clear

---

[5] Friedrich Nietzsche, *Daybreak*, 5 [*Sämtliche Werke, Kritische Studienausgabe (KSA)* 3: 17].

[6] For a concise overview, see Jef Huysmans, "International Politics of Insecurity: Normativity, Inwardness and the Exception."

[7] See Daniel Frei, *Sicherheit: Grundfragen der Weltpolitik*, 9.

[8] On the various metaphors implicit in the term "security" within political scientific discourse, see Paul Hilton, *Security Metaphors: Cold War Discourse from Containment to Common House*, 79–102.

how such investigations can shed light on nonpolitical or nonmilitary usages of "security." Political theory has much to say about the concept or concepts of "security," but generally neglects the term's elasticity and its historically shifting applicability. To speak with Saussure, political science concerns itself with security's referential, extralinguistic "meaning" yet fails to determine its systemic, intralinguistic "value."[9] Ever so quick to name or identify the issue, this kind of determining strategy begins to look like a scheme of avoidance, denial, or disavowal, latching onto presumed facts that invariably stifle a more involved and therefore disconcerting genealogical evaluation. The disciplinary motive to secure security reveals a tautology that speaks for itself.

Traditionally, international relations scholarship has proceeded by way of two major orientations, realist and liberal, that attempt to define the proper aim of public security policies. Realism adopts a statist approach that attends to the improvement of security by developing more effective policies, programs, and legislation. Based often explicitly on a notion of sovereign statehood reaching back to Thomas Hobbes, *Realpolitik* pinpoints and subsequently addresses national vulnerabilities and weaknesses, all with an eye toward increasing the state's strength, so as to protect territories, regimes, or populations. This kind of work profits from quantitative methods of risk analysis and statistical probability that essentially attempt to reduce contingency and foster predictability in very specific circumstances.

In contrast, liberal-minded critiques, which uphold a long tradition from John Locke to John Stuart Mill, opt for more qualitative modes of analysis. They renounce abstraction and protest the concrete sacrifices that individuals are compelled to make upon the altar of the state. In a word, liberalism laments that care for the nation trumps more personal concerns. Theorists like Ken Booth, to select a representative example, thus recommend: "*Emancipation* should logically be given precedence in our thinking about security over the mainstream themes of *power and order*."[10] Such work is particularly apt in moving attention away from purely statist concerns to what international policy makers call "human security," as defined by the United Nations Development Program:

> The concept of security has for too long been interpreted narrowly: as security of territory from external aggression, or as protection of national interests in foreign policy or as global security from the threat of nuclear holocaust. . . . Forgotten were the legitimate concerns of ordinary people who sought security in their daily lives.[11]

---

[9] See Ferdinand de Saussure, *Course in General Linguistics*, 111–20.

[10] Ken Booth, "Security and Emancipation," 319 (emphasis added). Equating security with emancipation has been the chief component in what has come to be known as the Aberystwyth School. For an extensive discussion of this position, as well as the comparable positions of the "Paris" and "Copenhagen" Schools, see the manifesto authored under the name C.A.S.E. collective: "Critical Approaches to Security in Europe: A Networked Manifesto."

[11] United Nations Development Program, *Human Development Report, 1994*, cited from Roland Paris,

Accordingly, liberal theorists laudably redirect the study of security along more humanitarian lines, tackling issues dealing with human rights, health, food and water supply, and the environment. In battling basic human needs, a liberal paradigm frees security studies to develop strategies of aid and support rather than refine policies of aggression.

Despite their differences, both realist and liberal orientations still share many presuppositions. In addition to assuming that security's meaning can be conceptually fixed, both would also agree that security—understood either as the protection of the state or as the preservation of individual freedom and well-being—is a good, that is, something desirable. Dissident voices, still within the field of political theory, interrogate primarily this latter assumption. Mark Neocleous, for example, advances a complete reconsideration of the liberal project. In his view, the ideal of securing individual freedom is just as oppressive as defensive models of territorial or national security, insofar as it is still based upon "a particular vision of order."[12] In other words, liberal policy aims to ensure a protective order that is, in the end, a rigid design that the policy itself has instituted and wishes to preserve. The realists' *geopolitical* focus on defending territory has simply been replaced by a *biopolitical* focus on safeguarding human lives through different codifications and classifications. Although the objective for each is vastly different, the structure is essentially the same: geopolitical security must position itself against whatever threatens the land; just as biopolitical security must guard against whatever threatens life. In both cases, the aim is to secure by means of separation and insulation, by protecting something or someone from whatever is taken to be a source of insecurity.

Over the past decades, "critical security theory" has challenged the assumptions of both realist and liberal modes of thought.[13] With a recognizably constructivist turn, critical security scholars focus on historical and social determinants that contribute to the conceptualization of security issues. Members of the "Copenhagen School"—including Barry Buzan, Ole Waever, and Jaap de Wilde—point to the intersubjective conditions and various authoritative speech acts that identify security threats in relation to some established idea of normalcy.[14] The object of study, then, is better understood as dynamic processes of "securitization" and "desecuritization," which take place on both institutional and personal levels.[15]

"Human Security: Paradigm Shift or Hot Air?" 89. See also the essays edited by David Chandler and Nik Hynek in *Critical Perspectives on Human Security: Rethinking Emancipation and Power in International Relations*.

[12] Mark Neocleous, *Critique of Security*, 4.

[13] The term "critical security theory" served as the title of a conference in Toronto, held in May 1994. The essays are collected by Keith Krause and Michael Williams in *Critical Security Studies: Cases and Concepts*. For an excellent overview and analysis, see Krause and Williams, "Broadening the Agenda of Security Studies: Politics and Methods."

[14] The theoretical premises and methodological principles are fully outlined in Barry Buzan, Ole Waever, and Jaap de Wilde, *Security: A New Framework for Analysis*.

[15] See Ole Waever, "Securitization and Desecuritization."

Frequently, one can discern a strong debt to the Frankfurt School of social theory. Critiques launched, either explicitly or implicitly, from the standpoint of Max Horkheimer and Theodor Adorno's *Dialectic of Enlightenment* charge that realist and liberal formulations of security rest on a classical, essentializing conception of the subjectivity.[16] In brief, critical security theorists interrogate the validity of realism's state-oriented procedures and liberalism's individualist views by problematizing notions of the subject that appear to underlie both assessments. Whereas realists and liberals tend to transcendentalize a secured subject—be it the state, the territory, the regime, the population, or the individual—critics emphasize immanence by highlighting the subject's inherent fragmentation and processual constitution, its dependency and vulnerability, its embeddedness in the world. In this view, the subject is not a pregiven, ready-made entity, but rather one that is continually in formation. Instead of positing a prior, stable subject to be guarded, critical theory claims that the subject comes into being only through security measures. The subject is originally formed by security initiatives rather than being already in place, awaiting subsequent protection. This view is a corollary to the idea that the subject is not autonomous but rather a product of hegemony or more blatantly coercive measures. In general, dissident security theorists recoil at any supposition of identity and argue instead on the premise of difference. Therefore, any strict, isolating division between some integral subject and a purely extraneous threat stands to be revaluated in order to rethink the metaphysical logic that reinforces and promulgates misleading dichotomies.[17]

Although still working within the parameters of political thought, many critical theorists appreciate the need to reconsider security from outside a political frame. Scholars like Michael Dillon and James Der Derian acknowledge that treating the topic of security with political philosophical concepts alone invariably leads to reductive lines of inquiry. Put simply, they recognize that problems of security cannot be solved by security measures. Nietzsche often steps in as one who can offer an alternative mode of thinking through the implications of "securitization." The philosopher's ebullient aphorisms are persistently solicited to propose a new kind of politics. In Dillon's *The Politics of Security*, Nietzsche provides many of the insights that would allow us to interpret the "will to secure" as the motivating drive behind precisely the kind of political thinking that must be overcome. In his introduction, Dillon quickly enlists the erstwhile Wagnerian to sound the opening harmonies of a *Zukunftspolitik*, a politics of the future: "Is it not the *instinct of fear* that bids us to know? And is the jubilation of those who attain knowledge not the jubilation over the restoration of a sense of security?" In response, Dillon submits the following gloss in a decidedly Foucauldian key:

---

[16] A comprehensive review of this approach with ample bibliography may be found in Richard Wyn Jones, *Security, Strategy, and Critical Theory*.

[17] See, e.g., Robert Walker, "Polis, Cosmopolis, Politics."

Hence: security as knowledge (certainty); security's reliance upon knowledge (surveillance); security's astonishing production of knowledge in response to its will to know (calculability); and the claim of knowledge which gives security its license to render all aspects of life transparent (totality). All these constitutive elements of our contemporary manifold politics of security excited my suspicion because they comprise a monumental enterprise of power-knowledge whose insatiable maw threatens to consume not only all thought, and not only that relating to the question of the political, but of what it is like to be human.[18]

This epistemological and moral critique ably discloses the shortcomings of conventional security studies by alluding to part of the key term's semantic range. Moreover, Dillon's subsequent analyses of Martin Heidegger's antimetaphysical provocations as well as his own penetrating reading of Sophocles' *Oedipus the King* convincingly exhibit an awareness of the need to be more attentive to language issues and move the discussion of security past an exclusively political philosophical discourse. Dillon is, indeed, cautious to resist forgetting *security*'s multiple functions across time and cultures, a forgetting that would prefer to stabilize and control the word by means of an extralinguistic reference. To this end, he insists on language's autonomy. Words like security "slip and slide, evade our grasp and convey both more and less than we intend. They do this both because they have a history and because when we use them we set them off again on their historical way." For Dillon, the viability of politics depends on respecting open-endedness, on letting the term *security* and its shifting implications persist despite "the designs that might be made upon it."[19] An adherence to the word as historically contingent will thus "impede the impulse to treat the founding of politics in security unthinkingly, as if security provided a secure ground"[20]—hence, the need for philological deceleration as Nietzsche describes it.

Dillon demonstrates well that philological work need not be unpolitical. Concerning security, he repeatedly turns to unabashedly negative assessments like the one cited above: security as an "insatiable maw" that swallows up thinking as well as our very humanity. The strong image may lead one to recall "Le Voreux," the ominous, voracious coal mine that haunts Zola's politically charged *Germinal* (1885). Such a judgment sufficiently illustrates the political agenda that motivates Dillon's analyses, analyses that in the end must negotiate security's semantic vagueness with the author's own desire for political reform. Yet, it is this kind of decision that, despite Dillon's philological carefulness, ultimately returns philology to its traditional position as handmaiden to a superior

---

[18] Michael Dillon, *Politics of Security: Towards a Political Philosophy of Continental Thought*, 17. The Nietzsche citation is from Walter Kaufmann's translation of *The Gay Science* (§ 355), 301.

[19] Dillon, *Politics of Security*, 114.

[20] Dillon, *Politics of Security*, 116.

science: in this case, although not as the *ancilla theologiae*, still as the *ancilla politicae*.

James Der Derian works in a similar vein, treating the imbrication of security and power with utmost suspicion:

> No other concept in international relations packs the metaphysical punch, nor commands the disciplinary power of "security." In its name, peoples have alienated their fears, rights and powers to gods, emperors, and most recently, sovereign states, all to protect themselves from the vicissitudes of nature—as well as from other gods, emperors, and sovereign states.[21]

With a light nod to Heidegger, Der Derian argues that sovereignty not only perpetuates a falsifying "ontotheology" that obfuscates the mutually constitutive relation between subject and object but also, in doing so, provokes unspeakable violence. He continues:

> In [security's] name, weapons of mass destruction have been developed which have transfigured national interest into a security dilemma based on a suicide pact. . . . in its name billions have been made and millions killed while scientific knowledge has been furthered and intellectual dissent muted.[22]

In line with most critical security theorists, sovereignty with its attendant transcendent force is especially dangerous: a security purchased by reifying and excluding the other harbors an insidious threat, because it deludes citizens into believing that they can live without relating to the outside. This delusion is the means by which a state's security policies try to establish legitimization; and it is the law's inclination to sanction injustice that Der Derian above all wishes to expose. His repeated and ironic invocation, "in the name of security," points to an institutional, quasi-ecclesiastical quality, one that should call attention to the term's dogmatic power.

For Der Derian as well, Nietzsche is *the* crucial thinker who can cure us of our security mania. Nietzsche has demonstrated how the will to self-preservation, as well as the corresponding will to truth, contravenes the will to power that is life itself, a life that is ceaselessly expanding, overwhelming all limitations and plowing through every obstacle, be it the borders that define the state or the confines that constitute the individual subject. It is out of fear for the unforeseeable danger implicit in life's expansion that motivates what Der Derian disparages as the "security imperative": "The fear of the unknown and the desire for certainty combine to produce a domesticated life, in which causality and rationality become the highest sign of a sovereign self, the surest protection

---

[21] James Der Derian, "The Value of Security: Hobbes, Marx, Nietzsche, and Baudrillard," 25 (emphasis added).
[22] Der Derian, "The Value of Security," 25.

against contingent forces."[23] Like Dillon, Der Derian shares Nietzsche's judgment that the instinct of fear drives us to assent to a mortifying security. To elaborate, he cites a passage from Nietzsche's *Twilight of the Idols* (1888):

> The causal drive is thus conditional upon, and excited by, the feeling of fear. The "why" shall, if at all possible, not give the cause for its own sake so much as for a *particular kind of cause*—a cause that is comforting, liberating and relieving.[24]

Like Nietzsche, Der Derian distrusts the "drive" to convert the new into the known and therefore concludes by renouncing security altogether as something inhibitive. Instead, one should embrace the new and rejoice in the radical insecurity that characterizes the real.

> [Nietzsche] recognizes the need to assert heterogeneity against the homogenizing and often brutalizing forces of progress. And he eschews all utopian schemes to take us out of the "real" world for a practical strategy to celebrate, rather than exacerbate, the anxiety, insecurity and fear of a new world order where radical otherness is ubiquitous and indomitable.[25]

Here, in the final sentence of his essay, Der Derian's political program is particularly pronounced. The remedy for our debilitating will to security, which keeps us locked into patterns of questionable legitimization and complacency, is achieved by encountering alterity. Rather than remain safely ensconced within identity, we must open up to difference, including above all self-difference. Instead of retreating before fear, we should anxiously accept and joyfully celebrate whatever may come. In brief, instead of security, we should appreciate the value of insecurity, even the insecurity that renders problematic the word "we"—a pronoun, incidentally, that Nietzsche at one point claims to have used only out of "courtesy."[26]

One could argue that Der Derian's concluding gesture merely replaces security with insecurity and thereby perpetuates the very problem he hoped to solve. How can this oppositional gesture override the work of something as fundamental as the "security imperative"—a command that orders experience by ordering oppositions? If we secure the world by introducing dichotomies like the one between the known and the unknown, then opposing the secure with the insecure unwittingly expresses a will to security that turns out to be much more difficult than expected. This difficulty was not lost on Nietzsche. In the text that Der Derian cites, it is noteworthy that Nietzsche does not chal-

---

[23] Der Derian, "The Value of Security," 34.

[24] The passage is from the fifth aphorism of the section entitled "The Four Great Errors": Friedrich Nietzsche, *Götzen-Dämmerung, KSA* 6: 93 (emphasis in original) [*Twilight of the Idols*, 180].

[25] Der Derian, "The Value of Security," 42.

[26] See, e.g., *Götzen-Dämmerung, KSA* 6: 77; p. 169 in Norman's translation, where *höflich* is rendered as "polite."

lenge all causality but only—with Nietzsche's own underscoring—"a *particular kind of cause*" (*eine* Art von Ursache), which he carefully distinguishes from "the cause for its own sake" (*die Ursache um ihrer selber willen*). Nietzsche discourages us from asking a *certain kind* of why, arguably so that we may never stop asking why, so that we may never settle for that which is "comforting, liberating, and relieving." In a parallel manner, Der Derian "asserts heterogeneity" by implementing oppositional techniques, not to give primacy to the knowable—or the "securable"—but rather to demonstrate that there is no securitization without considerable, appropriative violence. That said, as in the case with Dillon, Der Derian's political agenda inevitably reduces philology to an ancillary role. The excavation of security's historical ambivalence is undertaken in order to arrive at a nonambivalent political position.

The indeterminacy that inheres in the word security—as the condition of being either carefree *or* careless—motivates political thinking and can even lead to political action. A decision is reached; a thesis is ultimately formulated. In order to solve the indeterminacy of the word "security," one must choose one over the other. For example, among realists, such indeterminacy may prompt the conclusion that security must be freedom from existential threats to the state; among liberals, that it must be freedom from individual needs; while among dissidents security is judged to be simply an apparatus that consigns us to carelessness. The consequence is that any determined thought or act might imperil future thinking and acting. With strikingly mad logic, resolving the problem of security, deciding whether it frees us from care or makes us negligent, is a gesture that stabilizes security as a univocal concept. Decisions of this sort thereby affirm our positions but only at the risk of falling into thoughtless intransigence.

Unless, of course, one continues to ask why. Philology would then be seen as instigating an unending politics, as a method that proceeds not by positing any *thesis* but rather by moving more carefully, perhaps *athetically*, taking a step back for every step forward. For the same reason, philology would be indispensable not simply for political critique and activism but also for all manners of securitization. Theories of interpretation that fix assured methods and codes for understanding, systems that aim to establish a transcendental ground of being or truth, techniques for creating inner tranquillity and constancy, psychoanalytic economies that constitute self-consciousness or safeguard the ego's integration of unconscious drives—all are justifiably conceived as differing types of security projects. These correlations are not empty analogies. In tracing the word's historical, metaphorical, and cultural paths, the following chapters focus less on what security is and more on the shifting ideas, meanings, and figurations associated with the term. Although poised to be an alternative to a purely political approach, a philological investigation can still complement political choices, even if only by complicating them, at the very least because philology would curtail the speed that ideologies, institutions, and power structures require for their efficacy. A philological disposition halts the ready slide into all manners of acquiescence. It prevents the headlong rush into those established conventions of truth that are presented as beyond debate and instead raises problems and questions of meaning at the very moment of meaning formation, that is, before meaning has become ossified and proffered as second nature. Oscillating persistently between languages, cultures, and discursive histories, philology tarries upon the liminal zones, at the very thresholds of translation, inquiring into the conditions of translatability itself.

Without making any claims of comprehensiveness, I focus on the changing modalities, valuations, and iterations of security and care and thereby hope to offer some insight into what is gained and what is lost when care, however conceived, is removed. My approach is admittedly episodic, almost kaleidoscopic, and resists formulating a single, overarching narrative. This choice is again motivated by a philological ideal, one committed to historicity without falling into the temptation of constructing a grand, teleologically driven history. As Edward Said has argued, philology is above all a technique that should disrupt or erupt universal, traditionally "humanist" verities by engaging in what we could describe as a more human humanism—namely, a humanism understood as a process within historical contingency, "as an ongoing practice and not as a possession."[27] Philology thus stands to supplant not only the idealized subject but also any species of post-structuralist, lifeless subjects with a vital, insecurable sense of humanity. Along these lines Emily Apter remarks that "the human is ushered in as an emergency measure, promising, however utopistically, to put nothing less than life itself back on the table without resubjectivizing it in a necromantic or postmodern guise."[28]

With its responsibility to the historical alterations within the gift that is language, philology—slowly, humbly, and carefully—may provide a privileged means for holding determinations at bay, for perpetuating community and its constitutive communication, not by fixing a word's properties conceptually, with sovereign authority, disciplinary control, or tired complacency, but rather by pursuing its transit through time and across cultures and thereby allowing it to be translated, over and over again, on the basis of its very untranslatability.

Thus speaks our modern Zarathustra: "[Philology] itself will not 'get everything done' so lightly: it teaches how to read *well*, that is, slowly, profoundly, considerately and cautiously [*rück- und vorsichtig*]."[29] Nietzsche's "consideration" (*Rücksicht*) and "caution" (*Vorsicht*) testifies to both his *atheism* and *athetism*—a backward and forward gaze, emulating both Epimetheus (*epimētheia*, "afterthought") and Prometheus (*promētheia*, "forethought"). Taken together, they combine into a modality of care, a respect toward language, toward textual

---

[27] Edward Said, *Humanism and Democratic Criticism*, 6.

[28] Emily Apter, *The Translation Zone: A New Comparative Literature*, 26.

[29] Friedrich Nietzsche, *Morgenröte*, KSA 3: 17 [*Daybreak*, 5 (slightly modified)].

traditions of the past infused with futurity. It should be noted that in Goethe's *Festspiel* "Pandora" (1808), the daughter of Epimetheus and the stepdaughter of Prometheus is Epimeleia or "Care" herself. Nietzsche's doubled regard may not provide decisive political answers, but it is able to delineate the preconditions for possible solutions, even those for which we are not yet ready. By way of an investigation into the construction of meanings, philology demonstrates that, if and when we do arrive at a political solution, the time for it may have already passed.

Through patient, historically conscious attention, comparative philology respects the material reserve of words and staves off their dissolution into the conceptual rigidity of unequivocal sense. It strives to excavate the hidden, preconceptual substrate of thought by attending to the process of meaning formation before meaning is definitively accomplished. In this sense, philology would hardly seem to be a discipline at all. As Peter Szondi argues, with philology there is no body of knowledge that it seeks to master, no specific object to comprehend. Instead, it tirelessly if not infinitely works to grasp the way knowledge itself is constructed.[30]

A philological study of the term "security" would not only solicit new interpretations of security theories and critiques but also do so by exploring the vocabularies, images, and embedded metaphors that have formulated and continue to formulate these discourses. Through an explicit interdisciplinarity, which is the earmark of its nondisciplinarity, a philological approach to security can penetrate the fortress that would protect the topic kept behind the manned walls of international relations and political science. It liberates security from its disciplinary holding cell. Of course, this rescue mission can become just as problematic, especially if it simply transports security studies from one academic discipline to another. However, if the inherently inter- and nondisciplinary nature of philology is honored, it could produce a valid opening: one that points to future communication between different fields without being reducible to any single one.

Rather than understand philology as an authoritative discipline to determine stable meaning or still the flux of polysemy, it could be employed as Paul de Man once suggested, namely, as a subversive tool for examining the production of meaning itself. For de Man, philological techniques are fueled by "the bafflement that such singular turns of tone, phrase and figure [are] bound to produce in readers attentive enough to notice them and honest enough not to hide their non-understanding behind the screen of received ideas."[31] This wonder before the word itself, this dogged suspension of understanding, would in

---

[30] Peter Szondi, "Über philologische Erkenntnis," in *Schriften*, 1: 263 ["On Textual Understanding," in *On Textual Understanding and Other Essays*, 3]. On the difficult relation between philology and science (*Wissenschaft*) in Szondi's essay, see Thomas Schestag, "Philology, Knowledge."
[31] Paul de Man, "The Return to Philology," in *The Resistance to Theory*, 23.

turn recalibrate the "turn to theory" specifically as a "return to philology"—"to an examination of the structure of language prior to the meaning it produces"[32] De Man's insistent concern with "the structure of language" removes texts from the influence of authorial intention and thereby aligns philology with his broader assessment of language as rhetorical and mechanical, as operating beyond human, subjective control. Philological attentiveness, then, would renounce the careless securement of established significations and instead, to quote Barbara Johnson, "open up irresolvable difficulties, *resistances* to meaning, or other, unexpected meanings."[33]

Werner Hamacher's recent reflections on philology follow suit by pressing the tension between schemata for the production of meaning and communicative expression—that is, between language's *formal conditions*, which in themselves mean nothing, and its *significations*, which are grounded in subjective intention. Hamacher regards philology's traditionally ancillary role, one that establishes readable texts but refrains from interpretation, as the mark of its *Unmündigkeit*, of its minor or minority status, which renders it incapable of speaking for itself. Philology's word is the *word in itself* that is subordinate to "a more powerful, guiding, dictatorial meaning," just as "the child relates to the knowing adult." Philology's word is the impotent *thing* that is absorbed and mobilized by powerful—and, ultimately, political—discourses. Hamacher presses the simile into a striking metaphor: philology's word, the object of its minor attentions, is "the immature, unspeaking child [*das unmündige Kind*] that supposedly finds its determination in the arms of responsible, mature [*mündigen*] meaning—but the child in its arms is dead."

> It is dead because [philology's] language should merely be the derivate of a meaning, and it can be obliterated there, where this meaning is first captured and institutionally fixed. The death of the word in meaning, which philology has always abetted, by having placed itself in the position of the *infans* vis-à-vis the omnipotent matrix of meaning, this death of philology in the mother-text is the—very real—consequence of the phantasm of semanticism.[34]

This arresting image of the immature, nonspeaking child (*unmündig, in-fans*) who dies in the embrace of a speaking mother only makes more vivid the essential distinction between secured meaning and the nonmeaningful structures of meaning, which should orient philological research and keep it watchful, warding off the infanticidal impulses of semanticization.

Hamacher's portrayal of philology as *unmündig* is highly suggestive, clearly alluding to Immanuel Kant's famous definition of "Enlightenment" as "man's

---

[32] De Man, "The Return to Philology," 24.
[33] This formulation is from Barbara Johnson's brief but provocative consideration of de Man's "Return to Philology" essay: "Philology: What Is at Stake?" 28.
[34] Werner Hamacher, *Für die Philologie*, 24.

emergence from his self-incurred immaturity [*selbst verschuldeten Unmündig-keit*]."[35] The implication that Hamacher seems to make is that philological practice is preenlightened, indebted (*verschuldet*), or even guilty (*schuldig*). As Kant continues, "*Immaturity* is the inability to use one's own understanding without the guidance of another." Enlightenment is thus associated with the critique against dogmatism and metaphysical speculation. In this sense, Kant's epistemology can be said to implement a number of security measures insofar as it protects the knowing subject from the "noumenal," that is, from everything that the subject can never know for sure. As the later generation of German idealists would indicate, Kantian critique secures the subject's knowledge by renouncing inaccessible noumena in favor of accessible phenomena. Bearing this in mind together with Hamacher's provocative allusion, we may ask: Is philology perhaps a refusal *to dare to know* (*sapere aude*--Kant's Horatian tag to characterize the Enlightenment project)? How, then, should this refusal be understood? Is it a sign of philology's dependence on dogma? Is it a mark of cowardice that recoils from questioning? Or is it not, rather, an affirmation of its resistance to reducing everything to phenomenal objects of understanding? Is philology's immaturity nothing less than an unwillingness to take up residence within the protective framework of the categories of understanding, an aversion to rest *assured* within the epistemological fortification that Kant so painstakingly constructed? Would it not, finally, be philology itself that abides with the meaninglessness of the "thing in itself"—*das Ding an sich*—the Thing that is necessarily elided by the subject's understanding?

Slavoj Žižek, writing on Friedrich Schelling, explains: "[Kant] sets up the network of the conditions of possible experience in order to *make sure* that the actual experience of the real, the encounter with the Thing, will never take place, so that everything the subject will effectively encounter will be the already gentrified-domesticated reality of representations."[36] Kant fought valiantly against dogmatic slumber, but his battle harbors a threat of a different kind of acquiescence, which philology alone may be capable of disturbing. If the *security* of the sovereign and autonomous subject rests, as Kant indeed would insist, on *no longer caring* about inaccessible noumena, then philology's cognitive inability becomes surprisingly capable of addressing the gap that haunts and desecures all phenomenal knowledge. That is not to say that philology would provide authoritative or dogmatic insights into noumenal reality. Quite to the contrary, it stands to expose the vulnerability of every subject position that carelessly ignores the "thing in itself" so as to know its "objects" safely and carefree.

---

[35] Immanuel Kant, *Beantwortung der Frage: Was ist Aufklärung?* (1784), in *Gesammelte Schriften*, 5: 35 ["An Answer to the Question: 'What Is Enlightenment?'" in *Political Writings*, 54].
[36] Slavoj Žižek, *The Indivisible Remainder*, 74 (emphasis added).

Handle with Care

[W]e question barricades.

John Ashbery, "Finnish Rhapsody"

THE BURROW

THERE CAN BE NO SECURITY without care. The desire to protect oneself and others, the need, according to the instinct of self-preservation, to foresee dangers and preempt their deleterious effects, the commitment required to locate and identify threats, to discover and then remedy vulnerabilities, all ostensibly demand caution, alertness, and ingenuity, usually by implementing our capacity to calculate risk and anticipate contingencies. Without care we would leave ourselves offguard, exposed to fortune, adrift upon the high seas of a perilous existence, on the verge of falling into any number of horrific, even lethal situations. There can be no security without care, but not simply because "care" (*cura*) is first required in order to be eliminated in *securitas*. Although *security* arguably names a state free of concern, one would still have to take into account the concern needed to remove concern.

As his body began to succumb to tuberculosis, Franz Kafka, former officer and safety expert at the Workmen's Accident Insurance Institute (Arbeiter-Unfall-Versicherungs-Anstalt) in Prague, left us a keen and provocative statement on these matters. In one of his last stories, *Der Bau* (*The Burrow*, 1923– 24), the tiny, foraging animal knows all too well that the protection of his day-to-day life demands constant awareness. Although he has completed the construction of what appears to be an impenetrable, inviolable refuge, he realizes that he can "scarcely pass an hour in complete tranquility."[1] Worry cannot for a moment be forgotten. Attentiveness can never be relaxed. In brief, Kafka's creature is terrified, and it is this terror that motivates all his cares. From the very opening sentence of *Der Bau*, Kafka immediately, albeit lightly, alludes to the necessary imperfection that riddles but also constitutes every security proj-

---

[1] Franz Kafka, "Der Bau," in *Gesammelte Werke*, 8.166 ["The Burrow," in *The Complete Stories*, 325].

ect: "Ich habe den Bau eingerichet und er scheint wohlgelungen" (I have constructed the burrow and it appears quite successful, 165/325). Needless to say, what merely *appears* to be secure can never be entirely foolproof; and, in fact, for the remainder of Kafka's story, the subterranean creature wrestles with gnawing doubts and troubling concerns. Threats from without (for instance, other burrowing animals) and threats from within (like the underground monsters of legend) keep the narrating mole awake and ever watchful.

This insomniac concern, however, is not entirely a problem. If the creature was perfectly sealed up, absolutely secured, then he would almost certainly be exposed to danger. The burrow's threshold, camouflaged by moss, is a case in point. The entranceway is no doubt "secured"—"it is as secured [*gesichert*] as anything in the world can be secured"—yet Kafka, as his official writings attest, would acknowledge that continued security depends on a fundamental insecurity. For example, in his 1914 "Jubilee Report" for the institute, Kafka points out that in "quarry work, the main issue is not actually the use of safety devices . . . rather the exercise of caution in quarrying."[2] A modicum of danger produces heightened awareness: safety becomes unsafe when it is too safe. Thus, in *Der Bau*, the structure must be secure, but not so secure that it would tempt the dweller to be incautious.

> [The entranceway] is as secured as anything in the world can be secured, certainly, someone can step on the moss or break through it, and then my burrow would lie open, and anybody who liked—please note, however, that quite uncommon abilities would also be required—can make his way in and destroy everything for good. At that one spot in the dark moss I am mortal [*sterblich*] and in my dreams I often see a greedy muzzle sniffing around there persistently. It will be objected that I could quite well have filled in the entrance hole too, with a thin layer of hard earth on top and with loose soil further down, so that it would not cost me much trouble to dig my way out [*Ausweg*] again whenever I liked. But that plan is impossible; prudence [*Vorsicht*] demands that I should have a way of leaving at a moment's notice if necessary, prudence itself demands, unfortunately so often, to risk one's life.

In addition to providing a fast means of escape, the thinly camouflaged entranceway works to maintain alertness. The possibility of invasion, however remote, prevents the burrower's comfort from sliding into treacherous complacency. The defect, therefore, is a source of vital energy. Paradoxically, the single gap in the fortification's design introduces an element of weakness that reinforces the creature's capacity for self-defense. The structure's fragility corresponds to his own frailty, which pragmatically maintains his vigilance. "At that one spot in the dark moss I am mortal"—the structure's gap is a reminder of

---

[2] Kafka, "Jubilee Report: Twenty-Five Years of the Workmen's Accident Insurance Institute," in *The Office Writings*, 316.

mortality and may even be Death itself; but it is this architectural and existential flaw that keeps the creature alive. It correlates to his *careful* "prudence" (*Vorsicht*)—the Prometheus-like ability to foresee future occurrences, including, of course, his own destruction. The desire for maximum security demands that he renounce total security.[3] The prudent concern to save his life necessarily puts his life in danger. Were he to forget his vulnerability, he would run the greater risk of having his security slip into laxity.

Both self-directed and altruistic care are always linked to inevitable evanescence, because one cares only for that which will one day pass away. If an object could never be lost, it would never call for concern. If a being were imperishable—if one's own self were perfectly indestructible—there would be no occasion for anxiety, nothing to cause worry. The will to secure bespeaks a desire to fix or set in place that which is shifting and shifty, constantly in motion, and, like the real future, threatening constant change. The longing for security—the concern to be without concern—is driven by the wish to render the future motionless, to wrest it from its own futurity and set it firmly in the present, where it could be safely assessed. But this desire to fix the future hinges on the recognition that what is to come is highly mobile and impossible to predict exactly. Indeed, to deny the future of its contingency is arguably to commit an act of gross negligence, to fall into *imprudence*, which would severely undermine any hope for security.

This principle of hope is precisely what Walter Benjamin glimpses in Kafka's animals and their exemplary powers of reflection. In reading *Der Bau*, Benjamin first observes how the burrowing creature "flits from one worry to the next." This "worry" or "concern" (*Sorge*) "nibbles at every anxiety with the fickleness of despair [*Verzweiflung*]." Benjamin then offers the following interpretation, which he applies to all of Kafka's animals: "What corruption is in the law, anxiety is in [the animals'] thinking. It messes a situation up, yet it is the only hopeful thing about it."[4] Corruption unsettles the basis of legal statutes, yet its emergence also prevents the law from becoming rigid in mechanical, unreflective legalism. The only hope for the law is the potential for the law to be transgressed. Similarly, in the case of Kafka's *Burrow*, the creature's chance for survival stands in direct proportion to his "worry" or "anxiety"—two good translations for the *cura* that *securitas* aims to dispatch. The removal of all concern may leave the creature untroubled, but it would also make him foolish. In Benjamin's German, the two (*zwei*) options—the lack of disturbance and the absence of caution—produce the ambiguity (*Zweideutigkeit*) that characterizes despair (*Verzweiflung*); and it is this despair, in turn, that serves as the prerequisite for hope. It responds to a gap in the system that destroys the system's totality but also maintains its futurity. In the same way, the burrow's pregnable

[3] Cf. Hermann Wiegand, "Franz Kafka's 'The Burrow' ('Der Bau'): An Analytical Essay," 156.
[4] Walter Benjamin, "Franz Kafka," in *Gesammelte Schriften*, 2: 431 [*Selected Writings*, vol. 2 (1927–34), 810].

entranceway compromises the creature's safety but also holds open an exit, an *Ausweg* that gives birth to future contingency, whether for good or ill. Prudence teaches that contingencies are unavoidable, which turns the dream of total security into a most unwise desire to avoid the unavoidable. Thus, the animal is secure only as long as he remains insecure. It is the burrow's lack of complete protection that ensures the inhabitant's capacity for self-defense. His mortality saves his life.

THE MATERNITY WARD

Perhaps encouraged by technological advancement, scientific progress, miraculous breakthroughs in medicine, or a steady decrease in crime, we may have become so infected with dreams of invulnerability or possible deathlessness that we would deny our very human nature. The obsessive concern for security could be read as an attempt to distract ourselves from a frightening admission of our mortality, an apotropaic gesture aimed at warding off what can never be prevented, or a vain hope in the perfect efficacy of our calculations.

In her recent memoir, *Insecure at Last*, Eve Ensler frustratingly relates the problem of security to a desire to transgress our human finitude:

> What does anyone mean when they speak of security? Why are we suddenly a nation and a people who strive for security above all else? In fact, security is essentially elusive, impossible. We all die. We all get sick. We all get old. People leave us. People surprise us. People change us. Nothing is secure. And this is the good news. But only if you are not seeking security as the point of your life.[5]

The main cause of Ensler's complaint is the barrage of institutions that claim to provide safety and thereby nourish society's craving for security. Her conclusion ("nothing is secure") corresponds to the basic premise behind the vigilance worked into Kafka's *Burrow* but pursues a much different course by introducing an aspect of heteronomy. Despite the fact of a governing fear, Kafka's burrower is the autonomous sovereign of his castle, albeit without any subjects to lord over. He builds the elaborate structure with intense care and perpetuates his concern by leaving his work imperfect. This combination of diligence and incompleteness could serve as a model for an ideal democratic institution, provided the burrow was populated: a place where occupants would carefully participate in the institution's construction as an ongoing project, never complete, never perfect. In contrast, the collective conjured by Ensler—"a nation and a people who strive for security above all else"—is compelled to relinquish its care to transindividual agencies that assume all care. Perfect security is pur-

---

[5] Eve Ensler, *Insecure at Last: A Political Memoir*, xiii.

chased with mass carelessness, a refusal to acknowledge the fact that "security is essentially elusive, impossible." The desire for total protection hands the individual over to totalitarian designs. In the end, this refusal is equated to forgetting the fact of the mortality that defines our humanity and should motivate our continued concern.

Critics of the dream of complete security point to its potential to reduce life to lifelessness, not necessarily by mortifying—by taking life away—but more deviously by removing mankind from the existential temporality that constitutes life itself. This effect is somewhat congruous with the concept of *reification* as developed by Georg Lukács in a line of argumentation that is indebted to Karl Marx as well as to Max Weber, especially the latter's classic analysis of modernity's "iron cage" (*stahlhartes Gehäuse*)—a "housing as hard as steel," which is a far cry from Kafka's mossy, porous burrow. Weber's hyperrational, hyperefficient structure immures the individual in suffocating bureaucracy—perhaps the very thing that Kafka feared and longed to escape.

Among those within this sociological tradition is Jean Baudrillard, whose early work focuses on the loss of individual freedom to the forces of abstraction, which for him comprises the greatest source of alienation. Baudrillard identifies security with state "blackmail" and speaks of its booming industry, which converts all manners of accidents, diseases, and threats into "capitalist surplus profit." For example, in referring to seat-belt laws, Baudrillard complains of "the worst repression, which consists in dispossessing you of your own death."

> Thus car safety: mummified in his helmet, his seatbelt [*ceinture de sécurité*], all the paraphernalia of security, wrapped up in the security myth, the driver is nothing but a corpse, closed up in another, non-mythic, death, as neutral and objective as technology, noiseless and expertly crafted. Riveted to his machine, glued to the spot in it, he no longer runs the risk of dying, since he is *already* dead. This is the secret of security, like a steak under cellophane: *to surround you with a sarcophagus in order to prevent you from dying.*[6]

Baudrillard's interpretation of what he calls the "security myth," however disingenuous, points to a powerful protest: the security campaigns promoted by state offices—the warnings upon warnings that society's ideological assembly line spews out on a regular basis—offer us a gift of immortality (preventing us "from dying"), which is another way of saying that they take away our (mortal) life. The security "sarcophagus" takes life away, insofar as human life is defined as that which is exposed to the unforeseeable, that which is vulnerable to chance, and that which is ultimately, therefore, grounded in finitude. As Baudrillard would point out, an *immortal life* is a contradiction in terms. To live is

[6] Jean Baudrillard, *Symbolic Exchange and Death*, 177.

to be able to die; and the security technologies that would forestall this end end up defusing potentiality, preventing life itself from living.

Reduced to being "steak under cellophane," the flesh and blood of the secured citizen is nothing more than a piece of meat preserved for the state's consumption. In Baudrillard's logic, society's consumer is thus made consumable. We have, in a sense, abandoned Kafka's *Burrow* and entered into his *Penal Colony*, where the harrowing pins torture the condemned man strapped to the apparatus that destroys the body in order to produce an image of transcendent, unimpeachable Justice. As Baudrillard announces on the very first page of his study, this kind of operation—redeeming the contingency of loss by purportedly destroying contingency—is sanctioned by the "Law of the Father," which establishes a system of "symbolic exchange" designed to mitigate a fear of castration but in fact perpetuates a collective death drive.[7] Thus, the term "security" itself, so exceedingly present in our quotidian dealings with the world and with ourselves, comes across as an infernal machine persistently producing all manners of apprehension precisely by promising to keep anxiety at bay.

One need not pursue the implication, common in classical psychoanalytic theory, that the maternal dyad—presumably lost in the symbolic "Law of the Father"—would somehow counter the security problem outlined by Baudrillard. Indeed, the realm of the mother can be just as insidious. Elfriede Jelinek's *Klavierspielerin* (*The Piano Teacher*, 1983), for instance, presents the symbiotic mother-daughter relationship distinctly in pathogenic terms.[8] Erika Kohut, Jelinek's distraught protagonist, links her excessively controlling mother to the "grid system" of the musical staff, which "has tied her in an untearable net of directives, ordinances, and precise commandments, like a rosy ham on a butcher's hook [*am Haken eines Fleischhauers*]." Jelinek has recourse to nearly the same butcher metaphor employed by Baudrillard in order to expose security's menace. And she is equally explicit: designed to protect, such measures fatally paralyze. "This provides security, and security engenders fear of the insecure [*Sicherheit erzeugt Angst vor dem Unsicheren*]."[9] The person obsessed with security is caught within a vicious circle, a *Teufelskreis*, one that is especially malicious insofar as it manifests itself within a private, domestic space that presumably should instill a sense of comfort. The mother's neurotic solicitude, her exaggerated and frequently violent curatorship, might have aimed to prevent, bind, and contain but instead has traumatized the child into yet another species of lifelessness.

It was the object-relations psychologist, Heinz Kohut—Erika's namesake— who comprehensively analyzed infantile rage against the maternal caregiver, whose promulgation of her offspring's dependency banefully perpetuates

---

[7] Baudrillard, *Symbolic Exchange and Death*, 1.

[8] Cf. Barbara Kosta, "Inscribing Erika: Mother-Daughter Bond/age in Elfriede Jelinek's *Die Klavierspielerin*."

[9] Elfriede Jelinek, *Die Klavierspielerin*, 204 [*The Piano Teacher*, 190 (slightly modified)].

weakness.[10] In removing her daughter's care the mother removes the child's privilege of self-inflicted risk and autonomy. Security, here, is but a euphemism for imprisonment. For Jelinek, this ceaseless, maternal care with its "directives, ordinances, and precise commandments" again readily translates into the kind of sovereign concern familiar from totalitarian regimes. Matrophobia is symptomatic of political oppression, which paves the way for self-destructive masochism. Once again, one is reminded of the "peculiar machine" in Kafka's *Penal Colony*, which similarly engages in "precise commandments" and realizes the officer's masochist desires. In Jelinek's novel, the preservation of an ideal or an ideology, here efficiently performed by maternal vexation in concert with the Vienna conservatory, cannot fail to recall other institutions explicitly and ironically designed to maintain the "security" of the populace: the Soviet KGB (Комитет государственной безопасности [Committee for State Security]), the Securitate police of communist Romania, and the notorious East German Stasi (Ministerium für Staatssicherheit [Ministry for State Security]). Throughout the twentieth century, there has been no lack of victims who suffered from the "butcher's hook" of reigning power—*am Haken eines Fleischhauers*—not least of all those who fell beneath the swastika (*Hakenkreuz*) that continued to haunt Jelinek's Austrian imaginary.

Still, Jelinek's critical representation of this nightmarish maternity ward—together with Ensler's misgivings and Baudrillard's suspicions—should not detract from the possible benefits and advantages of a maternally coded security. In the novels of Herta Müller, for example, we encounter a much different portrayal of the mother and, incidentally, of music in the form of dissident folksongs. Müller, who consistently turns to her own upbringing in German-speaking regions of Transylvania under Nicolae Ceausescu's iron-fisted rule, counters the communist oppression of the Romanian Securitate with instances of maternal care that provide a sincere sense of personal security. Born in 1953, only seven years later than Jelinek, Müller interestingly draws from the same Habsburg legacy that the Viennese Nobelist finds so burdensome. In her own Nobel acceptance speech (2009), "Jedes Wort weiß etwas vom Teufelskreis" (Every Word Knows Something about the Vicious Circle), Müller illustrates how a mother's concern works to protect the daughter from the devastating mechanism of state security.

To tell her story, Müller focuses on a simple, almost trivial ritual: every morning, as she left home, her mother would ask if she had a handkerchief. As Müller explains, she always failed to take one, not out of forgetfulness but rather because her feigned negligence offered an opportunity for reassurance: "The handkerchief was the proof that mother protects me in the morning."[11] The ritual is described as "an indirect tenderness," an expression of love disguised in

---

[10] Heinz Kohut, *The Search for the Self: Selected Writings, 1950–1981*.

[11] Herta Müller, "Jedes Wort weiß etwas vom Teufelskreis," in *Immer derselbe Schnee und immer derselbe Onkel*, 7.

the form of a question: "Do you have a handkerchief?" As Müller accumulates sketches of life in the factory, this everyday piece of linen emerges as symbol of the certainty of familial structure and guardianship. Banished from her office after refusing to sign an admission of collaboration with the regime, she sets up a makeshift workplace in the factory's staircase, placing the handkerchief upon the step for her seat. She reflects on the precise arrangement of the handkerchiefs folded in a special drawer at home: on the left, those for father and grandfather; on the right, those for mother and grandmother; and warmly nestled in the middle, those for the child. She speaks with her fellow Romanian poet Oskar Pastior, a survivor from a Stalinist camp. Rather than address recent allegations that Pastior may have been involved with the Securitate as an informant, she simply listens to his story, how he held on to his mother's handkerchief through five years of hard and demoralizing labor. The touching account contributes to Müller's reflections on handkerchiefs, which demonstrate that this ordinary article can secure a sense of humanity in the midst of grossly inhuman and inhumane circumstances.

Müller harbors no delusions about the cloth's fragility. She can never be charged with denying the facts of human mortality and state-driven abuse. She relates how her grandmother kept a snapshot of the bloodied corpse of her son, who had enlisted with the SS and was killed in battle. Beside the gray heap of mangled flesh a white handkerchief could be seen upon the black field, a faint memorial to the individual whose life was lost well before his death. And when Müller's mother was herself picked up by the police, it occurred to her to grab the handkerchief in her pocket, which she subsequently used to clean the holding cell while she anxiously awaited interrogation. Again, the gesture is a weak but infinitely powerful attempt to retain agency, to secure herself from the security measures designed to break her. Müller's speech concludes: "Can it be that the question concerning the handkerchief has never meant the handkerchief but rather the acute solitude of mankind?"[12] Not despite but rather because of this fundamental solitude, human *care* consists not only in the will to protect oneself and others but also in acknowledging one's stark inability to do so absolutely.

SECURITY MADNESS

The recent interest among feminist and psychology theorists in formulating and prescribing an "ethics of care," sparked by the work of Carol Gilligan, corresponds to Müller's attempt to discover an opening, however slight, to reconnect morality and politics.[13] Gilligan's distinction between a "universal moral-

---

[12] Müller, "Jedes Wort weiß etwas vom Teufelskreis," 21.
[13] The major impetus for the movement towards an ethics of care is Gilligan's *In a Different Voice: Psy-*

ity" based roughly on Kantian notions of abstract, formal principles and a "contextual morality" grounded in interdependence and mutual responsibility usefully separates state-sponsored policies of removing care from an individual's recognition that true security is necessarily provisional.[14] If state security aims to render citizens carefree, individual security recognizes the perils of surrendering care to an impersonal system.

Ethical issues are by definition those that deal with values; and it is immediately clear that security rests on some concept of value. From the perspective of the state, it is easy to see that security policies in international affairs frequently consist in the imposition or promotion of a set of normative values, implicitly or not, either with sincere intent or as a pretext for exercising power and control. The clash of different subjective values or different perspectives has always revealed the ambiguity of military campaigns. President George W. Bush's moniker for the War in Afghanistan, "Operation Enduring Freedom," could not, indeed, be more ambiguous, designating a value both noble and terrifying: an attempt to prove the *durability* of "freedom" against tyranny as well as an opportunity to learn how devastating this "freedom" can be to *endure* among the Afghan population. Yet such mobilizations of power are not the only manner by which the question of value enters into an analysis of security. From an individual standpoint, security has to do with persons, institutions, and objects that are invested with personal value. We wish to secure what we are afraid of losing, what has value for us. The acknowledgment of the role of subjective valuation bears other important implications that confirm the ethical dimension of security, that is, the subject's insoluble relation to the other. Given the subject's own investment of value to the threatened object, we could say that the security threat is not solely produced by the attacker but also by the fearful person, who determines what is or is not an object under threat.[15] Terrorism is efficacious only when it aims at that for which we care as thinking, feeling subjects. To a certain degree, therefore, both the potential assailant and the potential victim author the dangerous scenario.

Ethical considerations disclose how security values articulate a distinction between interdependence and unilateral action, between relatedness and segregation. In her reflections written in the aftermath of the September 2001 terrorist attacks against the United States, Judith Butler elucidates a notion of fragile subjectivity constituted by otherness and the limitations of believing that this mutual relation can somehow be ignored:

---

chological Theory and Women's Development. On the implications for political theory, see also Selma Sevenhuijsen, *Citizenship and the Ethics of Care,* and Virginia Held, *The Ethics of Care: Personal, Political, Global.*

[14] See also Joan Tronto, *Moral Boundaries: A Political Argument for an Ethic of Care,* 26–27 and 101–4.

[15] Cf. J. Peter Burgess, *The Ethical Subject of Security: Geopolitical Reason and the Threat against Europe,* 14. Throughout, Burgess analyzes the various ethical ramifications of security projects under discussion here.

One insight that injury affords is that there are others out there on whom my life depends, people I do not know and may never know. This fundamental dependency on anonymous others is not a condition that I can will away. No security measure will foreclose this dependency; no violent act of sovereignty will rid the world of this fact.[16]

The "precarious life" that Butler wishes to investigate creates a tension between integration and disintegration. On the one hand, security names a desire to maintain the integrity of the object of care, be it our lives and the lives of our loved ones or, to revert to today's buzzwords, "freedom" or the "homeland." On the other hand, security policies aim to disintegrate the external threat and thereby, as Butler underscores, threaten to foreclose the care that constitutes a shared experience of mourning and grieving, an interdependent, groundless ground in loss.

The emphasis on care and the lament for its absence characterize many critiques of today's security concerns and the policies that perpetuate them. Scholars and journalists, particularly in Europe and the United States, have of late frequently and despairingly referred to the "security craze" or even "madness"—in German, Sicherheitswahn—which they regard as rampant. Typically these denouncements adduce the staggering amounts of money spent each year on security-related projects and contracts by governmental agencies and private corporations.[17] They consider the broad provision of services to combat all manners of threats, including the availability of insurance for every conceivable danger and for every potential disaster, as evidence that the desire for security has reached pandemic proportions. They despair that these phenomena are on the whole delusional (wahnhaft) and constitute disproportionate reactions to fantastically exaggerated menaces and are in fact little more than fearmongering strategies. With its insinuation of morbidity, the term Sicherheitswahn suggests that a common, understandable—perhaps universal—preoccupation has today turned into a societal neurosis, into a mass pathology, or at the very least into a rather curious, fashionable trend. Although commonly translated as "delusion," the word Wahn may indeed also be used to designate a popular "fad," as if the security craze were nothing but some new-fangled rage.

While conceding that measures against actual dangers are self-evidently justified, those who disparage an excessive attention to security issues invariably point to overlapping problems.[18] Skeptics may strive to expose how the insis-

---

[16] Judith Butler, *Precarious Life: The Powers of Mourning and Violence*, xii.

[17] For a provocative overview and cultural analysis of our contemporary security industry, see the various essays in *Cultures of Insecurity: States, Communities, and the Production of Danger*, J. Weldes et al., eds.; and, more recently, Pino Arlacchi, *L'inganno e la paura: Il mito del caos globale*.

[18] The titles of some recent German publications are sufficiently telling: Elisabeth Blum, *Schöne neue Stadt: Wie der Sicherheitswahn die urbane Welt diszipliniert* (Nice New City: How Security Madness Disciplines the Urban World); Thomas Darnstädt, *Der globale Polizeistaat: Terrorangst, Sicherheitswahn und das Ende unserer Freiheiten* (The Global Police State: Fear of Terrorism, Security Madness and the End of our Freedoms); and Ilija Trojanow and Juli Zeh, *Angriff auf die Freiheit: Sicherheitswahn, Überwachungs-*

tence on security is but a base expression of the state's oppressive power, how threats are exploited in order to enhance authoritarianism or to realize imperial or tyrannical desires. The political theorists, social scientists, and cultural critics who represent this trend belong to a liberal tradition insofar as they relate what they see as an inflated, worldwide spread of security concerns to a corresponding decrease in fundamental human freedoms and human rights. Such hypersecurity, they claim, offers no security at all, but rather the very opposite, insofar as citizens are expected to make sacrifices that ultimately make them insecure, now at the mercy of transindividual power. Critics bemoan how state-driven propagation obscures or even prohibits what should be our primary concern, namely the need to secure our own freedom: whether from fear, from despotism, or even—albeit ironically—from *security* itself.

A corollary problem emerges with the state's prioritization of territorial and civil defense, which tends to be understood as a vast apparatus that socially constructs our collective insecurities. Torin Monahan thus sees the explicit emphasis of the U.S. Department of Homeland Security—essentially, its overriding priority to protect the population from "external" threats like terrorist attacks or environmental disasters—as neglecting other problems that are just as real and just as urgent: "homelessness," "imprisonment," "domestic violence," "chemical exposure," "automobile accidents," and so forth.[19] Further, ever more efficient policies and technologies may provide a deceptive sense of being fully secure, which may then lead to reckless behavior. An all-too-sure ground may cause someone to take ever-greater risks, unleashing the adverse effect, again, of making someone less secure than otherwise.

Certainly, it would be misleading to suggest that the high prevalence of state-centered security issues always elicits disapproval. The counterposition to the denunciation of an exorbitant and superfluous concern for security is an insistence, frequently lodged by the Right, that this elevated attention is simply a necessary development in an increasingly vulnerable world. Self-styled realists claim that we care so much about safety and defense because we have no choice to do otherwise. Following a common narrative, the turn to security began as a reconfiguration of policy demanded by the new international landscape that materialized in the years after 1945. Here, security was understood as a strategy that could adequately address the historically unprecedented problems and potentially horrific consequences of the burgeoning Cold War. For proponents of this worldview, today's amplification of security concerns, especially those connected with terrorism, is hardly fear mongering but rather an unavoidable response to continual changes within the socioeconomic dynam-

---

staat und der Abbau bürgerlicher Rechte (Attack on Freedom: Security Madness, Surveillance State, and the Destruction of Civil Rights). See also the collection of essays edited by Hans Fricke, *Politische Justiz: Sozialabbau, Sicherheitswahn und Krieg* (Political Justice: Social Destruction, Security Madness, and War).

[19] Torin Monahan, *Surveillance in the Time of Insecurity*, 2.

ics of an ever more complex global context. Accordingly, security measures do not rescind our freedoms; on the contrary, they uphold them precisely by shielding us from threats to our very existence. Hardly instruments of oppression, security programs fulfill the state's core obligation to protect its citizens.

Whereas some regard the incessant attention to safety as our necessary fate, opponents understand security itself as a pestilential menace that we should struggle to eradicate. The former would grant that we are mad about security but only because we are living in a mad world; the latter, in contrast, would demonstrate that it is security madness itself that deludes us into discovering more threats than truly exist or goads us to produce more perils than necessary. Critics thus argue that we are desperately in need of a *cure*, because these policies and precautions are at bottom ways of inducing fear among the populace, a fear that manipulates the citizenry to relinquish rights that should be inalienable. Instead of securing ourselves from phantasmagorical menaces, we should protect ourselves from this very real threat to our freedom. All the same—the counterargument runs—fear can have a salutary effect, keeping individuals wary and vigilant, averting hazardous complacency, and therefore making everyone safer. Is it not some vague idea of freedom, these latter voices would argue, that itself counts as a phantasm? Are we to purchase our liberties with vulnerability, despair, and suffering? What is more insane: the so-called security madness that governs our quotidian existence or the obstinate denial that security issues do in fact demand constant concern?

Perhaps, in the case of security madness, it would be advisable to attend to Pascal's judgment and simply recognize that we are "so necessarily mad that not to be mad would be to give a mad twist to madness."[20] Rather than work to dismiss or justify today's widespread concern for security, we should attempt to understand what precisely constitutes these concerns: What or who is being secured, through which agency, by what means, at what cost? And what does such security entail: true safety from an outside danger or a psychological, wholly subjective mitigation of fear, regardless of whether the menace (or the safety) is real? Does our collective longing for security, for putting all concerns to rest, contradict or underscore our exaggerated restlessness, our need for constant innovation, information, and news updates? How can a desire for security be reconciled with an abhorrence of keeping still?

AUTOIMMUNITY

Today it has become increasingly clear that conventional paradigms of defense are obsolete. Conventional military strategies no longer suffice to fight against the complex networks that operate apart from a definable, localizable center. A

---

[20] Pascal, *Pensées* (1670), 412 (414), in *Œuvres complétes*, 549 [*Pensées*, A. J. Krailsheimer, trans., 148 (modified)].

product of the information age, aggressive organizations are capable of communicating across channels that are difficult to trace, plotting horrifically efficient schemes that rarely issue from a single, originating point. In *Networks and Netwars* (2001), John Arquilla and David Ronfeldt, two researchers associated with the RAND Corporation, offer typologies of how adversaries now exploit various organizational designs to mount their attacks: "from simple chain or line networks, to less simple hub or star designs, to complex all-channel designs, any and all of which may be blended into sprawling multihub and spider's-web networks."[21] The shift entails a collapse of the vertical, hierarchical forms of organization into decentralized, horizontal patterns, which introduces new problems of targeting. "Ideally, there is no single, central leadership, command or headquarters—no precise heart or head that can be *targeted*."[22]

Samuel Weber grants this difficulty, yet insists that, despite its amorphous or acephalous nature, the threat must still be delimited, fixed, and brought into scope. The response is always an act of isolation that separates the danger from its surroundings and thereby reduces the chance for distraction or misaim. "Targeting the enemy as a self-contained objective to be subdued or destroyed also creates a sense of common purpose and cohesion that, temporarily at least, can mitigate the isolation of the viewer by rendering the enemy more 'imaginable' and hence more manageable."[23] Yet here, by way of his reading of Freud, Weber hits upon a further problem. The destruction of the other reveals that securing our survival is indebted to this other; and any denial of this indebtedness becomes a source of guilt—a failure to acknowledge what is owed. Weber continues:

> The result is a dangerous and destructive spiral of guilt, fear, and aggression that ultimately tends to turn the targeting "inward" against oneself: the "enemy" is no longer simply "out there" but is now feared to have infiltrated the innermost reaches of domesticity.[24]

Such a reading reinforces Weber's initial, etymological insight, namely that the English *target* reaches back to a word for "shield."

Weber's analyses give sharper, more profound focus to critiques that deplore how security for one implies insecurity for another. Without question, in the words of one international relations scholar, "Seeking after security for oneself and being a cause of insecurity for others are not just closely related; they are the same thing."[25] Experience amply demonstrates how the securement of a territory, population, or individual is gained at the expense of whatever or whoever is perceived to constitute a major threat. Security requires a demonization of the

[21] John Arquilla and David Ronfeldt, *Networks and Netwars: The Future of Terror, Crime, and Militancy*, xi.

[22] Arquilla and Ronfeldt, *Networks and Netwars*, 9.

[23] Samuel Weber, *Targets of Opportunity: On the Militarization of Thinking*, 60.

[24] Weber, *Targets of Opportunity*, 60–61.

[25] R. N. Berki, *Security and Society: Reflections on Law, Order and Politics*, 32.

other: the integrity of the inside is rendered coherent by means of violence directed to the menacing outside. And this strategy, often performed in the name of "preemption" as opposed to "deterrence," again discloses the debt that occasions what Weber calls above "a dangerous and destructive spiral of guilt, fear, and aggression." Thus, in demanding more security, more insecurity is unwittingly produced. This logic also lies at the base of Giorgio Agamben's recent lament over the frequent slippage of security policies into violence. "A state that has security as its only task and source of legitimacy is a fragile organism; it can always be provoked by terrorism to turn itself terroristic." In this regard, security forges a "clandestine complicity" with its presumed opposite as "the hunt for security leads to a worldwide civil war which destroys all civil coexistence."[26] Security measures end up provoking more fear than they assuage.

As Weber suggests, this issue touches on what Jacques Derrida identified as the political problem of "autoimmunity," namely, how democracies may suspend or even destroy their democratic premises for the sake of preserving the democracy. In his essay "The Reason of the Strongest (Are There Rogue States?)" ([2003] 2005), Derrida alludes to the dissolution of Algeria's democratic government and the imposition of military rule in 1992 in order to prevent a projected victory of the antidemocratic Front Islamique du Salut party.[27] The logic is that free elections should be renounced when a party against democracy is likely to be elected. In light of this logic, "democracy has always been suicidal"—an idea that relates back to what Derrida in an earlier essay portrayed as the "death-drive that is silently at work in every community, every *auto-co-immunity*," "a principle of sacrificial self-destruction ruining the principle of self-protection."[28] Here and elsewhere, Derrida employs the biomedical concept of autoimmunity to analyze this autodestructive principle. Just as an organism's immune system begins to attack its healthy cells, so the preservative tactics of a democratic community start to dismantle the foundation upon which that community rests.

Like Agamben, Derrida regrets how a democracy chooses to mime its enemies, "to corrupt itself and threaten itself in order to protect itself against their threats."[29] The gross injustices committed by U.S. authorities at Guantánamo Bay that refuse most detainees the right to counsel and the right to trial is a clear illustration of how democratic ideals are obliterated for the sake of protecting a democracy. This blatant dismissal of the stipulations of the Geneva Convention does not simply represent a sovereign's legal right to suspend the law but shows how protective operations can eat away at the very institutions they are designed to shield.

[26] Giorgio Agamben, "Security and Terror."
[27] Jacques Derrida, *Rogues: Two Essays on Reason*, 33.
[28] Jacques Derrida, "Faith and Knowledge," in *Acts of Religion*, 87. For a probing analysis of autoimmunity and politics in relation to Derrida's broader project, see Martin Hägglund, *Radical Atheism: Derrida and the Time of Life*, 164–205.
[29] Derrida, *Rogues*, 40.

This autoimmunitary menace, which feeds on a simple but nonetheless confounding logic, need not be restricted to national affairs. On a related, more personal level, there are the paralyzing consequences of constant worry, fear, and anxiety. Both the public preponderance of security warnings and the individual obsession with prevention can be stifling, something that intimidates movement in a world now regarded as frighteningly dangerous. Here, too, security triggers a kind of autoimmune debility, insofar as safety is achieved through a curtailment of activity, which may impede growth, improvement, and general profit, foreclosing opportunities and stifling life. In short, such measures preserve existence at the cost of existence itself.

Roberto Esposito has analyzed at length the full ramifications of immunity projects that protect life by means of negating life. He pursues the link, indicated by Derrida above, between immunity and community. Like *securitas*, *immunitas* is constructed with a privative prefix (*in-*): from a strictly etymological perspective, "immunity" names the condition wherein the *munus* (task, obligation, duty) is lacking or has been negated. In Roman law, the opposing term is *communitas*, the "community" constituted by individuals who share the obligatory *munus*. The person who is immune is the one who has been freed of the debt that not only is owed to the community but also forms the community's cohesion. Therefore, this exemption preserves propriety in the strongest sense, for it permits the individual to hold on to a possession or property instead of surrendering it to the realm of the "common" (*commune*); it prevents the singular entity from being subsumed into the collective. Esposito stresses how the common threatens to transgress the borders that secure the private. In this regard, the principle of the common resembles a kind of contagion that, from the standpoint of the individual, poses the risk of disintegration and entropic dissolution. "Common life is what breaks the identity-making boundaries of individuals, exposing them to alteration—and thus potential conflict—from others."[30]

Whereas the community is formed by means of a sacrifice or expenditure, by giving something away, the private individual is preserved by a refusal of that gift. The early Christian Church understood quite well that it was the *munus* of Christ's sacrifice upon the cross that was capable of forming the community, precisely by producing the obligation to give back: *religio* is founded on an act of communal binding, *obligare*.[31] The ligaments of communal life ultimately spell the death of the proper. In order to counter this absorbing trend—and, indeed, in order to secure that the community of individuals continues to flourish—it is necessary to immunize the community by means of law. "The law responds to this unsustainable contamination by reconstituting the limits threatened by the connective power of the *munus*."[32] Law, therefore, literally exhibits a *privative* function. It secures the private. Thus, legal power overlaps

[30] Roberto Esposito, *Immunitas: The Protection and Negation of Life*, 22.
[31] Esposito, *Communitas: The Origin and Destiny of Community*, 6–11. Esposito's comments here overlap with Georges Bataille's notion of "expenditure."
[32] Esposito, *Immunitas*, 22.

with modern immunology, whereby disease is combatted not by expelling it entirely from the organism but rather by allowing a minuscule portion of its negative force within. Esposito presses this logic to its paradoxical conclusion: "It would appear that to ensure common life, law is forced to put something inside it that maintains it beyond itself; to make it less common or not common—in other words, immune."[33] The paradox consists in introducing a second sacrifice that counters the originary sacrifice that establishes the community so that, "by immunizing life from community, law ends up sacrificing the intensity of life to the need for its preservation."[34]

In Esposito's reading, the classic Hobbesian paradigm sets the stage for a scandalous problem: the sovereign's capacity to honor its founding obligation of providing security is premised on the idea that common life, left to its natural powers, would ultimately destroy itself. The "war of all against all" that notoriously characterizes the state of nature compels a denaturalization of life's powers. "Only by negating itself," as Esposito explains, "can nature assert its own will to live. Preservation proceeds through the suspension or the alienation of that which needs to be protected." In seeking safety, therefore, life must ultimately turn against itself. "In order to be saved, life has to give up something that is integral to itself," namely, its *natural* right.[35] Nietzsche's critique of the Leviathan state is voiced precisely from this vitalist position:

> The state is a clever institution for the protection of individuals against one another; but if one exaggerates its refinement, it will in the end enfeeble the individual and, indeed, dissolve him—that is to say, the original purpose of the state will be thoroughly frustrated.[36]

Like Jelinek's domestic, maternal prison, the most sophisticated civil institutions exaggerate by taking the immunological paradigm too far. Immunization turns into a grave autoimmunitary problem, when the antibiotic agents turn against the very life they were designed to sustain. Law, which should balance the vital impulses of the common with the limitations of the proper, becomes a parody of itself when it oppresses life entirely.

In line with Benjamin's insights on Kafka cited above, we see how rigid legalism, in striving to heal all wounds, denies mankind the vulnerability that motivates care. It consigns citizens to mindless inactivity. As Hannah Arendt would remark, it aims to establish a politics to end all politics, insofar as politics is based on concerned action. In removing all threats, it works to abolish mortality; and, in doing so, it eliminates what Arendt terms our "natality"—"the capacity of beginning something anew . . . the political activity par excellence."[37]

---

[33] Esposito, *Immunitas*, 27.
[34] Esposito, *Immunitas*, 27.
[35] Roberto Esposito, *Bios: Biopolitics and Philosophy*, 58–59.
[36] Nietzsche, *Menschliches, Allzumenschliches*, § 235, *KSA* 2: 197 [*Human, All Too Human*, 113 (modified)]. Cf. Esposito, *Bios*, 91–92.
[37] Hannah Arendt, *The Human Condition*, 9.

One must be wary of a state that preserves life by taking life away. In promising deathlessness, total security produces but a stillborn citizenry. In contrast, the dank burrow conjured by Kafka, the construction that retains "that one spot in the dark moss," the portal that opens onto the light of day as well as unforesee-able danger, is a healthy womb.[38]

SECURARE AND SE CURARE

Müller's brief anecdote of the handkerchief contrasts the state's oppressive secu-rity measures with the fragile security offered by the mother. Although the mother's concern can never fully protect the daughter, it is this partial failure that saves the child's life. From a historical perspective, the state, too, may adopt a security policy that similarly maintains a kind of breathing room, which is designed to make life live in a way that is both analogous to and quite different from the scenario that is conjured by Müller. The late work of Michel Foucault, for instance, relates an understanding of security to a particular vitalist dis-course. In his 1977–78 lectures at the Collège de France, entitled *Security, Ter-ritory, Population*, Foucault announced as his theme a new "device, system, or apparatus of security" (*dispositif de sécurité*) that must be considered alongside the systems of "sovereignty" and "discipline," which he discussed in previous courses. For Foucault, who is interested in examining varying political tech-nologies of power, security becomes a crucial concept, wherein the *population* becomes the privileged object of governance, as opposed to *territory* or the *people*. Whereas sovereignty executes its power upon a territory and a disci-pline exerts power on individual bodies, "security is exercised over a whole population."[39] Structures of legalism, which are grounded in codes that distin-guish "the permitted and the forbidden," and structures of discipline, which establish what is "obligatory," are modified by security measures, which move beyond both juridical permission and disciplinary coercion. In brief, mecha-nisms of security are not solely based on the sovereign-subject relationship of prohibition and obedience. Instead, a "new economy of power" acknowledges that it is the free-moving population that is the source of a state's affluence.

It should be noted that the "population" is not a mere collection of individu-als but more specifically an object or category of *statistics*, ascertained through methods of calculation and probability. In Foucault's scheme, whereas a terri-tory is controlled through delimitation and people are corralled into disciplin-ary spaces where they can be observed by panoptical authority, a population is allowed free circulation. As Foucault points out, movement is here promoted rather than inhibited because it is regarded as instrumental in increasing the prosperity of the nation. This idea is historically linked to the emergence of

[38] Cf. Verne Snyder, "Kafka's 'Burrow': A Speculative Analysis."
[39] Michel Foucault, *Security, Territory, Population: Lectures at the Collège de France, 1977–1978*, 11.

mercantilism, neoliberalism, and the ideology of laissez-faire, which still manages and regulates but on an immanent plane of policing, which is distinct from transcendent positions of reigning and commanding. In this regard, liberal theorists who caution against trading in freedom for security are ignorant of the power of the security dispositif, which functions by way of and not against liberties. For Foucault, in contradistinction to the right of the sovereign, security measures do not exercise the power to *take away life* but rather the power to *make life live*, which is the general characteristic of biopower.[40]

As an object of biopower, Foucault's population is ultimately very far from Müller's individual. The population is wholly an object of statistics, an object of calculation, quantified by the state and qualitatively different from a collective of singular persons. Thus, although associated with an increase of life and discourses of liberty, the security paradigm is based on very precise techniques of ordering.

> The population can only be the basis of the state's wealth and power in this way on condition, of course, that is framed by a regulatory apparatus [*appareil*] that prevents emigration, calls for immigrants, and promotes the birth rate. . . . In short, it requires an apparatus that will ensure that the population, which is seen as the source and the root, as it were, of the state's power and wealth, will work properly, in the right place, and on the right objects.[41]

The security dispositif perpetuates life and encourages mobility, which is to say it *compels* life's flourishing. In other words, security is constituted by a statistical, measurable *norm* that is derived from its concern with the population's movement and productiveness. The concern for the population, therefore, is ultimately a concern for the state and only nominally a concern for the individual who is readily reduced to the statistical norm. Whereas the handkerchief in Müller's tale makes the daughter careful, the apparatus in Foucault's scheme promises—and thereby threatens—to make the population free from all care.

For Foucault, the link to normality not only replaces people with a population but also distinguishes security from sovereignty, which, in the classic formulation of Carl Schmitt, rests on the logic of the *exception* from the norm. Foucault's analysis therefore illuminates many aspects of our present age of security: the porosity of borders, including the dissolution of bounded selfhood, which promotes trade and travel but also engenders uncertainty and fear; the fragility of threshold zones, which calls for security control; the prioritization of productivity and the degradation of idleness; the abnormalization of any deviance from the statistical majority; and so forth.[42] Yet, as convincing and rele-

---

[40] See Michel Foucault, *"Society Must Be Defended": Lectures at the Collège de France, 1975–1976*, 241.

[41] Foucault, *Security, Territory, Population*, 69.

[42] See, e.g., Michelle Perrot, Michel Foucault, and Maurice Aguilhon, *L'impossible prison: Recherches sur le système pénitentiaire au XIXe siècle*, 103–4.

vant as Foucault's genealogies of power and knowledge may be, his strict distinction between sovereignty and discipline on the one hand and security on the other fails to account for the present conjunction of sovereign authority, surveillance, and security measures that have been circulating at least since the 9/11 terrorist attacks against the United States. The insurance model traceable to the birth of mercantilism and cameralism may function well on statistical measurements of probability and risk, but the specter of worst-case scenarios, a clear throwback to the Cold War's fears of global annihilation, invariably transforms a politics of the norm into a politics of the exception. That is to say, whereas a model of insurance may mutualize episodic danger across the entire population, security against a *total* threat cannot be so readily disbursed. As Didier Bigo concisely notes, "Insurance can cope with catastrophe but not with Armageddon."[43]

Foucault himself perhaps sensed the insurmountable difficulties of keeping the security dispositif free from methods of surveillance and exceptional or constituting power. As the 1977–78 lectures demonstrate, barely a month after optimistically broaching the topic of security, he rather abruptly abandons the theme and moves, instead, to the different but related subject of what he calls "governmentality"—an historical species of power that he links to a Judeo-Christian tradition of "pastoral care." Interestingly, the turn marks a decisive shift from issues of *security* to issues of *care*—above all, to issues of a moral philosophical *care of the self* (*cura sui*), which will unfold across the subsequent lectures and the later volumes of the *History of Sexuality*. Scholars have been perplexed by Foucault's sudden break, the way he drops the topic of "security" in favor of an analysis of "pastoral care" and "care of the self."[44] How should the two domains be brought together? What is the genealogical link between them? Without delving further at this point into Foucault's exposition on these matters, it is important to note an oddly provocative juxtaposition, one, moreover, that Foucault and Foucauldian theorists, at least to my knowledge, never explicitly address. In associating an idea of *securing* with a notion of *self-caring*, Foucault essentially overlaps the "elimination of care" (*securare*) and the "cultivation of self-care" (*se curare*). What might justify this seemingly contradictory conjunction?

SICHER MACHT LUSTIG!

In Foucault's explicative scheme, discipline works upon *people*, attempting to regulate every aspect of their lives, and therefore practices protectionism. Secu-

---

[43] Didier Bigo's essay, "Security: A Field Left Fallow," in *Foucault on Politics, Security and War*, Michael Dillon and Andrew Neal, eds., 112.

[44] For some representative views, see Bigo, "Security: A Field Left Fallow"; François Ewald, "Norms, Discipline and the Law"; and Colin Gordon, "Governmental Rationality An Introduction," in *The Foucault Effect: Studies in Governmentality*, Graham Burchell, Colin Gordon, and Peter Miller, eds., 1–51.

rity, on the contrary, focuses on the *population*, which is allowed to act "naturally." Instead of mechanisms of protectionism, we are dealing with ideas of deregulation and neoliberalism. Thus, the focus on the security (*sécurité*) of the population differs from the classical theory of the safety (*sûreté*) of the Prince. The Machiavellian problem ("how to keep the sovereign in power") cedes to the core problem of security ("how to ensure circulation for the sake of the State").[45] Extrapolating from Foucault's analysis, we can observe how, by the twentieth century, the various individual, collective, and governmental demands to secure and be secure with an emphasis on increasing and improving life broke through all bounds, pushing security measures to the brink of autoimmunity. Today, the ongoing transformation of politics into biopolitics is discernible whenever state power glides from national and global to domestic and private spheres, where it is capable of touching on or tapping into the most intimate parts of our lives. The resonances may be quite disturbing, even if entirely unintentional.

Recently, at the Grunewald station in Berlin, I was personally struck by the poster that encouraged the prevention of sexually transmitted diseases: a lemon sheathed with a colored condom and the whimsical tag: *Sicher macht lustig!* (Safe is fun!). The sight should not have been that surprising: the poster, which at the time was plastered across the city's transportation system, had been seen before. On one level, the advice was noble enough, based of course on distressing statistics, a humanitarian service in the name of Enlightenment or *Aufklärung*, published in fact by Germany's Federal Center for Health Education (Bundeszentrale für gesundheitliche Aufklärung). The public announcement justifiably addressed the urgent need to protect oneself against the spread of serious and too often life-threatening diseases, above all acquired immune deficiency syndrome. The global AIDS epidemic certainly deserved precautionary measures, yet it was difficult not to balk at the ad's rhetoric, which attempted to persuade an audience to be safe because being "safe" or "secure" (*sicher*) is "fun" (or even "funny"—*lustig*). Colored condoms introduce a dose of levity to a very serious affair, yet what are we to make of the implication that the prerequisite for enjoyment is being worry free, that pleasure is possible only when one can control pleasure's consequences, when it is believed that the future and its contingencies can be domineered? Although the intervention encourages prudence in one area of experience, it cannot preclude recklessness in another. Protection may promote promiscuity, which itself would hold other, incalculable risks—psychological, emotional, or moral.

The torrent of associations that this poster triggered could hardly be contained. For instance, the opening of Horkheimer and Adorno's *Dialectic* of 1944 instantly came to mind: "In the most general sense of progressive thought, the Enlightenment has always aimed at liberating men from fear and establishing

---

[45] Foucault, *Security, Territory, Population*, 65.

their sovereignty."[46] That political and social organizations persist in dominating nature, despite the threat of self-destruction, is perhaps evident above all in today's micromanagement of everyday life. How far can this *lust* for security go? When will it cease to be fun or funny? In addition to questioning the equation of pleasure and safety, in addition to protesting the insinuation that personal intimacy is potentially hazardous, I shuddered at the bald historical reality of the Grunewald station itself. It was impossible to ignore behind my back the vacant platform memorialized as Gleis 23, which witnessed mass deportations in a past that is not yet—nor never could or should be—sufficiently passed, when biopolitical masters named "hygiene" the order of the day, when work was cruelly promised to make you free—*Arbeit macht frei!* However unfair or unjust, this horrific line intruded as a chilling correlate to the kitschy tag glaring above the protected lemon: *Sicher macht lustig!* Prophylaxis, I concluded, had never been so problematically fruitful, never so potentially unnerving, replete with conflicting emotions, painful images, and human shame.

PHYSICIANS OF THE SOUL

The operative premise of all biopolitical paradigms is that the state is a vast organism that requires physiological research, pathological diagnoses, and medicinal, curative prescriptions. Hence, the biologization of the political fades into the politicization of the biological. Thus, as Foucault observed, the primary right of biopower to "make live" is always counterbalanced by the right to "make die." Contagions must be identified and eliminated from the corporal state; sickness must be addressed, diagnosed, and ultimately healed. This is precisely where Roberto Esposito locates the inherent contradiction of "immunitary logic." Especially in the Nazi biopolitical mechanism, one discerns a tension "between a politics of increasing the birthrate and the antinatalism produced first by a negative eugenics and then by the elimination en masse of pregnant mothers": "on the one side, the exhibition and the strengthening of the generative capacity of the German people; on the other, the homicidal fury that is destined inevitably to inhibit it."[47] Sadly, biopolitics is all-too-often a mask for thanatopolitics. The removal of care implicit in such security measures may eradicate concern, but it does not erase the violence of removal itself—a violence that is merely transferred and perpetually enacted. State measures are therefore pharmocological in every sense: both cure and poison. Immunity invariably dovetails into autoimmunity.

Before the state turned into a living body—before it "truly" became an organism instead of the merely "artificial" or "metaphorical" body purported by

---

[46] Max Horkheimer and Theodor Adorno, *Dialectic of Enlightenment*, 3.

[47] Esposito, *Bios*, 169.

Hobbes—the moral philosophers of the Hellenistic schools developed extensive health programs to cure the soul of its travails. For the Epicureans and the Stoics, philosophy should adopt a medical approach, discovering norms by means of an immanent investigation of living things, as opposed to applying norms that others presume to be transcendentally fixed. Renouncing the realm of ideas or a theory of Forms, these Hellenistic and, later, Roman thinkers essentially practiced a therapeutic "care" (*epimeleia, cura*) that was utterly devoted to the singular case at hand, a concern that was, as Martha Nussbaum describes it, "committed to the amelioration of human life."[48] In principle, what was targeted was any excessive "desire"—*orexis*, literally a "reaching out" for something, an overextension of the soul driven by beliefs, whether true or false. For Epicurus, *orexis* was essentially a disturbance, a baneful concern that disrupted mental serenity. The Epicurean project—and here it would fully agree with the intentions of the Stoics—could therefore be understood as a concern to remove concern. Therapeutic care—*epimeleia*—would name another manner of "reaching out"—*orexis*—but here, specifically and impossibly, as a desire to extirpate desire. The story of "security" begins with these concerned doctors of the soul and, as we all know, does not end with the lethal doctors of the camps. In a provocative sense, it is the history of our collective *anorexia*.

Benjamin discerned in Kafka's burrowing animal a "concern" (*Sorge*) that "nibbles at every anxiety with the fickleness of despair." Here, *Sorge* is a disabling care or worry that feasts upon everything that is bothersome to the soul, a gluttonous worry unable to get its fill, gnawing away at the fabric of our being—indeed, like a mole frantically digging through the damp earth. The concerns, which come from nowhere and everywhere, like the unlocalizable sounds that haunt the creature at the end of *Der Bau*, eat away from within and act as a motor of self-consumption or self-undermining. These biting concerns render the entire writing project frightfully insecure. Kafka, like his "Hunger Artist," may flirt with asceticism, with a sublimating anorexia—he may impose upon himself the strictest of regimens and stuff Ohropax into his hypersensitive ears in order to write—yet the security thus achieved becomes but a prelude to deathly stillness, if the *curae* cease to reemerge. Whereas security makes the work possible, insecurity gives writing hope, even if it makes it impossible.

Kafka, both the writer and the security expert, no doubt recognized the double bind implicit in the concern for security. For him, this self-extirpating desire—the concern to be without concern—seems to present itself as an impossibility, one that is nonetheless motivational. In a significant letter to Max Brod from June 1921, Kafka identifies the relationship that Jewish writers have to the German language as one of groundlessness. However, "the despair over this," Kafka writes, "was their inspiration."[49] He goes on to link this inspiring despair with a series of impossibilities:

---

[48] Martha Nussbaum, *The Therapy of Desire: Theory and Practice in Hellenistic Ethics*, 41.
[49] Kafka, *Briefe*, 337.

[The] impossibility not to write, the impossibility to write in German, the impossibility to write otherwise [*anders*], and one could almost add a fourth impossibility, the impossibility to write (for despair was certainly not something that calms through writing, it was an enemy of life *and* of writing, writing was here only a provisionary arrangement [*Provisorium*], as for someone who writes his last will shortly before he hangs himself—a *provisorium* that can well last a whole life).

The parenthetical proviso that Kafka appends to his list of motivating impossibilities staves off death by keeping death perennially in view.[50] It may therefore be linked to the cautious "prudence" or "provision" (*Vorsicht*) that allows the burrowing creature to keep his structure vulnerable, imperfect. Whatever security the burrow provides can be granted only by means of desperate—and therefore inspiring—insecurity.

"I have constructed the burrow and it appears quite successful." The burrow is not only the structure built by the story's narrator but also *The Burrow* written by the story's dying author. With the opening sentence, the reader enters a labyrinth analogous to the underground maze that houses the creature. The burrower who digs "inside the earth"—*im Innern der Erde*—also arguably excavates, by way of an anagram, "inside speech"—*im Innern der Rede*. The safe house of language, including the fortress of tradition, is here undermined and rendered insecure, which instills both despair and hope. Again, the burrow, which has just been completed, only *appears* to succeed. The story's gambit may be alluding to the bold optimism famously announced by Horace in the concluding poem to his third book of *Odes: Exigi monumentum aere perennius* (I have constructed a monument more lasting than bronze, *Odes* 3.30.1). Horace, of course, is referring to his well-built poetry, which can now serve as a means to secure his immortal fame. As long as his poetry continues to be recited, the poet shall live—*non omnis moriar* (I shall not die entirely, 6). The gnawing, never-sated concern that motivates Kafka's writing digs into the Horatian monument and underscores the threat latent in eradicating worry. For the *monumentum* is both a memorial and a warning (*monere*), a poetic security project and a gravestone. *Non omnis moriar*—the poet will not die entirely, which means part of him must. If only provisionally, Kafka's biting concern counters the anorexia that would assign the text to the security of the tomb.

---

[50] For an extended interpretation of this letter, see Michael Levine, *Writing through Repression*, 150–51. I am highly indebted to Levine's comments on an earlier draft of this section.

PART TWO

Etymologies and Figures

Directories and Figures

A Brief Semantic History of *Securitas*

WHAT DOES THE TERM "security" express? What are or have been its semantic functions: its shifting cultural connotations and its divergent discursive values? Before examining the figures and metaphors that have been deployed to think about security across the ages, it would be useful to outline the main stations along the word's complex itinerary through historical usage. The cursory overview in this chapter simply intends to mark the major turning points of this history, beginning with ancient Rome and concluding with seventeenth-century Europe, so as to help organize the more in-depth analyses that follow.

TRANQUILLITY OF MIND (*ATARAXIA, APATHEIA*)

The word *securitas* emerges in the first century BC in the philosophical writings of Cicero, who in fact may have coined the term. It is a nominalization of the adjective *securus*, which is attested earlier. For Cicero, in general, *securitas* removes a *cura* that is negative and psychological, expressing an aggravation of the soul, an oppressive source of anxiety that disrupts one's emotional stability. Here, *securitas* denotes a mental state of calm and should be distinguished from *salus*, which in republican usage represents safety from physical harm and therefore health. Although the two states may clearly overlap—one is calm, when one is safe—it is important to emphasize the psychological dimension of *securitas*, especially because it is just as possible to be calm in the midst of danger, whether out of fortitude or out of ignorance.

Whereas *salus* targets a palpable threat, *securitas* addresses the tribulations that arise from within the soul. A key passage is found in Cicero's *De officiis*:

> There must be freedom [*vacandum . . . est*] from every disturbance of the mind, not only from desire and fear but also from distress, from the mind's pleasure and anger, so that there may be present the tranquillity of the mind and the security [*tranquillitas animi et securitas*] which brings not only constancy but also dignity. (*Off.* 1.69)

The list of disturbing passions is presented as what must be eliminated (*vacandum est*)—a privative gesture that underscores the removal grammatically expressed by the prefix *se-* in *securitas*. "Desire," "fear," "distress," "pleasure," and "anger" are regarded as examples of *curae* that disquiet the philosopher's composure and jeopardize his dignity. *Dignitas* implies worth, a moral quality of being suitable for a particular task. Without security, in thrall to worrisome concerns, the man not only fails to achieve "steadiness" (*constantia*) but also proves unfit for the tasks set before him. He is thrown off balance and is marked off as incapable, if not altogether impotent. The emotions enumerated here—desire and fear, distress, pleasure, and anger—should be regarded as the *curae* that will be absent in *securitas*, hence the peace of mind (*tranquillitas animi*) associated with private life, far from the onerous troubles of the political sphere. Within the historical context of *De officiis*, the absence of *cura* corresponds, at least in part, to Cicero's physical withdrawal from the Forum. Alone in Tusculum, sundered from the madding crowd, the former statesman can turn inward, reflecting on his life and its circumstances. No longer harried, he can gather the fruits of serene isolation and thereby come into *securitas*—almost a sinecure (< *sine cura*, "without care"), in which benefits are great without the taxing toil of administrative concerns and the contingencies of political life.

In iconic fashion, the word *securitas* reflects Cicero's movement away from the city. Although the prefix *sē-* may be understood as either the accusative or ablative form of the third-person pronoun *sui*, lexicographers have argued that the ablative ("by or from himself, herself, or itself") is originary. It is therefore not entirely by linguistic accident that the German reflexive pronoun (*sich*) is still audible in *Sicherheit*. The link to the ablative already introduces a sense of removal or withdrawal *from*, insofar as the primary force of the ablative case is one of separation (*ablativus* < *ablatus* "taken from"), which is generally used to express syntactic relations of privation, source, cause, agency, or comparison.[1] The syntagma *se-cura* vividly conjures a scene in which care has been taken away or one has moved away from care. *Se-* is also cognate with the adversative conjunction *sed* ("but rather"), which again suggests a turning away, a physical or mental conversion from its object, a move to the side.[2] *Sed* (or *se*) is also an attested archaic Latin preposition meaning "aside, apart from." Latin vocabulary provides many examples that emphasize the basic senses of apartness and detachment implicit in the prefix, for example: *secessio* "withdrawal, separation" (< *se* + *cedo*, "go, move"); *secretus* "that which has been set aside or put away" (< *se* + *cerno*, "distinguish, mark off"); *seductio* "a leading or drawing aside" (< *se* + *duco*, "lead"); and *separatio* "a setting apart" (< *se* + *paro*,

---

[1] See J. H. Allen and J. B. Greenough, *New Latin Grammar for Schools and Colleges, Founded on Comparative Grammar*, §§ 398–401.

[2] See Alois Walde, *Lateinisches etymologisches Wörterbuch*, s.v. "sēd, sē," 613. For this chapter, in addition to Walde's dictionary, I have referred primarily to Emile Boisacq, *Dictionnaire étymologique de la langue grecque*; Pierre Chantraine, *Dictionnaire étymologique de la langue grecque*; Alfred Ernout and Antoine Meillet, *Dictionnaire étymologique de la langue latine*; *The Oxford English Dictionary*; Emile Littré, *Dictionnaire de la langue française*; and Wolfgang Pfeifer, *Etymologisches Wörterbuch des Deutschen*.

"prepare, arrange, order"). To be *sober* means to be removed from wine (< *se* + *ebrius*, "sated with drink, drunk"); and to be sluggish (*socors*) is to be without spirit (< *se* + *cor*, "heart"). In this grammatical economy, we could say that the ablative object governed by *se*- has been removed, put off to the side, taken from one mental or physical place and put somewhere else.

Cicero's acceptation of "security" clearly turns on this sense of elimination. The term further collates ideals familiar from Hellenistic moral philosophy, encompassing Epicurean *ataraxia* (freedom from disturbances) and Stoic *apatheia* (freedom from passions [*pathē*]). These major terms, constructed with the Greek alpha privative, similarly denote the process of removal lexically marked by the prefix *se*- and aim toward the realization of the good, happy life (*eudaimonia*, *makariōs zēn*) or what the Romans would call the "blessed life" (*beata vita*).[3] In the *Tusculan Disputations* we read:

> How can anyone be in possession of that desirable and much-coveted *securitas* who has, or may have, a multitude of evils attending him?—for I now call freedom from distress [*vacuitatem aegritudinis*] *securitas*, on which freedom a happy life [*vita beata*] depends. (*Tusc.* 5.2)

The statement closely rehearses one of the principal motives of Hellenistic thought as found, for example, in the *Letter to Menoeceus*, where Epicurus posits "the soul's freedom from disturbance [*ataraxian*]" to be the "end [*telos*] belonging to the blessed life."[4] Thus Cicero, on vacation in the country, learns how to vacate the perturbances that make him miserable.

Later, for Seneca, the equation is perfectly clear: "What is the blessed life?—*securitas* and lasting tranquillity."

> How does a man reach this condition? By gaining a complete view of truth, by maintaining, in all that he does, order, measure, fitness, and a will that is inoffensive and kindly, that is intent upon reason and never departs therefrom, that commands at the same time love and admiration. In short, to give you the principle in brief compass, the wise man's soul ought to be such as would be proper for a god. (*Ep.* 92.3)

Perhaps more emphatically than with Cicero, *securitas* here constitutes an accomplishment. Grounded in a transcendent position above all contingency, the philosopher reaches security and thus touches on the divine sphere, where he is no longer ruffled by disturbances:

> For while the sum and substance of the happy life is sound freedom from care [*solida securitas*], and while the secret of such freedom is unshaken confidence [*inconcussa fiducia*], men gather together causes for worry [*sol-*

---

[3] For representative texts and commentary, A. A. Long and D. N. Sedley, eds., *The Hellenistic Philosophers*, 1: 394–401.

[4] Long and Sedley, *The Hellenistic Philosophers*, 2: 116.

licitudinis . . . causas], and, while traveling life's treacherous road, not only have burdens to bear but even draw burdens to themselves. (*Ep.* 44.7)

Seneca may be employing a subtle etymological figure to emphasize his point: "sound security" (*solida securitas)* is a security that is whole or undivided (*solidus < sollus*, "complete," related to Greek *holos*), a holistic integrity, moreover, that is "firm" and "unshaken" (*inconcussa*) and can therefore be played against the "worry" (*solicitudo*) that literally spells a "whole [*sollus*] that has been shaken [*citus*]." The remedy for the treachery one encounters on the road is to find a firm foundation—what Descartes will call a *fundamentum inconcussum.* Yet, as the *se-* prefix implies, concerns are not entirely annihilated in *securitas* but simply put off to the side, where they can no longer affect one's disposition. Accordingly, Seneca celebrates the achievement of *securitas* but without ignoring his human condition: "What a wonderful privilege, to have the weaknesses of a man and the serenity of a god [*securitatem dei*]!" (*Ep.* 53.12). For Seneca, all the while mindful of mortality, *securitas* cannot eradicate physical death but only the psychological fear of death.[5]

This godlike yet human accomplishment is postulated on what Michel Foucault has analyzed as "technologies of the self," which point back to the Socratic practice of self-concern: the *epimeleia heautou* ("care of the self") that forms a resilient selfhood through attentive spiritual and physical exercises (*meletai*).[6] The philosopher, in addition to striving to "know himself," should train his mind and body to become impervious to circumstance, to become capable of withstanding strong emotions and overwhelming impulses—a state that both Cicero and Seneca explicitly identify as *securitas.* Thus, a concept of security comes to be implicated in the historical development of the individual subject. As Foucault notes,

> [W]ith this notion of *epimeleia heautou* we have a body of work defining a way of being, a standpoint, forms of reflection, and practices which make it an extremely important phenomenon not just in the history of representations, notions, or theories, but in the history of subjectivity itself.[7]

The *construction* of an inviolable self literally depends on proper *instruction*, on building a subject that can weather all kinds of trouble, foreseeable or not. Among the ancient moralists, this arduous process of subjectivization is based on a simple premise: because future, external circumstances can never be predicted with certainty, it is wise to turn attention inward. In order to stabilize the self, one must devote vigilance and diligence to internal representations. To secure the self, one must care for the self. That is to say, one can be "free from care" only if one conscientiously practices philosophy "with care" (*cum cura*).

---

[5] See Seneca, *Ep.* 36.11.

[6] For Foucault's discussion, see especially *The Care of the Self: The History of Sexuality*, 39–68; and *The Hermeneutics of the Subject: Lectures at the Collège de France, 1981–1982*, especially 1–19.

[7] Foucault, *The Hermeneutics of the Subject*, 11.

For Cicero and Seneca, therefore, security is not attained simply through withdrawal from the tumult of political life but rather through the *careful* practice of cultivating a self that continues to be embedded in and constituted by a community. Thus secured, the philosopher—like the enlightened exile from Plato's cave—may return down to the dark and delusional realm of politics. Self-directed stability, achieved through reflection, ultimately prepares one to reenter the fray. In the Platonic dialogue *Alcibiades*, Socrates informs the young and ambitious Alcibiades why, before entering public office, it is first necessary to "take care of oneself" (*heautou epimeleisthai*, *Alc.* 1.127e). Learning to attend to oneself is the prerequisite for attending and therefore governing others. In giving the name *securitas* to this accomplishment, Roman Stoicism thereby anticipates the argument, subsequently exploited, that correlates the security of the public with the security of the caretaker. Self-government prepares one for political governance.

Balancing Act (*euthymia*)

In the passage from *De officiis* cited above, *securitas* brings about not only internal "constancy" but also the "dignity" that proves one's capacity to perform a task or carry out a public office. This subtle link between inner and public security is discernible elsewhere in Cicero's treatises, again with Platonic overtones relating to the well-known analogy between the city and man. In *De finibus*, Cicero takes *securitas* to be a synonym of *euthymia*, "cheerfulness" (*Fin.* 5.23), a term immediately linked to Democritus, who defined "wisdom" (*sophiē*) as that which "rids the soul of suffering or passions [*pathē*]" (Diels-Kranz B31). *Euthymia* literally denotes a balancing of the *thymos*, a word that has a venerable career in the history of ancient Greek literature.[8] In the Homeric epics, it essentially refers to the body's emotive organ, which produces strong feelings, incites passions, and arouses action. Associated with spiritedness or impulsiveness, *thymos* is often understood as the seat of indignation.[9] Later, within the topography of the Platonic tripartite soul, *thymos* assumes a crucial role, insofar as it occupies the position directly between the mortal drive of desire (*epithymia*) and the higher, immortal faculty of reason (*logos*). The extensive anatomy lesson of the *Timaeus* teaches that the area of the soul that contains the *thymos* is to be found between the diaphragm and the neck, that is, physically higher than desire's place in the belly but lower than reason's home in the head. So placed, the *thymos* is able to work together with *logos* in suppressing the "tribe of de-

---

[8] For a comprehensive account with ample bibliography, see William Harris, *Restraining Rage: The Ideology of Anger Control in Classical Antiquity*. For further examples of "balancing" in Democritus, see Diels-Kranz B224, 231, 281, and 285.

[9] For a general overview, see Bruno Snell, *The Discovery of the Mind in Greek Philosophy and Literature*, 9–15; and Harris, *Restraining Rage*, 52–54.

sires" whenever they refuse to obey the command from the "citadel of reason" (*Tim.* 70a). For Democritus, *euthymia*, which again Cicero aligns with *securitas*, is the cheerful disposition when the soul's impulsiveness is dominated by reason as opposed to being domineered by base desires.

In the ideal city of Plato's *Republic*, which is constructed by Socrates on analogy with the individual soul, *thymos* is associated with the guardians, the spirited class of security forces trained to ward off menaces from without as well as threats from within. Socrates muses that a successful guardian should be like a watchdog, an animal characterized by "high-spiritedness" (*thymoeidēs*), for *thymos* is something "unassailable and invincible" (*Rep.* 375a–b). In the later iconographical tradition, security is frequently depicted as a dog contrasted with the rabbit that represents fear. As for the republic, the city's safety must rely on the thymically driven watchmen, yet there remains the inevitable problem of controlling their aggression. How can the citizens be sure that the guardians, who are essentially personifications of *thymos*, will not turn their canine spirits upon each other or even upon the city's inhabitants? "It is necessary that they be gentle toward their own people but harsh toward their enemies" (375c). Faced with this problem, Socrates' exposition turns to the centrality of education. By training the strength of the guardians' bodies and cultivating the virtue of their souls, the ideal city will reap the benefits of the soldiers' ferocity without suffering any of the consequences.

Positioned at the border that separates the city from its environs, the *thymoeidetic* guardians are topographically correlative with the *thymos*, which is stationed between the immortal (rational) and the mortal (irrational) parts of the soul. Just as the *thymos* may form alliances either with desire or with reason, so the guardians must exhibit opposing capacities to be either gentle or fierce. Bearing Plato's pit-bull guardians in mind, we again see that, although *securitas* does not initially constitute a political term, the sense of civic protection and safety is never too distant.

Fully in line with a Stoic tradition, Cicero strives toward a *securitas* that would quell the impulsiveness of the passions. As later in Seneca, the "care of the self" is the method by which the emotions are educated, trained to serve the sovereignty of reason. For the Stoa, the mind's *logos* is therefore identified as the *hēgemonikon*, the authoritative, governing part of the soul likened to a military commander (*hēgemōn*) as well as the ruling principle of the cosmos.[10] Through the mechanisms of domination belonging to discipline, the careful instruction and construction of the self brings the body's emotive energy into line with rational behavior. Likewise, the philosopher is concerned with the inner dynamics of his soul in order to be ultimately free of these concerns. Although Cicero never explicitly describes it in this fashion, *securitas* is the order achieved by reason's domination.

[10] On the *hēgemonikon* as the governing principle of the soul, see Zeno, *Stoicorum Veterum Fragmenta (SVF).* 1.39. For the cosmological function, see Chrysippus, *(SVF)* 2.186, 192, and Cleanthes, *(SVF)* 1.112.

From Plato onward, the ideal city, whose ternary structure reflects the tripartite soul, represents an ordering that strives to conceal the violence of rational domination. Domination implies conflict: a struggle between two distinct parties. Here, in the political-psychological model that Plato establishes, the fight is between the rational and the irrational parts of either the city or the soul. Structurally, as we gradually move toward modern political philosophy, it would be useful to bear in mind this basic distinction between the dualism of disciplinary action and the threefold, pyramidal configuration of the order that results from this primary adversarial relationship.[11] The violence of the *cura sui*—the pain involved in physical and spiritual exercises, the taming of our impulses, the domestication of our dogged desires—exhibits itself as a fight between two opponents; yet it advances to the stability of *securitas* only when reason is at the head, leading the bodily appetites along with the help of its soldiery.

The basic conflict between *two* sides—which is contingent insofar as any side may triumph—is neutralized by the architectonics of *three* estates. Later modes of theological and juridical legitimization aim to establish an order akin to the inner, Stoic *securitas* whereby all cares should be put to rest. Yet this construct hovering above the soul, the city, and the world can never fully eradicate the violent work that takes place on the battlefield of immanence, of one against another. The self-curatorial struggle is barely concealed by reason's power. As the middle, third term, the well-balanced *thymos* of *euthymia* becomes the earmark of a secure order that strives to mask the simple domination of *logos* over the body. Violent dualities are quelled by stabilizing triads.

Sophocles provides a subtle but powerful indication of this matter in *Oedipus Tyrannus*. The central act of violence that motivates the plot (from outside the frame of the staged tragedy) is arguably Oedipus's murder of Laius, which, as the prophecy foretold, occurred "where three roads meet" (*Oed. Tyr.* 716, 730, and 1398–99). Oedipus is a hero consistently marked by "three": the fated "triple ways"; the exposure "three days" after birth (717–18); and the "three legs" of the Sphinx's famous riddle. The riddle, which Sophocles also did not represent on stage, was easily solved by Oedipus because he himself always walked with a staff. This walking stick, moreover, reflects a threefold function as cane, weapon, and scepter. We could say that the hero embodies the "three," which deems him capable of saving and protecting the city. This capacity seems to rest in a sovereign, trinitarian power that is thoroughly transcendent. Thus, he solves the Sphinx's riddle in the abstract, giving the species name "man" as his winning answer.

Oedipus himself, of course, is the exception to the rule he discovers: whereas infants crawl on all fours, he, with ankles bound, hobbled on three; and whereas healthy adults saunter confidently, he has always needed the cane's support to

---

[11] The distinction between the conflict of the two and the order of the three is suggested by Foucault, *Society Must Be Defended*, especially 16 -19.

prevent himself from falling. Perpetually three-footed, Oedipus is apparently not affected by the course of time that defines human life; his position thus comes across as noncontingent, unchanging, secure. As a consequence, he knows "man" in general but fails to know himself. The knowledge (*mathos*) that Sophocles' play famously transmits through suffering (*pathēi*) is nothing other than what one learns when one stumbles to the ground. The threefold security that Oedipus procures is also the cause of the city's devastating plague. The ternary order he establishes cannot mitigate the binary, parricidal violence that placed him on the throne. When one approaches a fork in the road—on the ground, and not from a transcendent, bird's-eye view—one does not see three roads but only two.

SAFETY AND DEFENSE (*ASPHALEIA*)

Whereas with Cicero the notion of *securitas* tends to adhere to the private realm, with the collapse of the Roman Republic the term begins to be employed in a decidedly public fashion. Throughout the imperial period the term came to denote an idea of military or governmental protection—not a condition to be achieved privately, away from the urban center, but rather within the city's sheltering walls. Velleius Paterculus, for example, writing nearly eight decades after Cicero's late works, used the term to describe the removal of the threat of civil war that the emperor had achieved for the populace.[12] Later still, under Nero's reign, an altar to the goddess Securitas was established in the Forum and coins were minted bearing the inscription *Securitas Augusti* and, later, *Securitas publica*. The tradition continued throughout the century, with the figure of personified *Securitas* appearing as a woman, sitting or leaning against a column, holding a scepter, a cornucopia, or a wreath.[13] The implication of these accoutrements of power, benefaction, and glory is that the emperor was now represented as the person who had taken on all the *curae* of the state and its citizens. That is to say, the individual is not secure in the Stoic sense of contemplative tranquillity accomplished through the practice of philosophical training. Rather every citizen is worry free thanks to the efforts and success of the governing power. Certainly, the *securitas* enjoyed by the individual retains its psychological or emotional valence, yet the agency responsible for this composure is now located externally rather than internally. Thus, Tacitus, who had been condemned to silence under Domitian, celebrated the public and consequently private security that was reestablished with the accession of Nerva and Trajan:

[12] Velleius Paterculus, *Hist. rom.* 2.89, 98, and 103. On the emergence of this sense of *securitas* in the imperial period, see Hans Ulrich Instinsky, *Sicherheit als politisches Problem des römischen Kaisertums*.

[13] In addition to *Securitas Augusti* and *Securitas publica*, inscriptions include *Securitas perpetua, Securitas rei publicae, Securitas orbis, Securitas populi Romani, Securitas imperii, Securitas temporum, Securitas saeculi*, and so forth. See Instinsky, *Sicherheit als politisches Problem*, 21–26.

Now at last the spirits are reviving. At the first dawning of this most fortunate age [*beatissimi saeculi*], Nerva Caesar at once combined principles formerly incompatible, monarchy and freedom. Day by day Nerva Trajan is enhancing the happiness of our times. Public security [*securitas publica*] has not merely inspired our hopes and prayers but has gained the assurance [*fiduciam*] of those prayers' fulfilment. (*Agricola* 3.5; Birley, trans.)[14]

The idea of civil defense, of course, did not originate with the establishment of imperial might. However, in former republican usage the meaning of protection against both external aggression and internal discord was instead expressed by the word *salus* (which yields English *safety* and *salvation*). Up until Augustus's accession, political-civil safety was neatly distinguished from Stoic security as psychological tranquillity. In denoting corporeal health, prosperity, and preservation, *salus* was precisely what the Republic and its appointed leadership rendered to individuals and to the state. Self-therapy produced *securitas*; state therapy engendered *salus*. A temple to the goddess Salus, high upon one of the summits of the Quirinal, overlooked the city; and the "safety or the security of the people"—the *salus populi*—was perceived as a fundamental good among the citizenry. As Cicero famously expressed it: *Salus populi suprema lex esto* ("Let the safety of the people be the supreme law," *De legibus* 3.3.8).

From the time of Augustus onward, this sense of protection was fully conveyed by *securitas*. The earlier republican distinction between *salus* as "bodily safety" and *securitas* as "peace of mind" here started to become less rigorous. As Seneca himself notes, the *securitas* of the populace was now wholly linked to the *securitas* of the sovereign.[15] A major split, then, in the word's history is between an inner, psychological sense of composure and an external, physical sense of administered safety. This latter, public meaning should no longer be understood as a translation of Hellenistic *ataraxia* or *apatheia* but rather as an extension of another privative term in Greek, *asphaleia*, "steadfastness, stability," literally: "prevention [*a*-] from stumbling [*sphallein*]"). The numismatic convention of depicting Securitas leaning against a column speaks to this idea of physical stabilization and further recalls Oedipus propped upon his staff. Although for Cicero, and subsequently for Seneca, *securitas* can allude to a metaphorical fortification of the self, *asphaleia* tends to express a more corporeal or existential assurance from danger, especially as it occurs in the military *History* of Thucydides. (In Hobbes's translation of Thucydides, *asphaleia* is consistently rendered as "security.") Still, the term is also employed figuratively: in the philosophical discourse of Plato, for example, an argument is *asphalēs* when it cannot fail or fall (*sphallein*), when its certainty is irrefutable.

---

[14] For a similar sentiment, see Pliny the Younger, *Panegyricus* 34 and 80. Cf. Andrea Schrimm-Heins, "Gewißheit und Sicherheit: Geschichte und Bedeutungswandel der Begriffe certitudo und securitas," 1: 139.

[15] Seneca, *De clementia* 1.19.5–6. See also, Seneca, *Ep.* 73.2. For analysis, see Schrimm-Heins, "Gewißheit und Sicherheit," 1: 138.

Asphaleia plays a prominent, albeit polyvalent role in Epicurean philosophy. On the one hand, negatively construed, the term is linked to the wish for *"protection* from others," which is misguided insofar as those desirous of such "security" believe it can be attained through wealth, through being "famous and ostentatious" (*Principal Doctrines* 7).[16] In another statement, which will similarly be taken up and fully developed by Lucretius, Epicurus again alludes to the notion of *asphaleia* as protection and cites its mortal limitations. "Against other things it is possible to obtain security [*asphaleian*]. But when it comes to death we human beings all live in an unwalled city" (*Vatican Sayings* 31).[17] On the other hand, *asphaleia* is not always what we would call a "false sense of security" but rather may be achieved in a philosophically viable manner, for example, through friendship—"within our mortal limits nothing enhances security [*asphaleian*] more than friendship" (*Princ. Doct.* 28).

A word with clear conservative connotations, *asphaleia* guarantees that institutions will not crumble. In civil language, it describes unassailable, quasi-divine permanence, like the "eternally steadfast [*asphales*] abode of the gods" described by Homer (*Od.* 6.42) or the "infallible [*asphalē*] statutes of the gods" invoked by Sophocles' Antigone (*Ant.* 454). In the prologue to *Oedipus Tyrannus*, Thebes' priest prays that the young ruler who defeated the Sphinx may once again save the city, but this time "with security" (*asphaleiai*, *Oed. Tyr.* 51). In addition to notions of civil and legal stability, there are also clear moral implications. Creon, angered by Oedipus's rash insinuations of conspiracy, admonishes his king: "In time you will know everything with certainty [*asphalōs*]" (614); and this sentiment is immediately corroborated by the chorus: "Those who are quick of temper are not safe [*ouk asphaleis*]" (617). More concretely, security also inheres in the *asphalt* that sets things in place. In the Septuagint, it is the pitch (*asphaltos*) that Noah uses to fix the timber of his ark, so that he may ensure safe passage through God's wrath (Gen. 6:14). According to Herodotus, *asphaltos* is the bitumen retrieved from the banks of the Euphrates, which cemented the thick walls of Babylon and protected the city on the plain from invasion (*Hist.* 1.178–79). In its modern form, *asphalt* will pave urban paths, either for the businessman whose hectic schedule allows little time for contingency or for the flâneur who yearns for the freedom to dream. Baudelaire, whose splenetic poetry trips on the uneven paving stones of modernity, will reveal the cracks in the city's efforts to secure timeless ideals.

Negligence (*acedia*)

A concern (*cura*) troubles the mind, spurring it into action, and may therefore be viewed as either inhibiting or productive. Pestering cares may render us in-

---

[16] Cf. Lucretius, *De rerum natura* 5.1120–35.
[17] In Long and Sedley, *The Hellenistic Philosophers*, 1: 150.

secure and can even be paralyzing, but they may also instigate means or processes to put those cares to rest. A fear of falling into danger, an apprehension of loss, a brooding anger, or an obsessive desire—each identifies *cura* as a potentially motivational distress. Yet, this same restlessness is also discernible in positively valued *curae* that are related to matters of intellectual effort like *labor* "work, toil," *opera* "service, attention," and *studium* "eagerness, endeavor." Good farmers display *cura* for their crops and shepherds show *cura* for their flocks, parents exercise *cura* for their children and the pious practice *cura* for the gods—activities that concretely assign *cura* to the areas of cultivation, provision, and reverence.[18] Evident here is the desire to proceed *carefully*, with an *accuracy* that corresponds to deep commitment. An individual beset with this species of *cura* works assiduously to overcome barriers and is fully involved in an enterprise that vividly bears its goal in mind, be it a successful harvest, an offspring's welfare, or the gods' placation.

In post-Augustan usage, *securitas* in the positive senses of tranquillity and stability continues to occur together with *securitas* as *carelessness*, that is, as the baneful negation of attentiveness or diligence. Quintilian, for example, employs *securitas* to express a fault common among students, one that hampers education: "In praising the student's speaking, [let the teacher be] neither stingy nor lavish, since the former engenders a loathing for work [*taedium laboris*], while the latter causes carelessness [*securitatem*]" (*Inst. orat.* 2.2.6). The teacher must ward off the kind of security that breeds overconfidence and hence *inaccuracy*. Furthermore, *securitas* may convey a sense of damaging impudence or disrespect. In pleading a case, for example, one should not display too much confidence, because a judge generally "hates self-assurance [*securitatem*]" (4.1.55). Similarly, a defendant ought to be dissuaded from exhibiting an "offensive assurance" (*invisa securitas*, 6.1.34). Seneca, too, although he generally aligns *securitas* with Stoic imperturbability, also on occasion uses the term to denote idleness and negligence. In *De beneficiis* he commends the difficulty of probing, philosophical questions, for "these, which appear subtle and tricky, remove carelessness [*securitatem*] and laziness [*segnitiam*] from our thinking" (*Ben.* 5.12.2). In both of these passages, "security" implies an adverse loss of concern, a cognitive failure that leads to recklessness or heedlessness. Free from care, the *secure* student or thinker is exposed as an insouciant fool.

Although Cicero fairly consistently deploys the term *securitas* to denote the absence of harmful concerns, he does on occasion question the moral implications of removing care altogether. In *De amicitia*, for example, he clearly expresses misgivings regarding this otherwise vaunted ideal:

> O distinguished wisdom! Truly, they seem to remove the sun from the world, those who remove friendship from life; nothing that we have from

---

[18] For a comprehensive investigation of Latin usage, with ample citations, see Manfred Hauser, *Der römische Begriff Cura*.

the immortal gods is better than friendship, nothing more delightful. What indeed is this so-called security [*quae est enim ista securitas*]? In appearance it is certainly enticing, but in reality it is in many cases to be repudiated. For it is improper not to undertake some honorable matter or action, or to lay aside what has been undertaken, in order that you may not be troubled [*sollicitus*]. If we flee from care, we must flee from virtue [*quod si curam fugimus, virtus fugienda est*]. (*Amic.* 47)

Insofar as it eliminates care, *securitas* threatens to remove the individual from relationships that define the best and most pleasing aspects of human life, leaving him or her isolated in a deficient, eclipsed world. The allure of a transcendent, philosophical position may on the surface promise a carefree existence, but in the inescapably immanent reality of our lives, both in the world and among others, any such promise seduces us into a carelessness that renders virtue impossible. *Quod si curam fugimus, virtus fugienda est* (If we flee from care, we must flee from virtue.) To emphasize the point, Cicero continues, "It is necessary that virtue disdains and loathes with some care [*cum aliqua cura*] those things that are contrary to virtue, as when kindness rejects malice, temperance lust, and fortitude cowardice" (*Amic.* 47). Moral excellence (*virtus*) demands an engagement practiced "with care" (*cum cura*) as opposed to the indifference implied in a state "free from care." Rather than bestowing a relieving *apatheia*, *securitas* can also reduce someone to sheer apathy.

The polyvalence of concern leads to many distinct evaluations of security. An important oscillation is clear in the work of Augustine. For him, true *securitas*—or "reliable security" (*firma securitas*)—is possible only with God, that is, in the eternally blessed state in which the saved will at last be removed from the anxiety that constitutes earthly existence.[19] As Augustine later explains, the troubles linked to weakness and sin, and the anxiety that these faults invariably breed, ultimately constitute the value of this kind of security: "The greater the danger in the battle, the greater the joy in the triumph" (*Conf.* 8.3.7).[20] Essentially, danger remains indispensable for the redemptive project:

> But not even the saints and faithful worshipers of the one true and most high God are safe [*securi*] from the [demons'] manifold temptations and deceits. For in this place of weakness, and in these wicked days, this worried concern [*sollicitudo*] is not useless, in order that this security [*securitas*], where peace is most complete and most certain [*pax plenissima atque certissima est*], may be sought with more fervent longing. (*Civ. Dei* 19.10)[21]

---

[19] See, e.g., Augustine, *Confessions* 2.6.13. For a good overview, see Andrea Leisner, *Zwischen Weltflucht und Herstellungswahn: Bildungstheoretische Studien zur Ambivalenz des Sicherheitsdenkens von der Antike bis zur Gegenwart*, 15–18.

[20] Augustine, *Confessions*, H. Chadwick, trans., 137.

[21] With regard to this particular problem, see also *Civ. Dei* 19.27.

It is the lack of security that causes security to be desired. Hence, for Augustine, God has by design created a world that is replete with worry and difficulties. Needless to say, Augustine does not deem this intention as an example of divine sadism; rather it is proof of God's mercy, insofar as it gives less "occasion to find sweet pleasure in what is not [God]" (*Conf.* 6.6.9). The faithful must endure a realm wherein fullness is shattered (*solli-citudo*) so that ultimate reintegration with the divinity persists as the sole aim of life. Analogous to Quintilian's pedagogical advice against *securitas* as negligence, Augustine, the former scholar of rhetoric, claims that to be utterly secure in this world would threaten true security with God. It would deceive us with a resting point, when the only valid resting point should be in the light of divine grace.

For Augustine, feeling secure may also be associated with a particularly political form of complacency. In the *Civitas Dei*, he observes how the Roman Republic degenerated into weakness and carelessness after its glorious triumph in the final war against Carthage:

> When the last Punic war had terminated in the utter destruction of Rome's rival, . . . then the Roman Republic was overwhelmed with such a host of ills, which sprang from the corrupt manners induced by prosperity and security [*prosperitate ac securitate*], that the sudden overthrow of Carthage is seen to have injured Rome more seriously than her long-continued hostility. (*Civ. Dei* 3.21)

The Roman triumph—an accomplishment of prosperity and security—is in fact more baneful than the former military threat. As already suggested, to fail to recognize one's continued vulnerability is to suffer from the carelessness of a security that leaves one more vulnerable than ever. Security from risks holds risks of its own.

Throughout early Christian usage, *securitas* tends to be regarded pejoratively in this sense of negligence. Specifically, it is associated with a caricatured portrayal of Epicureanism, aligned not necessarily with *ataraxia* but more frequently with *akēdia* ("indifference, torpor," literally: the negation of "care" [*kēdos*]). The Latinized term *acedia* initially characterized a monk's loss of interest in the ascetic life and a sinful desire to rejoin the world.[22] Following Gregory the Great, Christian theologians ultimately define *acedia* as one of the seven mortal sins, a terrifying fault that stems from pride (*superbia*) and invariably ends in melancholy (*tristitia*), where all occupation, spiritual as well as physical, has been supplanted by detrimental boredom, lethargy, and complete insouciance. Hence, Robert Burton, in *The Anatomy of Melancholy*, warns that "many a carnal man is lulled asleep in perverse security" and elsewhere cites the authority of Saint Jerome: "*Ubicunque securitas, ibi libido dominatur*—lust and security domineer together."[23]

---

[22] See R. Hauser, "Acedia," 73–74.
[23] Robert Burton, *The Anatomy of Melancholy*, Part 3.4.2.6 and Part 3.2.2.1 (vol. 3, 425 and 63).

Mortal's Chiefest Enemy

With the Christianization of the empire, positive connotations of *securitas* more or less vanished from political and religious usage, save for some formulaic vestiges heard in early liturgy. Otherwise, it was mostly in legal contexts where *securitas* served prominently as an ideal of guarantee in oaths, pledges, and contracts. The later link between securitization and mercantile insurance has its roots in this usage. When the term resurfaced in civil and theological thought during the Reformation, it again betrayed the ambivalence that has always characterized its usage. Whereas Thomas Hobbes deploys "security" in the sense of Thucydides' *asphaleia*—namely, as the stability that follows removal from the worrisome state of nature—William Shakespeare leaves us with a memorable figuration of an abusive sovereign, one who procured power for himself by violent means and dangerously dreams of putting every concern to rest:

> Sleep that knits up the ravelled sleave of care
> The death of each day's life, sore labour's bath
> Balm of hurt minds, great nature's second course,
> Chief nourisher in life's feast.
>
> (*Macbeth* 2.2)

The implicit term here is *security*, which promises to restore a mind perplexed by haunting troubles. The remedy that removes care is therefore equated with gentle, restorative sleep, with a refreshing bath or a satisfying meal. Yet, this security is also portrayed as a death, insofar as a life perfectly without care is a life taken out of time, which is to say no life at all. The "chief nourisher in life's feast" points toward an entirely carefree, nonexistent existence. Here, the afterlife is emphatically *after life*. As illicit sovereign or delusional *chief*, Macbeth aches for this "chief nourisher"—a feast fit for a king, an eternal subsistence that would presumably secure his authority and his power. Of course, he will learn too late, as the witch goddess Hecate predicts in the following act, that "security / Is mortal's chiefest enemy" (3.5). When the fighting energy of care is relaxed, when it is lulled to sleep in security's warm bed, the sovereign principle— whether embodied by the individual philosopher or the king of Scotland— readily degenerates into complacency. Tellingly, in *Eastward Hoe* (1605), the Jacobean satire written by Ben Jonson, George Chapman, and John Marston, Security is the name of a miserly creditor—"the father of destruction" (2.2).

As we shall see, in the sermons and writings of Martin Luther, this doubled valuation is articulated by the distinction between the secular, temporal kingdom and the religious, eternal kingdom. Whereas Luther grants that public security is a good provided by worldly governments and its magistrates, he continues to portray individual security as an evil disposition, symptomatic of the slothful and the proud, who neglect careful examination of scripture or are wrongly confident of their state of grace and salvation. In one's quotidian dealings in the community—in work, commerce, and personal interaction—the security established and maintained by public institutions and ministers is recognized as beneficial, if only because it grants the individual the peace of mind to hearken to the Gospel. However, an inner feeling of security whereby the crucial importance of the Word does not receive assiduous attention is utterly baneful. In this latter case, Luther asserts, *nihil est pestilentius securitate* (Nothing is more pestilential than security).[24] Luther's theory of "two realms" therefore fully accommodates the operative ambivalence of the key word: a faithful Christian could expect to be carefree in terms of this world but should never be careless in terms of the other.

ESCAPE FROM NATURE

A positive sense of security gradually established its position as a central topic in political philosophy primarily in the work of Thomas Hobbes. Throughout, the affirmation of security as a good is fundamentally connected with the power of sovereignty to alleviate the cares and concerns of its subjects. The state emerges as an institution that protects its citizens from all varieties of existential threats, from external aggression as well as from internal discord. "The office of the sovereign (be it a monarch or an assembly) consisteth in the end for which he was trusted with the sovereign power, namely, the procuration of *the safety of the people*, to which he is obliged by the law of nature."[25] Sovereign power alone is capable of preventing crime, averting civil discord and, if necessary, defending the populace against enemy aggression. For Hobbes, who witnessed at first hand the brutal excesses of the English Civil War, the natural rapacity and cruelty of mankind called for a ruling body whose claims to legitimacy consisted in establishing safe conditions. Hobbes invokes Cicero's *salus populi* to define the ruling body's function as the provision of security, which is henceforth utilized as a means for legitimizing power. The noun "procuration"—which corresponds to the verb *procurare* (to take care of, attend to, look after) in the Latin version of *Leviathan*—makes clear how this office has assumed the *curae* that are thereby removed from the citizens' thoughts. The sovereign, therefore, is specifically a *procurator*, that is, the one who manages concerns on behalf of another. The citizen is *securus* because the ruler works *cum cura*.

The evocation of the Ciceronian ideal of the *salus populi* is also a plea for the necessity of maintaining the safety of the regime. So horrific are the ravages of war, in whatever form, that an individual would readily exchange certain liber-

[24] Martin Luther, *Werke* (Weimarer Ausgabe), 25: 331. See Schrimm-Heins, "Gewißheit und Sicherheit," 1: 207–12.

[25] Thomas Hobbes, *Leviathan*, 30.1, 219 (emphasis in original).

ties for a measure of security. To cite the well-known Plautine tag that Hobbes used in his dedicatory letter to *De cive* (1651): *homo homini lupus* (man is a wolf to man).[26] Sovereign power therefore assumes the role of trainer in order to domesticate humanity's natural inclination to savagery and predation. According to Hobbes, this wolfishness is attributable to the innate, quasi-mechanical force of "natural right," the drive to pursue one's own desires, which inevitably come into conflict with another's desires; and it is thanks to a second natural drive—the impulse toward self-preservation—that motivates the way out of such frightening circumstances, namely and somewhat paradoxically by willingly surrendering one's proper will:

> The only way to erect such a common power, as may be able to defend them from the invasion of foreigners, and the injuries of one another, and thereby to secure them in such sort, as that by their own industry, and by the fruits of the earth, they may nourish themselves and live contentedly; is, to confer all their power and strength upon one man, or upon one assembly of men, that may reduce all their wills, by plurality of voices, unto one will: which is as much as to say, to appoint one man, or assembly of men, to bear their person; and every one to own, and acknowledge himself to be author of whatsoever he that so beareth their person, shall act, or cause to be acted, in those things which concern the common peace and safety; and therein to submit their wills, every one to his will, and their judgments, to his judgment.[27]

Security is therefore purchased with individual submission and suppression. One's proper desire must yield to a common will, which is henceforth identified as the sovereign's: "For they could not be persuaded to oppose the security of the very thing which gave them their own security."[28] It is mankind's moral freedom that, suspending natural drives, provides the means for self-preservation; but this is possible only by renouncing at least some degree of that very freedom. Liberty is expressed through the restraint of liberty.

All the same, the citizen should gratefully become a subject in order that the threat of violent death may be defused. Throughout Hobbes's reflections, it is fear that motivates acceptance of the covenant with the ruling body, whether monarchical or parliamentarian. This fear constitutes the origin and guide of human existence. In the autobiography that he composed in Latin verse, Hobbes relates rather fancifully how his mother, terrified by the invading Spanish Armada, prematurely gave birth to "twins, both me and fear at the same time" (*geminos, meque metumque simul*).[29] With fear as his brother or *Doppel-*

---

[26] Thomas Hobbes, "Epistle Dedicatory to the Right Honourable William Earl of Devonshire," *De Cive*, in *On the Citizen*, 3–4. The phrase is taken from Plautus, *Asinaria*, 495.

[27] Hobbes, *Leviathan*, chap. 17, 109.

[28] Hobbes, "Preface to the Readers," *De cive*, 9.

[29] *T. Hobbes Malmesburiensis Vita* (1672), printed in *The Metaphysical System of Hobbes*, vii.

gänger, Hobbes views any fraternity or any community whatsoever as a cause for fright. To ward off the hostility vividly represented by the Spanish ships, Hobbes conjures the Leviathan, the great beast of the sea, whose massive might can check the violence discernible in every human being. Ungoverned, roaming savagely in the state of nature, individuals would enter into conflict whenever they would come together, fighting to the death in order to satisfy their immediate wants and desires. Individual equality spells the equal capacity to kill and therefore the impossibility of enjoying any security. "The cause of men's fear of each other lies partly in their natural equality, partly in their willingness to hurt each other. Hence, we cannot expect security from others or assure it to ourselves."[30]

As in Roman imperial practice, it is here where securitization begins to follow an economy that guides the exchange of concern from citizen to the state and thereby introduces the possibility of abuse. Attention to the security of the individual tends to shift to the security of the governing body, for it is argued that the procuration of safety itself needs to be secured. It is perhaps valid to claim that the office should be secure, lest concerns over existential threats return to the people; but legitimization becomes questionable when the securement of the state trumps the citizens' well-being, when the provision of security becomes a base expression of power. It is not simply a horrific irony that within totalitarian-minded regimes of the twentieth century bureaus explicitly founded to provide security have historically done so by spreading widespread fear among the citizenry. The tactics of abusive organs of the state are arguably always at the ready wherever power is exercised over a population. As Marc Crépon claims, state apparatuses are explicitly charged with inspiring fear so as to maintain the need for security: By exposing the people to a permanent menace, to perpetual insecurity, such organizations legitimize their existence.[31] One could interpret the path to abuse according to shifting locations of concern. What appears to be an abuse of power or nefarious legitimization is, at least on one level, the conversion from the care for the individual to the care for the state, for that which exceeds the individual. Such techniques of securitization are dehumanizing, insofar as their concerns fall completely beyond the human. The greater irony, then, is that precisely by instilling *insecurity* among the populace, by depriving its subjects of the *privation of concern*, agencies like the Soviet KGB and the East German Stasi also allow their human subjects to continue to care and therefore to remain human.

---

[30] Hobbes, *De cive*, chap. 1, 25–26.
[31] Marc Crépon, *La culture de la peur: 1. Démocratie, identité, sécurité*, 49.

5

The Pasture and the Garden

Homo curans (II)

IN ORDER TO SPECIFY FURTHER the semantic ramifications of Latin *cura*, and hence *securitas*, it is fruitful to take an even closer look at the Hyginus fable with which this study began.

> *Cura cum quendam fluvium transiret, vidit cretosum lutum, sustulit cogitabunda et coepit fingere hominem. Dum deliberat secum quidnam fecisset, intervenit Iovis; rogat eum Cura, ut ei daret spiritum, quod facile ab Iove impetravit. Cui cum vellet Cura nomen suum imponere, Iovis prohibuit suumque nomen ei dandum esse dixit. Dum de nomine Cura et Iovis disceptarent, surrexit et Tellus suumque nomen ei imponi debere dicebat, quandoquidem corpus suum praebuisset. Sumpserunt Saturnum iudicem; quibus Saturnus aequus videtur iudicasse: "Tu, Iovis, quoniam spiritum dedisti <animam post mortem accipe; Tellus, quoniam corpus praebuit> corpus recipito. Cura quoniam prima eum finxit, quamdiu vixerit, Cura eum possideat; sed quoniam de nomine eius controversia est, homo vocetur, quoniam ex humo videtur esse factus.*[1]

When Cura was crossing a certain river, she saw muddy clay and, thinking, took it up and began to mold a man. While she was pondering to herself what in fact she had made, Jupiter came by; Cura asked that he give him a spirit, and the man obtained it easily from Jupiter. When Cura wanted to grant the man her own name, Jupiter prohibited it and said that his name must be given to it. While Cura and Jupiter were disputing over the name, Tellus rose up and said that it ought to have her name, since indeed she had provided her own body. They selected Saturn as judge; and Saturn seemed to them to have judged fairly: "You, Jupiter, since you have given the spirit, <take the soul after death; Tellus, since she provided the body,> should re-

---

[1] Hyginus, fable 220. The Latin text is from Hyginus, *Fabulae*, P. K. Marhsall, ed., 171–72. The emendation was suggested by H. J. Rose, *Fabulae*, ad loc.

ceive the body. Since Cura first molded him, let Cura possess him as long as he should live; but since there is a dispute over the name, let him be called *homo*, since he appears to have been made from *humus*.

By means of a common folk etymology, mankind's nature is linked to the soil (*humus*) that has been formed by or with Care. As noted in chapter 1, the fable passes from an account of physiospiritual creation to an account of designation—two distinct gifts that constitute the essence of mankind. Upon succeeding to persuade Jove to "give [the clay figure] a spirit" (*ut daret spiritum*), Cura sparks a dispute over what name it "must be given" (*dandum*). Through a light use of polyptoton—through the repetition of inflected forms of the verb for giving (*dare*)—the fable asks us to cross quickly from anthropogony to anthropology or from anonymity to nomination, and consider both components as donations.

Strikingly and uniquely, it is Cura who fashions the first man from clay and not Prometheus, who, according to Ovid, "mixed earth with fresh flowing waters" to create human forms.[2] Yet, despite reassigning the artisanal role to a female figure, Hyginus's fable does retain some aspects of the Ovidian myth. As a personification of concern, Cura certainly shares some characteristics with Prometheus, the doomed Titanic hero whose name implies "forethought." The one whose mind is trained on the imminent future is the one most beset by apprehension. As a common noun, *cura* and its verbal form *curare* often occur as synonyms for *providentia* and *providere*. According to Priscian, both terms are adequate translations of the Greek notion of "thinking or seeing beforehand" (*pronoein; Inst. gramm.* 3.350.11).[3] It is perhaps Cura's Prometheanism that makes her liable to enter into disputes with Jupiter, the lord of the gods. As a woman, Cura simply converts Prometheus's presentiment and concern for mankind into a mother's vexation.

Perhaps the most important difference between Hyginus's story and Ovid's is that the former elides the aspect of imitation. In Ovid, Prometheus "fashioned human beings in the image of the gods [*in effigiem ... deorum*] who command all things."[4] As in the Hebrew Bible, God or the gods serve as the model. The phrase *in effigiem deorum* closely corresponds but vastly simplifies the account in Genesis, where man is created "in our image and likeness" (1:26). The dual Hebrew terms צלם (*selem*) and תומד (*d'mut*)—translated in the Septuagint as εἰκών (*eikōn*) and ὁμοίωσις (*homoiōsis*) and as *imago* and *similitudo* in the Vulgate, respectively—may underscore the continuity and discontinuity implicit in every imitation. On the one hand, these terms of resemblance assert the dignity of mankind: it is a similarity to God that distinguishes human beings from every other animal. On the other hand, they serve as a humbling re-

---

[2] *Quam [sc. tellurem] satus Iapeto, mixtam pluvialibus undis (Met.* 1.82).
[3] For further examples, see Hauser, *Der römische Begriff Cura*, 4 n. 14.
[4] *finxit in effigiem modernatum cuncta deorum (Met.* 1.83).

minder of humanity's creaturely status as copies. We may take the two Hebrew terms as simply forming a hendiadys or follow a more Christian interpretation, first put forward by Ireneaus, and distinguish the *semel* as man's reason (i.e., as a "natural" image of God's mind) and the *d'mut* as man's moral excellence (as a "supernatural" likeness to the divine)—in either case, the issue of resemblance clearly relates mankind to his Creator.[5] We could say that resemblance establishes an idea of paternity, as it occurs in Genesis 5:3, where Adam begets Seth "in his own likeness [*semel*]." In passing over this element of imitation, Hyginus would seem to deny the child of care any certainty of his origin. This narrative gesture—this glossing over the motive of imitation—may relate to the fact that "man" is not named after any one of his creators. The myth, therefore, offers no concrete ground that would secure the being's participation in its source. The child of care is from the beginning overburdened with worries.

The absence of imitation in the Hyginus fable so disturbed Hans Blumenberg that he suspected authorial suppression. Why did Cura "cross" the river, when she could have easily happened upon the muddy clay by walking alongside the bank? Was it not precisely her reflection in the waters that drove her to fashion a figure in her own image? Blumenberg understands the fable as a rehearsal of the Gnostic myth, in which Wisdom (Sophia) decides to create her own duplicate after regarding her beauty in a mirror. It is through this act of vanity that she produces the material world, which henceforth longs for redemption. Blumenberg admits that a personification of Concern could not readily be presented as vain, yet he also suggests that the fable's suppression of imitation was made in deference to Jupiter's invisible contribution to the figure's birth.[6] In this interpretation Hyginus sacrificed man's certainty in order to underplay the uncertainty that every father must bear concerning his spiritual offspring. As Freud was fond of reminding us: *Pater semper incertus est.*[7] This insecurity typically passes on to the son. Thus, Homer's Telemachus complains regarding his relationship to Odysseus: "My mother indeed says I am his, but surely I do not know: who has ever known his own parentage?" (*Od.* 1.215–16).[8] Often, across multiple literary traditions, the son's sole inheritance, his only endowment, is precisely this lack. The strict codes of patriarchal order may be nothing more than a response to this deficit, which could also uncover the hidden source of filial obligation.

A philological peculiarity in Hyginus's text could reinforce Blumenberg's reading, even though he neglects to mention it. Throughout the story, Jupiter is referred to specifically as *Iovis*—the genitive form of *Iuppiter*, which is here used as a grammatical nominative. Because the story is in prose, metrical issues

---

[5] For a comprehensive overview of the long interpretive tradition concerning Genesis 1:26 with ample bibliography, see J. A. Clines, "The Image of God in Man."

[6] Hans Blumenberg, *Care Crosses the River*, 139–41 [*Die Sorge geht über den Fluß*, 197–200].

[7] Sigmund Freud, "Der Familienroman der Neurotiker" (1908), in *Gesammelte Werke*, 7: 229.

[8] Cf. Blumenberg, *Care Crosses the River*, 142 [201–2].

play no role. Why, then, does Hyginus depart from classical usage and use the genitive form in place of the expected nominative? Ancient grammarians had already recognized that the name *Iuppiter* could be explicated as *Iovis-pater*; and one could hence argue that the appearance of *Iovis* alone also marks the absence of the paternal designation. The *pater* is literally elided, obliterated. In a myth so concerned with matters of nomination, it is striking that the paternity of the "father of the gods" is thus erased.

At any rate, for Blumenberg, Saturn's decision is robbed of its basis because the issue of resemblance has been suppressed. Human concern is divorced from its grounding in mankind's capacity for reflection. Yet, as I have already suggested, the groundlessness itself, rather than being viewed as a pious lacuna, could be shown to contribute to the literal meaning of man as an insecure child of care. The subsequent conflict over the name, then, would appear to be an attempt to remedy an altogether other type of insecurity. The ensuing philological controversy over the creature's name strives to resolve the issue of the figure's proper being, without the aid of physical resemblance, without the talent for self-reflection.

In my view, the debate over the name revolves on whether humanity is essentially atemporal (Telluric matter or Jovian spirit) or instead fundamentally constituted by time and history. To settle the matter, the contesting parties summon Saturn. As the god of agriculture and former ruler of the golden age, Saturn has always been known for his fairness; and here he serves as a true sovereign insofar as he is called upon to decide. Without further argument, his judgment is accepted by all disputants as just: death will render the two aspects of mankind back to their original spheres, the material body to earth and the immaterial spirit to the heavens; yet "as long as he is alive," man will be possessed by and therefore belong to Cura. Man is alive—living in time—as long as Cura can keep her animated clay intact. Should the figure have been called Tellus or Jupiter, history would be merely an episode or a digression, without any substantial relevance. In fact, history would not even have the chance to begin. If Earth or Jupiter had triumphed, man would be named into the namelessness and timelessness of pure matter or pure spirit.

Saturn, the sickle-bearing god, arrives to make the cut, to perform the critical gesture that not only severs mankind from perfect Tellurian and Jovian security but also consigns humanity to an unstoppable flow of moments, each one vanishing as soon as it occurs. Saturn's association with the Greek god Kronos, together with the conflation of Kronos with Chronos (Time), was well established and frequently exploited in Hyginus's day;[9] and we could therefore conjecture that it is Time who insists that man live with *cura*, with worry and

---

[9] The conflation of Kronos and Chronos reaches back at least to the 6th century BC in the cosmogonic writings of Pherecydes and is further discernible in Pindar's *Second Olympian Ode* and in a number of Orphic fragments (e.g., frag. 68 Kern). Plutarch asserts that the identification of the Titan god and Time was common among Greek intellectuals (*De Iside et Osiride*, 32). For ancient testimony, see G. S. Kirk, J.

anxiety. This reading therefore approaches the interpretation of the fable that Martin Heidegger put forward in *Being and Time*, which we shall discuss in chapter 14. For now, it is important to note that the sovereign power of time commands that the creature should not be named after its caring mother. Its name will not refer back to its initial creator. Certainly, this decision is not unrelated to the elision of imitation noted by Blumenberg. The two major paradigms that Foucault identified in the historical production of meaning—resemblance and representation—both fail to secure the being consigned to live *cum cura*. Only history, beyond the limits of resemblance and representation, can provide the categories of meaning, a meaning that cannot shed its temporality and therefore its *provisionality*.[10] It is this *Promethean* commitment to time that prevents or disrupts any definitive, fixed meaning. Cura, posing as the wily Titan, can secure her creature only in insecurity.

Insofar as man lives within the constant passage of time, so Hyginus appears to suggest, mankind is prohibited from fully experiencing the stable security of the earth and the incorporeal security of the sky. It is important to note that this prohibition is not based on any "fall" from a previous paradisiacal state. Rather, the Tellurian and Jovian versions of security, which are explicitly designated by Hyginus as postmortem and implicitly as timeless, can never be experienced, simply because experience requires a subject living in time. Hyginus's man would have to be alive to experience his death, which means, of course, that he is not in fact dead.

Consigned, then, to time, mankind's relation to Care becomes clearer. The man possessed by care—*homo curans*—worries about that which can change, transform, or vanish, including, above all, himself. Again, care is an expression of mankind's mortality. In his last epistle, Seneca accordingly distinguishes human from divine being: both god and man are endowed with the power of reason, which alone accomplishes the Good; yet, in the case of the immortal god, "nature perfects the Good," whereas in the case of mortal man, it is "cura" that works toward this achievement (*Ep.* 124.14).[11] The Stoic *cura sui* comprises an endless task and requires a lifelong commitment, one that should never be abandoned. In pressing the terms of Hyginus's fable, we may be left with a scandalous problem, namely that the preoccupation with security should be understood not merely as an infinite task but rather as one that is entirely impossible: a concern for being fully without concern. However, the labor implied in Seneca's sense of *cura* may point a way out of this aporia. The Stoic practice of *cura*

E. Raven, and M. Schofield, *The Presocratic Philosophers*, 56–57. See also Erwin Panofsky's far-reaching study, "Father Time," in *Studies in Iconology: Humanistic Themes in the Renaissance*, 69–94.

[10] I am referring, of course, to the major paradigm shifts (resemblance, representation, and history) that organize Foucault's classic study, *Les mots et les choses* [*The Order of Things: An Archaeology of the Human Sciences*].

[11] *Haec duo [deus et homo], quae rationalia sunt, eandem naturam habent, illo diversa sunt, quod alterum immortale, alterum mortale est. Ex his ergo unius bonum natura perficit, dei scilicet, alterius cura, hominis.*

sui is sustained by this impossibility, which motivates the need for constant attentiveness, education, and exercise. Hyginian Cura, too, is after all an artist and man is her fiction (*et coepit fingere hominem*), a *figure* educated or brought out by care. Rather than view mankind's perennial longing for security as the history of a desire to evade time and its contingencies, there remains the possibility of limited security, provided we remain careful. Tellurian fixity and Jovian freedom are not absent in a life *cum cura* but rather are held together through Cura's tender efforts. The dream of being perfectly without Cura may express a death drive, a mad wish to rejoin the stillness of the earth or the redemptive bliss of the spirit; yet at least a measure of stability and even a modicum of salvation, just enough to survive, may be gained as long as we remain vigilant. In fact, without this watchfulness we may be utterly lost.

FELIX CULPA

The Hyginus fable insists that *care* should possess mankind—*Cura eum possideat*—which is to say that, if ever removed from care, humanity would be robbed of its humanity. Interestingly, the similar story of mankind's formation in the book of Genesis takes place in a garden, which would normally be a place requiring careful attention. The gardner is, indeed, the paradigmatic caretaker. Yet, in the Hebrew account, the first humans inhabit a garden where everything is already provided. This carefree existence may account for other reversals that the biblical story reveals in comparison with the Roman fable.

In both narratives, language supplements the fashioning and animation of the first human being. However, whereas Hyginus assigns Cura with the task of granting a name (or a noun—*nomen*), in Genesis man is formed precisely to serve as the name giver. It is Adam himself, the "red clay" (*adamah*) that has received God's breath, who subsequently gives a name for every category of creature (Genesis 2:19–20). In the Hebrew account, the divine creation itself is originally anonymous, outside history and without time; and it is man's act of naming that pulls timeless creation into history, into circulation. Insofar as Adam's naming relates the creation to him, language transforms nature into a human environment, the earth into a world.[12] With Hyginus the structure is similar, but here it is Concern herself who is concerned about granting a name: as though the historical and temporally contingent condition of mankind—anthropological worldliness—also has its source in Anxiety.

As already suggested, for Adam the name giver nature is originally a realm that is wholly *carefree*. The Garden of Eden is replete with animals, fruits, and fresh water. No work is required. Every desire is instantly gratified, even before it is desired. It is God who preemptively recognizes a possible longing for a

---

[12] See Franz Rosenzweig, *The Star of Redemption*, 186–88.

helpmate and consequently creates woman from Adam's rib while he blissfully sleeps. In assuming all care, God, the shepherd of men, deprives the human couple of care. Overprotected and fully secure, these beneficiaries of divine gifts lack the lack that drives human endeavor, commitment, and responsibility.[13] This lack of every lack has serious consequences: their security has left them defenseless against the serpent's alluring speech. It is precisely their *carelessness* that causes them to fall out of paradise and fall into a life of concern. Read together with the Hyginus fable, we could say that their reckless behavior unwittingly causes them to become truly human. Exiled from the Garden, they can begin to cultivate their own gardens and care for their own lives, tilling the *humus* that requires attention, devotion, and vigilance.

WHAT BURNS THE HEART

In the sixth book of his treatise *De lingua latina*, the ancient grammarian Varro offers a provocative etymology of the word for "care":

> *Cura, quod cor urat; curiosus, quod hac praeter modum utitur. Recordari, rursus in cor revocare. Curiae, ubi senatus rempublicam curat, et illa ubi cura sacrorum publica; ab his curiones.* (De ling. lat. 6.46)

> *Cura*, because it burns the heart [*cor urat*]; *curiosus* [an inquisitive or curious person], because he takes advantage of it beyond measure. *Recordari* [to remember, to call to mind], to call back again into the *cor* [heart]. The *curiae* [the halls of the Senate], where the Senate *curat* [takes cares of] the affairs of the state, and where there is the public *cura* of the sacrifices; from these, the *curiones* [priests of the curiae].

Varro's derivations clearly reinforce Quintilian's wariness, cited in the preceding chapter, over the *securitas* that characterizes pupils who are no longer driven by the inflaming passion to improve style. We could say that when a student is negligently "secure," his *heart* no longer *burns* for learning, that he fails *to call to mind* (re-cor-dari) the principles of his training and good breeding. Varro's explication, however fanciful, can also motivate a crucial and long-standing idea of political supervision, namely that people may enjoy *securitas*— a life *free from concern*—only because the governing bodies of the *curiae* have taken on all concern.

The noun *cura* commonly takes a genitive object (e.g., *cura deorum* "service to the gods" or *cura libertatis* "concern for freedom"); and is often conjoined with a referential dative, as in the common phrase *cura alicui esse* "to be an object of one's care or attention." Owing to the breadth of its basic meaning,

---

[13] See Robert Pogue Harrison's insightful interpretation in *Gardens: An Essay on the Human Condition*, 7–9.

cura may be applied to multiple contexts. In political discourse *cura* involves the management of state affairs and public administration, whereas in the social sphere it belongs to the task of "legal guardianship" (*curatoria*; Fr. *curatelle*). Similarly, the attentive physician bestows *cura* on the patient in order to effectuate a *cure*. Therefore, the magistrate, the medical doctor, and the guardian may each be designated as a *curator*, specifically as someone who administers a *curatio*. It is important to note that these governmental, iatric, and custodial notions of *cura* all include a fundamentally teleological force, which marks the kind of diligence that struggles to prevail despite all manners of resistance. Thus, specific knowledge (*scientia*) is generally called for. However, the teleology that steers *cura* to its end remains necessarily transcendent, if only for the simple reason that perfect achievement of the goal of concern would spell the end of care.

This combination of restless attentiveness and skillful knowledge shows up in further discursive contexts. For example, in his treatise on agriculture, Columella teaches that one can never yield a crop "unless *cura* is exercised diligently and knowledgeably" (*De re rustica* 4.3.4). The same industriousness is understandably discernible in artistic activity: in Vergil's *Aeneid*, Vulcan promises Venus that he will fully engage his "careful labors" (*curae*) in forging Aeneas's shield (*Aen.* 8.401). Likewise, in his *Ars amatoria*, Ovid proclaims his allegiance to a Callimachean ideal when he refers to his treatise on women's cosmetics (*Medicamina facei feminae*) as a "slight book, but [written] with great care" (*parvus, sed grande cura, libellus, Ars amat.* 3.206).

Like most general terms, the sense of *cura* acquires greater specificity depending on its contextual application. In love poetry and elegy, *cura* denotes the painful trouble and upsetting problems of erotic passion. Through metonymy, *cura* may come to name the beloved, the very object of desire.[14] It is, indeed, often the case that the *cura* bestowed upon an object transforms the object itself into a *cura*. Thus, in connection with military discipline, *cura* stands for the Greek *meletē* (care), which refers to the repeated drills and exercises that tone the body as well as the vigilant alertness that military training aims to accomplish. Analogously, in the field of rhetoric, *cura* is the *meletē* of ongoing practice and attentive memorization which Quintilian, for example, regards as a necessary component in the orator's training, namely, as that which supplements inborn genius (*ingenium*).[15] Henceforth, *cura* names the completed oratory or literary work itself. Throughout, *cura* as the concern for an object becomes *cura* as the object of concern.

Despite these well-attested usages, *cura* does not always receive a positive valuation. Quintilian also warns against excessive *cura* in the preparation of speeches, especially when it causes the work involved to become ostentatious

[14] For representative examples from Roman elegy, see, e.g., Propertius 1.5.10, 1.8a.1, 1.11.5, 1.15.31, and Tibullus 4.11.

[15] See Quintilian, *Inst. orat.* 3.1.22 and 7.1.40.

and thereby mars the delivery with artificiality (*Inst. orat.* 8 Proem. 23). This threat of excessiveness will, after Apuleius, attach itself to the problem of "curiosity" (*curiositas*), which describes an inquisitiveness that implies being meddlesome and prying. As we have seen, already with Varro, the *curiosus* is someone who goes "too far" (*praeter modum*) in his inquisitiveness. Along these lines, precisely because *cura* denotes engaged attention to an object, a person, or a task at hand, it may be construed either in the positive senses of diligence and mindful exertion or in the negative senses of anxiety and apprehension. The concern that one exercises in pursuing a project, the care that one devotes to oneself or to another, and the attentiveness that characterizes one's occupation may all readily become a troubling preoccupation, a disturbing source of worry, and a cause for excessive anguish.

The following lines from Terence's *Phormio* are exemplary in describing the labor implicit in *cura*, as well as the term's potential ambivalence. Toward the end of the comedy, Chremes offers the nurse Sophrona his reflections on happy accidents:

> quam saepe forte temere
> eveniunt quae non audeas optare! Offendi adveniens
> quicum volebam, atque ut volebam, collocatam filiam.
> Quod nos ambo opere maximo dabamus operam ut fieret,
> sine nostra cura, maxima sua cura, haec sola fecit.
>
> (*Phorm.* 757–61)

How often by random chance do things come about that you wouldn't dare hope for! Upon returning I found my daughter matched with the very person I wanted, and just as I wanted. That which we were both attending with greatest effort to bring about, she has done by her own great diligence [*cura*], without our exertion [*sine nostra cura*].

Here, it is the daughter's *cura* that accomplishes the goal of the father's work (*opere maximo, operam*), even though the father's "careful exertion" (*cura*) did not ultimately contribute to the achievement. The "security" implicit in the father's actions (*sine nostra cura*) refers to the inefficacy of his striving. Nonetheless, *cura*—both the father's and the daughter's—expresses the kind of intentionality that is strongly attached to a deep-felt longing. It describes the steady occupation that is necessary for accomplishing one's goals, successful or not, directly or indirectly. As such, *cura* also denotes a concern that reflects a degree of uncertainty. It is clear, then, how the difficult work that characterizes *cura* can readily turn into obsessiveness, into compulsive expectation. Earlier in Terence's *Phormio*, Chremes' son, Antipho speaks of "this perpetual anxiety [*quotidiana cura*] that would torment his mind" (1.3.160). The fact that any careful occupation may graduate to a preoccupation accounts for much of *cura*'s ambivalence.

In its negative connotation, the attention one devotes to a person or object has converted into something fearful and worrisome. In this case, *cura* becomes synonymous with *sollicitudo* (disquiet) or *metus* (fear). Latin poets, especially, often present these more negative aspects of *cura* as part of an experience that borders on anxiety. Vergil's Anchises, for example, confesses a disquieting concern when he first sees his son Aeneas approach him in the underworld. The father's shade stretches out his arms, relieved that the awaited time has in fact arrived, that "his anxious concern [*cura*] has not deceived him"(*nec me mea cura fefellit, Aen.* 6.691). Before the happy outcome or in circumstances of utter despair, the *cura* is felt as sheer anguish for mortals who must suffer from the unforeseeability of the future. Thus, also in the *Aeneid* 6, Vergil places the *ultrices Curae*—frightful personifications of vengeful anxiety—at the portal to the underworld, where they traffic with all that menaces mankind:

> *Vestibulum ante ipsum primisque in faucibus Orci*
> *Luctus et ultrices posuere cubilia Curae,*
> *pallentesque habitant Morbi tristisque Senectus,*
> *et Metus et malesuada Fames ac turpis Egestas,*
> *terribiles visu formae, Letumque Labosque.*
>
> (*Aen.* 6.273–77)

> Before the entranceway itself and in the foremost jaws of Orcus
> Grief and the vengeful Curae have laid down their beds,
> and pale Diseases live there, and sad Old Age,
> and Fear and ill-advising Hunger and foul Want,
> shapes terrible to see, both Death and Toil.

Cura may be discernible in the hard-working magistrate or committed statesman, but the same term can also designate an unsettling, haunting anxiety, a paralyzing preoccupation that thwarts an individual's free movement. Vergil's description of hell's entranceway conjures a realm of *cura* that is itself defined as a lack or an absence. Together with Disease, Fear, Hunger, and Want, the "vengeful Curae" characterize Orcus as a site of privation, as a place where health, composure, and satiety remain painfully remote.

Through the Darkest Valley

Concepts of *securitas* derive not only their ambivalence from differing values of *cura* but also their claims to universality, insofar as concern can well identify a core aspect of the human condition. To care for others and for oneself represents a responsibility that many would claim to be a fundamental trait of humanity. It is the responsibility that accompanies concrete being in the world: attending to a singular need and formulating how that need should be addressed under the particular circumstances at hand. It exhibits commitment, devotion, and mutual recognition, all of which reveal that care is grounded in temporality, contingency, and the possibility of loss. What burns the heart is a desire to hold on to something that at any moment may be lost. As indicated above, care is generally reserved for that which may one day disappear, including one's own life: if an object or a person were not subject to time, there would be nothing to care for. We care because we are mortal.

The link between human care and mortality is retained in many languages. It should be noted that, despite near synonymity and homophony, the English *care* is not cognate with Latin *cura*. *Care* rather derives from the Old English *caru* or *cearu*, a word for "anxiety" that is related to Old Saxon *kara* (sorrow), Old High German *chara* (a lament), and Gothic *kara* (trouble, grief). It appears in the modern German adjective *karg* (gaunt, meager), which originally describes the frugality that accompanies mourning, as well as *Karfreitag* (Good Friday). Besides the word *care*, the sense is still retained in the modern English adjective *chary*.[16] Analogously, the German *Sorge*, which commonly translates *cura* and *care*, is related to the English *sorrow*. A certain grief therefore tints the care for persons and objects, as though the attentiveness and awareness involved were motivated by the acknowledgment of eventual evanescence and bereavement. This association between concern and mourning is further heard in the Greek *kēdos*, a general word for the care or trouble one bestows onto others and specifically the word that denotes the funeral rites for the dead. It is arguably the desire to stave off disappearance or ruination that turns every careful task into a security project, into a concern for removing concern.

The tradition of the "care of souls" (*cura animarum*) belonging to the Christian pastorate exemplifies the link between care and human mortality. Throughout Church history, ministers have been explicitly entrusted with assisting the faithful through religious, psychological, and moral difficulties with an aim toward spiritual healing and, ultimately, salvation. Consolation, guidance, admonition, and penance have consistently been the hallmarks of this venerable practice that attempts to secure the well-being of the protégé. One could therefore regard this work essentially as an *ars moriendi*, techniques in the *art of dying*, that is, as a preparation for the final reconciliation, the extreme atonement.[17] Ideally, the pastor would exhibit the engaged, relational approach implicit in the term *cura*. Already in the Middle Ages, it was recognized that the cleric's work must attend to the particular problems and circumstances of the penitent seeking care. The major reforms of the Fourth Lateran Council of 1215 placed especial emphasis on the administration of penance, which conse-

---

[16] Altogether, these words belong to an Indo-European cluster of verbs denoting "call, cry, or scream," evident in the Greek *gērus* "voice, speech" and the Latin *garrire* "chatter," which gives us the English *garrulous*. Middle High German *karmen* "whimper, wail," Old Irish *gairm* "call, scream," and Ossetic *zaryn* "song, lamentation" are traceable to the same Indo-European stem.

[17] See John T. McNeill, *History of the Cure of Souls*.

quently occasioned numerous theological treatises in the form of confessional aids for training the clergy. In general, these manuals stressed the importance of considering each case individually. "The priest was expected to diagnose the moral condition of the penitent as a physician would diagnose the physical condition of his patients. Penance was no longer to be imposed mechanically according to preexisting lists of stock penances but was dependent on the discretion of the priest [penitentia arbitraria]."[18] Thus, the curate's task retained the iatric and custodial connotations familiar from the classical Roman tradition.

The theological model for this understanding of clerical ministry is well established in the Gospels, which present the image of Christ as the Good Shepherd. In the Temple courtyard at Jerusalem, Jesus responds to the Pharisees' questions:

> I am the good shepherd. The good shepherd lays down his life for the sheep. He who is a hired hand, and not a shepherd, who doesn't own the sheep, sees the wolf coming, leaves the sheep, and flees. The wolf snatches the sheep, and scatters them. The hired hand flees because he is a hired hand, and doesn't care [ou melei] for the sheep. I am the good shepherd. I know my own, and I'm known by my own; even as the Father knows me, and I know the Father. I lay down my life for the sheep. I have other sheep, which are not of this fold. I must bring them also, and they will hear my voice. They will become one flock with one shepherd. Therefore the Father loves me, because I lay down my life, that I may take it again. No one takes it away from me, but I lay it down by myself. I have power to lay it down, and I have power to take it again. I received this commandment from my Father. (John 10:11–18)

Jesus' self-portrayal is a clear allusion to Ezekiel 34:11–16, where the Hebrew God appears explicitly as a shepherd intent on retrieving and restoring the dispersed flock. In the Christian gospel, what further distinguishes the *pastor bonus* is existential commitment and authentic concern. As a mortal *curator*, he places his own life in the line of danger, so as to save the sheep. *Cura* establishes a deep relation of belonging and mutual recognition—"I know my own, and I'm known by my own"—and it is on the basis of this communal bond that the shepherd is willing to lay down his own life. Community is born of this self-sacrificial gift. Through his mortality—through the possibility of his own death—he gives the gift of a life that cannot be taken away.

> My sheep listen to my voice; I know them, and they follow me. I give [didōmi] them eternal life, and they shall never perish; no one will snatch them out of my hand. My Father, who has given [dedōken] them to me, is greater than all; no one can snatch them out of my Father's hand. I and the Father are one. (John 10:27–30)

---

[18] F.N.N. Diekstra, "Confessor and Penitent: Robert de Sorbon and the *Cura Animarum*," 157–58.

Pastoral care hinges on such notions of giving: The faithful are a gift given from the Father; and Christ, who is one with the Father, in turn grants eternal life, a life where death is no longer of concern.

The imbrication of shepherd and flock means that the pastor, in addition to being prepared to sacrifice his own self, must at times be willing to sacrifice the entire herd for the sake of a single sheep:

> If a man owns a hundred sheep, and one of them wanders away, will he not leave the ninety-nine on the hills and go to look for the one that wandered off? And if he finds it, truly I tell you, he is happier about that one sheep than about the ninety-nine that did not wander off. In the same way your Father in heaven is not willing that any of these little ones should perish. (Matthew 18:12–14)

The shepherd's *cura* finds expression in the sensitivity and devotion he gives to the individual. The decision to save one at the risk of the rest is grounded in the same logic of sacrifice, whereby a carefree life is gained by giving life away. Just as all are saved by the possible death of the single shepherd, so the individual is rescued by the possible death of all.

THE CONCERN TO BE WITHOUT CONCERN

As mentioned previously, Foucault focused on the techniques common to both the Hellenistic schools and the Christian pastorate in order to elaborate what he called "governmentality." The model for this innovative form of governance departs significantly from Greco-Roman political theories and instead shares more with Eastern ideas of "shepherding." Foucault notes that the Greek gods, in being transcendentally distant from human affairs, were never understood as shepherds, unlike the Hebrew God who, as we have seen, is characterized as the "shepherd of men." The shepherd is powerful only insofar as he guides the movement of a flock in pasture, as opposed to overseeing a fixed territory. Similarly, the Hebrew God wanders with his Chosen People, or better: he manifests himself when the flock is on the move.

Pastoral power is primarily beneficent; it is specifically aimed toward the salvation of the flock, dealing with every individual: the *pastor* "must keep his eye on all and on each, *omnes et singulatim*"[19] To this end, the shepherd is willing to sacrifice himself for the flock, while also standing ready to neglect the entire multitude for the sake of a single sheep. This criterion of "the sacrifice of one for all and the sacrifice of all for one" renders the shepherd a nonviable metaphor for the sovereign among the Greeks.[20] Yet, abetted by the institution

---

[19] Foucault, *Security, Territory, Population*, 128.
[20] Foucault, *Security, Territory, Population*, 129.

of the Christian pastorate, we arrive at a paradigm of governance that better addresses the needs and desires of the population, one that knows how to manage among the collective rather than control it from above. This paradigm allows Foucault ultimately to link pastoral power to the institution of the police. As in the *cura animarum* tradition, it is the singular lives of individuals—of individuals as living beings—that constitute the object of administrative concern. Thus, for Foucault, politics becomes biopolitics.

Especially important is that the criterion of *omnes et singulatim* reveals how mechanisms of security operate with a dual focus: the power to "totalize" and the power to "individualize." While technologies of the self produce a secure subject, the same preoccupation with individual lives can work toward subsuming these individuals into the collective. What we would today call the distinction between individual security and state security has its originating impetus here. The *cura sui* that forms the subject is complicit with an *ars moriendi*, insofar as the process of individual subjectivization is but a preparation for death into the totality of the political community. The theological program of sacrifice, whereby one secures life by putting one's life at risk, here becomes the basis for the state's rationale.

Needless to say, there have always been dissident voices to protest the dissolution of the individual into the state: voices that uphold the singularity of care and renounce the security of the whole. The formula (*omnes et singulatim*) that Foucault recognizes as operative in the concern for security may provide the benefits of subjectivity, but at too great—too fatal—a cost. The concern for removing all concern is here regarded as a death trap. Security grants identity but seals this achievement with a gravestone. Proponents of a human care that does not seek resolution in care's removal recognize that the subject is sacrificed to the very institutions that make the subject a subject. Their resistance finds expression in constant striving, in remaining at sea, in restlessness, anxiety, and concern. This insistence on a mode of infinite caring does not deny the individual's mortality. Rather, it is precisely holding on to the singularizing force of one's own death that saves the individual from a totalizing mortification. Care, no less than security, is a gift. However, whereas the gift of security fills a lack—a lack of identity, subjectivity, being—the gift of care grants the lack itself.

EPICURUS

Epicurus set up his school in a garden removed from the *polis*. The moral philosophical ideal of *ataraxia* could be achieved only in a place of cultivation, far from the distressing concerns of politics and society that torment the soul, but not without the concerns that make a garden grow. The fear of death cannot be conquered by safety measures but only by accepting the fact of mortality. The security that Epicurus promises is one that requires constant care, a gift that imposes an obligation to give back as long as one lives. In Epicurus's judgment, the political and social realms produce anxiety by promulgating false and erroneous beliefs. In one regard, such beliefs are sources of *cura* because they disturb the mind; but in another regard, they instill fear because they threaten individuals with a carefree and therefore careless existence. In an extreme view, governments that claim to confer perfect security appear to make its subjects lie down in green pastures. Instead, for the Epicureans, ensconced in their all-too-human garden, the benefit of being entirely without concern is reserved exclusively for a posthumous existence, which is no existence at all. Throughout the Roman Empire, latter-day Epicureans expressed their central claim upon their gravestones: *Non fui, fui, non sum, non curo* (I was not, I was, I am not, I do not care).

Security on the Beach

> To shield politics from the perils which are immanent to it,
> it has to be hauled on to dry land, set down on terra firma.
>
> Jacques Rancière, *On the Shores of Politics*

THALATTA

THE INFINITE VARIETIES OF CARE and the ways to deal with them coalesce into master metaphors that organize and motivate thinking about security. Reference has already been made to some examples: the solicitous mother, the garden, the pasture, and so forth. Without question, one of the most enduring paradigms for expressing different attitudes toward security is the dichotomy between the land and the sea.

Throughout Greco-Roman culture, the sea constituted a persistent source of concern. Any desire to quit the firmness of the land, where nature provided all that was needed for the sustenance of human life, would invariably be regarded as some kind of transgression. Even in the most justifiable cases, seafaring was believed to be somehow excessive, a departure from the norm. The practical dangers involved in venturing off coast would appear to reinforce the general unease. Traditionally, an individual or a collective took to ship for any number of reasons, from improving living circumstances—for instance by means of trade, emigration, or colonization—to exploring the unknown, from fleeing political oppression to waging war. Regardless of motive, the decision to set sail was rarely made lightly and generally only after one seriously considered the hazards involved and made adequate plans. Propitiatory sacrifices to assure fair weather and smooth sailing were often the rule. Still, no amount of preparation would entirely alleviate the anxiety that must have tainted the moment of leaving port, for once the hawsers were cut, the party drifted into vulnerability, soon to be exposed to the possibility of violent winds, sudden squalls, and unanticipated nocturnal tempests. Shipwreck remained a very real and frightening threat.

Archaic literature is fully cognizant of these perils. It is highly noteworthy that Odysseus, epic poetry's best-known adventurer, roams the seas not by will but by compulsion. The *Odyssey* offers vivid testimony to the frightening events that were imagined to lie in store for any navigator who was bold enough or unlucky enough to travel so far from home. Accordingly, within the poem, the nurse Eurykleia caringly warns and pleads with Telemachus, attempting to dissuade the young man from setting out on a sea journey in search of news about his father. "It is not at all necessary for you to suffer evils and wander upon the sterile sea" (*Od.* 2.369–70). In addition to being the site of severe hardship and difficult travails, the sea's surface is frequently described by Homer as "sterile" or "infertile" (*atrugetos*), as a desert that yields no fruit or crop (*trugē*), a terrifying place of *devastation*. Here, it is assumed that Telemachus's expedition would indeed be fruitless, if not disastrous, were it not for the fact that he proceeds under Athena's guidance (*Od.* 2.372). However, for mortals without this divine privilege or for those like Telemachus's father who are subject to a god's wrath, embarkation would remain highly troublesome and demand utmost caution.

Homer's apprehension seems to reflect the major consensus. According to Diogenes Laertius, when Pittacus of Mytilene (fl. 650 BC), one of the Seven Sages of Ancient Greece, was asked to name what was "trustworthy," he immediately proclaimed, "the land"; and he consequently defined the "sea" as "the untrustworthy."[1] To negotiate with the sea could be likened to doing business with an immoral, deceptive partner bent on defrauding or destroying. Apparently, even for this successful general of sea-girt Lesbos, putting one's trust in the capricious and undependable element of the waves would be placing oneself in a most precarious situation.

That said, it was precisely the treacherous nature of the sea that held out some promise to mortals. As Pelops reminds Poseidon in Pindar's *First Olympian*:

> ὁ μέγας δὲ κίνδυνος ἄναλκιν οὐ φῶτα λαμβάνει.
> θανεῖν δ᾽ οἶσιν ἀνάγκα, τί κέ τις ἀνώνυμον
> γῆρας ἐν σκότῳ καθήμενος ἕψοι μάταν,
> ἁπάντων καλῶν ἄμμορος;

(Ol. 1.81–84)

> Great danger does not seize the cowardly man.
> Since it is necessary that he die, why should anyone sit
> in darkness, stewing inglorious old age in vain,
> without a share in all fine things?

By engaging with the untrustworthy sea, one went out to meet an open-ended future, an incalculable temporal zone where things could go bad but also, just

---

[1] "πιστόν, 'γῆ': ἄπιστον, 'θάλασσα.'" (Diogenes Laertius 1: 4.77).

as probably, turn out quite well. As Aristotle notes, the idea of "fortune" (*tychē*) always includes both "good fortune and bad"—*eutychia* and *dystychia* (*Rhet.* 2.12.1389a). Restricting oneself to dealing exclusively with the trustworthy would be to limit one's chances, to rest content with the calculable. The sea's untrustworthiness creates a gap in the future, which could also constitute an opportunity. Therefore, together with the fundamental, anthropological fear of the high seas' many obvious perils, there was the possibility that this very danger could serve as a testing ground for heroic feats, transforming navigation into a chance for cultural recognition and celebration. Seafaring might lead to a horrific death or to utter disappearance into an unmarked grave, but it might also generate great profit and power.

Of course, even if one should enjoy a safe return, the troubles linked to the transgressive act of seafaring would not be entirely eliminated. Should the enterprise succeed, such rewards and accomplishments would stand to provoke a further menace, namely the haughtiness or *hybris* that would elicit retribution. Sailing connects by art what is separate by nature. Thus, to embark upon a hazardous sea voyage and return unharmed would be to court the possibility of moral or theological condemnation. A safe outcome would not conceal the fact of original excessiveness and therefore not exclude the subsequent risk of overweening pride. It is as though, once taken, the exorbitant step away from the shore, like any immoderate gesture, continued to be liable to serious limitation or correction. In the well-known choral "Ode to Man" in Sophocles' *Antigone*, the ability to span the sea by ship is the very first example that demonstrates mankind's monstrous and stunning "uncanniness" (*Ant.* 322–37).

In no small measure, all of these alternatively positive and negative assessments contribute to the ambivalence that defined the sea as an area of concern and worry, as a locus of *cura*, and thus as a realm of general insecurity in contrast to the relatively greater security afforded by life on sturdy land. This pattern underlies the genre of the propempticon, a poetic prayer for safe voyage. In *Odes* 1.3 Horace employs this form to evoke Vergil's journey to Greece. A direct address to the ship reminds the vessel of its obligation (*debes*) to return the precious cargo entrusted to it (*creditum . . . Vergilium*) without injury (*Odes* 1.3.5–6). The poem then continues to describe seafaring as a "forbidden crime" (*vetitum nefas*, 26), insofar as it disregards the separation of lands imposed by a "prudent god" (*deus . . . prudens*, 21–22).

Such concerns persisted throughout ancient culture. In his probing study, *Thalatta*, Albin Lesky ascribes a general leeriness to an archaic substrate within the Hellenic mind. He argues that the Indo-European Hellenes, who migrated from the north, were originally unfamiliar with the open sea, as opposed to the indigenous peoples who inhabited Ionia, Boiotia, Achaia, and the Peloponnesus. Lesky first draws up linguistic evidence to support this claim, namely the fact that every Indo-European language possesses a word for the sea derived from the root **mari*, except Albanian and Greek; and that the Greek term *thal-*

atta (or *thalassa*), which refers primarily to "saltwater," is of pre-Hellenic origin.[2] As for Greek words for "sea" that do belong to the Indo-European family, it can be shown that they are figurative applications: *pontos* stems from the radical **pent* (walk, go), as in *patos* (path) and the verb *pateō* (walk)—hence the Latin *pons* (bridge); and *pelagos* is related to **p(e)lag* (broad, flat), as in the Latin *plaga*, which originally denotes a "hunting net" laid out upon the ground and only consequently refers to a "stretch or tract of land." For Lesky, the use of these metaphors suggests that the open sea, when first encountered by the northern migrants, was an entirely strange domain, hitherto unknown from experience, and hence a source of uncertainty and fear.[3]

A vestige of this archaic ignorance of the sea is discernible in the third book of the *Iliad*. Before Menelaus and Paris enter into their duel, Agamemnon pronounces a formulaic oath, calling upon the entire world to stand as witnesses: Zeus and Helios of the sky, the rulers of the Underworld, and all the rivers and earth are summoned, yet there is no mention of the sea.[4] The prayer's formal language appears to point back to a time when the sea did not belong to the general worldview, when the open waters were simply not a part of life experience.[5] After the Hellenes had occupied the coastal lands, the sea's presence may have become undeniable, but the vestigial feeling of its strangeness remained, continuing to cause strong emotional effects of insecurity.

One may pause to consider the historical context of Lesky's study. Because it was published in 1947, reflections on an "Aryan" fear of the sea and compelled migration are hardly innocent. Although he was certainly not politically active in the Third Reich, Lesky was a member of the NSDAP. Without speculating too far, it is worth bearing in mind how this scholar, when faced with impending catastrophe, turned to the fearsome sea, as if he would find there some metaphorical relief for general malaise. Tellingly, in 1942, the juridical scholar and politically outspoken theorist Carl Schmitt published a popular book for his eleven-year-old daughter, Anima, entitled *Land and Sea*.

But to return to the metaphorical complex: Emile Benveniste's study of the Vedic Hymns corroborates Lesky's thesis by specifying the meaning of the Sanskrit *pánthāh*, which is cognate with the Greek *pontos* and the Latin *pons*. Distinct from other Sanskrit terms for "path" (e.g., *yāna-* [a soul's journey], *mārga* [the path taken by wild animals], *adhvan* [a cleared path], and *rāthya* [a wagon-path]), *pánthāh* names a way fraught with "incertitude and danger," given to "unforeseeable detours"—a passage outside the norm. As Benveniste explains,

---

[2] Albin Lesky, *Thalatta: Der Weg der Griechen zum Meer*, 7–9.

[3] Lesky, *Thalatta*, 11–13.

[4] "Father Zeus who rules from Ida, most glorious, most great, and Sun, who beholds all things and hears all things, and the rivers and the earth, and you in the world below who take vengeance on deceased men, whoever has sworn a false oath, be our witnesses, and guard over these faithful oaths" (*Il.* 3.276–80).

[5] Lesky, *Thalatta*, 15–16.

the *pánthāh* is "not traced out in advance nor regularly trodden. It is more a 'crossing' [*franchissement*] risked across an unknown and often hostile region, a way opened by the gods at the rushing waters, a traversal [*traversée*] through natural obstacles, or the route that birds make up in space, all in all a path in a region prohibited to normal passage, a means of traveling a perilous or uneven terrain [*étendue périleuse ou accidenté*]."[6] Greek literature, the *Odyssey* above all, is replete with examples demonstrating that, even after the arts of shipbuilding and navigation had long been developed, dread of the sea's unforeseeable paths persisted, and horror before the hostile waves prevailed.

NE PLUS ULTRA

The danger that Benveniste vividly conjures, detectable in the semantic substrate of the term *pontos*, tinges the Greek relation to the sea, which is further evident in the common preference, straight through the classical period, of sailing within sight of land. The hundreds of islands and miles of coastline that dominate the Greek world furnished a modicum of orientation, which would at least partially assuage the fright that the waters inspired. The Mediterranean as a whole would come to be considered as a great but bounded space in which the perils of navigation could be manageable to a certain extent. The concrete boundary to this relatively reassuring space was the Straits of Gibraltar, identified by the Greeks as the Pillars of Heracles.[7] If losing track of the coast would instill greater fear within the sea, then crossing past this threshold into the boundless Atlantic would engender a forbidding horror that few would dare to brave. It was broadly acknowledged that from this point outward there would be little chance of ever returning safely. In myth, the site was said to mark the final and westernmost point of Heracles' laborious adventures, seeking the cattle of the Erythian monster Geryon. Thus, as Strabo reports, the Pillars marked both "the boundary of the inhabitable world [*oikoumenē*] and the expeditions of Heracles."[8] The two imposing promontories that flank the exit from the Mediterranean could therefore serve as the line separating the comprehensible and the incomprehensible, the humanly attainable and the unattainable, the bounded and the boundless. Strabo's term for "the inhabitable world" (*oikoumenē*), which is first found in Herodotus, denotes the entire realm of human existence, relations, and intercommunication. Any movement past this domesticable realm is by definition a passage into the inhuman.[9]

---

[6] Emile Benveniste, *Problèmes de linguistique générale*, 1: 297–98.
[7] The exact location of the ancient "Pillars" has been disputed since antiquity. For an overview of the debate, including a consideration of recent archaeological evidence, see Gary Turnquist, "The Pillars of Hercules Revisited," 13–15.
[8] Strabo, *Geography* 3, 5.5.
[9] Cf. James Romm, *The Edges of the Earth in Ancient Thought: Geography, Exploration and Fiction*, 37.

Hence, beyond serving as a geographical marker, the Pillars of Heracles were regularly taken up by lyric poetry as a metaphor for the absolute limit to human possibility. Pindar employs the topos regularly as a check to mortal striving, for example, in the stunning conclusion to the *Third Olympian*:

> εἰ δ᾽ ἀριστεύει μὲν ὕδωρ, κτεάνων δὲ χρυσὸς αἰδοιέστατος,
> νῦν δὲ πρὸς ἐσχατιὰν Θήρων ἀρεταῖσιν ἱκάνων ἅπτεται
> οἴκοθεν Ἡρακλέος σταλᾶν. τὸ πόρσω δ᾽ ἔστι σοφοῖς ἄβατον
> κἀσόφοις. οὔ νιν διώξω: κεινὸς εἴην.
>
> (*Ol.* 3.42–45)

> If water on the one hand is best, and gold the most revered of
>   possessions on the other,
> now then Theron, reaching the furthest with his accomplishments,
>   grasps
> from his home the Pillars of Heracles. What lies beyond is inaccessible
> both for the skilled and the unskilled. I shall not pursue it: I would be
>   inane.

Within the context of the epinician genre, the *ne plus ultra* motif distinguishes the victor's achievements by implying that they are so great as to require a reminder of mortal limitations. Sailing to the very edge of the bounded sea is a forceful figure for how much has been attained as well as how much must remain forever out of reach.[10] Theron, ruler of the Greek colony of Sicilian Akragas, is already safe, insofar as he now enjoys such greatness from the secure ground of his home (*oikothen*), without embarking on any further voyages. Instead, he should let Pindar's song spread his fame as far as possible.[11] Still, although the poetic voice can travel far, proclaiming the fame and glory (*kleos*) of the athlete, the song, too, like the victory it celebrates, must be restricted to the realm of human possibility. To this end, the coordinating conjunctions of the protasis (μέν ... δέ [on the one hand ... on the other]) juxtapose the natural elements of water and gold, which should be read as relating the poet's contribution (the song that flows like water to distant lands) to his patron's accomplishment (the victory that like gold is revered by all).[12] Despite the naturalness of these elements and their intimations of immortality—the ubiquity of water,

---

[10] Pindar also utilizes the Pillars of Heracles figure in *Nemean* 3.20–23 and *Isthmian* 4.11–14. On limiting human achievement in the epinicia, see Gian Franco Gianotti, *Per una poetica pindarica*, 129–30; Thomas Hubbard, *The Pindaric Mind: A Study of Logical Structure in Early Greek Poetry*, 11–27; and William Race, *Style and Rhetoric in Pindar's Odes*, 191–95.

[11] On epinician poetry as a communicating voyage, see Leslie Kurke, *The Traffic in Praise: Pindar and the Poetics of Social Economy*, 46–52.

[12] Hubbard suggests this reading, *Pindaric Mind*, 14. For an example of the association between epinician song and water, see *Nemean* 7.61–63, where the "glory" (*kleos*) that poetry confers is likened to "streams of water" (ὕδατος ὥτε ῥοάς). On the poetic juxtaposition of water and gold, which also occurs in the famous opening of Pindar's *First Olympian*, see Gregory Nagy, *Pindar's Homer: The Lyric Possession of an Epic Past*, 278 n. 21.

the imperishability of gold—both the watery song and the golden conquest need to be limited, kept within the bounds of the human condition. The skillful knowledge or *sophia* implicit in the final lines therefore refers to *laudator* and *laudandus* alike; hence the subjective intrusion—a typical "break-off formula" in Pindar—which closely aligns the poet's achievement in song with the victor's in the Olympian games: just as Theron cannot go any further, so the poet must bring his poem to a close. To travel beyond this limit would be "inane" or "empty" (*keinos*) praise.

"What lies beyond" the humanly inhabitable and humanly comprehensible may be physically unattainable but not necessarily unimaginable. Insofar as it intimidates passage, it is analogous to a sacred space, an area that is "not to be trodden" (*abaton*), a region that may become the subject of mythological treatment or theoretical speculation.[13] Although conceived as a great "river," the Ocean was believed to be endless, stretching out far into the distance, perhaps reaching all the way to the celestial dome.[14] Encircling the known world, Ocean was identified in epic poetry as the "edges of the earth" (*peirata gaiēs*) and was accordingly placed around the outer border of the Shield of Achilles in book 18 of the *Iliad*.[15] In this regard, the ocean's edge, beginning at the far side of the Pillars of Heracles, demarcates an extreme point, a *peirar*, of the humanly inhabitable earth, of the *oikoumenē*. From the human, "economic" perspective, the waters on the other side of this boundary are boundless. Reminiscent of Anaximander's principle of "the infinite" or "the boundless" (*apeiron*), the open seas could be considered as an immeasurable yet immanent, physical realm of primordial indifferentiation, a formless mass that precedes all forms, suffering no division, admitting no order.

For this reason, Ocean plays a crucial role in a number of cosmogonic accounts. For example, at one point in the *Iliad*, Ocean is identified as the "origin of the gods" (14.201) and according to the Neoplatonist Damascius, ancient Orphic writings posited the ocean's waters as the primal substance, out of which the inhabitable earth emerged through a process of cosmological solidification and sedimentation.[16] The security of the land, its amenability to order, measure, and assignation, could be understood as having been wrested from a primeval fluidity. This ordering is consistently exemplified by the accession of the Olympian pantheon, whose vanquished opponents would need to be relegated to the region of disorder. Thus, in Hesiod's *Theogony*, this outermost limit, precisely as the *peirata gaiēs*, is the murky, dank place where Zeus consigns the Titans, Gi-

---

[13] See, e.g., Sophocles, *Oedipus at Colonus* 167 and 675.

[14] For an overview of descriptions of Ocean, see Lesky, *Thalatta*, 58–87.

[15] For πείρατα γαίης, see *Iliad* 8.478, 14.200; *Odyssey* 5.463, 11.13. On the varied uses and senses of πεῖραρ in epic and lyric poetry, see Ann Bergren, *The Etymology and Usage of πεῖραρ in Early Greek Poetry*.

[16] For an extensive analysis of these oceanic cosmogonies, including Damascius's account, see Jean Rudhardt, *Le thème de l'eau primordiale dans la mythologie grecque*; and Romm, *The Edges of the Earth*, 20–26.

ants, and monsters he has defeated—all that which "must be overcome before the universe can be properly ordered."[17] The fear of an open sea, populated by horrific dragons, fiendish beasts, Scylla and Charybdis, the Aspidochelone, and even the Leviathan, was in no small measure the dread of being swallowed up into this whirlpool of loathsome confusion.

THE SHORE

The experiential shore is a paradigmatic boundary. In dividing the land from the sea, it provides the model for determination, for that which produces meaning by imposing structure, by extracting something definable from the murky confusion that lies outside. Secure—immovable, unassailable—knowledge begins where solid ground differentiates itself from the flowing waters of the restless, boundless, and sterile sea. Unlike a property line, whose validity and legitimacy rest on social conventions or ultimately, as Rousseau surmised, on the force of language itself, the shoreline's status as border would appear to be independent of verbal representation, cognitive mediation or legal fiat. We do not need to be *told* that the beach marks a frontier; we can simply be *shown* that this is the case, concretely and immediately. *Here* the land ends; *here* the sea begins. *Here* you are safe, able to breathe; *there* you must swim if you are not to drown.

There are at least two ways to approach this self-evidence. On the one hand, deixis would suffice and render semantics superfluous. In pointing to the shore—however irregular it may appear, however much it may shift with the tide—we seem to indicate a measure on earth that precedes any naming or signification, a line or caesura that is in itself prehistorical and prehuman. On the other hand, deixis could be regarded as already belonging to a semanticizing process. In constituting a perceptible edge, the coast furnishes a limit that functions as a phenomenon—that is, as an image for a subject—and thereby articulates any number of extrapolations and interpretations that necessarily take place in time, within history. In this regard, the physical immediacy of the shoreline can only be posited as that which has already been sublated into meaningful space. Theorists of social space have long acknowledged the dialectical process that obtains between pure reference and signification. Edward Soja, for example, explains, "Space itself may be primordially given, but the organization, use, and meaning of space is a product of social translation, transformation and experience."[18] Accordingly, the distinction between the conventionality of the property line and the naturalness of the shore becomes far less rigorous.

---

[17] Romm, *The Edges of the Earth*, 24. For exemplary passages in Hesiod, see *Theogony* 517–20, 621–23, and 807–13.

[18] Edward W. Soja, "The Socio-Spatial Dialectic," 210.

As a purely *natural* border, the shore demarcates an enclosed area that ante-dates history and thereby provides the ahistorical ground upon which history unfolds. In contrast, as a *meaningful* space, the coast offers itself as a line that organizes patterns of thought that reflect historical change. These two aspects should not be considered separate: it is through the interference of the geomor-phic space—through its inevitability, through its obstinate reality—that histori-cal usage finds its motivation. The shore, then, is a paradigmatic boundary, not simply because it divides the land from the sea but also because its presence in nature, together with the historical strategies developed to interpret this pres-ence, has consistently served as a model for articulating the mutual interference of space and time.

Thus, well past the historical particularity of the ancient Greek world, the securing antitheses that the coastline generates pervade literary texts from across cultures and periods, from the Epic of Gilgamesh to Melville's maritime parables and beyond. Philosophical or theoretical discourse as well has again and again been inclined to adopt this topographical mode, especially when it proceeds critically, that is, when it focuses on a *crisis* that, like all crises, re-sembles and perhaps draws its dichotomizing power from the divisive shore. The directions and significances of these antithetical orderings vary and di-verge considerably. To take but a few representative examples: in his *Critique of Pure Reason*, Kant contrasts the terra firma of the categories of understanding with the turbulent but seductive waters of metaphysics:

> We have now not only traveled through the land of pure understanding, and carefully [*sorgfältig*] inspected each part of it, but we have also measured it, and determined the place for each thing in it. But this land is an island, and enclosed in unalterable boundaries by nature herself. It is the land of truth (a charming name), surrounded by a broad and stormy ocean, the actual seat of illusion, where many a fog bank and rapidly melting iceberg pretend to be new lands and, ceaselessly deceiving with empty hopes the voyager looking around for new discoveries, entwine him in adventures from which he never can escape and yet also never bring to an end.[19]

According to Kant, the "careful" work of the critical philosopher has secured the terrain of cognition, yet only by bracketing out the encompassing waves or *vagueness* that he ascribes to idealism's excesses. In this case, epistemological truth is purchased with insularity.

The very same dichotomy, however, may just as well be reoccupied by new terms, for example in the lucubrations of Gilles Deleuze and Félix Guattari, who also posit two distinct poles, although now open to contamination and mutual modification, namely the nomadic, unhindered, "smooth space" of

[19] Immanuel Kant, *Kritik der reinen Vernunft*, in *Gesammelte Schriften*, 4: 294–95. English translation (slightly modified) from *Critique of Pure Reason*, 354.

movement at sea against the sedentary "striated space" of movement on land.[20] Instead of cordoning off, like Kant, epistemological certitude from a deceptive realm, Deleuze and Guattari would rather demonstrate how the "deterritorial-izing" force of the former elicits the territorializing tactics of the latter. "The sea is a smooth space par excellence, and yet was the first to encounter the de-mands of increasingly strict striation."[21]

These varying examples of modern interpretation arguably reach back to ancient conceptions, which distinguished the security of dry land from the in-security—or lesser security—of the sea. To trace the development of this basic antithesis and its shifting evaluations is to begin to assess how notions of secu-rity arose and were modified and complicated over the course of history.

In antiquity, through its formal division of terrestrial and aquatic existence, the shore delineated immanent topographies of thought that were able to ar-ticulate a far-reaching series of experiential oppositions that contribute to some sense of security: between stability and instability, solidity and fluidity, safety and danger, calculability and incalculability, familiarity and strangeness, one world and the other. The shore itself, of course, could be regarded from either side of these divides. From the perspective of the land, the littoral formed a natural threshold where the ground of day-to-day life opened onto the vast, limitless expanse. The beach thereby furnished an evocative and ambivalent topos, fraught with affect, particularly in epic poetry. For the solitary, the coast became a privileged site for contemplation, for working matters through, a fit-ting place for indulging in melancholy or hatching plans. In its dynamic bound-lessness, the breadth of the sea could inspire or condemn; it could invite an ac-tive overcoming of limits or presage a passive submission to superior powers.

Thus Achilles, after quarreling with Agamemnon, sorrowfully tarried on the beach, "gazing upon the boundless sea [ἐπ' ἀπείρονα πόντον]" (Il. 1.350). Thus, Dido watched her harbors empty out, "beating her charming breast with her hand" (Aen. 4.589). The waterfront afforded a spectacle that might be alluring or dreadful. The surf, birthplace of Aphrodite, encouraged children, like Nausi-caa and her maidens, to play and frolic, but also elicited strong passions. The beach ignited many a daring spirit, like Vergil's Misenus, the Trojan trumpeter who, peering out from the shore, audaciously and fatally challenged the gods with a conch shell (Aen. 6.171–74). At times, one shore could summon nostal-gia for another, as when Odysseus sat upon the sands of Calypso's isle, "looking out on the barren sea, shedding tears" (Od. 5.84). In this way, the security of the land could come to be perceived as constraining or mortifying, immuring the subject who therefore longed for the waves that would flood over every barrier and wash away every obstacle.

[20] Gilles Deleuze and Félix Guattari, A Thousand Plateaus: Capitalism and Schizophrenia, 474–500. On the ancient land-sea dichotomy and the philosophical tradition of binary logic, see Irad Malkin, "Postco-lonial Concepts and Ancient Greek Colonization."
[21] Deleuze and Guattari, A Thousand Plateaus, 479.

From the perspective of the sea, the coast was most frequently a sign of safe return, a welcome sight of relief and rest. As a shipwrecked victim of Poseidon's implacable wrath, Odysseus regarded the Phaiacian shores as a joyous "shelter from the wind" (*Od.* 5.443). The harbor consoled and renewed hope, offering respite from exhausting trials, signaling the end of a journey or the restitution of stability. Yet glimpsing a beach that was recognized as hostile or dangerous would spur travelers to hasten on their way, as Odysseus's companions did, when nearing the shores of the Sirens, no doubt spotting, as Circe had warned, "a heap of bones of decomposing bodies with rotting flesh" (*Od.* 12.45–46). Viewed from the sea, the beach generally meant the presence of others, be they inimical or friendly, human or monstrous. Whenever Odysseus landed on an unfamiliar shore, he first had to consider the nature of its inhabitants: "Are they arrogant and wild and not just, or are they hospitable and god-fearing in their thoughts?" (*Od.* 6.120–21)

In separating solid ground from flowing waters, the shore differentiated two modes of human existence and two opposing paths of orientation. The seafarer, pioneer, or explorer approached the world differently than the farmer, shepherd, or artisan did. Terrestrial life proceeded by tilling fields, laying foundations, erecting institutions, mapping borders, and perhaps drawing up property lines. The well-grounded populace was able to move about on sure footing, settle down, and establish a territory. This stable base provided a defined position from which any number of identities may be forged—be they civil, cultural, social, or individual. Upon the good earth, mankind knew where it stood. By contrast, life upon the high seas was compelled to face nearly constant difficulties. With the shore no longer in sight, navigation demanded specialized technical skills and pragmatic knowledge. Perilous contingencies were more likely and less foreseeable.

Two ancient Greek words for "way" illustrate the land-sea dichotomy with particular force: *hodos* and *poros*. The *hodos* is a road marked out upon the ground, which provides an enduring line that leads from starting point to destination and thereby also enables a clear return back. In antiquity, the *hodos* was the surest means of conveying travelers, goods, and armies, a vital channel of communication, an unambiguous sign of civilization, an index to the *oikoumenē*. Evidence reaching back to the Mycenaean age indicates the development of paved roadways, whose functionality was later enhanced by ramps, mountain passages, and rest areas. In the classical period, *hodoi* were commonly associated with a single territory, like the Sacred Way (*hiera hodos*) that led from Athens to Eleusis, though, as Pausanias reports, there were also "highways" (*eutheiai hodoi*) that connected Athens to Boiotia and Argos to Epidauros (Paus. 9.2.1; 2.25.10). The road was a securable artery, like the route from the port of Piraeus to the Athenian center, which was constructed within the Long Walls during the Peloponnesian War and played a key role in protecting citizens from Spartan hijackers. The passage's legible inscription in the ground gave shape to the terrain and thereby contributed to the maintenance of civil identity, an idea reinforced by the common practice, dating back to archaic times, of burying the city's dead along major roadways. The first epitaphs were intended for wayfarers.

Assured conveyance, convertibility, and memorialization were functions denied to a *poros*, the word for "way" that was commonly associated with water. Hesiod speaks of the "Ocean's way" that Heracles crossed to slay Orthus and Eurytion (*Theog.* 292–94); and Homer's Odysseus confesses that his encounter with Scylla and Charybdis was by far "the worst ever suffered in searching the passages of the sea [*porous halos*]" (*Od.* 12.258–59). The waves' surface admitted no inscription. A sea journey could never be perfectly retraceable. In navigating, a helmsman had to deal with any number of sudden conditions that often required impromptu action.

Cognitive implications follow suit: the *hodos* provides the ground for stored wisdom (*sophia*) by laying out a clear *method* (*met-hodos*) that allows a thinker to travel assuredly from past experience to present circumstance, whereas the *poros* calls for ad hoc measures, drawing less from a sophical body of knowledge and relying more on spontaneous, frequently "cunning knowledge" (*mētis*).[22] The seafaring Odysseus, precisely as the man "of many devices" (*polumētis*), was a document in such craftiness against the relentless fury of Poseidon. On this basis, *poros* came to denote a way of achieving or accomplishing something arduous. The word therefore can frequently be translated as "resource." *Poroi* were the "ways and means" for overcoming Herculean difficulties, routes for escaping evils, but also the contrivances that instigate further risk. Through the elaborate framing devices of Plato's *Symposium*, we learn from Apollodorus's account of Socrates' account of Diotima's speech that *Poros* is the father of Desire. The erotic call of the sea was therefore as seductive as it was frightening. It promised great profit but threatened grave danger. Philosophers shuddered at the specter of *aporia,* and sailors trembled at the thought of being lost at sea. To fail to find one's "way" out of an argument was provocatively analogous to missing out on the "funerary care" (*kēdeia*) that would insure public, posthumous memory.

In brief, throughout this long tradition, the shore represented the threshold between the securable and the insecurable. More specifically, as we have seen, it was the border between boundedness and boundlessness, which meant between method and waywardness, between tightly sealed identity and porosity. As a clear limit, then, the coast served as the site for decision-making. Should one keep to the steady but unspectacular income of the land; or should one set out for great rewards at sea, regardless of risk? Should one follow the dictates of law or surrender to a realm where law has no hold? Understandably, the word

---

[22] The distinction between *sophia* and *mētis* is fully explored in the classic study by Marcel Detienne and Jean-Pierre Vernant, *Les ruses de l'intelligence: La mètis des Grecs.*

poros is related to the word for "trial" or "attempt" (*peira*), and its Indo-European root can be still be heard in English *experience* (Gk. *empeiria*; L. *experiri* [to try, test]), *peril* (L. *periculum*), and perhaps even *pirate* (Gk. *peiratēs* [one who makes a hostile attempt]). Humanity may derive its basic orientation from its terrestrial, sedentary standpoint, but it turns to sea as a realm that urges passing "through" (L. *per*). In brief, the *poros* could be conceived as the "limit" (*peras*) of the possible, as the "boundary" (*peirar*) within the *apeiron*, determining a path through the lawless origin of the law.

HESIOD'S NAUTILIA

The so-called Nautilia section of Hesiod's *Works and Days* (618–94) stages and complicates the antithesis between terrestrial security and thalassic insecurity. Over the course of lauding the prudence of steady work and the humble gratification of an agrarian life, the poem shifts abruptly to a cautious assessment of the sea's temptations:

Εἰ δέ σε ναυτιλίης δυσπεμφέλου ἵμερος αἱρεῖ,
εὖτ᾽ ἂν Πληιάδες σθένος ὄβριμον Ὠαρίωνος
φεύγουσαι πίπτωσιν ἐς ἠεροειδέα πόντον,
δὴ τότε παντοίων ἀνέμων θυίουσιν ἀῆται·
καὶ τότε μηκέτι νῆας ἔχειν ἐνὶ οἴνοπι πόντῳ,
γῆν ἐργάζεσθαι μεμνημένος, ὥς σε κελεύω.

(*WD* 618–23)

But if desire for turbulent seafaring seizes you,
when the Pleiades, fleeing the mighty strength of Orion,
sink into the murky sea,
then there blows with rage winds of all kinds;
and then no longer keep your ships upon the wine-dark sea,
remember to work the land, as I am bidding you.

The sea intrudes by way of an impulsive "desire" (*himeros*) that forcefully "seizes hold" of the subject. The implication is that the decision to abandon the land has little to do with well-considered planning or sagacious reflection. Rather, the thought of seafaring flashes suddenly into consciousness and violently snatches the individual away from quotidian routine. From the start, Hesiod suggests that this unexpected craving is perverse: whereas "impulsive desires"—*himeroi*—are generally aimed toward something pleasurable, here the desire is for the "turbulent, stormy, or boisterous" (*dyspemphelos*) life at sea. This association of *himeros* with a realm described as *dystopic* is altogether striking and unusual.[23] The perversity of this desire is compounded by its occa-

---

[23] This point is raised by Ralph Rosen, "Poetry and Sailing in Hesiod's 'Works and Days,'" 103.

sion, late October, when the constellation of the Pleiades sinks below the horizon, when wintry storms are already astir. Much more than a straightforward, meteorological identification of the season, mention of the Pleiades "sinking" constitutes a dark allusion to the likely fate of those struck with the passion to sail. From the perspective of the shore, such yearning is simply a foolhardy leap into danger and therefore difficult to justify. At moments like these, it is recommended that one recall the merits of working the land as well as correct an attitude that is recklessly oblivious to peril.

Hesiod's *Works and Days* belongs to the ancient tradition of wisdom literature. Essentially an exhortation to work hard and respect justice, the poem consistently extols the virtues of keeping to the land, a recommendation that correlates to a deep fear of the sea. Adherence to the land further confers a sense of personal identity. Inspired by the Muses, Hesiod is the first poet in the extant literature who speaks in the first person; and his name, in addition to legitimizing further the claims made, may allude to the proclivities of the singer's persona, however speculatively. The clearest etymology that comes to mind would be to take *hesi-* as an aorist form of *hēdomai* (enjoy, take delight) plus *hodos*—that is, *Hēsiodos* as "he who takes delight in the road"[24]—a poet, therefore, of calculable industry, traceable paths, and assured method, that is, one who avoids the unforeseeable, watery paths of the open sea.

The principal addressee of *Works and Days* is the poet's brother Perses, a figure portrayed as lacking the values upheld in the poem. An indolent and morally suspect young man, Perses apparently squandered his share of the paternal inheritance and subsequently bribed local rulers to award him Hesiod's own half of the farm (*WD* 37–39). For the poet, Perses is exemplary of an age mired in corruption, one that is prone to litigation and averse to earning fairly. Faced with this black sheep of a brother, Hesiod offers instruction on the virtues of hard, honest work in conformity with the seasons, for it is only such labor that is just and therefore rewarded by Zeus. Under Olympian governance, "Justice" (Dikē), the daughter of Zeus, ultimately triumphs over "arrogance" (*hybris*, [*WD* 217–18]), like the arrogance discernible in those who shun upright labor. Essentially, idleness disrespects Justice and thus elicits the god's punishment. The poet is clearly concerned for his brother, lest he incite the god's anger. However, Hesiod's lessons are not entirely given altruistically, for the man, who like Perses has harmed Justice, risks exposing his family and even his entire city to Zeus's wrath (*WD* 238–47).[25] In setting Perses to work, in

---

[24] For this and other possible etymologies, see Glenn Most's introduction to his edition and translation of Hesiod's works, *Hesiod: Theogony, Works and Days, Testimonia*, 1: xiv–xv and 176–77.

[25] A comparison of the two Prometheus episodes from the *Theogony* and from *Works and Days* illustrates divergent consequences: in the *Theogony*, the Titan himself is punished for his crime (*Theog.* 521–25), whereas in *Works and Days*, the mortals under Prometheus's care are punished, without mention of what becomes of their caretaker.

teaching him to earn rather than steal, Hesiod not only serves his divine patron but also helps to maintain the moral order that preserves generations and upholds their political community.[26]

Hesiod's poem suggests that the city would prosper if no one ever deviated from the just path. Peace would course through the land, and the people would no longer be plagued by "war," "famine," or "disaster." The only concern (*memēlota*), in fact, would be to work the fields: an honest activity that could supply everybody's needs and wants (*WD* 226–31). Hard work, then, should be the sole object of concern, which would banish all other cares. This ideal community would closely resemble the prior golden race of man, which Hesiod had described as a period when men "lived liked gods, possessing a carefree heart [*akēdea thymon*], far from toil and misery" (*WD* 112–13).

This former state of having a "carefree heart" ostensibly occurred before Prometheus's deception, which caused Zeus to "devise baneful cares [*kēdea lygra*] for humans" (*WD* 49). The Olympian ruler does not simply impose necessary labor on mankind, he destroys a prior *security*—a freedom from cares, a freedom from *kēdea*—by introducing fresh and "baneful *kēdea*."[27] The golden race of men had "all the fine things" in life and enjoyed the earth's benefits without toil: "since the life-giving soil bore fruit of its own accord" (*WD* 116–18). Now, the land must be cultivated with difficultly. All the same, these painful concerns should not be deemed entirely baneful. To be sure, the present compulsion to work is a punishment for the Titan's trick, but it is also an opportunity to improve one's lot, for the necessity of labor is congruent with the necessity of leading a just life, which fairly earns divine benefits.

Pious workers would therefore "flourish forever with good things" (*WD* 236). Tellingly, Hesiod further qualifies this scenario of justice by eliminating the desire for the sea, for "[these hard workers] no longer travel on ships, for the life-giving soil bears fruit" (*WD* 236–37). As the poem goes on to assert, remaining at one's hearth and suppressing all desire to quit the land are crucial for maintaining the good life, a life without lack and without care:

οὐδὲ τό γ᾽ ἐν οἴκῳ κατακείμενον ἀνέρα κήδει.
οἴκοι βέλτερον εἶναι, ἐπεὶ βλαβερὸν τὸ θύρηφιν.
ἐσθλὸν μὲν παρεόντος ἑλέσθαι, πῆμα δὲ θυμῷ
χρηΐζειν ἀπεόντος

(*WD* 364–67)

For indeed what lies stored up in the home does not cause a man to
care.

---

[26] On the political ramifications of Hesiod's poem, see Robert Bartlett, "An Introduction to Hesiod's *Works and Days*."

[27] Cf. Jean-Pierre Vernant, "At Man's Table: Hesiod's Foundation Myth of Sacrifice," in *The Cuisine of Sacrifice among the Greeks*, Marcel Detienne and Jean-Pierre Vernant, eds., 79.

It is better for things to be at home, since what is outdoors is harmful.
It is good to take from what is there, but woe for the heart
to need what is lacking

Through ordinances of justice, executed by means of a system of rewards and punishments, Zeus prepares the way for regaining paradise, where tranquil existence and freedom from want are secured, as long as the citizenry diligently works within the dictated bounds. The path toward destroying this perpetual peace is therefore clearly marked: anyone who is dissatisfied with the gifts of bountiful earth, anyone who disdains what is present, anyone who is struck with a longing to transgress the threshold, is already upon "the smooth road" (*leiē . . . hodos*) to evil (*WD* 288). In fleeing the home, especially to board a ship, after Zeus himself has rendered seafaring unnecessary, the adventurer threatens the security of all. Embarkation would introduce new and troubling concerns.

The Nautilia episode that follows later in the poem brings to the fore the negative aspects of maritime enterprises:

οὔ μιν ἔγωγε
αἴνημ'· οὐ γὰρ ἐμῷ θυμῷ κεχαρισμένος ἐστίν·
ἁρπακτός· χαλεπῶς κε φύγοις κακόν· ἀλλά νυ καὶ τὰ
ἄνθρωποι ῥέζουσιν ἀιδρείῃσι νόοιο·
χρήματα γὰρ ψυχὴ πέλεται δειλοῖσι βροτοῖσιν.
δεινὸν δ' ἐστὶ θανεῖν μετὰ κύμασιν

(*WD* 682–87)

I myself do not
praise it [seafaring in springtime]; for my heart takes no pleasure in it:
a stolen moment: you would have difficulty avoiding trouble;
but even this men do in their ignorance;
for property is life for miserable mortals.
And it is a terrible thing to die upon the waves.

Given the likelihood of encountering danger or, at worst, perishing at sea, only fools would leave the land and seek wealth off shore. Yet the poet's emphatically personal dislike appears to be justified more specifically on the moral, theological, and even political grounds established earlier in the text. In brief, sailing is fundamentally unjust, hubristic, and civically disastrous, insofar as it would incite Zeus's wrath on the entire populace.

Still, Hesiod's misgivings regarding seafaring could not discount pragmatic considerations. Despite his own antipathy toward the sea, he must concede that it is not merely base greed or the vain lust for possessions that compels men to sea travel but also the visceral pain of poverty and hunger. Zeus may have prepared the path for an ideal and just life of work, where economic scarcity would no longer be a problem, but the real conditions of human society, saturated in "baneful cares," are far from perfect. Sometimes agriculture alone is insufficient; sometimes it is necessary to set sail. Hence, in lines devoted to the righteous acquisition of wealth, Solon condones trading by sea as a legitimate alternative to farming, despite the likelihood of being "tossed by difficult winds" and risking one's life (frag. 13.43–46). As Hesiod reports, the need to improve one's lot in this manner was very much a part of his own family's history: "Your father and mine, most foolish Perses, used to sail [plōizesk'] on ship since he did not have a fine life" (WD 633–34). The iterative verb for sailing indicates that the decision to brave the waters was no singular, mad impulse—not a perverse desire—but rather one that was grounded in a realistic assessment of present circumstances, "fleeing not abundance, not wealth and happiness, but rather base poverty, which Zeus gives to men" (WD 637–38). In this case, sailing appears to find its justification.

All the same, unlike Solon's example and the example of Hesiod's father, the "sudden impulse" to sail among the poet's contemporaries, "foolish Perses" included, is described not as a viable alternative for satisfying basic needs but a dangerous supplement aimed toward greater profits and luxury.[28] Hesiod is perhaps addressing his Boiotian compatriots, who were attracted to the exportation of grain. He seems to have in mind those who are never satisfied with what is present, those who disdain what is available at home. Hesiod's fear of the sea coincides with his more general fear of retribution. If sailing threatens the just, how much more does it threaten those who fail to be content with a simple life? The way to attain a happy life may never be absolutely secure, but limiting acts and desires that are inherently transgressive may persuade Zeus to allow prosperity and withhold catastrophe. Hesiod's prayer, at the head of the poem, emphatically exhorts the god to judge "with justice" (dikēi, WD 9). In the hope for security, mortals should perform their work in accordance with justice, so that Zeus may respond with justice. Yet, even when the community acts justly, security may elude it. After all the evils and plagues escaped from Pandora's jar, "hope" alone remained beneath the lid (WD 96).

As Hesiod's honest father learned firsthand, among the "gifts" that Zeus offers to mankind there is "base poverty." The things that the gods send are neutrally appraised, both benevolent and malicious, somewhat like Pandora, a "beautiful evil thing" (kalon kakon, Theog. 585).[29] The Hesiodic corpus is generous with structuring ambiguities of this sort. In the opening lines of Works and Days, the powers of Zeus are portrayed as thoroughly neutral: the ability to grant men renown and to plunge them into obscurity; the power to strengthen and to weaken; to lower the proud and raise the humble—such is achieved "by the will of great Zeus" (WD 4). The theme of neutrality directly continues with

[28] At Works and Days 689 it is clear that the sailor is an entrepreneur who intends to profit from a farming surplus. See Martin West's edition, Hesiod: Works and Days, 313.
[29] In Works and Days, the Pandora episode (54–105) directly precedes the account of the Ages of Man.

the presentation of two kinds of personified "Strife" (Eris), the one who incites quarrels and war, and the other who encourages healthy competition, stirring even the indolent to work (*WD* 11–26). Analogously, Zeus punishes mankind by imposing necessary labor, but labor is also the means by which workers can satisfy their needs. Justice is introduced into the world in order to award human society with possible security, but only by punishing the venturesome ones who impulsively abandon their fields, follow the allure of the sea, and thereby threaten to disturb the peace. Seafaring is an evil—difficult, troublesome, and risky—yet it is also, at times, the only way to combat the evil of poverty. The father's journeys ultimately brought the family to Ascra, "a wretched country village," but one "near Helicon" (*WD* 639), that is, close to the home of the Muses who inspired the shepherd Hesiod to song. The only time the poet traveled by ship was to perform in a rhapsodic contest, in which he was awarded first prize (*WD* 650–59).[30]

Because in a necessarily evil world sailing is a necessary evil and therefore a potential good, Hesiod can only moderate rather than eliminate it. Upon conceding the possible (albeit doubtful) legitimacy of a sudden impulse (*himeros*) to sail, Hesiod instructs his dishonest brother:

Εὖτε ἂν ἐπ' ἐμπορίην τρέψας ἀεσίφρονα θυμὸν
βούληαι χρέα τε προφυγεῖν καὶ λιμὸν ἀτερπέα,
δείξω δή τοι μέτρα πολυφλοίσβοιο θαλάσσης,
οὔτε τι ναυτιλίης σεσοφισμένος οὔτε τι νηῶν.

(*WD* 646–49)

If ever you turn your witless heart to commerce,
and should want to flee need and joyless hunger,
I shall show you indeed the measures of the loud-roaring sea,
even though I know nothing of seafaring nor of ships.

Like their father, Perses may long to find a way (*poros*) out of penury and hunger by trading upon the seaway (*emporia*). In that case, Hesiod will indicate "measures" that should limit when sailing may take place. As usual, the poet is keen to define the proper season, which navigation, like agriculture, must obey.[31] Here, the term "measures" (*metra*) further links seafaring with song. However, whereas Hesiod, precisely as a poet, has skilled knowledge (*sophia*) of measures in song, he claims no such knowledge regarding the sea—"even though I know [*sesophismenos*] nothing of seafaring nor of ships.[32] Showing compensates for a lack of knowing. The sea's incalculability admits no sure

---

[30] The links between seafaring and Hesiod's approach to poetry are broached by Gregory Nagy, "Hesiod," in *Ancient Greek Authors*, 66; and further explored by Rosen, "Poetry and Sailing."
[31] The crucial importance of the right season (τὸ ὡραῖον)—the "days" of the poem's title—is emphasized throughout the Nautilia. See *Works and Days* 617, 630, 642, and 665.
[32] Cf. Rosen, "Poetry and Sailing," 101.

method of knowledge, yet the prudence that poetry imparts can at least minimize risk.

By following the proper measure, the seafarer would show respect for Justice and in return expect some security upon the insecurable waves. Zeus, however, is not bound to justice: *Dikē* is after all his daughter; and the divine ruler need not respect the ordinances he himself proclaims. Any expectation for fair compensation must remain uncertain, like "expectation" or "Hope" itself (*Elpis*), the one evil that fails to escape from Pandora's jar (*WD* 96).[33] Even if the sailor attends to the right season, there is no guarantee that disaster will be averted: embarking in late summer would appear to prevent the chance of shipwreck and death at sea, "unless indeed Poseidon the Earthshaker is not favorable, or Zeus the king of the immortals wishes to destroy" (*WD* 667–68). In breaching the boundary of the shore, regardless of the time of year and regardless of motive, the navigator is still exposed to the arbitrary, capricious wills of the Olympian sovereigns. The mortal realm, at the shore's edge, is characterized by impermanence, in contrast to the home of the gods, which is perched atop "snowy Olympus," far away from the sea and therefore permanent: "eternally immovable" or "forever secure" (*asphales aiei*, *Theog.* 117, 128).

THE PHILOSOPHICAL SPECTACLE

In his concise study, *Shipwreck with Spectator*, Hans Blumenberg adopts the land-sea dichotomy as a central "thought model" for understanding historical shifts in formulations of the meaning of human life.[34] In addition to Hesiod's Nautilia, Blumenberg cites the proem to the second book of Lucretius's *De rerum natura* as his primary exemplum. As discussed above, although for Hesiod the extrajuridical zone is a realm to be feared, its attractions cannot be readily discounted. As Blumenberg rhetorically questions, "What could have motivated the move from land to sea but a refusal of nature's meager offerings, the monotony of agricultural labor, plus the addictive vision of quickly won rewards?"[35] Seafaring may be fraught with danger, but its potential benefits— proportionate to the high risks—remain strongly seductive.

It is the will to resist this enticing temptation that appears to motivate the Lucretian position. The crucial passage opens the second book of *De rerum natura*, where the person trained in philosophy is depicted as a spectator, safely possessing "an inviolable, solid ground for his view of the world."[36]

---

[33] There is, of course, a long and rich tradition of interpreting the significance of *elpis* in this episode. For an exemplary reading, which reviews some of the main arguments, see Vernant, "At Man's Table," 78–86.

[34] Hans Blumenberg, *Shipwreck with Spectator: Paradigm of a Metaphor of Existence*, 8.

[35] Blumenberg, *Shipwreck*, 9.

[36] Blumenberg, *Shipwreck*, 26.

Suave, mari magno turbantibus aequora ventis,
e terra magnum alterius spectare laborem ;
non quia vexari quemquamst iucunda voluptas,
sed quibus ipse malis careas quia cernere suave est.

(*De rer. nat.* 2.1–4)

It is sweet, when on the great sea the water is stirred by the winds,
to watch from the shore another man's struggle;
not because someone else being shaken is a delightful pleasure,
but rather because perceiving from what evils you are spared is sweet.

As Blumenberg stresses, for Lucretius the sweetness or "pleasantness" that characterizes this removed standpoint should not be understood as consisting in the pleasure one enjoys before another's suffering but rather as the security of the position attained by means of philosophical reflection. The safe harbor, then, is the philosopher's own self-consciousness, a sound mooring that can withstand "the whirl of atoms out of which everything that he observes is constituted, including himself."[37] In a word, the materialist worldview offers to mankind stability, for it allows us to neglect the reality that neglects us; it teaches us how to be indifferent to an indifferent environment. Like a god, the philosophical subject is withdrawn from the world and thereby immune from its incalculable effects.

Blumenberg's reflections provide a useful starting point for a consideration of the conceptualization of security. Lucretius's proem is commonly proffered as a vivid illustration of *ataraxia*, Democritus's and Epicurus's key term for the peace of mind that is posited as the supreme gift that one may expect from the philosophical life, an ideal that Cicero repeatedly identifies as *securitas*. Lucretius describes this acquired repose or impassiveness as enjoying the security of the shore, which is here contrasted with the turbulence or insecurity of the sea. By Lucretius's day, the image had become proverbial: a fragment of Archippus (fl. 410 BC) reads "How sweet to view the sea from the land, mother, if one never sails upon it" (Kock frag. 43); and Cicero later deploys the image to express his animosity toward his political enemies: "I desire to watch their shipwreck from the shore" (*Att.* 2.7.4).

Lucretius may temper the sentiment's harshness by denying a simple case of *Schadenfreude* ("not because to see someone else being shaken is a delightful pleasure"), yet the dark implications nonetheless remain. For now, what is important in this passage is that the philosopher may observe the anguish of the world, unaffected. Thus, the "delightful *voluptas*" described in Lucretius's lines specifies the meaning of the "pleasure" or *hēdonē* conventionally associated with the Epicurean school. Specifically, what appears to be at stake is the "catastematic" pleasure of being free from pain and anxiety, as opposed to the "ki-

---

[37] Blumenberg, *Shipwreck*, 26.

netic" pleasures of the body and imagination.[38] That is, *voluptas* is here conceived as a mental "passion" or "emotion" (*pathos*) as opposed to *voluptas* as a corporeal sensation.

Lucretius's Epicureanism does not claim that human existence is free from danger but rather that fear and anxiety can be and must be overcome. Through the use of our intellect and understanding, Lucretius hopes that we may become "instructed" (*perdocti*, 3.473), that we may conquer the fear of death, which is the primary cause of turmoil and despair in the world. The continuation of the proem from book 2 addresses this hope:

> *suave etiam belli certamina magna tueri*
> *per campos instructa tua sine parte pericli.*
> *sed nihil dulcius est, bene quam munita tenere*
> *edita doctrina sapientum templa serena,*
> *despicere unde queas alios passimque videre*
> *errare atque viam palantis quaerere vitae,*
> *certare ingenio, contendere nobilitate,*
> *noctes atque dies niti praestante labore*
> *ad summas emergere opes rerumque potiri.*
> *miseras hominum mentis, o pectora caeca !*
> *qualibus in tenebris vitae quantisque periclis*
> *degitur hoc aevi quodcumquest ! nonne videre*
> *nil aliud sibi naturam latrare, nisi utqui*
> *corpore seiunctus dolor absit, mente fruatur*
> *iucundo sensu cura semota metuque ?*
>
> (5–19)

> It is also sweet to behold great battles of war
> arrayed over the fields without your part in the peril.
> But nothing is sweeter than to occupy
> high sanctuaries serene, well fortified by the teachings of the wise,
> from where you can look down on others and see them wandering
> here and there, going astray as they seek a way of life,
> as they rival each other with their wit, as they dispute in their claims
>   for nobility,
> as they strive night and day with surpassing effort
> to rise up to the highest and to take possession of the world's riches.
> Oh, miserable minds of men, oh blind hearts!
> In what darkness of life, in how many dangers
> is whatever part of life spent! Do you not see
> that nature barks for nothing other than this:

---

[38] With regard to the distinction between catastematic and kinetic pleasure in this passage, see Cyril Bailey's commentary in *Lucretius: De rerum natura*, 2: 796.

> that pain be absent, disjoined from the body, that she may enjoy in mind
> a sense of pleasure, removed from care and fear?

Lucretian philosophy offers mortals serenity comparable to the gods'. The transcendent position (*despicere*) relocates the sage far from the deafening commo-
tion of existence, far from the aimless striving and violent contention that
would ensnare humanity in countless dangers. The fortification of Epicurean
therapy protects us from miserable pain and thereby permits us to realize what
our natures should truly desire, namely *ataraxia*. Although Lucretius does not
employ the term *securitas*—its syllabic form could never conform to the poem's
dactylic meter—the term is concretely discernible in the passage's final syntagma: *cura semota* (removed from care). The perfect participle of the verb
semovere, also built with the prefix (*se-*), allows this phrase to capture the primary sense of *securitas*. In fact, Lucretius engages an entire program of elimination underscored by *se-*, the prefix of apartness: *corpore seiunctus dolor, cura
semota metuque*—an eradication of pain, concern, and fear that is achieved explicitly through distantiation.

However, with one threat expunged, another, perhaps more insidious menace may surface. Mindful of Hyginus's anthropology, which describes human
life explicitly as an existence *cum cura*, we may question a philosophical attitude poised to leave us careless. Internal evidence from Lucretius's poem, not
discussed by Blumenberg, can begin to point in this direction. By quickly com-
paring the proem of book 2 to other passages of *De rerum natura*, some troubling conclusions emerge that necessarily qualify Lucretius's primary claims.
We note that elsewhere in the poem, in acquiescing to the security of distance,
the subject also approaches a moribund state. In book 3 we learn of "the unperturbed repose of death" (*leti secura quies*, 3.211); and further along, that death
is "more secure than any sleep" (*omni somno securius*, 3.977). As later books
assert, to be removed from biting concerns is to live like "the gods, who lead a
life without care" (*deos securum agere aevum*, 5.82, 6.58). A life without care is
divine, for the life of the gods is one that is "removed and disjoined far from our
affairs" (*semota ab nostris rebus seiunctaque longe*, 1.45)—a description that
perfectly corresponds to the language from the opening of book 2. Moreover,
Lucretius disparages the sated life of the "fool" (*stultus*) as "carefree or careless
repose" (*securam . . . quietam*, 3.939).

Thus, in Lucretius, the state of being *securus* may be divine, stultifying, or
lethal. A life perfectly removed from dangerous existence is indeed a kind of
death, insofar as life appears to be consigned to motionlessness if not lifelessness. It would appear that, for Lucretius, the dream of complete *securitas* is both
divine and foolish, an assessment that need not be regarded as a contradiction.
Security is divine because it liberates us from fear; but it is foolish insofar as it
deprives us of the very mortal transience that defines human existence. In making us like the gods, security literally dehumanizes, for a nonhuman humanity

is absurd. One might well conclude that security is potentially paralyzing, not because it saves our lives, but because it takes away our mortality. Epicurean tranquillity would seem to be valid only when danger, including the threat of death, is kept in view rather than extirpated entirely.

LYRIC INFALLIBILITY

Securitas in its positive sense implies a firm foundation for judgments and actions unimpeded by vexatious doubt. In ancient Greek, this connotation is forcefully expressed by *asphaleia*, a term that eliminates the fear of "stumbling, tripping, or falling" (*sphallein*). Political applications of the term are attested early on. Although the verb *sphallein* is initially connected in archaic poetry with wrestling, in political contexts the term *asphaleia* describes an institution's resistance to being overthrown. For Aristotle, *asphaleia* may vividly convey a sense of security that is crucial to a functioning democracy, namely, a forum where opponents can struggle without causing either side to "stumble."[39] Like *securitas*, *asphaleia* addresses risks. However, whereas *securitas* tends to denote a psychological discharge—eliminating the *fear* of falling or the *apprehension* that one might stumble—*asphaleia* generally deals with a physical menace, that is, the concrete possibility of ruin. All the same, the inner, emotional stabilization conveyed by *securitas* is also operative in *asphaleia*, even though the metaphorical ramifications significantly differ.

The following fragment of Archilochus serves as a useful example, one that is not very distant from the roaring surf:

θυμέ, θύμ᾽ ἀμηχάνοισι κήδεσιν κυκώμενε,
†ἀνάδευ δυσμενῶν† δ᾽ ἀλέξεο προσβαλὼν ἐναντίον
στέρνον †ἐνδόκοισιντ᾽ ἐχθρῶν πλησίον κατασταθεὶς
ἀσφαλέως· καὶ μήτε νικέων ἀμφάδην ἀγάλλεο
μηδὲ νικηθεὶς ἐν οἴκῳ καταπεσὼν ὀδύρεο,
ἀλλὰ χαρτοῖσίν τε χαῖρε καὶ κακοῖσιν ἀσχάλα
μὴ λίην, γίνωσκε δ᾽ οἷος ῥυσμὸς ἀνθρώπους ἔχει.

(frag. 128 West)

My heart, my heart, troubled by unmanageable cares,
emerge, ward off the hostile ones and cast against them
your chest, among the beamlike spears of the enemies stand close,
securely; and do not gloat openly in victory
nor when defeated fall down lamenting at home,
but rejoice in joyful times and grieve in bad times
not excessively, know what rhythm holds mankind.

[39] See Aristotle, *Politics* 6, 1319b.

This passage, preserved by Stobaeus, can only be read without the benefits of papyrological evidence. Still, even with the multiple philological cruxes, the basic sense of the adverb *asphaleōs* (securely) can be ascertained. Hardly having recourse to metaphors of containment, protection, or distance, Archilochus encourages his heart, his *thymos*, to stand tall amid danger. Rather than immure or distance himself from hostilities, the soldier-poet refuses to stumble (*sphallein*) beneath the weight of his concerns or cares (*kēdesin*). In place of refuge, Archilochus gives us a security based on gathering strength and braving the storm. He resolves not to succumb to any countering force, neither to the internal weight of his fears nor to the external violence of enemy assault. The privative function is still operative, but here what is absent is specifically the anxiety that would cause flight or surrender. Rather than supplying shelter, *asphaleia* impels confrontation. Instead of implementing means of prevention, it instigates engagement. With security, spear in hand, the subject leaps into the fray.

Although taking place on land, the battle scene evokes danger at sea. The participle *kykōmene* (troubled) also appears in Archilochus's fragment 106, where it explicitly describes a storm upon the open waves. Martin West suggests that the verb bears direct relation to the word *kyma* (wave).[40] In the *Iliad* the river Skamander, outraged by Achilles' murderous fury, "makes all its waters turbulent [*kykōmenos*]" in an effort to protect those bodies still breathing (*Il.* 21.235). Moreover, the ancient commentator Heraclitus notes that Archilochus compares war to a storm at sea (frag. 105 West). On the basis of these passages, in returning to fragment 128, Michael Theunissen recognizes a "second image" superimposed upon the battle evoked in Archilochus's poem: the struggle of one army against the other correlates to a ship's struggle against the turbulence of the storm-tossed waters.[41]

Like many Greek poets, Archilochus appeared to harbor a deep fear of the sea. In describing the colonizing expedition from his native Paros to Thasos, where the battle of fragment 128 may have taken place, the poet confesses his need to drink a good deal of wine in order to withstand his nausea (frag. 4 West); and according to ancient testimony, Archilochus composed a great elegy for his brother-in-law, who perished in a shipwreck, lamenting the victims identified as "the painful gifts of lord Poseidon."[42] This kind of thalassophobia contributes strongly to the Lucretian proem discussed above. The philosophical, transcendent position—"removed from care" (*cura semota*)—is preferable to the fearful realm of sea.

However, as we see in Archilochus, a different species of security—*asphaleia*—is still possible upon the rough waters. For him, it is explicitly a question of "rhythm." Waves create a rhythmic pattern, an ebb and flow that can be

---

[40] Martin West, *Iambi et elegi Graeci ante Alexandrum cantati*, ad loc.
[41] Michael Theunissen, *Pindar: Menschenlos und Wende der Zeit*, 173.
[42] ἀνιηρὰ Ποσειδάωνος ἄνακτος δῶρα (frag. 12 West; see also frag. 13 West).

observed, anticipated, and also feared. The final extant line of fragment 128 speaks of the *rhythmos* that "holds mankind." This grip suggests heteronomy and inevitability, and therefore recommends moderation both in joy and in grief. In the fragment's opening image it is the "unmanageable cares" that trouble the heart, perhaps like a formidable wave. The poem's subject cannot fight against them; there is no "means" or "contrivance" (*mēchanē*) to ward off these debilitating concerns that leave one in a state of utter "helplessness" (*amēchania*). Instead, the heart is encouraged to endure. Most of the various conjectures for the crux of line 2 corroborate the force of the wave imagery: Wolfgang Schadewaldt's proposal, ἀναδύευ (emerge!), suggests that the subject has been overwhelmed by these waves of concern and must now rise to the surface in order to survive; and Theodor Bergk's earlier emendation, ἀνὰ δ᾽ ἔχευ μένων (stand firm!), depicts a subject who is standing, say on board a ship, and must remain standing.[43] The "security" (*asphaleia*) promoted here does not shy away from the mortality that defines the human condition but rather faces it stoutheartedly.

A call for a similar kind of security is heard in another fragment, where Archilochus expresses distaste for well-groomed generals:

> οὐ φιλέω μέγαν στρατηγὸν οὐδὲ διαπεπλιγμένον
> οὐδὲ βοστρύχοισι γαῦρον οὐδ᾽ ὑπεξυρημένον,
> ἀλλά μοι σμικρός τις εἴη καὶ περὶ κνήμας ἰδεῖν
> ῥοικός, ἀσφαλέως βεβηκὼς ποσσί, καρδίης πλέως.

(frag. 114 West)

> I do not love the tall general or the one who struts
> or the one who exults in his curly locks or is cleanly shaven,
> rather for me let him be someone short, even bow-legged,
> walking secure on his feet, full of heart.

Again, as in fragment 128, security consists in holding one's ground and launching into battle with resolute conviction. It is a soldier's ideal of bravery that welcomes treacherous onslaught and cares little for pretty appearances. Archilochus's preferred general draws his value from an internal source of security as steadfastness. The series of antitheses—tall and short, refined handsomeness and plain homeliness, self-aggrandizement and self-effacement—vividly reinforce the sense of *asphaleia* at work. The poet's emphatically personal inclination for the tough, hearty, and austere is markedly distant from the heroic ideal proffered by Homer, where outer appearance and inner constitution tend to coincide to create a picture of glorious strength comparable to the gods. In the *Iliad*, for example, from the walls of Troy, Helen points out to Priam the leaders of the Achaean host—Agamemnon, Odysseus, and Aias—and how their bear-

---

[43] For a consideration of the various conjectures, see J. C. Kamerbeek, "Archilochea," 5–6.

ing and demeanor correspond to their lordly natures (3.191–224).[44] The inner
fortitude of Archilochus's exemplary general, on the contrary, amounts to a
bald discrepancy. Here, *asphaleia* is recognized in the courageous acts committed in the heat of the moment and less on show. As Hermann Fränkel observes,
"Humanity steps forward as it is, in heroic nakedness; with virile resolution it
strips itself of all restricting conventions and all meretricious adornment."[45] Security on the beach derives from this inner fortitude.

In the Wake of Poseidon

Across the ancient Greek city-states and provinces, Poseidon was commonly
named "the Securer"—Poseidōn Asphaleios—a cultic epithet perfectly appropriate for the god who is responsible for earthquakes and sea storms.[46] In ancient Greek culture and ritual, it is Poseidon's devastating power—consistently
linked to the sea and the might of horses—which must be appeased or tamed
so that he might grant the sure ground of *asphaleia* and prevent stumbling. His
marine and equine attributes work together with a capacity to lay down solid
foundations. In describing the temple to Poseidon at an Achaean harbor, Pausanias relates that, in addition to traditional local names, the god is addressed
by all men as "the God of the Sea" (Pelagaios), "the Securer" (Asphalios), and
"the God of Horses" (Hippios) (7.21.7).

Specifically, the force of *asphaleia* is resultative, a state that follows great
upset. Strabo tells how, following a horrific volcanic eruption beneath the waters surrounding the Therasian islands, courageous sailors from Rhodes traveled there to erect a temple to Poseidon Asphaleios. After the frightening flames
finally died down, freshly acquired security is to be celebrated and honored. In
particular, as we learn in the *Odyssey*, Poseidon protects sea voyages and can
also threaten shipwreck. Herodotus reports on the calamitous effects of a four-
day tempest that destroyed the Persian fleet off the coast of Thessaly, at which
point the Greeks proclaimed vows to Poseidon, poured libations into the sea,
and upon being spared by the storm, henceforth worshiped the god as "Savior"
(Sōtēr) (*Hist.* 7.192). It was certainly a reassuring sight for merchant ships arriving to Athens to spot the large temple to Poseidon Sōtēr at Cape Sunium.
This sense of security associated with the god persisted well into the Roman
epoch and can be found, for example, in Appian's account of Octavian's naval
preparations against Pompeius:

> Caesar [Octavian] sailed from Puteoli, offering sacrifices and pouring liba
> tions from the admiral's ship into the water to the propitious winds, and to

[44] See Rainer Nickel's commentary in *Archilochos: Gedichte*, 270.
[45] Hermann Fränkel, *Early Greek Poetry and Philosophy*, 150.
[46] For the relevant source material, see Friedrich Wieseler, "Poseidon Asphaleios." For a general account of Poseidon's attributes, see Walter Burkert, *Greek Religion*, 136–39.

Poseidon the Securer [Ἀσφαλείῳ Ποσειδῶνι], and to the tranquil sea, that they should become his assistants against the enemies of his father. (*Civil Wars* 5.11.98)

Poseidon Asphaleios is similarly beseeched in the event of earthquakes. As the "Earthshaker," the god fearfully manifests himself in great disasters on land, for example the massive tremors that rattled Sparta in 464 BC, which Thucydides interprets as divine retribution against the Lacedaemonians who blasphemously murdered suppliants from Poseidon's temple at Taenarus (*Hist.* 1.128.1). The god's seismic power should not be too rigorously distinguished from his jurisdiction over the sea. The natural philosopher Thales believed that the earth's land floated upon the ocean and that it quaked when the waters below were disturbed.[47] The traditional threefold allotment to the Olympians—the sea granted to Poseidon, the sky to Zeus, and the underworld to Hades—would confirm that the god who ensures safe passage upon the waves is also the one who maintains the land's solidity. Poseidon Asphaleios appears to embody the land-sea dichotomy that pervades metaphors of security. Waters are "secure" when they behave like land; and the earth resembles the sea when it trembles. The one who moves the ground is the one who stabilizes it.[48]

Although the Homeric epics nowhere name Poseidon (or rather, Poseidaōn) explicitly as Asphaleios, the god's prominence as the "Earthshaker" and Calmer of the seas sufficiently attests to his cultic role as the "Securer." Rather than consider Poseidon's complex and at times confusing presence within the epics, I shall restrict my reading to the well-known prophecy of what Odysseus is to perform for his final journey. The episode does not occur within the epic itself, but rather is foretold twice: first, by the seer Teiresias during the hero's descent into the underworld, and then in the penultimate book, when Odysseus relates his fate to his wife Penelope in Ithaca. These passages together constitute what is perhaps the most crucial narrative component for assessing those attributes of Poseidon that contribute to the land-sea constellation and the security issues it expresses.

In the eleventh book of the *Odyssey*, Teiresias first assures Odysseus that he will slay the suitors who occupy the halls of his palace at Ithaca. He then further prescribes what the hero is to do afterward: namely, he must take an oar and travel to a place where the inhabitants have no knowledge of the sea. When someone mistakes the oar for a "winnowing fan," Odysseus is to plant it in the ground and establish a cult to Poseidon, thus appeasing the wrathful god and bringing his wanderings and troubles to an end. To assess the significance of this final journey, it is worthwhile to consider the striking metaphors that Teire-

---

[47] The theory is cited and denounced by Seneca in *Natural Questions* 3.14 and 6.6.

[48] See Macrobius, *Saturnalia* 1.17.22: *Nec mirum, si gemini effectus variis nominibus celebrantur, cum alios quoque deos ex contrario in eadem re duplici censeri et potestate accipiamus et nomine, ut Neptunum quem alias Ἐνοσίχθονα, id est terram moventem, alias ἀσφαλίωνα, id est stabilientem, vocant.*

sias employs in order to specify his prophecy. Odysseus must carry the oar until
he comes across a people who have no experience of the shore:

> οἳ οὐκ ἴσασι θάλασσαν
> ἀνέρες οὐδέ θ᾽ ἅλεσσι μεμιγμένον εἶδαρ ἔδουσιν·
> οὐδ᾽ ἄρα τοί γ᾽ ἴσασι νέας φοινικοπαρῄους
> οὐδ᾽ ἐϋήρε᾽ ἐρετμά, τά τε πτερὰ νηυσὶ πέλονται.

(Od. 11.122–25)

> Men who do not know the sea,
> men who do not eat food mixed with salt;
> they know neither purple-cheeked ships
> nor well-fitted oars, which are wings for ships.

Teiresias's metaphors appear to be intended for those who have experienced sea
journeys: the ship's bow that looks like a cheek adorned with reddish purple
color; and the oars that like wings allow the vessel to soar. The latter image may
even further suggest that the act of venturing out on sea is as transgressive as
abandoning the earth for the air. In a rationalized version of the Icarus myth,
Pausanias explains that Daedalus invented sails, not wings, to flee Minos and
that it was Icarus's ship that was overturned, because he was an incompetent
helmsman (9.11.4–5). All of these associations are understandable for people
who are familiar with seafaring. Yet Teiresias is speaking of those who have
never had access to the shore. For them, an oar *qua* oar is an incomprehensible
object. The prophet continues:

> σῆμα δέ τοι ἐρέω μάλ᾽ ἀριφραδές, οὐδέ σε λήσει:
> ὁππότε κεν δή τοι συμβλήμενος ἄλλος ὁδίτης
> φήῃ ἀθηρηλοιγὸν ἔχειν ἀνὰ φαιδίμῳ ὤμῳ,
> καὶ τότε δὴ γαίῃ πήξας ἐυῆρες ἐρετμόν,
> ῥέξας ἱερὰ καλὰ Ποσειδάωνι ἄνακτι,
> ἀρνειὸν ταῦρόν τε συῶν τ᾽ ἐπιβήτορα κάπρον,
> οἴκαδ᾽ ἀποστείχειν ἔρδειν θ᾽ ἱερὰς ἑκατόμβας
> ἀθανάτοισι θεοῖσι, τοὶ οὐρανὸν εὐρὺν ἔχουσι,
> πᾶσι μάλ᾽ ἐξείης. θάνατος δέ τοι ἐξ ἁλὸς αὐτῷ
> ἀβληχρὸς μάλα τοῖος ἐλεύσεται, ὅς κέ σε πέφνῃ
> γήραι ὕπο λιπαρῷ ἀρημένον: ἀμφὶ δὲ λαοὶ
> ὄλβιοι ἔσσονται.

(Od. 11.126–37)

> And I shall tell you a sign quite clear, and it will not escape your notice:
> when another wayfarer who happens to meet you
> says you have a winnowing fan upon your bright shoulder,
> then fix the well-fitted oar in the earth,
> make worthy offerings to Lord Poseidon,

a ram, a bull, and a boar that mates with sows,
then go home and prepare sacred hecatombs
to the immortal gods who hold broad heaven,
to all of them, each in due order. And death away from the sea,
a death so gentle shall come to you, that will strike you
overhelmed by sleek old age: and the people beside you
will be blessed.

The scenario may well express the desires of a fatigued mariner who seeks re-pose from his risky life at sea. Odysseus should be relieved to learn that his di-vine and wrathful antagonist Poseidon will eventually be placated, and that once he has returned from this final journey, he will die a gentle death "away from the sea."[49] Moreover, the people assembled around him—his family, his comrades, his political community—will reap the benefits of a blessed life. Teiresias graciously offers this "sign" (sēma) so that Odysseus should no longer fear perishing in shipwreck, being lost at sea, and receiving nothing but an un-marked grave.

For someone tied to farming and utterly ignorant of navigation, an oar may indeed be mistaken for a winnowing fan. However, unlike Teiresias's initial metaphor, which regarded oars as wings, the image of the winnowing fan fails to indicate the object's primary function. Oars are like wings insofar as both are instruments of movement. But in Greek, the winnowing fan is literally a "chaff destroyer" (athērēloigon), that is to say, it separates the wheat from the husk. An oar may figuratively "cut" the waves, but it divides nothing.[50] One may move across the waves as a bird flies through the air, but water's fluid element suffers no separation, no cuts. The image of oars considered as wings communicates function, but the image of oars taken as a winnowing fan explains nothing rel-evant. Therefore, when Odysseus fixes the oar in the earth, it will serve as an empty signifier, a "sign" that for the landlocked tribe will refer to nothing ever experienced or seen. Odysseus must establish a cult that cannot be based on empirical knowledge or Erfahrung, but rather on pure belief.[51] For those who live entirely removed from the sea, Poseidon's capacity to settle the waters can-not be known. The resultative, maritime security that the god procures—the particular kind of blessed life he grants—cannot be understood, for there are no waters to secure. Unlike the "people" gathered around Odysseus at Ithaca,

---

[49] The phrase ἐξ ἁλός, which can mean either "out of the sea" or "away from the sea," has troubled scholars since antiquity (see Scholia ad Od. 11.134). I here follow Uvo Hölscher who compellingly argues that for Odysseus, who has been viciously pursued by Poseidon, a "most gentle death" can only be applied to one that takes place "away from the sea." Review of G. S. Kirk, Songs of Homer, 443; cited in William Hansen, "Odysseus' Last Journey," 42 n. 38. See Hansen's comprehensive review of the scholarship, 42–48.

[50] In his commentary, Eustathius takes the difference between a winnowing fan and an oar to be mini-mal since both are "blades": one cuts the land, the other the sea (ad Od. 11.123).

[51] Cf. Seth Benardete, The Bow and the Lyre: A Platonic Reading of the Odyssey, 93–94 and 152.

these people who never saw the sea can never know the true significance of this god-granted security, even though they can be taught to believe that it exists.

In any event, as soon as Odysseus plants the oar in the ground, his travails are over. Now, this gesture *can* be understood by his agrarian audience, accustomed as it is to the planting of a winnowing fan upright in a pile of grain, which signals that the harvest has come to an end.[52] In setting the oar in the soil, Odysseus, too, will express that his days of navigation are now behind him.[53] In this sense, Teiresias's precise instructions rehearse the prior plea of Elpenor, Odysseus's former comrade at sea. When Odysseus encountered Elpenor in the underworld, the perished sailor begged his captain to retrieve his body off the coast of Aiaia, prepare a grave, and fix his oar upon the mound (*Od.* 11.66–78). Odysseus promised that, once he reemerged into the land of the living, he would plant Elpenor's oar on the shore; and after hearing Teiresias's words, he learns that he will one day do the same for himself. Indeed, the "sign" (*sēma*) that Teiresias offers to Odysseus is nothing less than the hero's own symbolic "tomb" (*sēma*).[54] In pointing to the unknowable, the oar becomes a semiotic vehicle, available for resignification or refunctionalization. Specifically, it becomes a sign denoting that Odysseus's life—regarded as a sea voyage—will soon be over: landed, secure, and gently dead.

In book 23, now home in Ithaca, Odysseus must confess to Penelope that, although he has safely returned, there is still work ahead:

ὦ γύναι, οὐ γάρ πω πάντων ἐπὶ πείρατ᾽ ἀέθλων
ἤλθομεν, ἀλλ᾽ ἔτ᾽ ὄπισθεν ἀμέτρητος πόνος ἔσται,
πολλὸς καὶ χαλεπός, τὸν ἐμὲ χρὴ πάντα τελέσσαι.

(*Od.* 23.248–50)

Woman, we have not yet come to the ends of all our trials,
rather, there is still to follow unmeasured labor
complex and difficult, which I must complete entirely.

Read in relation to the Nautilia episode from Hesiod's *Works and Days*, the terms that Odysseus here uses would seem to imply another sea voyage. The immensity and difficulty of the anticipated trial resonates with the experience that would await Hesiod's seafarer. Odysseus's word for "ends" (*peirata*) further suggests a *perilous* marine excursion. Yet, as we know, the future journey will emphatically be taken on land, not only away from the sea but also in a place where the sea is entirely unknown. Although the land is eminently measurable, the work to be carried out on this last itinerary is "unmeasured" (*ametrētos*), a characteristic that essentially undermines the conventional, topographical dis-

---

[52] This interpretation is first proposed by Jane Harrison with reference to Theocritus *Idyll* 7.155ff.; cited in Hansen, "Odysseus' Last Journey," 38.

[53] Cf. Hansen, "Odysseus' Last Journey," 39.

[54] Cf. Gregory Nagy, "Sēma and Noēsis," in *Greek Mythology and Poetics*, 214–15.

tinctions of the land-sea dichotomy. Because the term *metra* is commonly associated with the image of a road (*hodos*), the immeasurability of this trial (and trail) further links it to the nonsophical nature of a *poros*, a way that frustrates familiar orientation. Again, knowledge (of the work's limits) is separated from belief (in the truth of Teiresias's prophecy). That the journey will in fact take place outside the narrative limits (*peirata*) of the *Odyssey* underscores the voyage's peculiar resistance to the "metrics" of Homeric poetry, which of course have never failed to chart the hero's movement at sea.[55] While the agrarian poet Hesiod simply confesses that he can only "show the measures of the loud-roaring sea" (*WD* 648), without "knowing" them—an admission that Gregory Nagy and others have understood as an incapacity to follow Homer's poetic "skill" (*sophia*)[56]—Homer here appears to regard an inland voyage to be beyond metrical treatment, at least in terms of the *Odyssey*.

Perpetual security may be enjoyed only by the gods, whose abode is "forever immovable," "forever *asphales*." In the archaic period, here represented by Homer and Hesiod, *asphaleia* is also a gift that may or may not be granted by the divine rulers in general and by Poseidon Asphaleios in particular. From the human perspective a degree of security can be gained from the gods by preferring the near over the far, the home (*oikos*) and the extended home (the *oikoumenē*) over the distant seas, and thus the just over the unjust. Yet, even when a mortal attends to these pious preferences, the reward of *asphaleia* still cannot be guaranteed. In setting Odysseus on a final journey of wandering, fate demonstrates that the land as well may become a kind of sea. Humans may expect security, but they can only believe in the probability of this expectation and never know it for certain. The land-sea dichotomy, therefore, is but one attempt to secure security, an attempt moreover that may or may not be efficacious.

[55] The points on "metrics" and "limits" are made by Alex Purves, "Unmarked Space: Odysseus and the Inland Journey," 8–9. My discussion on this episode is indebted throughout to Purves' reading.

[56] Nagy, "Hesiod," 66, and Rosen, "Poetry and Sailing." See also Carol Dougherty, *The Raft of Odysseus: The Ethnographic Imagination of Homer's* Odyssey, 21–25.

Tranquillity, Anger, and Caution

CICERO'S APPLIED ETHICS

IN THE SPRING OF 59 BC, as the First Triumvirate made a mockery of the constitution, Cicero was compelled to abandon politics and retreat to his sheltered villa at Antium. There were plans to write a geographical treatise, to chart the measure of land and sea, but inspiration was thin. As he explained to Atticus, here, in this quiet coastal town, he would simply indulge in idleness, either enjoying his books or "just counting the waves" (*Att.* 2.6). The distance from Rome afforded him the peace of mind that he would eventually call *securitas*, an inner sense of emotional stability that would have been difficult if not impossible to obtain in the present atmosphere of fractious politics. Still, despite the attractiveness of leading a tranquil life, we learn in the subsequent letter that the former consul's "soul would be delighted to do something in the Republic," to brave once again the treacherous waters of governance. Yet could he summon sufficient energy?

> Already long ago I was growing tired of being at the helm [*gubernare*], even when it was my right. And now that I am forced to leave the ship, not having cast aside the rudder, but rather having it torn from me, I want to watch their shipwreck from the shore [*cupio istorum naufragia ex terra intueri*]. (*Att.* 2.7)

Tossed off the ship of state and having reached the safety of the shore, Cicero settled for the position of the Lucretian sage, opting, at least for now, to view the catastrophe from the land, "removed from care" (*cura semota, De rer. nat.* 2.19). The vessel that should have piloted the populace across the tumultuous tides of this world had proved too weak to handle the ambitions of Crassus, Pompey, and Julius Caesar; and Cicero, having escaped at the last moment, was more or less content to observe the spectacle from afar. Yet that is not to say that he would not dive back in, should the opportunity arise.

Clearly, Cicero had never been one of those pure philosophers who could remain divorced from the political sphere for long. A renowned public orator and staunch defender of republican ideals and civic virtues, he successfully worked his way through the *cursus honorum*, serving as quaestor, aedile, and praetor before being elected consul in 63. Despite imposed exile, failed political maneuvers, and civil war, he continuously fought to reestablish his leadership role in the capital. However, with Caesar's dictatorship and assassination, and then with the frightening rise of Mark Antony, Cicero would suffer an almost complete disaffection with politics, spending more and more time in the safety of the country, now in Tusculum, where he would compose his major philosophical works—*De finibus, Tusculanae Disputationes*, and *De officiis*. Deprived of all political power, the statesman turned to intellectual matters. It is at this point that the term *securitas* first appears in his texts. But even now, he still appeared to be waiting for that day when he could reclaim his position in the Forum.[1] For Cicero, it could never be a question of adopting the *vita contemplativa* over the *vita activa*. Indeed, given the biographical context, any distinction between a philosophical and a political perspective would have to be seriously qualified. Cicero forever abided on the shore, occupying the hot, sandy threshold that separated the land of contemplation and the sea of civil discord, ready to turn in either direction.

Although Cicero never provided a sustained, comprehensive account of *securitas*, one can nevertheless determine the term's import by attending to its functions within the context of his arguments, explanations, and illustrations. Essentially, *securitas* numbers among those technical terms that Cicero selected to transmit Greek concepts for a Roman audience. Its initial significance, therefore, cannot be considered apart from a highly complex network of philosophical speculation and schemas, above all, Stoic theories of selfhood.[2] In order to ascertain what the term *securitas* denotes in this early usage, one must consider the inner core of one's being that moral precepts attempt to secure. That is, one must interrogate the constitution of the *self*: its composition, its relation to an individual's physiology, emotions or passions, its performative roles in society, and so forth—questions that are far from simple to resolve.

Although ancient psychology plays a decisive role in discovering what *securitas* originally secures, it is again impossible to ignore the political ramifications. Engaged with the moral and ethical aspects of Greek philosophy, the Roman concept of an individual's *securitas* invariably touches upon or even overlaps with public issues. The two domains simply cannot be held apart. For Cicero, the value of the doctrines gleaned from Academic, Peripatetic, and Stoic thinkers had always been grounded in their applicability to problems inherent in social life. Hardly confinable to a pure, abstract realm of theory, the

---

[1] See Ingo Gildenhard, *Creative Eloquence: The Construction of Reality in Cicero's Speeches*, 223–24.

[2] Among the most significant interventions, there is the work of Christopher Gill, above all *The Structured Self in Hellenistic and Roman Thought*, which has proved indispensable for this area of research. Other useful, general studies in English include Gretchen Reydams-Schils, *The Roman Stoics: Self, Responsibility, and Affection*; and Margaret Graver, *Stoicism and Emotion*.

conclusions generated by Hellenistic philosophers were persistently tested within the sociocultural milieu. This tradition of applied or practical ethics, forcefully instigated by Cicero and later elaborated by Seneca, courses through the entirety of Roman philosophical reflection, culminating perhaps in the late second-century, Stoic "meditations" of the emperor Marcus Aurelius. The secured self is always the embodied self and is therefore secured *in relation to* (and not necessarily *from*) social and civic experience. *Securitas* denotes a private condition of an individual's selfhood whose definition cannot neglect the fact of communal embeddedness.

In Stoic theory, the embodied self continuously negotiates internal and external experience. The "self is in essence a mediator, and not its own final end: it adjudicates between different demands in different circumstances and weighs business-as-usual against a philosophical ideal of living according to the rational order that shapes all of reality, including human beings."[3] Ethics and moral philosophy help the human subject to acquire knowledge concerning ideals and virtues, which should then be measured against the societal, political framework. The privative construction of *se-curitas*, therefore, should not be misconstrued as the privation of communal life. On the contrary, it should be taken as the removal of matters that obstruct the realization of a rationally sound disposition that can consequently ensure safe passage through circumstantial difficulties.

In Cicero's *De officiis* (On Duties), the public aspect of private *securitas* is especially clear. Although Cicero admits that there may be exceptions for men "of extraordinary genius" (*excellenti ingenio*), who could therefore be excused from civic service, those who are privileged to be educated are expected to enter into the political fray and serve their country:

> Those who manage the state no less than philosophers—for all I know, even more so—must acquire that greatness of spirit and indifference [*despicientia*] to human affairs of which I often speak, as well as tranquillity of mind and freedom from care [*tranquillitas animi atque securitas*], if they are to be without anxiety and live with seriousness and consistency. (*Off.* 1.72–73)

Clearly, philosophers who are withdrawn from public affairs would find it "easier" to enjoy *tranquillitas* and *securitas*, which suggests that the true task is for statesmen, whose engagement in political matters leaves them vulnerable to "greater emotions" (*maiores motus animorum*, 1.73). The acquisition and maintenance of "security" is therefore more fruitfully studied in the latter case; its significance comes more to the fore when viewed against a political backdrop. For Cicero, the term *securitas* may have more to do with individual psychology, but its value is better measured in relation to the public sphere.

[3] Reydams-Schils, *The Roman Stoics*, 13.

PATERNAL ADVICE

Composed in the autumn months of 44, *De officiis* emerged at a particularly difficult and apprehensive time for the philosopher-statesman.[4] Politically, Cicero was positioned to become one of the most powerful senatorial voices during the confused and tense aftermath of the dictator's assassination. Events led him to support reconciliation for the *liberatores* and argue for the peaceful restitution of republican principles, which would come to include the altogether demanding and delicate task of denouncing the ambitions of Mark Antony without alienating the Caesarian faction. After Antony's vicious attack against Cicero before the Senate in mid-September, the onetime consul retired to Tusculum to prepare his response, namely, the speech that would come to be known as the second *Philippic*, which Cicero in fact would never deliver. It is at this time as well that Cicero enters into correspondence with Octavian, who is very clear about his intentions to challenge Antony and to do so by working together with the Senate. All in all, civic duty was fraught with powerful animosity and precarious allegiances. Every philosophical ideal would ultimately be put to the most daunting and risky of trials.

Personally, as his letters repeatedly attest, Cicero was still mourning his beloved daughter Tullia, who passed away the year before in February 45. At present, the loving father was further overwrought with concern for his only remaining offspring, his son Marcus, who was desperately in need of assistance. The young man had been studying philosophy under Cratippus in Athens and was reportedly having problems, presumably regarding career decisions, which required the father's immediate attention. Given the unstable political climate in Rome and his desire to return to the Forum to set the Republic back on track, Cicero decided against making the sea voyage to the Greek capital and instead wrote his treatise "On Duties," which he warmly addressed to his son. In this work, political urgency and paternal concern are everywhere coincident. The father's solicitude for the well-being of his child finds its analogue in the senator's anxiety for the welfare of the state.[5]

De officiis is clearly Stoic, in both its theoretical orientation and its content. The title makes direct allusion to a text, no longer extant, by Panaetius of Rhodes—*Peri tou kathēkontos* (On Duty)—a topic that was of central importance for the Stoa. Works of the same title have also been attributed to Zeno, Cleanthes, Sphaerus, and Chrysippus; and it was Panaetius who, at the urging of Scipio Aemilianus, traveled to Rome in the mid-first century BC to introduce Stoic doctrines to the Republic.

---

[4] The earliest explicit reference that Cicero makes concerning the writing of *De officiis* is found in his letter to Atticus from late October 44 (*Att.* 15.13).

[5] On the interwoven themes of political theory and moral pedagogy, see A. A. Long, "Cicero's Politics in *De Officiis*," in *From Epicurus to Epictetus: Studies in Hellenistic and Roman Philosophy*, 307–34.

In his biography of Zeno of Citium, Diogenes Laertius provides a concise definition of how the word *kathēkon* (duty) is employed philosophically—a usage that is not irrelevant to a discussion of *securitas*.

> The term *kathēkon* was first employed in this way [i.e., concerning moral conduct] by Zeno. Etymologically, it is derived from κατά τινας ἥκειν [to reach down to some things]. It is in itself an activity appropriate [*oikeion*] to nature's arrangements. For, among the actions done on impulse, some are fitting or proper [*kathēkonta*], others are contrary to what is proper, and others are neither proper nor improper. Proper actions [*Kathēkonta*] are all those that reason [*logos*] compels us to do [*poiein*], as in honoring one's parents, brothers and country, and carrying on with friends; that which is improper, is everything that reason does not condone, such as neglecting [*amelein*] one's parents, paying no heed [*aphrontistein*] to one's brothers, not agreeing with friends, disregarding one's country, and so forth. Actions that are neither proper nor improper are all those which reason neither compels us to do [*prattein*] nor forbids, such as picking up a twig, handling a stylus or a scraper, and the like. (7.108–9; Hicks, trans.; slightly modified)

Etymology allows Diogenes to draw out the fundamental sense of *kathēkon* as being oriented by a clear goal, as *reaching toward* that which is "appropriate" or firmly "situated" (*oikeion*) "in accordance with nature" (*kata phusin*). The topic of "appropriateness" or "appropriation" (*oikeiōsis*) is of great significance for Stoic thinkers.[6] In general, it refers to the natural affinity that animals and human beings possess in relation first to themselves and then to elements of their environment, including their social setting.[7] Related to the word for "house" or "home" (*oikos*), *oikeiōsis* suggests a position one inhabits, the place where one morally dwells. It presupposes a specific self-awareness, the ability to know where one stands, to understand one's inner nature, and to make the right choices accordingly. What is "appropriate" or "fitting," therefore, is what the natural gift of "reason" (*logos*) dictates. To ignore this naturally rational course is to commit moral "mistakes"—what the Stoics refer to as *hamartēmata*. More specifically, in the case presented by Diogenes, it means to be "negligent" (*amelēs*) or "heedless" (*aphrontis*), two alpha-privative adjectives, which, incidentally, closely correspond to the later, negative sense of *securus* as "careless." It is noteworthy that the domains that Diogenes lists—kinship, patriotism, and friendship—locate the *kathēkonta* solidly within the realm of social and civic relations. In contrast, the individual who happens to reach for a dry twig, the solitary writer who manipulates his pen, or the private bather who quietly

---

[6] For a comprehensive account, see Troels Engberg-Pedersen, *The Stoic Theory of Oikeiōsis: Moral Development and Social Interaction in Early Stoic Philosophy*. For the concept's specific role in the work of Cicero, see Engberg-Pedersen's earlier article, "Discovering the Good: *Oikeiōsis* and *Kathēkonta* in Stoic Ethics," 145–83. See also Mary Whitlock Blundell, "Parental Nature and Stoic Οἰκείωσις."

[7] Blundell, "Paternal Nature," 221.

scrapes the oil and dirt from his skin all fall outside the societal frame. Consequently, their actions cannot be judged on their appropriateness. In Stoic theory, this third class of actions would be regarded as "indifferents" (*adiaphora*), that is, actions whose morality cannot be determined.

For the most part, Cicero's *De officiis* remains within the socially grounded categories of the appropriate (*kathēkonta*) and the erroneous (*hamartēmata*). In order to translate the Greek *kathēkon*, Cicero selects *officium*, a word that contains the verb of doing and making (*facere*), which correlates with the verbs of making and doing, *poiein* and *prattein*, attributed to Zeno. Generally speaking, *officium* denotes any kind of "service" or "courtesy" but more specifically comes to signify an "obligation" or "duty."[8] This latter sense, which implies a kind of compulsory gift, appreciably modifies the Stoic concept of the *kathēkon*, which does not necessarily convey the same obligatory sense. Conversely, the Greek sense of appropriateness implicit in *kathēkon* and *oikeiōsis* charges the commonplace meaning of Roman *officium* with a decidedly public aspect.

To equip his son with the necessary tools for the good life, Cicero outlines the details of these *offices*. Instead of "going down" (*kahtēkōn*) to Athens, the father stays behind to inscribe his reflections. In translating *kathēkonta* as *officia*, Cicero not only provides a Latin for a Greek term but also interprets and thereby converts the Stoic idea of appropriate action as relating to questions more pertinent to Roman culture. Whereas Zeno and Panaetius, from what can be gathered, addressed their program of practical ethics to a general audience, Cicero's explications are clearly intended for the ruling class.[9] The philosophical treatment of the *officia* that define Roman "honesty" or "moral rectitude" (*honestum*) is the appropriate gift that the esteemed father feels obliged to bestow, not only upon his ambitious son but also upon the young and future generations of leaders, who are in need of the correct "precepts" (*praecepta*) that would guide them along the right, antityrannical path.

As already suggested, *De officiis* was begun at a time when Cicero's role in public life was cast into serious doubt. The tension between the *vita contemplativa* and the *vita activa* is particularly discernible in the opening sentence of the first book, where Cicero celebrates the fact that his Marcus not only is studying with the eminent Cratippus but is also living in Athens: "The one is able to enrich you with knowledge, the other with examples" (*Off.* 1.1). The ideal of combining the benefits of *scientia* with *exempla*, of testing philosophical principles against urban experience, readily leads the author of the *Philippics* to remind his son that both his philosophical works and his public orations should be read "diligently" (*studiose*, 1.3). For "moral rectitude" (*honestas*) to be achieved, one cannot neglect the duties that one owes to the community (1.4). The theoretical working out of ethical principles is insufficient until one applies them to practical service within society.

[8] On Cicero's own defense for translating καθῆκον as *officium*, see his letter to Atticus, 16.14.3.
[9] See E. M. Atkins, "'Domina et Regina Virtutum': Justice and *Societas* in *De Officiis*."

To this end, Cicero tells us that he has adopted the method of Panaetius, who has divided ethical deliberation into three simple steps. First, one must determine whether an action is "morally right" or "wrong"—*honestum* or *turpe*. Second, one should question whether this action is "expedient" (*utile*) and in what sense: whether it would be conducive "to life's comfort or happiness" (*ad vitae commoditatem iucunditatemque*): to wealth, influence, and power, or even to being able to help one's friends. Finally, one must judge whether what is expedient conflicts in any way with what is morally right, whether the *utile* clashes with the *honestum*. Set up in this way, moral reflection potentially leads to mental unrest. When the useful appears to be directly opposed to rectitude, when the expedient can only be judged as *turpe*, then "the mind becomes distracted in its deliberation" and leads to a "doubtful concern [*ancipitem curam*] in its thinking" (1.9). Thus, quite early in the treatise, Cicero broaches the problem of *cura*, which will be implicitly addressed when he turns to the concept of *securitas*.

In this early passage, the "concern" or *cura* is split in two: it is *anceps*, literally "two-headed," which condemns the mind to a troubling state of doubt, pulling it in two directions, producing an uneasy *Zweideutigkeit*. Cicero only complicates the scenario by considering both morality and expediency in degrees, that is, by requiring that one also weigh which of two moral acts is more moral, which of two profitable acts is more profitable. In order to dispel this complex irresolution, in order to rid the mind of an *anceps cura*, Cicero recalls the two fundamental properties that define humanity: the instinct of self-preservation (*vitam corpusque tueatur*), which is bestowed by Nature; and the gift of reason (*ratio*), which enables one to comprehend temporal succession: to perceive causality, to draw analogies, and to anticipate future consequences (1.11). Thus endowed, the human mind is capable of ultimately discovering and adhering to morally correct judgments, which are always in accord with at least one of the four cardinal virtues: wisdom, justice, fortitude, and moderation.

The *anceps cura* that results from the conflicting demands of the expedient and the moral is in fact but one species of concern in these opening pages of *De officiis*. In discussing the virtue of "wisdom" (*prudentia*), Cicero admonishes the student from falling into two common errors: namely, treating the unknown as known; and devoting too much attention to obscure and abstruse matters. Throughout, the analysis turns on the issue of *cura*. "If these faults are avoided, the effort and *care* [*operae curaque*] given to issues that are morally right and worthy of thought will be justly praised" (1.19). A little further on, Cicero remarks on the difficulty of truly being *concerned* about others' affairs— *est enim difficilis cura rerum alienarum* (1.30). It should be stressed that, in these two statements, *cura* is presented in a positive light, as opposed to the earlier description of the bothersome *anceps cura*. As noted above, *cura* denotes a personal investment of time and attention, a mental engagement that is, in itself, morally ambivalent, as these few passages attest. Only by constantly weighing the objects of *cura* in view of the cardinal virtues can moral worth be ascertained. One may be concerned with what is either right or wrong; the *cura* may be either *honesta* or *turpis*. In general, then, one could say that the question of morality itself may be understood as the motivating force behind concern. *Cura* would seem to manifest itself precisely when the morality or appropriateness of an action falls into dispute or remains unclear.

To resolve these problems once and for all is to arrive at a condition that could quite justifiably be named *securitas*—a freedom from concern, a safe haven within the fortress of virtue, a state wherein all the difficult questions have at last been settled. We come, then, to Cicero's key definition:

> *Vacandum autem omni est animi perturbatione, cum cupiditate et metu, tum etiam aegritudine et voluptate animi et iracundia, ut tranquillitas animi et securitas adsit, quae affert cum constantiam, tum etiam dignitatem.* (Off. 1.69)

> There must be freedom from every disturbance of the mind, not only from desire and fear, but also from distress, from both the mind's pleasure and anger, so that there may be present the tranquillity and security of the mind, which bring not only constancy but also dignity.

The list of disturbing passions is presented as what must be vacated (*vacandum est*), a privative gesture that underscores the removal expressed by the prefix *se-*. Cicero is very specific: "Desire and fear, distress and pleasure, and anger" need to be shunted to the side, if the soul is to enjoy a carefree life. Cicero therefore provides a genealogy of *securitas* as *apatheia*, a brief account, entirely indebted to the Stoics, of how security is accomplished: destructive passions must be identified and summarily pushed away from the soul. Yet what can this genealogical account tell us about security's ontology, about what it in fact is?[10]

The list of five "emotions" poses interesting philological problems, but I shall restrict my comments to one.[11] Stoic theory consistently names only four, not five, *pathē*: desire, fear, distress, and pleasure. Elsewhere, for example in the *Tusculan Disputations*, Cicero upholds this common fourfold distinction.[12] In the *De officiis* passage, however, he departs from conventional practice and introduces *iracundia* ("anger," or more specifically, "a proneness to anger"). *Iracundia* would appear to stand for the Greek *thymos*, a *pathos*, certainly, but one that the Stoics tended to regard as a subspecies of desire (*epithymia*).[13] In isolating "anger" and placing it in emphatic final position, Cicero not only increases

---

[10] In her forthcoming work, Michèle Lowrie raises this point in connection with Cicero, *De finibus* 5.9.24–17.46.

[11] For a more detailed account, see Andrew Dyck, *Commentary on Cicero's De officiis*, 198.

[12] See, e.g., *Tusc.* 3.24–25.

[13] One could assume that Cicero's model, Panaetius, employed a fivefold scheme that granted anger an independent position among the passions, as is the case with Posidonius. Aulus Gellius reports a speech that Herodes Atticus made against the Stoic ideal of *apatheia*, in which more or less the same five passions are given: *aegritudo, cupiditas, timor, ira,* and *voluptas* (*Noct. Att.* 19.12.3). See Max Pohlenz, *Antikes Führertum: Cicero De Officiis und das Lebensideal des Panaitios*, n. 2, and *Die Stoa: Geschichte einer geistigen Bewegung*, 1.199. For further discussion, with bibliography, see Dyck, *Commentary*, 198–99. For a useful

the number of *pathē* to five but also suggests that this fifth passion is crucial for understanding what "security" and "tranquillity of the mind" mean.

If we read Cicero's list as a progression from *desire* to *anger*—as a long arc stretching from *cupiditas* to *iracundia* or, more vividly in Greek, from *epithymia* to *thymos*—we may discern a narrative of passion that moves from an attention to the near future ("desire" and "fear"), through obsessions concerning the present ("distress" and "pleasure"), before arriving at an emotion that could well characterize all passion in general ("anger"). With the term *thymos*, the focusing prefix *epi-* ("upon" or "on"), which defines "desire" specifically as a spirited heedfulness *upon* a particular object or person (*epi-thymia*), has vanished. *Thymos*, then, can be regarded as a fundamental passion prior to being attached to any specific object. This notion of potentiality is perhaps recognizable in Cicero's specific word choice, *iracundia*, which denotes an inclination or proneness to anger (*ira*), a sense that nicely captures the definition of *thymos* as an *orgē archomenē* (initial impulse) recorded by both Diogenes and Stobaeus.[14]

Cicero himself would hardly be troubled by accusations of departing from Stoic orthodoxy. Elsewhere, namely in his work on oratory, Cicero acknowledges that such philosophical nuances have little bearing on the work of the prosecutor embroiled in public life. In *De oratore*, for example, while admitting his profound admiration for the philosophical schools, he nonetheless asks:

> For what great and serious speaker, when he wants to make the judge angry [*iratum*] with his opponent, was ever hesitant simply because he did not know whether *iracundia* was a vehement passion of the mind [*fervor mentis*] or the desire [*cupiditas*] to avenge pain? (*Orat.* 1.220)

In other words, at least before a tribunal or a popular assembly, it would appear to matter little whether one treated anger as a species of desire or as a passion in its own right. Such academic hair-splitting would be irrelevant, if not altogether crippling in a public, prosecutorial context. However, in the philosophical realm of *De officiis*, such distinctions matter a great deal, not because Stoic theory should be reworked but rather because the promotion of anger as an independent *pathos* makes a crucial moral point.

As usual, Cicero applies philosophical learning to present purposes. According to Cicero, when the goal is a criminal conviction, it is perfectly legitimate to display one's anger as well as to incite anger in others. In contrast, for the philosopher, whose goal is the *securitas* and *tranquillitas animi* that provide the basis for virtuous and appropriate action, one must agree with the Stoics and eradicate anger altogether:

---

account, see Diogenes Laertius 7.110–14. For further citations, see the section "De Affectibus," in the *Stoicorum Veterum Fragmenta*, 3: 396–97, pp. 96–97.

[14] Diogenes Laertius 7.114; Stobaeus 2.91.10.

Truly, in all affairs *iracundia* must be repudiated, and it is to be desired that those who preside over the republic should be like the laws, which are said to move to punish not by *iracundia* but rather by uniform fairness. (*Off.* 1.89)

The opposed attitudes—the early justification of anger in *De oratore* and its later invalidation in *De officiis*—perfectly illustrate the statesman's eclecticism. The fine nuances of moral problems are certainly of great interest to Cicero in his philosophical works, but these same debates may prove to be a serious obstacle in the pursuit of public affairs. The *vita activa* proceeds according to much different standards. A pragmatist at heart, Cicero is careful not to become an ideologue.

The same point is raised in Cicero's speech for Murena. Here, while acknowledging the value of Stoic beliefs, Cicero stresses the infeasibility of adhering to them in a court of law. He refers to the exemplary Marcus Cato, who without equivocation followed the precepts of Zeno and the Stoa, including a straightforward denunciation of anger—*numquam ... sapiens irascitur* (the wise man never becomes angry, *Mur.* 62). Yet, a prosecutor who must deal with the case at hand can never say "never." Here, Cicero's teachers are the philosophers of the Platonic and Aristotelian schools, who are not so firm in their opinions but rather practice moderation and temperance (*moderati homines et temperati*, 63). Given the circumstances, the wise man is perfectly justified in becoming angry (*irasci non numquam*, 63). There is no question that Cato's commitment to Stoic virtue is laudable; however, in the "real world" of *veritas*, one must conclude that "the teachers of virtue would like to carry out their definitions of duties [*finis officiorum*] well past what is natural" and that "humanity, too, deserves praise" (*sed tamen est laus aliqua humanitatis*, 65). As Karl Galinsky comments on this speech, "[Cato's] flaw ... is his following a *doctrina non moderata* which is hard to endure in reality or for human nature.... Such a doctrine is fine as a *causa disputandi* but not *vivendi*."[15] The tumultuous life upon the high seas of politics demands ad hoc measures, lest the ship of state suffer a total wreck.

We could provisionally conclude that, for Cicero at Tusculum, the concepts of *securitas* and its close synonym *tranquillitas* have less to do with the messy realm of the human, where every opinion remains subject to modification, and relate more to the quasi-divine sphere of the "blessed life," the *beata vita*. Here, in this transcendent domain, rigid adherence to philosophical terminology is entirely in order. In the purely theoretical reflections that constitute the *Tusculan Disputations*, Cicero remarks:

But how can anyone possess that greatly desirable and coveted security [*maxume optatam et expetitam securitatem*]—for I now call freedom from

---

[15] Karl Galinsky, "The Anger of Aeneas," 338.

distress [*vacuitatem aegritudinis*] the security on which the blessed life [*vita beata*] is based—anyone for whom there is present or can be present a multitude of evils? (*Tusc.* 5.42)

The claim appears to be congruous enough with Stoic thought. The privation implicit in *securitas* corresponds to the evacuation of the manifold misfortunes, pains, and sufferings that plague the mind. All the same, the passage, one could say, barely rises above the level of abstraction. Of the four conventional *pathē*, only "distress" (*aegritudo*) is mentioned. By comparison, the lines from *De officiis*, which broach the subject of *securitas* within the context of Stoic emotion theory, are far more comprehensive and therefore potentially more concrete.

All in all, the problem of anger is no more than this: although rage may be useful and effective in defending and fighting against enemies within the public sphere, it threatens to disturb the mind. The very emotion that arrives to assist the statesman at a perilous moment can become a debilitating disturbance once that danger has past. Anger lingers well after the enraging circumstances. In the Forum, Cicero can condone *iracundia*; in his country estate, it must be eliminated. Yet, if this is indeed the case, how could *securitas*, so defined as the removal of anger, ever be possible in the distressing city?

THYMOS

Unlike *securitas*, the subject of anger received a great deal of attention from ancient authors and was comprehensively treated as a major theme among the Stoics. As mentioned, among the latter, from Chrysippus to Seneca, anger is consistently condemned. According to Lactantius, in his treatise *De ira*, the Stoics do not bother to discriminate between just and unjust anger: in any form, rage is inherently irrational and must be denounced.[16] The Stoic's unequivocal position does not respect the highly nuanced discussions of anger that can be found in the Platonic and Aristotelian traditions that often served as Cicero's models.

From the perspective of Greek emotion theory, *thymos* is but one term for expressing anger and therefore must be distinguished from other key Homeric words like *cholos* (the "bile" that rises in a fit of rage) and *mēnis*, the memorable, enduring "wrath" that furnishes the first, motivating word of the *Iliad*.[17] In addition, there is *orgē*, which denotes a sudden, angry urge. An in-depth review of the full semantic career of *thymos* falls well beyond the scope of this present study.[18]

---

[16] *Sed Stoici non viderunt esse discrimen recti et pravi ; esse iram iustam, esse et iniustam; et quia medelam rei non inveniebant, voluerunt eam penitus excidere. Stoicorum Veterum Fragmenta* 3.444, p. 108.

[17] Homer's vocabulary for anger is rich and highly nuanced. See P. Considine, "Some Homeric Terms for Anger" and "The Etymology of μῆνις." For further discussion and analysis, see Leonard Muellner, *The Anger of Achilles: Mēnis in Greek Epic*.

[18] A good deal of this history is succinctly covered in Harris, *Restraining Rage*, 50–70.

It is sufficient to note that by the fifth century both *thymos* and *orgē* are the most frequently employed terms to express a vast range of angry emotions.

It is in the realm of philosophy, notably in the developed system of Platonic psychology, where the functions of *thymos* and *orgē* take on greater precision. This specification hearkens back to the Homeric suggestion that *thymos* names the psychological seat of spirited anger. More importantly, for Plato, it rests on the threshold of mankind's inner faculties, lodged between the mortal and immortal portions, between appetitive desire and reason. In contrast to later Stoic theory, which regards the self as single and unified, the Platonic texts rigorously distinguish a rational (immortal) part from an irrational (mortal) part and subsequently place *thymos* in the middle position between the two poles. Thanks to this medial placement, *thymos* is able to communicate between the desires and reason. *Orgē*, however, fully resides and functions within the mortal site of irrational impulses. Within the topography of the Platonic, tripartite soul, *thymos* thereby assumes a crucial role. Although it clearly belongs to the mortal part of the soul, *thymos* nonetheless converses with the higher, immortal faculty of *logos*. Aristotle, too, consistently distinguishes the rationalizable *thymos* from the entirely irrational *orgē*.[19] When we turn to the Stoics, given their fundamentally holistic account of selfhood, it is no surprise that *thymos* is simply irrational—an *orgē* in its initial stages, as in the "initial impulse" or *orgē archomenē* of Diogenes, quoted above.

I have already proposed that in *De officiis* Cicero departs from his usual practice and may add anger to the list of Stoic *pathē* so as to illustrate the meaning of his neologism, *securitas*. That is to say, the decision to promote *iracundia* to the status of an independent *pathos*—and not just a species of *cupiditas*— may have something to do with the way *securitas* should be understood. The hypothesis is that "anger" must be regarded as distinct from "desire" in order to establish the meaning of security and its role in Ciceronian psychology.[20]

It is noteworthy that in *De officiis* Cicero tends to rely on the Platonic "part-based" model of the soul. At one point, still in the first book, he makes explicit reference to *orgē* as belonging to the irrational part of the dualistic mind:

> Indeed, the force and nature of our minds [*vis animorum atque natura*] are twofold: one part is placed in the appetite, which in Greek is the *orgē* that compels man here and there; the other is in reason, which teaches and explains what should be done and what should be abandoned [*faciendum fugiendumque*]. In this way, reason commands, appetite obeys. (*Off.* 1.101)[21]

---

[19] See, e.g., *Nicomachean Ethics* 3.8 1117a8.

[20] In broaching the topic of "Ciceronian psychology," I do not mean to suggest that the statesman-philosopher ever provided a systematic and coherent theory of the self that could be comparable to the ones developed by the Hellenistic schools. As Christopher Gill points out, Cicero is remarkably inconsistent on the subject: at times he bases his arguments on a Stoic "unified approach"; other times he reverts to the "part-based" model of the Academics. See Gill, *The Structured Self*, 214.

[21] See also *Off.* 1, 132.

Various reasons have been offered to explain Cicero's adherence to the Platonic model, despite the overtly Stoic orientation of *De officiis*. Brad Inwood and Richard Sorabji evoke the influence of Posidonius, who was presumed to expound the tripartition theory.[22] Carlos Lévy, who is intent on demonstrating Cicero's deep-seated affiliation with the Academics, sees this and analogous passages as evidence of his philosophical allegiance.[23] It should be borne in mind that *De officiis* is addressed to the statesman's son, who was studying with the Academician Cratippus; and that Cicero would therefore be prone to remain on familiar ground when instructing his beloved protégé. Christopher Gill thus concludes, "Cicero conflates the two kinds of models because the contrast between them had not yet been clearly defined as an explicit issue of debate."[24] But I would argue that the part-based model is deliberately posited by Cicero in order to modify Stoic thought, so as to ground his particular conceptualization of the *beata vita*, including the notion of *securitas*, which depends on an appreciation of the role *thymos* plays in Platonic psychology.

To illustrate, we need to recall the basic structure of Plato's ideal city that I briefly sketched in my fourth chapter. In the *Republic*, the *thymos*, precisely because of its medial position between the belly and the head, is free to ally either with *logos* or with the baser instincts of *epithymia* (*Rep.* 440d–e). Here, *thymos* specifically works in concert with *logos* in order to protect the individual from being wronged. Reason needs this spiritedness in order to offer a viable means of safety, just like Cicero must summon anger to win his case. Anger is the fuel. Similarly, *thymos* comes to be associated with the guardians who are assigned with the task of protecting the city from without and within.

The guardians enter early on in the *Republic*, when Glaucon expresses his dissatisfaction with the first kind of community that Socrates sketches in conversation with Adeimantus (*Rep.* 2.369b–372c). This initial scenario is based on an individual's lack of self-sufficiency and utter dependence, which lead him to associate with others who are themselves deficient in their own way, so that together they may satisfy each others' needs. Through mutual help and partnership, this simple *polis* would assure that all basic necessities are covered. Each member of the community would provide what the others lack and, in turn, receive from the others what he or she requires. Consequently, everyone would be able to "lead a peaceful and happy life" (372d)—fully content, in want of nothing. Glaucon steps forward and expresses his disappointment with Adeimantus's description. In brief, he is unimpressed with this colorless existence and disparagingly labels it a "city of pigs," a community that lacks all the com-

---

[22] Brad Inwood, *Ethics and Human Action in Early Stoicism*, 140–41; Richard Sorabji, *Emotion and Peace of Mind: From Stoic Agitation to Christian Temptation*, 103.

[23] Carlos Lévy, *Cicero Academicus: Recherches sur les Académiques et sur la philosophie cicéronienne*, 472–80. The doxography here and in the previous note is covered by Gill, *The Structured Self*, 214 n. 36.

[24] Gill *The Structured Self*, 214.

forts and conveniences that one normally associates with civilization, that is, with a "luxurious city" (372e). As Glaucon points out, human life is not defined by satisfying bare, animal necessities. Instead, it consists in desiring what is unnecessary. Once this idea is broached, the discussants must turn to the ways in which this higher standard of living could be achieved. First and foremost, the city would eventually have to acquire more territory, which would unavoidably lead to warfare with one's neighbors. War requires warriors; hence the demand for guardians.

In entertaining this modification of the simple *polis*, in considering this shift toward luxury beyond mere necessity, Socrates muses that a guardian should be like a watchdog, exhibiting a spirited form (*thymoeidēs*, 375a) that renders him "unassailable and invincible" (375b). The guardian's disposition, therefore, must be fundamentally duplicitous: exactly like a guard dog, gentle to family and friends but fierce to enemies. The problem, however, goes beyond mere duplicity. On the one hand, the city's continued safety depends on the thymic warriors; their willingness to fight is necessary for the protection of the citizenry. On the other hand, the selfsame characteristic of aggression stands to become a threat to the populace when there is no danger to face. The problem is analogous to the one Cicero faces in Tusculum: once allowing himself to become angry, how can he prevent rage from upsetting his peace of mind?

In returning to the passage from *De officiis* examined above, it appears that Cicero follows Plato in treating anger as an emotion distinct from desire. When we recall that, in *De finibus* (5.23), Cicero further equates *securitas* with Democritean *euthymia* ("cheerfulness," or "the right balancing of the *thymos*"), the problems of ambivalence become perfectly clear. Although *thymos* may be complicit with "desire" (*epithymia*), poised to hurl an individual's soul into a state of disarray and instability, it also stands ready to strike a deal with *logos* and thereby serve as the surest means of protection. In the latter case, *thymos* and *logos* together rein in appetitive drives and thereby curtail their deleterious effects. Although anger is an evil *pathos* or *perturbatio*, which threatens the individual's rationality and therefore must be eliminated (*vacandum est*), it can be domesticated in *euthymia*, that is, made to negotiate with *ratio*, and thereby safeguard the mind from all pathic disturbances. Anger thus becomes a *cura* that assists in the removal of *cura*, just as the guardians' violence is trained to quell violence. Police science (*Polizeiwissenschaft*) as it would develop in the eighteenth century is indeed but a footnote to these proceedings.

In the end, it remains doubtful whether Cicero would have ever discovered how to accomplish this balancing act: if the dignity and constancy of *securitas* were in fact accomplished in the Tusculum shade, how could it be maintained upon returning to the battlefield of Roman politics? How could the "safety and health of the people"—the *salus populi*—be achieved after its would-be spokesman had made himself immune to anger? How could the citizens relax carefree when they no longer care?

CAVEAT

A particular "folk" etymological tradition, which cannot be validated by the criteria of modern linguistics, takes *cura* to be a substantive built from the verb *cavere* (to beware, to take notice). Certainly, from a semantic point of view alone, the verbs of caring (*curare*) and taking notice (*cavere*) are closely linked, as many lexicographers willingly acknowledge.

Unlike the case of *cura*, the etymological web in which the verb *cavere* and its nominal form *cautio* are implicated has been convincingly established. The proto–Indo-European root for *cavere* is *(s)keu-*, which generates a vast array of terms denoting "looking, hearing, feeling, and paying attention." The list includes: the Sanskrit *kavis* (wise), cognate with the Modern German *klug* (clever); the common Greek verb *akouein* (to hear), and the noun *kudos* (glory, renown); and the German verbs *hören* (to hear) and *schauen* (to look). *Schauen*, in turn, yields the adjective *schön* (beautiful), which means agreeable to the eye.[25] As a removal of *cura*, *securitas* could here point to a condition of being *incautious*—being somehow blind and deaf to all that demands notice. Carefree and careless, the secured subject fails to engage in the world to which it none-theless belongs.

In *Odes* 1.14, Horace seems to employ this *figura etymologica* when he aligns his "concern" (*cura*) with an apostrophized plea to "beware" (*cave*).

> tu, nisi ventis
> debes ludibrium, cave.
>
> nuper sollicitum quae mihi taedium,
> nunc desiderium curaque non levis,
> interfusa nitentis
> vites aequora Cycladas.

(*Odes* 1.14.15–20)

> You, unless
> you must be the plaything for the winds, beware!
>
> Of late you have been for me vexatious trouble,
> now something to long for with concern not light,
> avoid the seas that flow about
> the shining Cyclades.

The poet expresses profound concern (*cura . . . non levis*) that the object of his attention is bound for shipwreck. Ever since Quintilian's influential reading, many have regarded this poem as an allegory of the "Ship of State," where the

---

[25] Cf. Walde, *Lateinisches etymologisches Wörterbuch*, s.v. "cavere."

poet names "the ship for the Republic, the waves and tempests for the civil wars, and the harbor for peace and concord."[26] Hence, Horace's *cura* is presumed to be political in nature. Although some scholars have called this interpretation into question, Quintilian's traditional reading, corroborated by ancient scholiasts, has found much support, including from critics who have worked to ascertain some specific event as the poem's historical referent.[27] Still, debates over the poem's definitive meaning continue to endure: while many persist in reading it as a political allegory, others, following William S. Anderson, regard it as an address to a beloved woman.[28]

We are dealing, then, with a case of either eroticized politics or politicized erotics. Certainly, within the context of the *Odes* as a whole, both areas of human experience—politics and love—consistently serve as sources of worry or anxiety for the poems' narrating *ego*. Given this broader context, the poem may be expressing the very ambiguity that has plagued the interpretive literature: namely, that the poet's *cura* stems from treating politics as a love affair and/or entering into personal intimacy as though it were a matter of civil business. As we have seen, the open sea has long been taken as the site of terrifying danger for those abroad and a cause of insecurity for concerned parties remaining on the shore. In Horace's poem the ship has become a "plaything for the winds," a source of urgent concern. Whether the vessel is being assaulted by the tempestuous threat of civil war or by competing and jealous lovers, it is explicitly identified first as something loathsome and bothersome (*sollicitum . . . taedium*) and then as a thing to be desired (*desiderium*). This ambivalence is crucial, for it is precisely the combination of loathsomeness and desirability—*taedium* and *desiderium*—that characterizes the *cura*. The object of concern disquiets and impassions or, rather, disquiets because it impassions and impassions because it disquiets. The expressed *cura*, whatever its referent, readily converts into a plea to make the addressee *aware* (*cave*). With the emphatic command that the beloved "beware," the narrator seems to beg that he himself become an object of *cura*: "Beware! Take notice of the dangers all about you and thereby take notice of me who is concerned for you! The fact that I am heavy with concern should cause you concern." Concern and wariness work together to express a shared intention, namely that the noticed object be borne in mind. The concerned poet desires that he become an object of concern.

[26] *navem pro re publica, fluctus et tempestates pro bellis civilibus, portum pro pace atque concordia dicit.* Quintilian, *Inst. orat.* 8.6.44.

[27] The principal opponents to the ship-of-state allegory are Charles Mendell, "Horace I.14"; and William S. Anderson, "Horace *Carm.* 1.14: What Kind of Ship?" As would be expected, historical conjectures generally involve Octavian—for example, his growing conflict with Mark Anthony prior to Actium or, later, the tension between republicanism and imperialism or, quite specifically, the perilous sea journey Octavian undertook in the winter of 30 BC from Samos to Brundisium. For a good overview of the various positions, with ample bibliography, see Ortwin Knorr, "Horace's Ship Ode (*Odes* 1.14) in Context: A Metaphorical Love-Triangle."

[28] I am indebted here to Michèle Lowrie's comments on *Odes* 1.14 in her forthcoming work.

BUILDING PROJECTS

Similar to the Ciceronian position in *De officiis*, Horace's *Odes* 3.1 contrasts the tranquillity of privacy with the anxiety of public ambition. In this first of the so-called Roman Odes, Horace employs *cura* to name the perplexity inherent to the public sphere. The poem essentially expresses a preference for the private life and serenity of his Sabine farm, far from political turmoil. The *ataraxia* that the poet enjoys in his refuge is vividly distinguished from the life led by the power-thirsty Romans, whose desire for luxury and prominence is exposed as a debilitating trap. As the poem's final line concisely relates, wealth invariably brings greater burdens (*divitias operosiores*, 48). In contrast, the poet opts for the "gentle sleep that does not scorn the humble cottage of the country folk and the river's shady bank" (*somnus agrestium / lenis virorum non humilis domos / fastidit umbrosamque ripam*, 21–23). Here, the security of a blessed life contributes to the opening definition of the poet's priestly role (*Musarum sacerdos*, 3)—a public office, no doubt, but one that is rigorously set apart from others.

At the poem's center we learn of vulgar entrepreneurs who contract slaves to realize their grandiose plans, which are regarded as little more than monuments to vanity. In the poet's judgment, their disdain for a simple agricultural life will be met by crippling vexations. The towers built to their glory, including the tall edifices of a political career wrought by hell-bent obsession, will no doubt be assaulted by biting anxiety:

> sed Timor et Minae
> scandunt eodem, quo dominus, neque
> decedit aerata triremi et
> post equitem sedet atra Cura.
>
> (*Odes* 3.1.37–40)

> but Fear and Threats
> climb up to the same spot as the master; and
> *she* withdraws not from the bronze galley, and *she* even
> sits behind the horseman—black, gloomy Care.

As in *Odes* 1.14, *cura* adheres to an object of desire, one that is moreover associated with travel. *Atra cura*—"black, gloomy Care"—will ambush those driven by material and political ambition. The poem further appears to allude to Hesiod's Nautilia in coding the sea voyage ("the bronze galley") as transgressive, something that is motivated by dissatisfaction with one's lot. In contrast, so the poet proclaims, "the stormy sea does not trouble the one who desires only what is sufficient" (*desiderantem quod satis est neque tumultuosum sollicitat mare*, 25–26). The longing for limitless horizons should be recognized as a lethal seduction toward uprootedness, toward losing one's position on the ground.

For Horace, the threat of "black Care" alone should recall the overachiever back to the moderate, carefree pleasures of the simple life. The ambitious, dissatisfied Roman is deprived of the "gentle sleep that does not scorn [*fastidit*] ... the shady riverbank" and instead plunges into the icy waters fraught with uncertainty and risk. Greed and lust for power make him "scornful of the land" (*terrae fastidiosus*, 36–37). Such an entrepreneur mistakes security as the ability to master nature. Instead of enjoying true *asphaleia*, he pours "unhewn stone" (*caementa*) into the shallow river to extend his dominion over given limits (34–37). His acts forfeit all caution. As we shall examine in a later chapter, Goethe's Faust—the overachiever par excellence—also takes on transgressive projects that extend human industry well past natural restrictions by constructing upon the water. At the conclusion of Goethe's tragedy, as Horace predicted, the everstriving hero is blinded by Care (*Sorge*).

Rather than fall back into the perilous realm of political intrigue and avidity, Horace represents himself as content with his quiet, shielded life on his Sabine farm. His opening ode in book 1 explicitly refers to his benefactor Maecenas as his "protection" (*praesidium*, *Odes* 1.1.2), not because he provides physical safety but rather because he guarantees the conditions necessary for the composition of poetry. For Horace, verse is what brings peace of mind:

> *Musis amicus tristiam et metus*
> *tradam protervis in mare Creticum*
> *portare ventis, quis sub Arcto*
> *rex gelidae metuatur orae,*
>
> *quid Tiridaten terreat, unice*
> *securus.*

(Odes 1.26.1–6)

> I, the Muses' friend, shall hand over sadness
> and fear to violent winds to bear to the
> Cretan sea; what king of the frigid shore
> beneath the Arctic sky is feared,
>
> what could terrify Tiridates, I am uniquely
> unconcerned.

Whereas the politically ambitious Roman of *Odes* 3.1 hurls cement into the river to increase his property holdings, Horace throws his fear and grief to the winds, expecting them to drown in the Cretan waters. Political topics such as the behavior of some Nordic tyrant (*rex gelidae ... orae*) or the terror that afflicts the Armenian sovereign (*Tiridates*) are of no concern to the poet. Royalty is a game either of causing fear or of being afraid, a game in which Horace—unconcerned, indifferent, *securus*—no longer wants to participate. Instead, all *cura* is to be eliminated so that he can cultivate his friendship with the Muses.

No dark, gloomy cura—*atra Cura*—will haunt him as it haunts "the bronze galley." As he famously prophesies in the epilogue to the third book, Horace's own monument—the poetry constructed in the *locus amoenus* of the Sabine estate—will be "more lasting than bronze" (*aere perennius, Odes* 3.30.1).

Unsafe Harbor

The art of composing verse may be facilitated by the removal of political concerns, but poetry, too, may become a concern, one moreover that could ultimately drag the poet back into the political arena, perhaps with dire consequences. At Rome, Ovid enjoyed the freedom to devote his poetic energies to create meticulously formulated works, to publish books written "with care" (*cura, Ars amat.* 3.206). There is evidence that Ovid was an intimate friend of Hyginus, the grammarian appointed by Augustus to serve as superintendent of the Palatine Library;[29] and it is at least suggestive to see in Ovid the artistry of Hyginus's Cura, who seeks both divine animation and a lasting designation. Like Phoebus, Ovid consistently exhibited the "paternal concerns" (*patrias . . . curas*) that define a father's profound love and his gravest fears (*Met.* 2.93–94). The composer of the *Metamorphoses* arguably applied such heedfulness out of consideration for his sophisticated, urbane readership, which expected nothing less than perfection.

Once exiled in Tomi, Ovid finds no use in taking pains to maintain this high standard: "Why should I polish my songs with anxious care?" (*Cur ego sollicita poliam mea carmine cura? Ex ponto*, 1.5.61). The nervous scrupulousness that once motivated his art (*cura*) has now been degraded to a despairing why (*cur*). The iconic positioning of the homophonic terms at the beginning and end of the verse emphasizes the fatal turn. As the exiled poet remarks elsewhere, the concern that used to distinguish his work has been replaced by despondent *curae,* which constantly eat away at his heart—*sic mea perpetuos curarum pectora morsus* (*Ex ponto*, 1.1.73). At Rome, the poet was *secure* but not without *cura,* that is, he cared about his work without being troubled by basic needs or lack of readership. Back then, with this existential security in place, he could use *cura* to compose polished verses. However, banished to the Black Sea, the poet now is faced with fresh and more urgent concerns; and it is this uneasy state that causes him to direct all his concerns to survival alone, with no concern left for his art.

Nonetheless, Ovid's concluding poem of the first book of the *Tristia* (1.11) alludes to the possibility that the care devoted to his work can alleviate the frightening concern over his impending exile—*omnis ab hac cura cura levata*

---

[29] See Suetonius, *De grammaticis*, 20. A long tradition identifies Hyginus as the target of Ovid's relentless diatribe *Ibis.*

mea est (Every concern [over the troubles ahead] was lifted by this concern [the composition of the present poem], 12). The repetition of *cura* at the line's caesura—and I can find no valid reason to reject it as dittographic—is striking, especially in connection with the participle *levata*. The vexatious concern is not eliminated but rather "lifted"—"lightened" or "mitigated" by a beneficial concern: *cura cura levata* (care by care lifted). Whereas Stoic practice works toward a blessed state that is removed from care, Ovid suggests that troubling anxieties can be dealt *cum cura*.

For Ovid, perfect "peace of mind" was possible only in the long vanished golden age, when there were no laws and hence no fear of punishment, when there was no lust for profit, no navigation, no imperial, Caesarian designs— "the pine was not yet cut [*caesa*] from the mountainside, descending into the flowing waves." In this portrayal, *security* has nothing to do with civil defense or vigilance: "deep trenches were not yet surrounding the towns . . . the carefree [*securae*] people carried on with gentle repose [*mollia . . . otia*]" (*Met.* 1.94– 100). Throughout the *Metamorphoses*, *securus* is understood in this positive sense of being free from *cura* as anxiety or worry. *Securitas* belongs exclusively to the remote golden age, before antagonism and struggle and crime. Now, for the poet of love, transformation, and ultimately exile, such security can never be an option. *Omnis ab hac cura / cura levata mea est*, "All my concern by this concern was lifted"—incapable of arriving at a state that is entirely worry free, the poet can only pitch one concern against the other. The difference between one *cura* and the next is a difference generated by time, by the gap or caesura that prevents a stable, fixed identity. If for Horace, security remains a viable possibility (however improbable), for Ovid it is crucial to remember that mankind is a child of Care and that the world, which provides the setting of human experience, is a time-bound realm utterly inundated by concern.

PART THREE

Occupying Security

Fortitude and Maternal Care

THE TERM SECURITAS is not explicitly employed as a political or philosophical concept in any sustained manner before the fourteenth century. Instead, other words served the semantic functions that today we would associate with "security," for example, terms for "safety" or "salvation," "certitude," and "peace"—*salus, certitudo,* and *pax.* Different arguments may be proffered to explain this phenomenon. Particularly compelling and provocative is the narrative postulated by Franz-Xaver Kaufmann: given the predominantly psychological sense of *securitas* as an internal stabilization—as a calming of inner, emotional disturbances—Kaufmann claims that security reenters European thought only when institutions offering external stabilization, above all the church and the empire, begin to weaken. In brief, problems of *certitude* come to be supplanted by problems of *security* when the individual human subject develops into the central producer of knowledge who rivals outside authorities.[1] Thus, the reemergence of *securitas* in political, philosophical, and even theological discourses is tied to general trends toward secularization.

Kaufmann's thesis has many clear merits. However, although processes of secularization can account for some features of usage, they are incapable of explaining all. Indeed, it would be misleading to think that *securitas* presents a univocal sense for the early modern and modern periods. Quite to the contrary, the word retains its ambivalence and semantic versatility, defining a state that is either carefree or careless or both—an ambivalence that, as we have seen, renders the term all the more ideologically useful. Theoretical positions for and against security turn on diverse understandings and interpretations, which ultimately reduce or hollow out the word's significance. Proponents of and opponents to some idea of security are thus capable of deploying specific meanings that occupy the term and enlist it to new ends. The meanings, values, and metaphors associated with *securitas* are thus engaged to address multiple issues in an extensive variety of historical contexts. These particular occupations of the word propel its semantic career forward in ever more complex directions, solving problems and raising fresh questions. Throughout, the figurations

---

[1] Franz-Xaver Kaufmann, *Sicherheit als soziologisches und sozialpolitisches Problem,* 25. See also, Schrimm-Heins, "Gewißheit und Sicherheit" 1: 127–28.

linked to "security" persist, however latently, waiting for their operative force to be activated at any point.

BEING WITHOUT

One of the earliest and perhaps richest illustrations of security's function in medieval thought is found in the elaborate fresco series painted by Ambrogio Lorenzetti for the Sala dei Nove in Siena's Palazzo Pubblico, completed in 1339: a large allegorical representation of Good and Bad Government extending across three walls. A simple scheme will help ground the description that follows.

Table 8.1. Lorenzetti, Allegory of Good and Bad Government, General Scheme

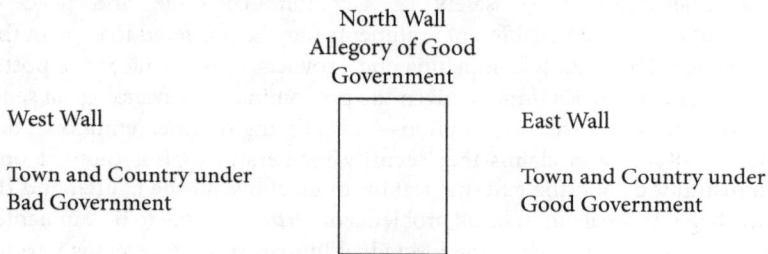

	North Wall Allegory of Good Government	
West Wall		East Wall
Town and Country under Bad Government		Town and Country under Good Government

Among the many figures that populate the murals is a personification of Securitas, which adorns the eastern wall of the chamber. An investigation of this figure in itself as well as in relation to the broader allegorical scheme will specify the significance of security in medieval political thought as well as point forward to later developments.

Lorenzetti equips his winged angel with a broad cartouche proclaiming the precise nature of her benefaction (Fig. 8.1):

SENÇA PAVRA OGNVOM FRANCO CAMINI
ELAVORANDO SEMINI CIASCVNO
MENTRE CHE TAL COMUNO
MANTERRA QVESTA DON[N]A I[N] SIGNORIA
CHEL ALEVATA AREI OGNI BALIA

Without fear let each man freely walk
and working, let everyone sow
while such a commune
will keep this lady in rule
because she has removed all power from the guilty.[2]

---

[2] This translation, which I have slightly modified, together with transcriptions and translations of all the inscriptions in the Sala dei Nove, can be found in George Rowley, *Ambrogio Lorenzetti*, 1: 127–29.

Figure 8.1. Ambrogio Lorenzetti, Securitas. *Sala dei Nove* (Eastern Wall, detail), Palazzo Pubblico, Siena (1338–39). Alfredo Dagli Orti / The Art Archive at Art Resource, NY

In this representation, Securitas appears as both the precondition for and the custodian of the peaceful city. The ageless Latin name, inscribed in gold at the maiden's head, passes into the Lombard vernacular to unfold the gospel of the elimination of everything that is bent on the destruction of civil order. The verbal declination produces a paradigm of beneficial negation—*securitas: sença paura*. In displaying Securitas hovering in the blue sky above the city gate, at the

Figure 8.2. Lorenzetti, *City at Peace* (Eastern Wall, detail). Erich Lessing / Art Resource, NY

threshold between inside and out, the fourteenth-century republic celebrates the absence of imminent danger. In order to emphasize security's function as an agent of removal, Lorenzetti places a gallows in her left palm.

Lorenzetti's masterpiece was commissioned in 1338 by Siena's ruling Council of "the Nine" ostensibly to illustrate the ideals, accomplishments, and aspirations of the republic. The figure of Securitas belongs to the long mural on the east wall depicting the city and countryside at peace (Fig. 8.2). Here, the citizens work in concert, unmarred by any disturbances: masons assist each other in construction; craftsmen toil together in their shops; and merchants display their wares for the passers-by. The best illustrations of this concord are a wedding procession and a group of maidens dancing in a round. The graceful movements rejoice in the soothing comfort of a life without worry. The smooth, broad street that connects the town and the *contado* reiterates the continuity between the separate regions that fall beneath Securitas's jurisdiction: fresh deliveries are brought in through the city gate, while a shepherd directs his flock out to pasture.

This idyllic scene stands in stark contrast with the one given on the western (sinister) wall facing directly opposite. The pandemonium represented here is the city ravaged by war, discord, and crime (Fig. 8.3). Murder and rape course through the town in flames. Ruin and confusion are rampant. The scene is dom-

Figure 8.3. Lorenzetti, *City at War* (Western Wall, detail). Scala / Art Resource, NY

inated by a personification of Tyranny, who sits upon his dark throne with all the vices in attendance. A pair of black, satanic goats prance about the tyrant's feet and, at the base of the podium, we find Justice, her feet bound, lying upon the street with her scales beside her, broken.

Figure 8.4. Lorenzetti, *Good Government* (Northern Wall). Erich Lessing / Art Resource, NY

Finally, on the shorter, central wall to the north, we find a complex allegory of good government, replete with figures of Justice and Sovereignty accompanied among other images by personifications of the cardinal and theological virtues (Fig. 8.4). At the feet of Justice, we find a figure labeled CONCORDIA, who gathers in her hand two cords that fall down from the scales above and passes them on to a row of twenty-four magistrates. Their hands bound behind their back with Concordia's cord, they line up to attend the king. At the bottom left, knights armed with spears lead shackled prisoners before the sovereign.

The cycle's main argument, distributed across these three large panels, appears to be fairly straightforward: if the ruling body attends to the virtues presented in the central mural, then the city can enjoy the prosperity and optimism portrayed on the right; but if these lessons are neglected, the horrifying rule of tyranny depicted on the left will overrun the unfortunate commune. Altogether, Lorenzetti presents a theory of security that ably coordinates theological and juridical ideals with concrete pragmatic concerns involving civil order, public welfare, and risk management.[3]

---

[3] On Lorenzetti's novel contribution to burgeoning ideas of public security, see Gerrit Schenk, "*Human*

Securitas's direct counterpart in the war-torn city is Timor, a personification of the "fear" that characterizes the populace burdened by violence and war (Fig. 8.5). A sword-brandishing demon, rendered in black and smoky grays, Timor spreads mayhem through the desolate countryside and the crime-infested city. This urban landscape represents a clear antithesis of the cultivated land and halcyon scene governed by Securitas. Timor is depicted as a harpy-like demon in tattered clothes, flying through the twin-towered gate. With malicious intent, he races toward the countryside and thereby suggests that the ill effects of tyranny emanate from within the city itself.[4]

In surveying the dystopia plagued by fear, it becomes clear that the *sença* implicit in and proclaimed by Securitas is specifically a removal of that which removes order, happiness, and well-being—a negation of a negation. This grammatical gesture is both elucidated and intensified in the banner presented by Timor. In striking fashion we discover that the unkempt demon also bears a message featuring the privative preposition "without":

P[ER] VOLERE ELBENPROPRIO I[N] QVESTA TERRA
SOM[M]ESSE LA GUISTITIA A TYRANNIA
VNDE P[ER] QVESTA VIA
NO[N] PASSA ALCVN SE[N]ÇA DVBBIO DI MO[R]TE
CHE FUOR SIROBBA E DENTRO DELE PORTE.

For wanting his own good on this earth
He has subjected Justice to Tyranny
Wherefore along this road
Passes no one without dread of death
Because robbery is outside and within the gates.

(Rowley, trans.; slightly modified)

If Securitas eliminates the negative function of fear (*sença paura*), then, in somewhat dizzying logic, Timor must be understood as negating a negation of negation (*non . . . sença dubbio*).

It would be useful to investigate—in a somewhat Foucauldian manner—the techniques of power involved in effectuating the removal of danger that defines defense. These techniques are discernible through Lorenzetti's modes of representation. It is at once noteworthy that Lorenzetti's representation of Securitas is presented in antique costume, which distinguishes her from the other, generally Byzantine-like depictions. Therefore, this allegorical personification of removal or distantiation is itself removed stylistically from the scene in which she appears. Her antique garb sets her apart. Yet this portrayal also underscores her

---

Security in the Renaissance? Securitas, Infrastructure, Collective Goods, and Natuarl Hazards in Tuscany and the Upper Rhine Valley."

[4] Diana Norman, "Pisa, Siena, and the Maremma: A Neglected Aspect of Ambrogio Lorenzetti's Paintings in the Sala dei Nove," 314.

Figure 8.5. Lorenzetti, *Timor* (Western Wall, detail). Scala / Art Resource, NY

close oppositional relation to the personification of fear. Iconically, Securitas's bright nakedness, barely covered by a diaphanous veil that wafts from the waist down, suggests juridical transparency. In contrast, fully cloaked Timor is an exemplum of opacity. His looming, kinetic energy swoops down swiftly to intimidate the unprotected, self-serving populace. Masculine Timor therefore counters the calm stasis of feminine Securitas, whose gentleness is reflected in the city's enterprises.

Although Securitas represents the antithesis of fear, the proclamation of her power (*sença paura*) reveals fear to be a necessary component of these secured projects. Lorenzetti compels the Sienese to face the sinister consequences of Timor, which at any point could reemerge. Like Archilochus's soldier, security depends on recognizing the "rhythm that holds mankind" (frag. 128)—the successive oscillation between prosperity and devastation, between order and strife. This positioning defines security as vigilance. Lorenzetti's representation also shows that fear is a crucial tool in security's arsenal. The gallows in Securitas's left hand serves as a forceful demonstration of the consequences of transgressing the republic's laws. The city and its environs certainly enjoy a secured peace; however, it is a peace gained through the active suppression of crime and the constant prevention of tyranny. In the peaceful republic, fear is not so much erased as it is instrumentalized, that is, knowingly integrated into the urban order. In other words, Securitas holds fearful threats of her own, namely the fatal repercussions of transgressing the laws established. While maintaining the crucial distinction between powerful acts that are sanctioned by the ruling body and criminal acts that constitute an assault against the city's ordinances or threaten a citizen's well-being, it is clear that Securitas and Timor, at least according to Lorenzetti's allegories, are both characterized by violence.

To be sure, the violence of each is differently targeted. Timor infects those who behave individualistically. Fear attends those who care exclusively for their own success, for their own property (*elbenproprio*), refusing to subordinate their private wills to the common weal. In this case the communal idea of justice for all has been supplanted by the tyranny of particular interests. With fear, the city's moral architecture is fractured and on the verge of collapse. Visually, we can say that anarchic fear is disseminated haphazardly along a horizontal axis, spreading through the populace without regard for any hierarchical ordering. In contrast, the fear-inspiring violence that security wields runs along a vertical axis, emanating from heavenly justice and distributed among the townspeople. The nonintegrative fear personified by Timor is therefore opposed to the integrative fear represented by Securitas.

A temporal distinction reinforces this spatial one. Whereas the sword of Timor constitutes a menace of death to come (*dubbio in morte*), the gibbet that Securitas exhibits manifests a death sentence already executed. Lorenzetti's notion of security would therefore appear to be more resultative than preemptive. The gallows indicates that the menace has been identified, duly processed, and properly disposed. Hobbes would concur: fear defines the original state; security is a result. However, this result must also act preemptively in order to prevent a return to the state of fear. In conjunction with its privative and resultative functions, security's preemptive capabilities must address a lack. Like mourning, it aims to remedy the effects of death, but since it is a death that has not yet happened, the work of security becomes a failed work of mourning—a melancholic gesture before an irremediable lack. Security is melancholy for future loss. It is within this odd, precarious temporality that Lorenzetti's subjects of security are carefree: no longer, but also not yet, crippled by fright.

REMEDIES FOR FORTUNE

The direct juxtaposition of Securitas and Timor explicitly occurs in the form of a philosophic dialogue found in a widely circulated text dating from the early twelfth century, the *Moralium Dogma Philosophorum*. The vast amount of extant manuscripts in the original Latin as well as in many European vernaculars attests to the book's extensive popularity.[5] Long ascribed to the twelfth-century Scholastic philosopher and humanist William of Conches, the treatise's authorship nevertheless continues to be debated.[6] In any case, it is clearly a compendium of classical passages on the four cardinal virtues (Prudence, Justice, Fortitude, and and Temperance) derived primarily from Cicero's *De officiis* and Seneca's *De beneficiis*. Among other writings interpolated into this volume is the *De remediis fortuitorum*, a demonstration of various "remedies for chance events" traditionally attributed to Seneca, which enjoyed equal popularity and would come to be employed by key authors, including Vincent of Beauvais (*Speculum historiale*), Petrarch (*De remediis utriusque fortunae*), and Roger Bacon (*Opus maius*).[7] The *De remediis* presents a dramatic exchange between two interlocutors. In multiple manuscripts the speakers are the personifications Reason (Ratio) and Feeling or Sensuality (Sensus); however the compiler responsible for the *Moralium dogma philosophorum* renames the pair as Securitas and Timor, respectively, and consequently entitles this subchapter *De securitate*.

In brief, Timor—which personifies principally the fear of death—attempts to unsettle Securitas's sure-footed composure by conjuring renewed scenarios of dread. Although such didactic expositions of the virtues and vices were extremely common throughout the Middle Ages, this interchange between Security and Fear is altogether unique. With Securitas taking the role of Reason and Timor playing the part of Sensuality, this text furnishes not only a script for Lorenzetti's visual staging but also a glimpse into how security was reinterpreted and reconceptualized within the context of medieval theory.

The *De securitate* section of the *Moralium dogma philosophorum* falls within a large chapter devoted to the theme of "fortitude." Following the list provided by Macrobius in his commentary on Cicero's *Dream of Scipio*, *securitas* is here named as the third quality of *fortitudo*, together with "magnanimity," "confidence" (*fiducia*), "high-mindedness" (*magnificentia*), "constancy," and "pa-

---

[5] For a bibliographic account, see John Holmberg's edition, *Das Moralium Dogma Philosophorum des Guillaume de Conches, Lateinisch, Altfranzösisch, und Mittelniederfränkisch.*

[6] Cf. John Williams, "The Authorship of the *Moralium Dogma Philosophorum*."

[7] See Robert Newman, "Rediscovering the *De Remediis Fortuitorum*."

tience" or "endurance" (*patientia*).[8] Each of these subdivisions usefully opens with a definition of the aspect's particular "duty" (*officium*). Thus, the *De securitate* begins: *Securitatis officium est contra aspera fortune solatium dare* (The duty of security is to give solace in face of adverse fortune).[9] In this regard, *securitas* explicitly contributes to the general merits of *fortitudo*, which is initially explained as "an assault that strikes back against adversity" (*retundens impetus adversitatis*, 30). This emphatically combative nature of fortitude—violence against violence—more or less characterizes every one of its subspecies; even *patientia* is understood as an active "rejoicing in hard times" (*gaudet patientia duris*). To behave with fortitude, and hence with security, is to engage concretely against peril, to hold danger in direct sight. In this way, *securitas* is related even more to Archilochian *asphaleia* and much less to Stoic *apatheia*, insofar as it does not shy away from active engagement with the enemy. Yet, what distinguishes *securitas* from early lyric *asphaleia* is its designation as a virtue in the thoroughly Stoic sense. The subsequent dialogic encounter between Securitas and Timor reasserts this distinction.

The general idea of security is significantly transformed by the *Moralium* text. Mindful of the passage's source in the *De remediis*, Securitas should be heard as the very voice of reason. Whereas Seneca would identify the positive sense of *securitas* as a state analogous to the *apatheia* that defines the blessed life lived in accordance with reason, the *Moralium* author suggests that security is reason itself. Moreover, this psychological quality should now be considered as demonstrating a particular aspect of fortitude or courage, a fundamentally active virtue whose confrontational character should modify any conception of Stoic impassibility. Still, despite these departures, such a description of *securitas* remains essentially associated with the ideals of classical Stoic theory and its later reception. The chapters on fortitude in the *Moralium* exhibit a strong indebtedness to a Ciceronian and Macrobian legacy. In this regard, the discussion is fully in line with medieval speculation on the nature of *fortitudo*, which invariably refers to *De officiis* 1.19–23 and to the Macrobius passage cited earlier. This tradition, in turn, has decisive roots in the Stoic interpretation of Plato and Aristotle.

From a Hellenistic philosophical viewpoint, fortitude (*andreia*), precisely as a virtue, must always be guided by the dictates of moral rectitude, so as to keep its assault free from the charge of mere belligerence. Here, *andreia* loses its earlier Homeric sense of masculine boldness and indomitable prowess—best exemplified in the heroic displays of Ajax or Achilles—and instead is allied with

---

[8] Macrobius, *In Somnium Scipionis* 1.8.7. Given Macrobius's strong predilection for the number seven, it is no surprise to find seven distinct aspects that elaborate the meaning of *fortitudo*. The author of the *Moralium Dogma Philosophorum* adheres to this list and its precise order, yet replaces *tolerantia* with *patientia* and altogether leaves out Macrobius's seventh entry: *firmitas* (steadfastness). See Thomas Aquinas's account in *Summa Theologica* 2.2 quaest. 128, art. 1.

[9] *Moralium Dogma Philosophorum*, Holmberg, ed., 32. All subsequent citations are from this edition.

virtuous and noble intent, which distinguishes such strength from mere audacity or base violence. Again, fear should play a constitutive role. A crucial passage is from Plato's *Laches*, where Socrates specifies *andreia* as the kind of "endurance" (*karteria*) that behaves nobly and not in a harmful or mischievous manner (192b–192d). In the dialogue, Socrates seeks a criterion that would set courage off from foolhardiness or recklessness and suggests that to exhibit true *andreia* it is necessary to possess sound knowledge of what should be dreaded, for "the fearless and the courageous are not the same thing" (197b). The Platonic theory of the educability of the soul's *thymos* from the *Republic* reinforces the connection between authentic courage, prudence (*sōphrosynē*), and wisdom (*sophia*). In contrast, a purely aphobic response to danger betrays pure irrational mindlessness.

Aristotle agrees that *andreia* should be understood as the virtuous mean between the bad extremes of "cowardice" (*deilia*) and heedless "daring" (*thrasytēs*).[10] The coward fears things he ought not to fear and the excessively brave man fails to fear what he should. *Andreia* on the contrary must remain "concerned with or face the fears" (*peri phobous, Eud. Eth.* 3.1228a). Without dismissing or retreating from fear, the courageous man must deal with perils reasonably, taking measures that correspond to the threat at hand. Virtuous courage, therefore, is based on a paradox: to display *andreia* a man must behave fearlessly before fearful things (*phobera*); yet, in order to recognize events or experiences as fearful, the courageous man must in some degree remain fearful. If he were not afraid, no experience would be fearful; and hence he would fall into the unvirtuous extreme of daring. However, if he is afraid, there emerges the possibility that he would slip into cowardice.

Fortitude is thus caught in the double bind that will come to characterize the practice of security. As for Aristotle, he attempts to extricate his argument from this potential *aporia* by reverting to reason or *logos*. Courage is "the pursuit of *logos*" (*Eud. Eth.* 3.1229a); and *logos*, it would appear, is capable of producing fortitude, not despite but because of the double bind. Virtue (*aretē*) is an achievement precisely because of its difficulty. It is better, then, to understand the Aristotelian mean less as "moderation" or "mediocrity," and more as a dynamic tension that negotiates two bad excesses. Provocatively expressed, the surest way to be courageous is to be fearless while being afraid.

In a similar discussion from the *Nicomachean Ethics*, Aristotle elaborates on this difficult ideal by broaching the ultimate test case for courage:

> What, then, are the kinds of fearful things with which the courageous man is concerned? Surely the greatest, because nobody is better able to endure dreadful experiences [*deinōn*]. Now the most fearful thing of all is death; for it is the limit [*peras*], and it is assumed that for the dead there is no good or

---

[10] Aristotle, *Eudemian Ethics* 3.1228a–b7.

evil any more. But it may be thought that even death does not in all its forms afford scope for courage—for example, death at sea or in illness.[11]

The limit that defines *andreia* is the threat of death but not all manners of dying. As Aristotle continues, courage is grounded in civil recognition. Presumably, a death at sea or a death in illness would fail to be acknowledged, because both fall beyond the limit of civil recognition. It appears that to succumb to sickness would be to suffer reduction to bare animal life, to move from *bios* to *zōē*, whereas to perish at sea would be to pass away far from the shores of communal existence. One may or may not fear shipwreck or illness, but in either case one has no opportunity to exhibit fortitude, for virtue cannot subsist without one's humanity or without one's society. Virtue is virtue recognized. The two major definitions of mankind that Aristotle has bequeathed to posterity—that man is both a "political animal" and an "animal possessing *logos*"—propels the societal exile as well as the bearer of bare life beyond the realms where recognition of fortitude may be gained.

What Aristotle requires, then, is a glorious death, particularly one that happens during warfare: "This is borne out by the honors paid to the fallen both in city-states and at the courts of monarchs" (*Nic. Eth.* 1115a). Aristotle may be alluding to a statement attributed to Heraclitus: "Souls slain in war are purer [*kathaṓterai*] than those [that perish] in diseases."[12] Confrontation with death, and even ultimate defeat, purifies one's actions. War is catharsis. Tellingly, Macrobius defines fortitude with its seven qualities specifically as a "political virtue" (*In Somn. Scip.* 1.7.5). When Cicero comes to grapple with the topic of fortitude, he likewise situates the discussion within the province of the political. For Cicero, the meaning of fortitude should be restricted to the strength that fights "for the common good" (*pro salute communi*) as opposed to aggression, which viciously serves selfish ends (*Off.* 1.62). The harmful or mischievous combatant conjured by Socrates is here identified as the one who neglects the community and instead pursues private interests.

Cicero's extended treatment of *fortitudo* in this part of *De officiis* includes passing comments on magnanimity, confidence, endurance, and so forth. It is also in these pages where one finds the key definition of *securitas* as the elimination of every perturbation of the mind, which affords "moral stability" (*constantia*) and "dignity" (*Off.* 1.69). Thus, by introducing nearly all the elements that will be featured in Macrobius's list, Cicero provides further authoritative basis for the subdivisions of *fortitudo* presented in the *Moralium dogma philosophorum*. However, as we have seen, regarding security, the duty described in the *Moralium* is explicitly understood as active consolation (*solatium*). That is, whereas Cicero understands *securitas* as the mental state that results from the

---

[11] Aristotle, *Nicomachean Ethics* 3.1115a; *The Ethics of Aristotle*, 127 (translation slightly modified).

[12] ψυχαὶ ἀρηίφατοι καθαρώτεραι ἢ ἐνὶ νούσοις (frag. 136). The fragment is preserved in a scholion to Epictetus. Text and translation in Kirk et al., *The Presocratic Philosophers*, 207.

evacuation of everything that disturbs (*vacandum . . . omni est animi perturbatione*), the *Moralium* author presents it as the giving of solace, a gift, moreover, that does not withdraw the subject from the opposing force. More distinctly, while Cicero tends to associate the achievement of *securitas* with the private contemplative life, the *Moralium*, precisely by naming security as a subcategory of fortitude, repositions the discourse within the realm of the *vita activa*.

To accentuate the confrontational aspect that *securitas* shares with the other kinds of political or civil fortitude, the *Moralium* passage quickly introduces an especially pugnacious antagonist. Timor emerges out of nowhere, ready to enter into striking conflict (*confligit*). His gambit has the concise force of a single word: *Morieris*—"You shall die" (33). Since *securitas* is an abstract virtue and cannot in itself die, the opponent's attack is clearly addressed to the mortal subject who displays or embodies security. The contest, then, should be read as an internalized fight over the soul, a *psychomachia* that pits a subject's fearful state against its secure, courageous state. And when the voice of fear speaks, it appears to ask: How can anyone be secure, if all are bound to perish? Again, as in Aristotle, death functions as the constitutive limit.

Securitas responds with lapidary statements reminiscent of standard Stoic arguments:

> This is human nature, not a punishment. Under this condition I entered [the world], that I should depart. It is civil law [*gentium lex*] to give back what you will have received. Life is a pilgrimage; when you will have walked much, you are to return. It is foolish to fear what you are unable to avoid. (33)

As Seneca tirelessly reminds his readers, the highest good is to live and act in accordance with nature.[13] Any denial of the mortality that defines human nature would be ill-advised, since it counters the very basis for rational comportment. Securitas therefore opens her rebuttal by recalling the natural necessity of death, which has always motivated Stoic fatalism as well as indifference. Because death is inevitable, it should not be a matter of any concern. Correspondingly, as Lorenzetti depicts her, Securitas stares at the death and destruction portrayed upon the facing mural with unflinching composure.[14] In this regard, her full-frontal stance is exemplary of *apatheia*, but it is an impassibility that presents itself in a far more confrontational manner than admitted by the Stoa.

Apart from comparison with the Stoics and more in line with the medieval context, such austerity may be well tempered by a Christian faith in salvation, whereby the end of life's journey is regarded as a return to a blessed state: death

---

[13] See, e.g., Seneca, *De otio* 5.1.

[14] Rosemond Tuve has demonstrated how the iconographical details of Lorenzetti's frescoes relate to the exposition of the virtues in the *Moralium Dogma Philosophorum*. "Notes on the Virtues and Vices," 290–95.

is not only a release from toil and pain but also the beginning of a supreme reward. As Securitas reminds the reader, *peregrinatio est vita*—"life is a pilgrimage." That is, we are all *peregrini*, pilgrims who live in a foreign land, far from our true heavenly home. To traverse the world of mortal existence is to be in exile. Christian theology inherits the classical notion of the *peregrinus* but is able to rectify the insecurities that were invariably attached to this designation. Unlike the *peregrinus* within the Roman Empire—who, until the Edict of Caracalla in AD 212, could never become a citizen and receive full protection under the *ius civile*—the Christian pilgrim no longer needed to fear a marginal, defenseless status. Rather, Christ himself, through incarnation, suffered from the same alien situation: "For I was hungry and you gave me something to eat, I was thirsty and you gave me something to drink, I was a stranger and you invited me in" (Matthew 25:35). For precisely this reason, the incarnate God indicates the way to ultimate salvation.[15] Christ's exile on this earth—his suffering, his humiliation, and expected exaltation—serves as the prototype for mortals and a vivid expression of their hopes for redemption.

This argument is consistent throughout the Middle Ages and contributes broadly to the formulation of the concept of fortitude. Contemporary with the earliest manuscripts of the *Moralium* are the writings of Bernard of Clairvaux, who effectively aligns martial courage with the security of postmortem compensation. In the opening exhortation of his *De laude novae militiae* (1129) Bernard encourages crusading knights to imitate Christ, who "by the strength of his own hands" (*in fortitudine manus suae*) vanquished the powers of darkness. Although there are soldiers who battle enemies and priests who fight against sin, the knight of the "new chivalry" combines both corporeal and spiritual aspects. "He indeed is a fearless [*impavidus*] knight, and one *secure* from every quarter [*et omni ex parte securus*], whose soul is dressed in faith just as his body is dressed in steel." Rather than describe this secure fortitude as the Aristotelian mean between extremes of recklessness and cowardice, Bernard theologically renames the poles in respect of body and soul and subsequently defines this Christian courage as their glorious conjunction, again in full imitation of the incarnate God. "Therefore go forth secure, knights [*Securi igitur procedite, milites*], and with undaunted will drive out the enemies of the cross of Christ, certain that neither death nor life can separate you from God's charity, which is in Jesus Christ."[16] The abbot of Clairvaux concludes these opening remarks with a statement that could well have been adopted by the *Moralium*'s Securitas: "How secure is life when the conscience is pure! How secure is life, when death is anticipated without fearfulness, when death is even longed for with sweetness, and welcomed with devotion!" (922C).

---

[15] On the shifting interpretations of the pilgrimage metaphor, see Jürgen Hahn, *The Origins of the Baroque Concept of Peregrinatio*, especially 19–20.

[16] Bernard of Clairvaux, *De laude novae militiae*, in J.-P. Migne, *Patrologia latina*, vol. 182: col. 922A.

Yet, in the *Moralium* Securitas does not allude explicitly to the Christian promise of salvation. On the contrary, she insists on human finitude, on the common condition that consolidates an earthly community: "I am not the first to die nor the last. All have preceded me, all will follow" (33). This observation is based not on any eschatology. Rather it marshals strength from a collective participation thoroughly motivated by the necessity of death that all hold in common. Timor recognizes this assurance through a feeling of community and aims his next thrust at robbing Securitas of this support as well: *Sed peregre morieris* (But you shall die away from home). Timor's adverb (*peregre*, "away from home") already weakens his argument, insofar as life in general has already been defined as a *peregrinatio*. As a mortal, one can never die apart from the larger community that contains all mortals. Thus, Securitas responds: "Sleep is no more grievous outside than at a home" (33). The pattern persists: Timor raises a series of circumstances that might make death appear more heinous—dying young, remaining unburied, suffering from malicious talk after one's passing, and so forth. To each attempt, Securitas answers as though in her own name: death is simply of *no concern*.[17]

SPECULUM REPUBLICAE

Lorenzetti's Securitas pictorially displays the fortitude that consoles without denying the human condition. Moreover, situated directly above the city gate, she arguably stands for the combination of two distinct civil ideals: *securitas interna et externa*. On the one hand, she denotes the tranquillity of a population working wthin a community and in accordance with justice; on the other hand, she symbolizes the good government's promise to prevent threats that would otherwise menace the people from abroad. As the protectress of the commune, she expresses the fruits of lawfulness within the confines of the republic and also shields the Sienese from outside aggression. A review of the larger context of Lorenzetti's composition demonstrates how each mode depends on the other.

On the central north wall we find two enthroned figures: on the left, the queenly image of Justice (IVSTITIA); and on the right a much larger depiction of a king. The fresco as a whole is thereby divided between a metaphysical conception of Justice to the west and a representation of terrestrial governance to the east. The metaphysical import of Iustitia is underscored by the figures that accompany her along the vertical axis: Wisdom (SAPIENTIA) at her head and Concord (CONCORDIA) at her feet. Correspondingly, the terrestrial monarch is flanked by the cardinal and civic virtues, which sit on either side along the horizontal plane. This metaphysical-terrestrial division is further strengthened by two distinct representations of Justice: in addition to the grand and majestic

---

[17] The same ensues as "Man" (*Homo*) comes to take Timor's place as Securitas' interlocutor.

figure of Iustitia in full regalia on the left, we find a different Iustitia upon the bench furthest to the right of the king. Whereas the enthroned Iustitia holds a pair of scales balanced by representations of "distributive" and "commutative" justice, the lesser depiction of the second personification holds a crown on her lap and an upright sword resting upon a severed head—symbols of just rewards and just punishment, respectively.[18] Thus, the mural suggests a separation between theoretical and practical concerns: we observe on the left a concise interpretation of an idea of justice that transmits eternal wisdom to the civil concord portrayed below—a fairly conventional depiction of the mediating force of justice (*Iustitia mediatrix*)[19]—whereas we are presented on the right with a scene familiar from the "mirrors of princes" (*specula principum*) tradition, which aimed to demonstrate how earthly rule should govern in respect of the cardinal virtues, as well as the theological virtues (Faith, Hope, and Charity) that float above the Sovereign's crown.[20]

The depiction of a single monarch would appear odd, given that Siena was constitutionally a republic. Nicolai Rubenstein first reconciled the disparity by taking the image of the king as a representation of the commune as a whole. This interpretation is supported by the Sovereign's garments in white and black, which are the colors of Siena's official shield, the *balzana*, as well as by the figure's exaggerated size. The pairs of initials inscribed on both sides of the Sovereign's crown, c.s. and c.v., evidently stand for *Civitas Senesis* (or *Comune Senarum*) and *Civitas Virginis*—the "city of the Virgin."[21] At the monarch's feet a she-wolf nurses the twins, Ascius and Senus, the children of Remus and mythical founders of the city. It is the magistrates and the citizens' representatives, therefore, who together execute the laws with fortitude, prudence, magnanimity, and temperance.

A full discussion of Lorenzetti's allegorical program and the textual traditions it reflects would take us too far afield.[22] Instead, I would like to focus on the figure of Peace (PAX) who is numbered among the virtues upon the monarch's bench yet is situated at the direct midpoint between the two enthroned

---

[18] The locus classicus for the distinction between distributive and commutative justice is found in Aristotle, *Nicomachean Ethics* 5.2.12–13. For Aquinas, see *Summa Theologica* IIa, IIae, quaest. 61, art. 1; as well as his commentary on the *Ethics* (*In decem libros Ethicorum Aristotelis ad Nicomachum exposito*), nos. 927–31; cited in Nicolai Rubenstein, "Political Ideas in Sienese Art: The Frescoes by Ambrogio Lorenzetti and Taddeo di Bartolo in the Palazzo Pubblico," 182 n. 29.

[19] For the textual tradition relating to the figure of *Iustitia mediatrix*, see Ernst H. Kantorowicz, *The King's Two Bodies: A Study in Mediaeval Political Theology*, 107–43. Lorenzetti's portrayal is briefly discussed on 112–13.

[20] See Rubenstein, "Political Ideas in Sienese Art," 180.

[21] See Rubinstein, "Political Ideas in Sienese Art," 180–81. Art historians have demonstrated that the extra C that partially appears to the left of the crown is not original.

[22] In addition to the studies cited above, see Randolph Starn, "The Republican Regime of the 'Room of Peace' in Siena, 1338–1340"; Jack Greenstein, "The Vision of Peace: Meaning and Representation in Ambrogio Lorenzetti's *Sala della Pace* Cityscapes"; Bram Kempers, "Gesetz und Kunst: Ambrogio Lorenzettis Fresken im Palazzo Pubblico in Siena"; and Quentin Skinner, "Ambrogio Lorenzetti's Buon Governo Frescoes: Two Old Questions, Two New Answers."

Figure 8.6. Lorenzetti, *Pax* (Northern Wall, detail). Alfredo Dagli Orti / The Art Archive at Art Resource, NY

figures: Iustitia and the Sovereign (Fig. 8.6). The compositional scheme clearly posits Lady Peace as a threshold figure. Resting upon a cushion propped up against a pile of discarded armor, Pax shares space with the Sovereign but re-clines toward Iustitia at her back. Moreover, she is pictorially distanced from the other personifications of the virtues, both by her position on the bench, which is at a considerable remove from the rest, and by her antique costume, which distinguishes her from the other virtues in contemporary dress. This liminal characterization may allude to the fact that Peace is not traditionally numbered among the cardinal virtues but rather is regarded as a beneficial result of virtuous governance. From another angle, we could understand Peace as playing her own mediating role, negotiating the realms of theory (justice) and praxis (sovereign rule). In either case, a focus on this border figure further differentiates the two seats of power that organize the north panel's composition. In other words, the central representation of Pax reveals the mural to be a republican version of the traditionally monarchical notion of "throne sharing" (*synthronismos*), whereby the Sovereign is described as one who shares his rule with Justice.[23] The cardinal and theological virtues associated with the Sovereign, together with the representations of distributive and commutative Justice deriving from wisdom, do not, then, create a general *speculum principum* but rather, more specifically, a *speculum republicae*.

The didactic message would not be lost on the Nine who, upon entering the Sala, were summoned to execute the commune's laws with righteousness and liberality. This overall sense is fixed by the text that is offered in the painted tablet at the bottom edge of the fresco:

QVESTA SANTA VIRTV LADOVE REGGE
INDVCE ADVNITA LIANIMI MOLTI
EQVESTI ACCIO RICCOLTI
VN BEN COMVN PERLOR SIGNOR SIFANNO
LOQVAL P[ER] GOVERNAR SVO STATO ELEGGE
DINO[N]TENER GIAMMA GLIOCHI RIVOLTI
DALO SPLENDOR DEVOLTI
DELE VIRTV CHETORNO ALLVI SISTANNO
P[E]R QVESTO CONTRIVNFO ALLVI SIDANNO
CENSI TRIBVTI ESIGNORIE DITERRE
PER QVESTO SENCA GVERRE
SEGVITA POI OGNI CIVILE EFFETO
VTILE NECESSARIO EDIDILETTO.

This holy virtue, wherever she rules
Induces to unity many souls
And these, gathered thus together,
A common good for their lord do make
Who, in order to govern his state, chooses
Never to keep his eyes turned away
From the splendor of the faces

---

[23] For a brief overview of this tradition in iconography, with ample bibliography, see Ernst Kantorowicz, "ΣΥΝΘΡΟΝΟΣ ΔΙΚΗΙ."

Of the virtues which stand around him
For this with triumph are given to him
Taxes, tributes, and lordships of lands,
For this, without wars,
Is followed then by every civil effect,
Useful, necessary and pleasurable.

(Rowley, trans., slightly modified)

In attending to the lessons contained on this north wall, the Nine can secure the city's peace, stave off wars (*sença guerre*), and lead the way toward beneficence, toward a state free of contingency (*necessario*)—a delight for all those who have pledged to work together for a common purpose. The *speculum* thus presented, from which the elected governors should "never turn their eyes" (*giamma liochi rivolti*), is subsequently reflected or projected, positively and negatively, upon the two urban landscapes that adorn the longer walls. The result of gazing upon the virtues is a thriving, harmonious city; and the result of neglecting such attention is a city afflicted with tyranny and crime. The effects of bad government, therefore, are essentially constituted by vanished virtues, by a privation of the good, a moral blindness, and hence a deficit of vision.

Once again, it is the figure of Pax that assumes the mediating role, for in reclining she gazes out toward the western wall, toward the depiction of the well-governed city. That is to say, within the mural, she is represented as a spectator of the related mural. Within Lorenzetti's didactic program, the figuration of Peace provides a model for the paintings' spectators to follow.[24] Her relaxed, almost erotically seductive posture suggests that peace is both desirable and henceforth immobile, not prepared for travel—she is the only one among the virtues who is barefoot, another iconographical detail that she shares with Securitas.[25] Thus, Pax gazes perpetually at the republic's accomplishments. "Never turn your eyes away from the splendor of the faces of the virtues" and you shall be enlightened. Specifically, you shall have the delight in seeing the effects of just governance—the prosperous city and fertile countryside depicted on the western wall, which is but a reflection of the northern. To keep one's eyes trained on the allegory of Justice and virtuous Sovereignty is ultimately to pursue the line of vision indicated by Peace; and from this depicted angle, it is fairly obvious that she is staring directly at Securitas, who shares her antique costume.

By means of the directing gaze of Pax, the removal of fear—*securitas* as *sença paura*—can now be concretely understood as premised upon the removal of conflicts: *sença guerre*. Securitas, in turn, stares straight across the hall to her demonic counterpart, Timor, who, as we have seen, also enunciates a privation, namely the complex negation of the negation of negation: *non . . . sença dubbio*. The triangulated configuration that thus emerges from the cross gazing of Pax,

---

[24] Thus, Jack Greenstein interprets the well-governed city as "literally a vision of Peace." "The Vision of Peace: Meaning and Representation in Ambrogio Lorenzetti's *Sala della Pace* Cityscapes," 498.

[25] Cf. Joseph Polzer, "Ambrogio Lorenzetti's 'Peace and War' Murals Revisited," 87.

Securitas, and Timor delineates vectors of elimination that specify the definitions of each personified term, all articulated by the preposition *sença*.

Table 8.2. Fear, Peace, and Security

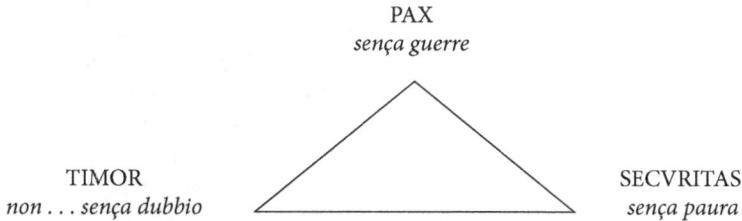

PAX
sença guerre

TIMOR   SECVRITAS
non . . . sença dubbio   *sença paura*

The opportunity for self-reflexivity that this *speculum republicae* affords is engendered precisely by this anaphora of *sença*, which could well be regarded as a phenomenon of pure *mise en abyme*.

Visually, Lorenzetti establishes a deep affinity between Pax and Securitas. As mentioned, both figures share the same classical antique attire: a quasi-transparent cloak that tightly fits the body's contours. Moreover, both occupy a crucial medial position: Pax sits directly between the enthroned figures of heavenly Justice on the left and the Sovereign on the right; Securitas hovers above the city gate, at the threshold between town and country. Most importantly, both are presented as agents of elimination: Securitas bears a gallows (dispatching the one who disturbs the civil peace); and Pax rests upon discarded armor (i.e., she is grounded on the cessation of war). To specify both peace and security as processes of removal (*sença guerre* and *sença paura*, respectively) is to identify the negative object of removal as a prerequisite. Quite simply, without care there would be no security and without war there would be no peace. Tellingly, the personified virtue that sits directly next to Peace on the Sovereign's bench is Fortitude.

There could be no security without care for the simple reason that security, precisely as a negation, must have something to negate. Political and theological theories from late antiquity into the medieval period consistently recognized this logic, which essentially belongs to a common understanding of "peace." In classical Latin usage, the word *pax* rarely denoted a simple absence of disorder or disturbance but rather a specific triumph over the privative events of war or discord. A nominal form of the verb *pacisci* (to strike a bargain, to enter into a contract or covenant), *pax* initially signified the *pact* that brought some interpersonal upset to an end. The politicization of the term occurred only around the time of the Social War (91–88 BC), when hostilities between Rome and neighboring cities were neutralized by treaties.[26] On this basis, we have Cicero's repeated association of *pax* and *concordia*, which is maintained

[26] See Stefan Weinstock, "Pax and the 'Ara Pacis.'"

throughout the medieval period. This notion of peace as the triumph over war and discord is linked to a prehumanist understanding that should be distinguished from the later view, explicitly pronounced by Thomas Aquinas, that peace is simply the absence of discord.[27]

This distinction implies a difference in anthropology. To understand peace as the mere absence of belligerence is to regard war as an accident. From this perspective, mankind is essentially sociable and benign, and peace is but a return to this original harmony. This line of thought would be Aquinas's operative premise. In contrast, to interpret peace as a victory over enmity is to recognize mankind as originally savage, ready to do violence unless prevented. This position is commonly associated with Cicero. In the *De inventione*, for example, Cicero alludes to a primal era "when men used to roam randomly in the fields in the manner of beasts," a time of utter lawlessness ruled only by individual cupidity and brute strength, until a "great and wise man" (*magnus . . . vir et sapiens*) eloquently introduced a system of education, with which he could render his fellow man "gentle and civilized" (*mites et mansuetos*).[28] A peaceful and concordant society, therefore, occurs through the offices of a powerful man, who is capable of persuading his neighbors to submit to his teaching and abandon their brutishness.[29] Peace is not had without a battle.

Centuries later, Giambattista Vico presses this practical wisdom to the point of aporia when he admits "that wars are waged so that peoples may live secure in peace" (*che le guerre si fanno perché i popoli vivano sicuri in pace*).[30] The problem would not have been lost to Vico's profoundly philological consciousness: wars are waged so that people may live without concern (of war), which alludes to the historical verity that all wars take place to end all wars. It is the mad logic that will weakly justify the oxymoronic notion of a "preemptive war," that is, a war waged to prevent war. In no small measure, Vico's repeated calls for a reconsideration of philology are motivated by a desire or need to engage in a political analysis that would disclose the often self-defeating mechanisms operative in our institutions.

The Sienese constitution of 1309–10 stated that the principal obligation of the Nove was to conserve the commune "in perpetual peace and pure justice." That is to say, should the "great and wise" ruling body dissolve, mankind's essentially divisive nature can at any moment reemerge. Thus, Security balances the gallows in clear view. Peace may rest upon the armor beneath her pillow once order has been achieved, but she cannot discard it. Likewise, Security must remain tirelessly ready to execute the established laws. More abstractly, when related to both triumphant peace and concord, Security reveals the indispensability of opposition. Aristotle's identification of the two bad extremes that

---

[27] This distinction is made and comprehensively analyzed in relation to Lorenzetti's frescoes by Quentin Skinner, "Ambrogio Lorenzetti: The Artist as Political Philosopher."

[28] Cicero, *De inventione* 1.2.

[29] Cf. Skinner, "Ambrogio Lorenzetti: The Artist as Political Philosopher," 17–18.

[30] From the Introduction to the 1744 version of *La scienza nuova*, 106 [*New Science*, 17].

delimit the virtuous mean of fortitude corroborates this crucial criterion. No security project can allow itself to be decimated by fear; however, being altogether blind to potential menace would result in sheer recklessness. Lorenzetti's composed maiden, who stares out at the sinister scene, is the figure of an idea of security as vigilance—as the fearless confrontation with recognized fear, as a disposition that is unafraid precisely by being afraid.

CRITIQUE OF FORTITUDE

In Lorenzetti's portrayal, fear is not completely vanquished but rather limited, controlled by keeping it in constant view. Across the well-governed city, the day-to-day business of the townspeople—at least for the moment, as long as justice is maintained—has become a sinecure: difficult travails are over; the remaining work, now equally distributed across the community and in harmony with nature, has been significantly reduced and promises great profit. Freed from the threat of Florentine aggression, the Sienese can continue to build and maintain their autonomous republic. As the lines written below the panel attest, by annihilating fear, security redefines "life" in Siena as something sweet, plentiful, and just:

> *Guardate quanti ben vengan da lei*
> *E come è dolce vita e riposata*

> Behold how much good comes from her [Justice]
> And how life is sweet and tranquil

As we have seen, Lorenzetti's presentation of *la dolce vita* consolidates ideals culled from a broad range of theological, classical, and prehumanist literature. Yet, the basic scenario is also more or less congruent with the gamut of modern political theory, where security, as the freedom from recognized fear, is routinely posited as the prerequisite for the liberty that defines the "good life" within the city. Hannah Arendt succinctly rehearses the standard plot that persisted throughout the seventeenth and eighteenth centuries: "The highest purpose of politics, 'the end of government,' was the guaranty of security; security, in turn, made freedom possible, and the word 'freedom' designated a quintessence of activities which occurred outside the political realm."[31] Certainly, for Hobbes, the security that the sovereign is compelled to provide is first and foremost security from "violent death"; but this duty should be further understood as producing the conditions for a satisfying, sweet life—one in which all species of dread have been checked so as to allow the maintenance of liberty.

With Hobbesian security, the notion of privation is never too distant, insofar as the commonwealth itself is inaugurated by means of a negation, namely, by dispelling the frightening circumstances that pervade the state of nature. On

---

[31] Hannah Arendt, "What Is Freedom?" in *The Portable Hannah Arendt*, 443.

this issue, Hobbes's presumed absolutism agrees with the legacy of liberalism that is otherwise conventionally opposed to it. Among liberal theorists, in an argument quite similar to Hobbes's exposition, security's privative function is again justified by being translated into a doubly articulated freedom, where the negative freedom from fear consequently permits the positive freedom to pursue individual or collective ends.[32] From John Locke to Jeremy Bentham, security is consistently identified as the necessary condition for happiness and the very ground of liberty. Along these lines, David Hume consolidates all potential threats beneath the rubric of some Machiavellian "fortune"—specifically, as that which may or may not happen to thwart an individual's intentions:

> Happiness cannot possibly exist, where there is no security; and security can have no place, where fortune has any dominion. Though that unstable deity should not exert her rage against you, the dread of it would still torment you; would disturb your slumbers, haunt your dreams, and throw a damp on the jollity of your most delicious banquets.[33]

Security's negating power to disencumber its subjects from debilitating hindrances and anxieties is thus legitimized. Even though Locke's state of nature, as the site of perfect liberty, is much more benign than Hobbes's, it still may be threatened; and it is for this reason that the strong securitization of civil society is summoned, an agreement among the people "to join and unite into a community, for their comfortable, safe, and peaceable living amongst one another, in a secure enjoyment of their properties, and a greater security against any, that are not of it."[34]

However, as today's critics of security's privations are keen to argue, this justification or legitimization should not go unchallenged. At what point, they ask, from a predominantly post-Orwellian perspective, does the drive to eliminate fear come to encroach upon human freedom or civil liberties? Late medieval culture and theories of governance also provided some alternatives to this typical security problem. A key area that might offer a critique of security as fortitude stems from the tradition of pastoral care as practiced in monastic communities. As indicated above, for Michel Foucault this alternative tradition eventually contributes to the formulations and techniques of security that take hold in the eighteenth century. As for the fourteenth century, one would have to move away from Europe's urban centers and focus instead on life within the cloisters.

Perhaps the most telling difference between legalistic-disciplinary rule and the pastoral rule of the monasteries is the coded masculinity of the former and the femininity of the latter. Caroline Walker Bynum has demonstrated that re-

---

[32] The classic formulation of "negative and positive liberty" is Isaiah Berlin, "Two Concepts of Liberty," in *Four Essays on Liberty*.

[33] David Hume, "The Stoic," in *Essays, Moral, Political, and Literary*, 150.

[34] John Locke, *Two Treatises of Government*, II.8 (§95), 330 (emphasis in original).

ligious authority figures of the twelfth and thirteenth centuries, particularly ab-
bots of the Cistercian Order, consistently reverted to maternal imagery to describe both Jesus' relationship to the church and their own spiritual work.[35]
Metaphors of nurturing, sheltering, and nursing portray a mode of governing
that essentially replaces fear with love. Thus, Bernard of Clairvaux advises those
preparing for the pastorate: "Learn that you must be mothers to those below
you, not masters; strive more to be loved, rather than feared."[36] Such instruction
is far removed from his encouragement to crusading knights, cited above. If
security forces are necessary for external threats (or foreign conquest), the contemplative life calls instead for tender care. A bishop is defined accordingly as
one who is obliged to give care to the weak—*curae teneris debitor.*[37] *Cura*, no
less than *securitas*, is a duty, an *officium* that ruling bodies owe to the ruled; and,
following the logic of exchange, the gifts of security and care each consequently
impose a duty in return. Generally speaking, where *securitas* demands obedience from its recipients, *cura* expects devotion.

Bynum's extensive essay offers a rich array of examples of this maternal solicitude. What is perhaps most intriguing are statements by Geurric of Igny,
who portrays God's love explicitly as a womb sheltering and nurturing the un-
born within, appropriately in his sermons for the Annunciation.[38] The monas-
tery itself becomes a kind of womb protected by care in face of love, which in
turn may serve as a political alternative for the walled city defended by security
in face of fear. The transcendence of Securitas, floating above ground with her
gallows, is thereby replaced by the immanence of Cura, within an amniotic
envelope that preserves the populace in safety. Given Siena's age-old devotion
to the Virgin Mary, we would expect this alternative to be frequently activated;
and we may even expect Lorenzetti's frescoes to reflect the effects of this softer
authority. Yet to what extent is this apparatus of maternal power a true alternative? Can this particular species of pastoral care always be understood as purely
beneficial?

Regina Coeli

The images of Lorenzetti's eastern and western walls, whose realism stands in
stark contrast to the blatantly allegorical design of the northern mural, insist on
immanence but hardly foreclose religious significance. The early modern theological priority granted to the spiritual over the material did not readily apply

---

[35] Caroline Walker Bynum, "Jesus as Mother and Abbot as Mother: Some Themes in Twelfth-Century
Cistercian Writing," in *Jesus as Mother: Studies in the Spirituality of the High Middle Ages*, 110–69.

[36] Bernard of Clairvaux, "Sermo XXIII: De tribus modis contemplationis circa Deum," in Migne, *Patrologia latina*, vol. 183, col. 885B. Cf. Bynum, "Jesus as Mother," 118–19.

[37] Bernard, *Tractat de iis quae circa ipsum sunt*, in Migne, *Patrologia latina*, vol. 182, col. 772C.

[38] Cited in Bynum, "Jesus as Mother," 121 n. 32.

to medieval religious experience. Historians of religion have stressed the concrete, sacramental nature of medieval devotion, which found expression in material and corporeal forms that later theologians would find either simpleminded or repulsive.[39] Arduous pilgrimages to holy sites, the veneration of relics, and the ingestion of Christ's flesh through the mystery of transsubstantiation all reflect a magical mode of thinking that betrayed a fundamental desire to encounter the transcendent by way of the immanent.[40] As many have argued, the later exaltation of the spirit at the expense of the tangible, together with a concomitant iconoclasm, should be attributed to the increase in literacy and the appearance of printing.[41]

In earlier forms of piety, it is clearly the incarnate Christ—God in his all-too-human flesh—who inspires intense worship. The centrality of the Virgin Mary, therefore, cannot be overstated, for it was the Blessed Mother who was responsible for Christ's human nature. His flesh was emphatically understood as hers, hence the unquestioned prominence of Marian worship across the Middle Ages.[42] Yet, Mary's role cannot be limited to individual devotional practices. Her power to act as a protectress, to intercede on behalf of the city, was consistently invoked and broadly celebrated. As we have seen, writers like Bernard of Clairvaux could here find their model for a use of authority that depended on love and care rather than fear and security. As a distinctly political Madonna, Mary would be revered as a provider of safety, watching over the community, as a mother would care for her children, that is, with worry and an instinct to shelter—*cum cura*.

Medieval Siena, whose cathedral had always been dedicated to the Holy Virgin, persistently exemplified this kind of political Mariology. The annual procession for the feast of the Assumption constituted a major event in the city: according to a public statute dating from 1200, every male citizen between the ages of eighteen and seventy was required to offer a candle; representatives from Siena's subject territories would follow suit on the next day, bearing specified quantities of wax; and anyone failing in this obligation would be severely fined. No one was exempt, no one immune. In one sense, through this act of ceremonious participation, the inhabitants of the town and *contado* expressed their submission to Sienese power and received in exchange the rights of protection and defense, which were directly procured by the city's patron, the Blessed Virgin. Here, the cult of the Virgin "assisted successive Sienese governments in their efforts to promote a particular civic ideology and spread its in-

---

[39] See, e.g., John Bossy, *Christianity in the West, 1400–1700*; and Carlos Eire, *War Against Idols: The Reformation of Worship from Erasmus to Calvin*, 1–18.

[40] Cf. Eire, *War Against Idols*, 11. On the conflation of magic and religious practices, see Keith Thomas's comprehensive study, *Religion and the Decline of Magic*.

[41] The thesis is forcefully presented by Lucien Febvre and Henri-Jean Martin, *L'apparition du livre* [*The Coming of the Book: The Impact of Printing, 1450–1800*].

[42] See Donna S. Ellington, "Impassioned Mother or Passive Icon: The Virgin's Role in Late Medieval and Early Modern Passion Sermons."

fluence well beyond the confines of the city itself."[43] Yet the efficacy of this ideology points to a deeper cause, one that lies beneath the level of mere political propaganda. The Virgin's divine gift of caring protection and defense imposes an obligation upon all the citizens, who now form a community based on this shared debt. That no one is immune from repaying during the feast of the Assumption means that no one can neglect to contribute the required gift (*munus*) that defines the *commune*.[44]

When Lorenzetti completed the frescoes in 1339, it had already been nearly four decades since the Sienese fought alongside German knights dispatched by the Hohenstaufen king Manfred of Sicily to defeat the Florentine forces at the Battle of Montaperti (September 4, 1260). From the vantage of European politics, the victory was crucial for the Hohenstaufen emperor Frederick II, who, supported by his Ghibelline allies, sought to wrest control of central Italy from the papacy and its Guelph allies. On a more local level, the event confirmed Siena's conviction that its commune was under direct protection of the Virgin Mary. An early chronicle of the confrontation by Paolo di Tommaso Montauri vividly relates how, on the eve of the battle, the city's mayor, Buonaguida Lucari, led the townspeople in a solemn procession to the Santa Maria Cathedral, where he made a vow at the Virgin's altar that, should Siena be victorious, the city would henceforth be dedicated exclusively to her.[45] Subsequently, according to popular opinion, the stunning victory of the Sienese Ghibellines, who were significantly outnumbered by the Florentine Guelphs by some ten thousand soldiers, was owed entirely to the city's devotion to the Virgin Mary. It was claimed that the Blessed Mother herself sent down a dense, moist cloud to cover Siena's men and thereby to protect them from assault.[46]

Orders for the Palazzo's decoration followed suit. Simone Martini's *Maestà* mural, which shows Mary crowned, holding the infant Christ and attended by a consortium of saints, graces the legislative chamber, the Sala del Consiglio della Campana, which is adjacent to the Sala dei Nove on the Palazzo's second story. Martini's fresco was finished around 1315 and served to reiterate Siena's long-standing indebtedness to the Virgin's guidance. As scholars have stressed, Martini's heavenly queen rehearses Duccio's Rucellai Madonna (1311), which adorns the altar in Siena's cathedral and which bears further witness to the cen-

---

[43] Diana Norman, *Siena and the Virgin: Art and Politics in a Late Medieval City State*, 43.

[44] Roberto Esposito has usefully analyzed how a "community" (*communitas*) names the collective of individuals who share some required duty. "[It] emerges that *communitas* is the totality of persons united not by a 'property' but precisely by an obligation or a debt; not by an 'addition' [*più*] but by a subtraction [*meno*]: by a lack, a limit that is configured as an onus, or even as a defective modality for him who is 'affected.' " *Communitas: The Origin and Destiny of Community*, 6 [*Communitas: Origine e destino della comunità*, xiii].

[45] See Norman, *Siena and the Virgin*, 3.

[46] For a contemporary account, see Angolo di Tura's *Cronaca* of 1338, which was included in Lodovico Muratori's *Rerum Italicarum scriptores: Raccolta degli storici italiani dal cinquecento al millecinquecento*, tome 15, part 6. Polzer, who refers to Angolo di Tura's chronicle ("Ambrogio" especially 99 n. 8), cites the edition produced by F. Iacometti and A. Lisini, *Cronache Senesi*.

tral role that the cult of the Virgin played in the city's self-representation.[47] In 1337, after Martini left Siena for Avignon, Ambrogio Lorenzetti was hired to decorate the Palazzo's façade with scenes from Roman history (no longer extant). In 1338 Lorenzetti was next charged with painting the allegories of Good and Bad Government. He duly acknowledges the Virgin's protection by placing the image of the Madonna and Child upon the shield of the Sovereign together with an inscription of Siena's official seal: *Salvet Virgo Senam veterem quam signat amoenam* (May the Virgin save Siena, the ancient, which she marks out as lovely).

Thanks to the Virgin's intercession, Siena had become a veritable *locus amoenus*. Sienese artists throughout the late medieval period repeatedly acknowledged their debt. In addition to hosting Duccio's painting for the cathedral's high altar and Martini's *Maestà* in the Palazzo Pubblico, both the town and the *contado* are saturated with Marian imagery, which consistently depicts the Virgin as protector and savior.[48] The vectors of elimination delineated by Lorenzetti's figurations of Pax and Securitas ostensibly derive their divine efficacy from the Virgin's icon inscribed upon the Sovereign's shield.

The Virgin's function as *protectrix* is clearly based on her role as mother, hence the prevalence of the Madonna and Child theme in works directly implicated in Siena's civic cult. Consequently, the dogmatic tradition that developed around Marian adoration assigned the citizenry to the position of a mother's children, a position that implies particular needs, desires, and wishes, which are, of course, the privileged object of study for psychoanalysis. Sigmund Freud famously acknowledged this component of collective infantilization in *The Future of an Illusion* (1927), where the bonds implicit in religion (*re-ligare*) effectuate a stabilization of societal life and offer consolation for the helplessness and vulnerability associated with the human condition. Thus, for Freud, the "infantile prototype" provides the structure for the phylogenetic development of religious devotion: "For once before one has found oneself in a similar state of helplessness: as a small child, in relation to one's parents. One had reason to fear them, and especially one's father; and yet one was sure [*sicher*] of his protection against the dangers one knew."[49] In Freud's account, this "infantile prototype" ultimately motivates a phylogenetic development:

> The gods retain their threefold task: they must exorcise the terrors of nature, they must reconcile men to the cruelty of Fate, particularly as it is shown in

---

[47] See James Stubblebine, "French Gothic Elements in Simone Martini's *Maestà*." Polzer relates both Martini's and Duccio's paintings to a no longer extant *Maestà* by a master named Mino, mentioned in a number of records collected in *Palazzo Pubblico: Vicende costruttive e decorazione*, but otherwise unknown ("Ambrogio Lorenzetti," 65–67; for bibliographical references, see 99 nn. 15 and 17).

[48] For a comprehensive account, see Norman, *Siena and the Virgin*.

[49] Sigmund Freud, *The Future of an Illusion*, 21 [*Die Zukunft einer Illusion*, in *Gesammelte Werke*, 14: 338].

death, and they must compensate them for the sufferings and privations which a civilized life in common has imposed on them.[50]

As this last point indicates, theology may be utilized to reinforce processes of socialization and address problems of collective preservation. Ferdinand Schevill's description of Siena's emergence from the feudal age explicitly as "a period of infancy" alludes to the social, economic, and political anxieties that could well reduce the people to a state of early childhood desperate for protection.[51] As the republic progressed in independence from the nobility and episcopal administration, it would understandably turn to religious support in its need for self-defense and self-reliance.

However, Freud's genealogy of religion is resolutely patriarchal: "[T]he terrifying impression of helplessness in childhood aroused the need for protection—for protection through love—which was provided by the father; and the recognition that this helplessness lasts throughout life made it necessary to cling to the existence of a father, but this time a more powerful one."[52] Freud's explication, which centers on the figure of the father, is hardly an adequate response to medieval Siena's cult of the mother. Were we to accept Freud's psychoanalytic explanation for the persistence of religious devotion, questions would still remain: Why do we witness the widespread, if not excessive, veneration of Mary throughout the medieval period? What specific purpose would doctrines of the Immaculate Conception, Virginal Motherhood, and the Assumption serve in relation to social and political life? How might the peace and security provided by the *Mater protectrix* differ from the benefits donated by the Father or the Incarnate Son?

Erich Fromm seized upon these questions in his essay *The Dogma of Christ*, written in 1930 when Fromm was still working closely within Freudian parameters. Throughout, Fromm's operative premise is that historical shifts in Christian theology are attributable to unconscious processes occasioned by changes in the early church's political, social, and economic conditions. Fromm argues the following: in its earliest manifestation, the collective psyche of the population felt disenfranchised and therefore flocked to Christian doctrine, which conflicted with Jerusalem's Pharisees, scholars, and aristocrats. This rebellious association was unconsciously driven to seek in Jesus the powerful son who would remove a hostile god and thereby deliver the people from their suffering. Through their feelings of helplessness and despair, the faithful could identify with the humiliated and crucified divinity. The passion of Christ could even serve as a prototype for the atonement of guilt invariably caused by parricidal wishes. Still, the latent wish persisted that

---

[50] Freud, *The Future of an Illusion*, 22 [*Zukunft einer Illusion*, 339].
[51] Ferdinand Schevill, *Siena: The History of a Mediaeval Commune*, 45.
[52] Freud, *Future of an Illusion* 38 [*Zukunft einer Illusion*, 352].

the messiah would ultimately vanquish the hateful father associated with the forces of oppression.[53]

Fromm shows that these early revolutionary tendencies started to diminish as Christianity spread across the Roman Empire, primarily through the agency of prominent women who were capable of winning over members of higher social classes. No longer a faith held exclusively by the proletariat, Christianity began to find its place among the ruling classes. Consequently, state authority could now be respected as paternalistic, that is, as a source of loving care and grace. Fromm cites the Edict of Caracalla, which for the first time allowed aliens to become Roman citizens.[54] The *peregrinus*, once tied to an uncertain and legally vulnerable status, could now enjoy the benefits of the *ius civile*. The pilgrim had been transformed into a protégé. The son, who was formerly viewed as an eschatological usurper, was now coextensive with the ruling father; and together this divine basis could support the protofeudal economy that characterized the late empire. The once imminent Apocalypse could be postponed indefinitely, if not forgotten entirely.

> The real historical world no longer needed to change; outwardly everything could remain as it were—state, society, law, economy—for salvation had become an inward, spiritual, unhistorical, individual matter guaranteed by faith in Jesus. The hope for real, historical deliverance was replaced by faith in the already complete spiritual deliverance.[55]

Through the benevolence and grace of the transcendent realm, the immanent had been secured. The aims of the state could be reconciled with the church.

For Fromm, then, the crucial theological shift, motivated by unconscious responses to sociohistorical circumstances, is an abandonment of the "adoptionist doctrine" (Jesus the man elevated to divinity) and the establishment of the "doctrine of consubstantiality" (God descended to humanity). In the former case Jesus was portrayed as a violent usurper, whereas in the latter he was characterized by forgiving care. Psychoanalytically, any remaining aggression toward the father could now be directed inward: an individual's sins, and not the power of the sovereign, were to blame for suffering in this world. This internalization only further reinforced social stability.

The doctrine of the consubstantiality (*homoousia*) of Christ the son and God the father, proposed by Athanasius and established by the First Council of Nicaea, posed the logical contradiction of two distinct bodies being a single person. In Fromm's view, the psyche could make sense of this paradox only by recalling intrauterine experience, where mother and child retain their individ-

---

[53] Erich Fromm, *The Dogma of Christ*, 37–45. As Fromm acknowledges, this thesis is first broached by Theodor Reik, *Dogma und Zwangsidee* (1927) [*Dogma and Compulsion: Psychoanalytic Studies of Religion and Myths*].

[54] Fromm, *Dogma of Christ*, 50.

[55] Fromm, *Dogma of Christ*, 53.

uality but nonetheless share a single body. Hence, Fromm draws his ingenious conclusion: "The strong, powerful father has become the sheltering and protecting mother; the once rebellious, then suffering and passive son has become the small child."[56] And it is this theological and psychic justification that, for Fromm, accounts for the prominence of Mary's cult in the Middle Ages.

Although retaining the Freudian equation of religion and illusion, Fromm's account remains more or less optimistic. In brief, Marian care allows her devotees to be secure: not entirely carefree, but rather sheltered, protected, and nursed. The fears that emerge from the seas of contingency are easier to weather with maternal support. Yet, as is the case with every gift, this security comes with a price. What Fromm neglects to consider are the specific implications of such infantilization. When the city becomes a womb or a maternally guarded home, movement is necessarily impeded and suffocation emerges as a threat. The immunity promised by this uterine space destroys community by annulling the lack that constitutes its living existence. Life is reduced to a prenatal plenitude, consigned to a paradisical non-time before birth. From another angle, a second threat is posited for those who desire to flee these immune, nonliving conditions. A premature birth into the world or an infant's unsupported sojourn could be characterized only as highly dangerous. The embryo is not yet truly living, and the infant torn from the mother's bosom barely has a chance to survive. Bernard of Clairvaux suggested that maternal care should replace fear with love, when in fact one fear—like the Timor that runs rampant under Security's gaze—is simply supplanted by other fears.

[56] Fromm, *Dogma of Christ*, 61.

Embarkations

And I saw a new heaven and a new earth:
for the first heaven and the first earth were
passed away; and there was no more sea.

Revelation 21:1
(King James Version)

Discord from the Sea

In 1425, for the thirtieth of his daily Lenten sermons offered to the people of Siena, the celebrated Franciscan priest and future saint Bernardino vividly conjured scenes from Lorenzetti's allegorical frescoes painted nearly a century before. Bernardino could rely on the citizenry's firsthand knowledge of and civic pride in these images that adorn the walls of the Sala della Pace. Of the three murals, he chose to open with an account of the eastern wall:

> Turning to peace, I see commerce all about; I see dances, I see houses being repaired; I see vineyards and fields being cultivated and sown. I see people going to the baths, on horses, I see girls going to marry, I see flocks of sheep, etc. And I see the man hanged in order to maintain holy justice. And for this reason, everyone lives in holy peace and concord.[1]

The anaphoric affirmation of sight (*vego . . . vego . . .* [I see . . . I see . . .]) is a typical ekphrastic device that accumulates details and provides a fairly comprehensive inventory of an image. Yet ekphrasis is rarely undertaken without some didactic purpose, and, accordingly, Bernardino quickly graduates to the level of evidence: distinguished from the beneficial *effects* of peace—the commerce, the dancing, and so forth—we behold the gallows, which constitutes the *cause*.

---

[1] Bernardino of Siena, "Questa è la predica de la concordia e unione che doviamo avere insieme" (This Is the Sermon on the Concord and Unity That We Must Have Together), in *Le prediche volgari*, 2: 266–67. For discussion, see Nirit Ben-Aryeh Debby, "War and Peace: The Description of Ambrogio Lorenzetti's Frescoes in Saint Bernardino's 1425 Siena Sermons," 275–76. I have used Debby's translation, slightly modified.

"And I see the man hanged [*E vego implicato l'uomo*] in order to maintain holy justice. And for this reason [*E per queste cose*], everyone lives in holy peace and concord." This final observation moves the scene from description to argument. Peace and concord are demonstrated to be an achievement that specifically results from bringing a malefactor to justice. There are serenity and joyful work for all, save for those found guilty of some crime. Execution of the city's laws is the originating factor of the contentment and harmony visible everywhere.

Lorenzetti himself pictorially marked off this piece of juridical theory from the generally mimetic representation of the town and the *contado* by having Securitas and her gallows occupy a transcendent position floating in the sky. What Bernardino sees is what Lorenzetti has given us to see, namely the quality of life in a society where security prevails. The "holy peace and concord" are but manifestations of this transcendent cause. To see her, to see Security, is to gaze through the genial behavior and complaisant enterprises that populate the scene. As an allegorical executioner, Securitas eliminates the forces, subjective or objective, that are bent on transgression or disruption. She introduces or restores stability by dispatching anything that would threaten civil order or individual well-being. With security, danger of all kinds has come under control.

When Bernardino's sermon shifts to the western wall, the terror caused by what the friar sees—murder, rape, arson, and pandemic anxiety—correlates to the sadness for what he no longer sees:

> In contrast, turning to the other side, I do not see commerce; I do not see dances, rather I see men killing each other; no houses are being repaired, rather they are being damaged and burned; the fields are not being cultivated; the vineyards are cut down; there is no sowing, the baths are not used nor are there any other delights. I do not see anyone going outside. Oh women! Oh men! The man is dead, the woman raped, no herds unless they are preyed upon; men treacherously kill one another; justice lies on the ground, her scales broken, she is bound, her hands and legs are bound. And everything that is done is done with fear [*con paura*].

While standing outside the Palazzo Pubblico, Bernardino's listeners are brought inside, into the Sala dei Nove. Through the activation of their collective imagination, the preacher places his audience in front of Lorenzetti's paintings, first to face the eastern wall's depiction of the town and country at peace and then to turn around and consider the picture of ruined social order upon the western wall. In selecting this sequence—first the town flourishing in security on the eastern wall, then turning to the city under tyranny to the west—Bernardino follows the order that any fifteenth-century visitor to the Sala would experience, walking through the only doorway cut into the western wall. Spectators were thus invited to regard the pleasant scene of a well-governed city only to discover afterward the depiction of mayhem and crime that had been unfolding behind their backs all the while. The contemplation of security ultimately yields to a sight of horror.

Bernardino stresses this fear-inspiring movement by relegating the scene of security to the status of being no longer seen. Yet he goes even further than Lorenzetti. He does not end his sermon with a description of social dissolution or with a statement on the constitutive necessity of fear. Upon lamenting what can be seen (murder, destruction) and what can no longer be seen (useful work, delightful activity), he compels the distraught spectator to take in other visions:

> But the Apocalypse, in the thirteenth chapter, shows war in the figure of a beast coming out of the sea with ten horns and seven heads, like a leopard, and with the feet of a bear. What do these ten horns signify, if not to be in opposition to the Ten Commandments? With its seven heads and therefore with the seven mortal sins, like a leopard and therefore like treachery; with its feet of a bear and therefore full of revenge. And yet, by forgiving, you end and eliminate war.

Having summoned the scenes of Lorenzetti's frescoes, Bernardino evokes yet another scene, one that cannot be found in any of the murals but rather only from a scriptural tradition. In this way, the friar identifies a different, altogether unseen cause, one that is beyond the paintings' frames.

The reference to the book of Revelation places the priest squarely on the shore along with Saint John the Divine—"And I stood upon the sand of the sea, and saw a beast rise up out of the sea" (13:1). The position may recall that of Vergil's Laocoon, the priest who watched in horror as the "twin snakes" emerged from the surf (*Aen.* 2.203–5). The coastline, which should maintain the separation of safe and unsafe zones, is also the privileged vantage of the watchman who would be first to discover a serious threat. Yet the Franciscan's evocation of the apocalyptic beast is not motivated by eschatology. Rather, he is driven by a concern for the daily lives of his followers and their need to restitute order for themselves and their society. Instead of involving an end of time, Bernardino points to the possible end of misfortune here and now, on a wholly immanent plane where there will be "no more sea" (Revelation 21:1). If the present-day social and political dissoluteness is essentially an occasion of failed vision (*non vego*), then the remedy consists in a prophetic conjuration of an invisible source of the catastrophe. Lorenzetti does not feature the sea in his frescoes, yet its deleterious power, according to Bernardino, is everywhere discernible. Bernardino conjures Lorenzetti's depiction of war—the term *guerra* can denote both an external and an internal conflict—so as to define precisely what must be eliminated. The means for its removal, however, is not some collective or military action but rather an individual's piety and his readiness to forgive his neighbor: "By forgiving, you end and eliminate war."

Bernardino's sermon clearly presents a tripartite scheme inspired by Lorenzetti's three murals; and by evoking peace and war, the friar closely adheres to his model. However, the final move to the judgment of sins is a decisive departure, for Lorenzetti's third scene, the central panel on the northern wall, the extensive allegorical study of Good Government and the attendant virtues, is entirely evaded. Bernardino thereby introduces a purely theological argument to displace a political one. Where Lorenzetti negotiates the contrast between the concordant and discordant cities with a reflection on political institutions and civil virtues, Bernardino introduces a moral interpretation employing eschatological imagery to present ends.

Whereas Bernardino restricts his ekphrasis to the two side panels, to the panoramic, more realistic depictions of peace and war, the reverse is true in today's scholarship. Given its rich iconographic detail and its illustration of many strands of classical, prehumanist, and Scholastic political theory, it is Lorenzetti's central mural on the northern wall that has by far received the most attention from modern historians, much more than the representations of the peaceful and war-torn cities.[2] This modern emphasis makes Bernardino's neglect especially curious. Bernardino's selectivity could certainly have been based on a desire to be as cogent and powerful as possible. His reputation as an eloquent, charismatic, and awe-inspiring speaker was already well established across the Italian states; and he reportedly attracted audiences in the tens of thousands.[3] His canonization in 1450, a mere six years after his death, testifies to the magnitude of his impact among the people. The Lenten sermon cited above provides sufficient hints of his accomplished skills in public oratory. Here, even in this brief excerpt, we can observe how artfully he manipulates rhetorical devices to enhance the force of his message with anaphora, deixis, and apostrophe. His presentation is a study in *enargeia*, which transforms the described scene into a living spectacle and the audience into engaged, participating witnesses. Clearly, the friar is using Lorenzetti's paintings to forge a link between the aesthetic realm and present experiential reality: the discord that you can view inside upon the western wall of the Sala dei Nove is in fact all around you in your everyday lives; and the solution is as simple as turning from one panel to the other, back to the depiction of serenity on the eastern wall: forgive one another and thereby eliminate war.

Bernardino doubtlessly limited his comments to Lorenzetti's stark opposition of peace and war in order to be perfectly clear before his massive and not entirely literate audience. A consideration of the northern wall's intricate allegorical scheme would certainly have complicated the preacher's message and

---

[2] Uta Feldges-Henning acknowledges and addresses this deficit in "The Pictorial Programme of the Sala della Pace: A New Interpretation." See also Greenstein, "The Vision of Peace."

[3] For a useful account of Bernardino's oratorical effectiveness, see Lina Bolzoni, *The Web of Images: Vernacular Preaching from Its Origins to St Bernardino da Siena*, 120–84.

could well have jeopardized the sermon's effectiveness. The simple antithesis between the flourishing city to the right and its sinister counterpart, with a final gesture to the provocative apocalyptic imagery, served the friar's purposes much better than any long digression into matters of juridical erudition. In this regard, Bernardino's approach is fully in line with the general program of Franciscan Observants, who tended to concentrate on issues of social reform and spiritual renewal, rather than busy themselves with the minutiae of Scholastic or humanistic debate. For Bernardino's purposes, Lorenzetti's realist representations of urban experience to the left and right of the hall would make a more immediate impression on the laypeople and take full advantage of Gregory the Great's well-known advice to employ images for instructing the illiterate.[4]

Historical circumstance also must have played a key role in guiding Bernardino's choices. The social and political climate that fostered the original composition differed significantly from the times that Bernardino and his fellow Sienese experienced. Between Bernardino's sermon and Lorenzetti's paintings lies the caesura of the Black Death of 1348, which severely affected Siena's population and, in the collective consciousness of the early Quattrocento, readily divided a time of former flourishing from present entropy. The year Lorenzetti finished his work, 1339, marked a culminating moment of prosperity for the Sienese republic. For decades the people had enjoyed internal stability and relative peace with neighboring cities, which provided the basis for a highly profitable wool trade, the founding of moneylending institutions, and the acquisition of resourceful territory. Politically, the commune had fully emerged from the feudal age, winning independence from both the episcopacy and the local nobility.[5] It was in this climate of extraordinary affluence and autonomy that the magistrates ordered construction of the impressive Palazzo Pubblico, which was completed in 1310, the year that also saw the redrafting and ratification of the commune's constitution, the first in Italian history to have been written in the *volgare* for the benefit of any literate citizen. Lorenzetti's grand allegorical design could therefore be viewed as a celebration of the civil order that was commonly believed to be responsible for the city's fiscal thriving and artistic brilliance.

However, 1339 was also the year when Siena's fortunes began to falter. As later chronicles report, a devastating crop failure was followed by famine and epidemic—a bitter foretaste of the plague that within a decade would claim Lorenzetti's life.[6] An increase in violent crime, attributed to the ravages of the deadly epidemic, was explicitly acknowledged by the Council of the Nine,

---

[4] Cf. Roberto Cobianchi, "Fashioning the Imagery of a Franciscan Observant Preacher: Early Renaissance Portraiture of Bernardino da Siena in Northern Italy," 60–61. Gregory the Great's recommendation to Serenus, the bishop of Marseille, can be found in Migne, *Patrologia latina*, vol. 78, cols. 1128–30. For general discussion, see Michael Baxandall, *Painting and Experience in Fifteenth-Century Italy*, 41–65.

[5] See Schevill, *Siena: The History of a Mediaeval Commune*, 45–71.

[6] See Polzer, "Ambrogio Lorenzetti," 64.

whose efforts to maintain public safety as well as their own protection ultimately failed in 1355, when a popular rebellion overthrew the government.[7]
From that point forward the city suffered steady regime changes, one as unstable as the next, which understandably led to severe economic depression and
civil unrest. The Papal Schism that marred the last quarter of the century reinforced the general sense among Siena's citizenry that order had deteriorated
under the weight of corruption, partisanship, and violence. By 1425, the year of
Bernardino's sermon, the once affluent and peaceful city had degenerated into
a state of perpetual crisis and terrifying insecurity.

Bernardino thus recalls the hall's conflict-ridden cityscape as a mirror image
of Siena's present catastrophe. Lorenzetti, who worked during a decidedly more
prosperous time, would instead employ these horrors as a cautionary tale, as a
preemptive call to remain loyal to the institutions of justice. In Lorenzetti's secular design, the central portrayal of sovereignty and civil justice serves as the
basis for the healthy and happy life on the eastern wall. But in Bernardino's reductive description, the functioning of government is irrelevant. A native of
Massa Marittima, which was annexed to the Sienese republic by the Nine in
1335, Bernardino presumably knew at first hand the intrigues and factiousness
of the commune's political organization. The miserable failure of constantly
shifting regimes to produce lasting peace would understandably cause one to
question the efficacy of any mundane government.

From Bernardino's perspective, which in this case is not dissimilar to Cicero's, in order to serve society it may be better to circumvent politics and focus
instead on individual morality. The friar thus interprets the sea monster of war
on a personal level, as the sinner who opposes God's law and is therefore prone
to treachery and vengefulness. In this reading, the pain and suffering of war are
not merely due to tensions between rival cities or political feuding, but rather
are manifestations of divine retribution designed to correct and discipline er-
rant lives. Bernardino's moralizing view can thus be inscribed in the Tuscan
tradition of the "merchant writers" (*mercanti scrittori*), who consistently understood war, discord, and disasters—like the Black Death—as divine punishment
for a society's sins.[8] Giovanni Villani, for example, explains: "All the plagues,
war, destruction and floods . . . came through the permission of divine justice
to punish sins."[9] Accordingly, Bernadino's account of Lorenzetti's political theoretical depiction is refunctionalized so as to speak to a different historical context. Contrary to Lorenzetti's original scheme, it is not the malfunctioning of

---

[7] On the dire circumstances following the plague and the city's police organizations, see William
Bowsky, "The Medieval Commune and Internal Violence: Police Power and Public Safety in Siena,
1287–1355."

[8] Debby, "War and Peace," 285–86.

[9] Giovanni Villani, *Cronica*, F. G. Dragomanni and I. Moutier, eds. (Florence, 1844–45), 2: 131; cited in
Debby, "War and Peace," 286. For other illustrative examples, see *Merchant Writers of the Italian Renaissance*, Vittore Branca, ed.

government that causes the effects of war and crime but rather the moral failings and transgressions of the city's individuals.

In brief, Bernardino passes over the allegorical representations of Lorenzetti's northern wall and attends to the realistic scenes of civil prosperity and civil unrest in order to provide space for his own allegorical intention, which he reveals in introducing the Apocalypse's watery beast. As a site of general insecurity and a source of visceral terror, the sea continued to furnish the imagery for staging a broad variety of conflicts, from interstate war and civil discord to interpersonal strife and individual emotional disruption. The political and social crises and emergencies that repeatedly punctuated fourteenth-century Europe thus had recourse to the land-sea dichotomy in order to articulate both hope and fear: security's potential victory over fear as well as the possible triumph of fear.

Self-Preservation

As a site of insecurity and uncertainty, nautical experience has consistently provided the terms for difficult questions in moral philosophy, for limit cases that test the validity of one's judgment. Cases where individual lives are threatened at sea furnish problems linked to the issue of urgency and the "state of exception" where conventional rules and ordinary values may be suspended. Such casuistical arguments classically reach toward conditions for moral laxity and especially thrive on the extreme example of shipwreck, an emergency situation that reevaluates interpersonal behavior and thereby questions the grounds for social relations. An oft-cited case entails two men who, struggling for survival upon the waves, come upon a single plank. How resilient is altruism or one's sense of *humanitas*? Can the ideal of virtue withstand an existential threat? Or will the instinct of self-preservation trump moral considerations? Can saving one's own life be justified when it is performed at another's expense?

Towards the conclusion of *De officiis* (3.89–90), Cicero adduces the problem of a sinking ship and contending survivors. He claims to have taken his examples from the work of Stoic philosopher Hecaton of Rhodes; and each case ostensibly challenges some basic tenet dear to the Stoa. The series of questions concerns two varying types of men striving to keep afloat and dealing with a single plank that can save only one of them. In each instance, the value distinctions maintained on land are seriously interrogated by the maritime emergency. To begin, we are asked whether a "wise man" (*sapiens*) should be allowed to wrest the plank away from a "fool" (*stultus*), if he is able to do so. The question is malicious insofar as it raises problems with Stoic ideals that value the sage's life above all. Hecaton's response artfully circumvents the utilitarian issue of value by alluding to another principle: The wise man would commit an "injustice" (*iniurium*) insofar as his act would ignore the doctrine that prior possession justifies continued possession.[10] The second question then pursues this principle and asks if the ship's owner has the moral right to take the piece of timber, because it in fact belongs to him. Again, Hecaton says no and clarifies that until the ship reaches harbor, the vessel belongs to the passengers. The examiner presses further: What if both were "wise men"? Who, then, should claim the plank for himself? Here, Hecaton reverts to the utilitarian argument that he implicitly rejected above: whoever is more valuable "either for his own sake or for the sake of the republic" should be the one to survive. With this response, the questioner raises a final point: What if the two wise men are equally valuable? Here, Hecaton can only concede that the result must simply be left to fate.

The steady onslaught of questions is aimed at dismantling Hecaton's assured Stoic method. It is an attempt to push the philosopher into an aporia. Curiosity is the propempticon to morality. The issues raised are highly reminiscent of the critiques lodged by the Academic skeptic Carneades, who notoriously debated with Chrysippus, the great explicator of the foundational Stoic doctrines of Zeno of Citium.[11] Cicero introduces this material as part of his general illustration of "justice" (*iustitia*), a legalistic notion that should demonstrate how any conflict between what is morally upright (*honestum*) and what is expedient (*utile*) is merely apparent. That is to say, a correct understanding of justice would reveal that true expediency is always in accord with moral rectitude. Yet Hecaton's final concession, which leaves the matter entirely to fate, cannot be applied to Stoic ideas of "appropriate action" (*oikeiōsis*), insofar as life itself is here treated as an "indifferent" (*adiaphoron*), that is, as an issue where morality is indeterminable. The conclusion only weakly supports the primary Stoic precept that virtue should not be compromised by the threat of death, that reason should not falter before the impulse of self-preservation.[12]

Without moving further into the intricacies of Stoic argument and evaluations, it is sufficient here to note that the emergency situation upon the high seas broaches serious moral problems, and also occasions philosophical positionings. Standard principles of utility, rights, and virtue, which orient behavior on land, are here rigorously challenged and forced into contradiction. Upon the waves, the issue of bare life—the spontaneous, animal drive for the simple *conservatio vitae*—can no longer be consigned to an earlier stage of philosophical development and must instead become a problem of pressing concern. Skeptics, therefore, love the ocean; but Stoics, too, can take advantage of nautical difficulties. The impasses can give rise to discovering new passages; *aporiae*

---

[10] See Dyck, *A Commentary on Cicero's De officiis*, 613. The principle of prior possession is attributed to Chrysippus, as reported by Cicero in *De finibus* 3.67–68.

[11] On the attribution of this kind of questioning to Carneades, see Malcom Schofield's chapter, "Morality and the Law: The Case of Diogenes of Babylon," in his *Saving the City: Philosopher Kings and Other Classical Paradigms*, 140–54.

[12] For a general account of these principles, see Nicholas White, "The Basis of Stoic Ethics."

may lead to fresh *poroi*. According to Diogenes Laertius (7.1.2), it was a ship-wreck that first led Zeno to pursue a philosophical life.

Traditionally, the laws that apply on land have difficulty being held at sea. Saving oneself at another's expense may be morally reprehensible and unjust, yet it is less clearly *criminal*. In other words, individual survival would appear to fall under the lawless law of necessity, under the canonical maxim that "necessity has no law" (*necessitas non habet legem*). Giorgio Agamben employs this precept in order to emphasize the paradoxical nature of the "state of exception." If necessity has no law, then two alternate juridical problems invariably emerge concerning the exception: on the one hand, the exception becomes "the legal form of what cannot have a legal form"; and on the other hand, the exception is revealed as "the relation that binds and, at the same time, abandons the living being to law."[13] As already noted, it is life itself, biological survival, that becomes an issue. And indeed the biopolitical implications of these tensions are never far from Agamben's considerations.

The core issue for Agamben's analysis is how the paradox of the included exclusion of bare life is historically transformed into a "technique of government," how the law is used to suspend the law and thereby allow the absorption of the legislative body into the executive.[14] The argument eventually turns to the Roman institution of *iustitium*, which named a suspension of the law courts or a juridical holiday. Agamben's primary source is a study by Adolph Nissen, *Das Iustitium* (1877), which cites Cicero's sixth *Philippic* where the statesman reiterates the need for closing the courts so as to deal fully against Mark Antony without any legal restrictions (*Phil.* 6.2). One is reminded of Cicero's legal problems in the aftermath of the Catiline affair. Here, with Cicero's reasoning, Antony would have no legal recourse to protection. Should he seek justice (*iustitia*)—like the Stoic Hecaton in the *De officiis* passage above—he would discover only that justice has come to a standstill (*iustitium*).[15] He would be tossed upon the seas of unlimited power, losing his life to the *aporia* caused by the exception. The laws that would provide safe harbor would no longer apply, because the gravity of the situation calls for the *necessary* removal of these constraints.

Immanuel Kant specifies the aporetic nature of the state of exception as the confusion of moral and juridical issues. Tellingly, in a passage not cited by Agamben, when he comes to cite the maxim *necessitas non habet legem*, Kant offers the example of the shipwreck:

> There can be no *penal law* that would assign the death penalty to someone in a shipwreck who, in order to save his own life, shoves another, whose life is equally in danger, off a plank on which he had saved himself. For the punishment threatened by the law could not be greater than the loss of his own

[13] Giorgio Agamben, *State of Exception*, 1. As Agamben subsequently shows, the maxim *necessitas non habet legem* may be found twice in Gratian's *Decretum*. For Agamben's analysis, see 24–26.
[14] Agamben, *State of Exception*, 2.
[15] See Agamben, *State of Exception*, 41.

life. A penal law of this sort could not have the effect intended, since a threat of an ill that is still *uncertain* (death by a judicial verdict) cannot outweigh the fear of an ill that is *certain* (drowning). Hence the deed of saving one's life by violence is not to be judged inculpable [*inculpabile*] but only unpunishable [*impunibile*], and by a strange confusion jurists take this *subjective* impunity to be objective impunity (conformity with law).[16]

Kant summons the lawlessness of necessity in order to convert the moral dilemma into a legal aporia, an impasse for legislators and therefore a source of confusion for jurists. For this reason, as Kant explains, objective law can never regulate subjective action. It is a notion that is analogous to Agamben's opening claim that a "political fact" is irreducible to the legal system. The shore represents the border between the clarity of moral-legal regulations and the baffling deregulation under the force of necessity. At sea, where the law's reach is suspended, charges of criminality or injustice cannot apply, no matter how immoral the acts may be.

To be sure, casuistry may just as well contaminate the soundness of judgments made on land. The beach stages problematic episodes especially when moral sanctions are sought for remaining inactive before witnessed emergencies like a shipwreck viewed from the shore. Can the decision to do nothing, to refrain from assisting another in danger, ever be morally justified? Is the concern for one's personal existential safety capable of allowing dispensation from acting virtuously? Here, the impulse of self-preservation is not spurred by the exceptional situation at sea but rather emerges upon the security of the land. Terra firma, which provides stability and comfort, may also entail a cold rigidity that has to do less with the suspension of the law and more with the degeneration of law into an inhuman mechanism. Here the heterogeneity of the moral and the legal, broached by Kant, is even further pronounced. Security on land may lead to inaction, which is as morally culpable as the violent acts committed through the insecurity of the sea.

This negative view is certainly valid, yet it does not exclude the converse. Although the exception may thus be used as a nefarious technique for encompassing bare life, it may just as well supply the gap in legalism through which the law can be reanimated, perhaps enabling a transition from "biopower" to what Roberto Esposito ordains as "biopotentiality" (*biopotenza*, as opposed to *biopotere*)—"a biopolitics that is finally affirmative. No longer over life but of life, one that doesn't superimpose already constituted (and by now destitute) categories of modern politics on life, but rather inscribes the innovative power of life rethought in all its complexity and articulation in the same politics."[17] The law's porosity may be the only means for preventing it from stiffening into cold mechanicity.

[16] Immanuel Kant, *The Metaphysics of Morals*, 28 [*Die Metaphysik der Sitten* (1797) in *Gesammelte Schriften*, 6: 235–36].
[17] Esposito, *Bios: Biopolitics and Philosophy*, 157 [*Bíos: Biopolitica e filosofia*, 172].

Ebb and Flow

It is precisely with this revitalizing purpose that Niccolò Machiavelli metaphorically abandons the safety of the shore in commencing his *Discourses* on Livy (ca. 1517):

> Although the envious nature of men, so prompt to blame and so slow to praise, makes the discovery and introduction of any new principles and systems as dangerous [*periculoso*] almost as the exploration of unknown seas and continents, yet, animated by that desire which impels me to do what may prove for the common benefit of all, I have resolved to enter through a route [*per una via*], which has not yet been followed by any one, and may prove difficult and troublesome, but may also bring me some reward in the approbation of those who will kindly appreciate my efforts.[18]

Machiavelli was well acquainted with the thrill and the lucrative promise of sea exploration. While still a young man at work in the Florentine Chancery, he shared an office with Agostino Vespucci, a cousin of Amerigo, whose recent discoveries redounded to the city's glory. For the political theorist, the resonant metaphor of a fresh, difficult, uncharted sea journey announces above all a *historical* consideration. Through a reading of Livy, Machiavelli aims to liberate political thought from universalist (nonhistorical) ideas of governance. Just as, in *The Prince (published posthumously* 1532*)*, the immorality of *virtù* challenges the moralist arguments for the legitimacy of hereditary monarchies, so here, in the *Discourses*, the necessity of time and temporal change disturbs customary, stabilized forms of civil order.[19] As Hannah Arendt reminds us, Machiavellian *virtù* includes the notion of virtuosity, an idea that responds to *fortuna* through impromptu performance and cunning know-how.[20] Contingent events, unforeseeable occurrences, and irreversible circumstances solicit performances that enable one to survive—as Odysseus was quick to learn—by abandoning accepted legal codes and reaching for whatever plank comes one's way.[21] Risk is the prerequisite for gain.

For this reason, Machiavelli spurns security as repose comfortably nestled within the confines of customary, perfectly legal institutions, which in fact eradicate the possibility of the political. "For the cause of disunion of republics is usually idleness and peace; the cause of union is fear and war" (*Disc.* 2.25.1).

---

[18] Niccolò Machiavelli, *Discourses on the First Ten Books of Titus Livius*, 1 (Introduction), in *The Prince and the Discourses*, 103 (translation slightly modified).

[19] Cf. J.G.A. Pocock, *The Machiavellian Moment: Florentine Political Thought and the Atlantic Republican Tradition*, 184.

[20] Arendt, "What Is Freedom?" 446.

[21] In *The Prince*, Machiavelli famously recommends that a leader "must have the mind so disposed that when it is needful to be otherwise, [he] may be able to change to the opposite qualities [and] act against faith, against charity, against humanity and against religion." *The Prince*, chap. 18, 65.

Discord cultivates alertness and introduces the conditions for civil engagement. Thus, he consistently follows the ancient Greek proverb: Ἀργία μήτηρ πάσης κακίας (Leisure is the mother of all evil), which likely stems from the Hippocratic corpus: "Idleness and lack of occupation seek out evil and are dragged toward it. Alertness, however, and exercise of the intellect bring with them something that helps to make life beautiful."[22] Machiavelli urges his readers to forsake the devil's playground of inactivity, which promotes complacency. He warns his readership of how civic incaution invariably leads to tyranny.[23] "Those are the best constituted bodies, and have the longest existence, which possess the intrinsic means of frequently renewing themselves, or such as obtain this renovation in consequence of some extrinsic accidents" (*Disc.* 3.1). Whereas Zeno begins his philosophical career upon reaching safe harbor, Machiavelli actively sets sail to save politics from philosophy. With his steady examination of ancient historiography, he courageously confronts the waves of envy and jealousy that aim to preserve the status quo by threatening to shipwreck any plot for governmental innovation.

According to Machiavelli, the envy invoked in the *Discourses'* opening sentence is symptomatic of the historical amnesia that results in idle indifference. The security thus achieved is baneful to the health of the republic, but this is not to say that Machiavelli disdained the *ataraxia* that accompanied historical research. Around the time of composing the *Discourses*, having suffered unspeakable torture and now banished from his home, he confessed to Francesco Vettori:

> I enter the ancient courts of the men of antiquity where affectionately received by them I pasture on that food that alone is mine and for which I was born, where I am not too timid to speak with them and ask them about the reasons for their actions; and they in their humanity answer me; and for four hours of time I feel no weariness, I forget every trouble, I do not fear poverty, death does not dismay me; I transfer all of myself into them.[24]

Through immersion in the ancients, Machiavelli suggests that the political problems of his day find important analogues in the strife that unworked the Roman Republic. However, the universalism that warrants his method of imitation should not be confused with an appeal to the universal or Catholic legalism proffered by the church. Machiavelli is writing precisely at that moment, instigated by the collapse of papal supremacy, when the notion of a world empire is ceding to a focus on the particular demands of the territorial state, when ecclesiastical dominance is yielding to civil power. Within this new secular framework, the only way to achieve security is by rejecting the security established by a supranational, religious system. Machiavelli approaches Livy like a

---

[22] Hippocrates, *Decorum* 1.7–10, in *Hippocrates*, 2: 278–79 (slightly modified).
[23] This point is analyzed at length in Ioannis Evrigenis, *Fear of Enemies and Collective Action*, 48–71.
[24] Letter dated December 10, 1513; cited in Sebastian de Grazia, *Machiavelli in Hell*, 26 (modified).

sea explorer because he is convinced that there can never be a noncontingent, universally accepted, moral basis for governance.

To dispense with the security of the church is not to disregard the desire for territorial security. Throughout the *Discourses*, Machiavelli repeatedly asserts the centrality of the latter. In the very first chapter, he emphasizes that the first cities were formed by dispersed inhabitants who desired "to live secure" (*vivere securi*), namely, to escape the dangers of external attacks (*Disc.* 1.1). It is the "prudent legislator" who, cognizant of his territory's specific vulnerabilities, lays the groundwork for "living securely" (*vivere sicuramente*, *Disc.* 1.2). Prudence, the capacity to anticipate peril—even to foresee the unforeseeable—is opposed to the dogmatic slumber that vicious tyrants inculcate; and it is in accord with prudence that the state's constitution should always remain open to reform and improvement. Herein lies the fundamental problem: a constitution is generally reformed only in time of danger; however this danger may destroy the state before it has a chance to adjust its laws. In order to prevent utter shipwreck, it is wise to acknowledge that none of the traditional forms of government—monarchy, aristocracy, and democracy—is ever absolutely perfect. Each model is prone to degeneration, an inevitable consequence of historical time and mankind's natural cupidity. Hence, Machiavelli sponsors a constitution that would allow all three forms, a supple system of checks and balances, which introduces stability precisely by resisting the stabilization of power. The "security of the people" (*sicurtà della Plebe*, *Disc.* 1.3) names the dynamic equilibrium that results from sustained antagonism, from a perpetual conflict among the classes. Thus, as Louis Althusser stresses, Machiavelli resorts to the "cyclical theory of history"—first broached by Polybius—as the only means for synthesizing the contradictory premise that informs his work: the immutability of the human condition, which itself is defined by inexhaustible mutability.[25]

Out of the ruins of papal supremacy, Machiavelli glimpses the import of the state's rising autocracy. Whereas in one sense we are dealing with a somewhat straightforward, secularizing transfer of power, in another sense we are faced with an entirely novel understanding of security, one that is no longer founded on the timelessness of the law but instead on the lawlessness of time. In his reading of Machiavelli motivated by Althusser's lectures, Michael Dillon adumbrates an idea of "factical freedom," which embraces the "freedom of the event" implied by the instability of human temporality. For Dillon, the Machiavellian moment consists precisely in this factical freedom, which should be distinguished from negative modes ("freedom from") as well as from positive modes ("freedom to"). The central role of *fortuna* in *The Prince* points to a "freedom for"—a freedom for assuming our "thrownness into time without law in order to bring law to time."[26] The perilous tranquillity of idleness results from neglect-

[25] Louis Althusser, *Machiavelli and Us*, 34–35.

[26] Michael Dillon, "Lethal Freedom: Divine Violence and the Machiavellian Moment."

ing this freedom, which constitutes the core force of *virtù*. In the end, Machiavellian time can be understood only as strategical, reading "the heterogeneous signs of the times in order to fashion timely interventions in the course of time, continuously seeking to secure itself against all the changing correlation of forces which distinguish the changing nature of the times."[27]

It is, indeed, at this moment, on the eve of the Reformation, when the European states began to cultivate a paradigm of security that would come to organize political thought for centuries to follow. Like islands scattered across the inhabitable main, each state would assume its sovereignty designed to protect its shores from without. Thus granted with nearly unlimited legitimacy, the newly configured political authority abandons traditional criteria of natural law: for the sake of the regime's security—and, concomitantly, the security of the populace—utility, expediency, and efficiency must trump morality. No longer subordinated to the universalizing claims of either the church or the empire, with the weakening of any supranational system, each particular state maintained a demand for safety as an end in itself and thereby justified whatever measures might be necessary to pursue that mandate. It is at this moment that security began to serve more forcefully than ever as a euphemism for base power. Consequently, as Machiavelli would recommend, the only means for ensuring against a slippage into tyranny was to direct the lessons of external contingency within, to check and balance the insular power by retaining the freedom for change. The true peril, therefore, would be when the regime forgets or ignores the fact that its dominion floats upon the unmanageable, incalculable sea of history.

[27] Dillon, "Lethal Violence."

Lingua Homini Lupus

SAFE AND SECURE IN THE ACADÉMIE

> Philology is that venerable art which demands of its devoted
> followers this above all—to step to one side, to take one's time, to
> become silent, to become slow—as a goldsmith's art and connois-
> seurship of the *word* which has to apply purely nice, cautious work
> and attains nothing if it does not attain it *lento*.
>
> Friedrich Nietzsche, *Daybreak*

CLAUDE FAVRE DE VAUGELAS, the seventeenth-century grammarian and one of the founding members of the Académie Française, was long reputed for his slowness. It was his colleague Vincent Voiture, who, broaching the topic of language change, likened Vaugelas to the exceedingly careful barber described in one of Martial's epigrams:

> *Eutrapelus tonsor dum circuit ora Luperci,*
> *Expungitque genas, altera barba subit.*
>
> (*Epigrams* 7.83)[1]

As the barber Eutrapelus goes round Lupercus' face,
And smooths the cheeks, another beard springs up.

To explain the allusion, Voiture concisely and despairingly adds *altera lingua subit*—"Thus, another language springs up." Martial's hyperbole forcefully communicates Voiture's frustration: as Vaugelas studies the French language with his typically excessive patience and caution, day-to-day usage alters the object of study significantly, suddenly, and more or less unexpectedly—*subito*. The beastly nature of modern discourse, which is as hairy as the lupine face of Martial's Lupercus, continues to grow incessantly and uncontrollably every time someone opens his or her mouth. The tonsorial philologist can hardly keep up. The care that the grammarian devotes to his project is helpless before the fact

---

[1] Cited in Paul Pellisson, *Histoire de l'Académie Française*, 2 vols. (first edition: 1653; completed by the Abbé d'Olivet, 1700), 1: 237. Cf. Zygmunt Marzys's introduction to his edition of Vaugelas's *Remarques sur la langue françoise*, 7.

that the object of his attentions can never be secured. The infinite evolution of living language invariably reveals the fatal shortcomings of any linguistic description bent on totality. Analogous to the task of Sisyphus, the work of the language police can never be complete; it can never arrive at a clean finish. *Lingua homini lupus*—Language is a wolf to man.

Vaugelas no doubt realized that every subsequent, individual enunciation destroys the finitude of language. As a comparison of Vaugelas's copious manuscripts with the published 1647 version of his *Remarques de la langue françoise* would reveal, the lexicographer never shied away from emending his observations according to innovative trends in current discourse.[2] Throughout, his work is motivated by the tension between contemporary usage and the dictates of what he refers to as "reason." A rational method, as Vaugelas understood it, should judge the spoken language in relation to the usage employed by established authors (*nos bons Autheurs*) and would ultimately impose stringent restrictions on what words should or should not be allowed to enter into the French lexicon.[3] Specifically, the glossary should include but one word for each thing. Two words for the selfsame thing would only lead to confusion and uncertainty. Yet, admittedly, the progress of human history and the transformative qualities of experience at times require new words, which could serve as adequate expressions under ever-changing circumstances. Vaugelas cares about language not despite but precisely because of its capacity to spring up anew. As a matter of philological prudence, any and all conclusions would have to remain provisional.

A particularly interesting case is the term *sécurité*, an apparently fashionable neologism that Vaugelas had been hearing of late among the "ladies of the court."[4] To ascertain the meaning and connotation of this trendy buzzword, Vaugelas quits his eavesdropping and reverts instead to his trusty male Authors, citing two sentences from François de Malherbe, whose demand for lexical purity did not inhibit him from employing the new term. What is intriguing is that the two citations that Vaugelas selects present widely divergent connotations, one negative the other positive. The first example links *sécurité* with a sense of shamefulness and torpor: *N'avez-vous pas de honte de vous plonger en une sécurité aussi profonde que le dormir même?* (Do you not feel ashamed of immersing yourself in a security as deep as sleep itself?); while the second example associates the term with something agreeable: *Jamais la fin d'une crainte n'est si douce qu'une sécurité solide ne soit beaucoup plus agréable* (The cessation of fear is never so sweet that a sound security would not be much more pleas-

---

[2] For a comprehensive analysis of Vaugelas's manuscripts and the *Remarques*, see Wendy Ayres-Bennett, *Vaugelas and the Development of the French Language*, 3–12.

[3] Claude Favre de Vaugelas, *Remarques sur la langue françoise vtiles à ceux qui veulent bien parler et bien escrire*, iii–v.

[4] The earliest citation of *sécurité* given by Godefroy is from 1444; however, the term does not enter into broad circulation until the sixteenth century. Frédéric Godefroy, *Dictionnaire de l'ancienne langue française et tous ses dialectes du IX au XV siècle*, s.v. "securité."

ant). Thus, Vaugelas has chosen two distinct usages that together demonstrate the ambivalence and complexity of the concept *sécurité*. Judging from Vaugelas's examples, *sécurité* refers to a condition or mental state that should be either disparaged or lauded, likened either to shameful idleness or to a pleasing sense of stability and confidence.

Both quotations are in fact taken from Malherbe's translation of Seneca's treatise *De beneficiis*; and each has undergone some degree of emendation. The first, negative example is from a passage where Seneca sharply distinguishes Stoic practice, which "takes pleasure in bestowing benefits to others," from Epicurean pleasure, which indulges in "sluggish idleness" (*inertis otii*) and merely seeks a "freedom from care" (*securitatem*) that is "quite similar to sleep" (*Ben.* 4.13).[5] Here, for Seneca, Epicurean "security" or "peace of mind" (*tranquillitatem animi*) is nothing other than mental laziness, which dozes off like "worthless pale bodies stuffed with food and drink" (*cibis potionibusque ... corpora ignavia pallentia saginare*). Epicureans, he charges, are secure through surfeit, wallowing in complacency and self-interest. Stoics, on the contrary, are altruistic and are even willing to undertake "dangerous services" (*beneficia ... periculosa*), "provided that they remove others from dangers" (*dum alios periculis extrahant*). Whereas Epicureans take refuge and languish in the security of their gardens, Stoics courageously enter into the fray, ready to face perils for the sake of their neighbors.

Vaugelas's second example boldly reverses this negative evaluation of *securitas* by presenting an altogether favorable illustration of the concept. It comes from the sixth book of *De beneficiis*, from an extended passage where Seneca reproaches those who maliciously pray for another's harm simply so that they may have the opportunity to save them (*Ben.* 6.25–29). "It is wicked to thrust [someone] into the water in order that you may pull him out" (*Nequitia est ut extrahas mergere*, 6.26). As Seneca stresses, it is not a benefit if someone removes a burden that he himself has inflicted. It is morally perverse to wish someone ill, to want to place him in a dangerous situation, even though it is only desired as an opportunity for glorious deliverance. "Consider how much torture it is to have been in need [of help], even if I will have received it. ... The cessation of fear, however pleasing, is never more pleasant than sound and unshaken security [*solida et inconcussa securitas*]" (6.28).[6] Opposed to Epicurean *securitas*—a carefree condition that Seneca disdains as careless idleness—Stoic *securitas* is that "sound and unshaken" state that he elsewhere equates with the *beata vita*. Being rescued from the perilous waters represents a lesser species of

[5] Seneca's text reads *Vobis voluptas est inertis otii facere corpusculum et securitatem sopitis simillimam appetere*, which Malherbe renders as *C'est votre plaisir de vous accoutumer à ne rien faire, de vous plonger en une sécurité aussi profonde que le dormir même* (François de Malherbe, *Œuvres*, 2: 103). Apparently, it was Vaugelas who interpolated the element of "shame." Vaugelas, *Remarques*, 43.

[6] *Quantum tormentum existimas, etiam si accepero, eguisse? ... Nullius metus tam gratus est finis, ut non gratior sit solida et inconcussa securitas.* Malherbe's translation is found in *Œuvres*, 2: 197.

pleasure than the calm enjoyment of resting on "solid" ground, in security "undisturbed" (*inconcussa*).

Vaugelas's philological *discussion*, therefore, is perfectly willing to shake things up. His carefully selected passages from Malherbe's Seneca translation desecure the sense of *securitas*, which is here presented in all the ambivalence that has haunted the term since the Roman imperial period. As we have seen, for the most part Seneca follows Cicero in regarding *securitas* positively and favorably, as a moral philosophical term that reflects the Stoic ideals of magnanimity, constancy, and good judgment in accordance with nature. For Seneca, nothing in this life, which is beset by contingency, can be enjoyable unless one has acquired the "freedom from care" that comes with spiritual exercises and prolonged contemplation, "for in them is *securitas*, without which nothing is pleasant [*iucundum*]" (*Ep.* 20.12). Elsewhere, however, Seneca expresses misgivings regarding *securitas* by associating it closely with idleness and negligence. We recall another passage from *De beneficiis*, not cited by Vaugelas, where Seneca praises the difficulty of philosophical questions, for "these, which appear subtle and tricky [*callida et insidiosa*], remove carelessness [*securitatem*] and laziness [*segnitiam*] from our thinking" (*Ben.* 5.12). Here, the "care of the self" (*cura sui*) needed for the attainment of blessed *securitas* clearly can never be relaxed, lest security degenerate into gluttonous complacency and torpor. Yet, how might this statement be reconciled with the previously quoted line that recommends the unconditioned pleasure of an *inconcussa securitas*? In Seneca, *security* apparently names both the highest ideal and the gravest error.

For Vaugelas, it is precisely the irresolvable ambivalence of *sécurité*—its vacillating nuances and contradictory values—that argues for its necessary inclusion in the French lexicon. Many of his seventeenth-century contemporaries would disagree, although for different reasons. In their view, the problem with this recently introduced term was due less to problems of ambiguity and more to the fact that the French tongue already had recourse to *sûreté*, a word that is also derived from the Latin *securitas* and therefore presumably designates the very same condition of safety or being protected. Why, then, would it be necessary to have both *sécurité* and *sûreté*? Dismissing this etymological argument, Vaugelas's careful ear hears a crucial difference: "I foresee that this word [*sécurité*] will one day be of great use, because it perfectly expresses that assured confidence [*confiance asseurée*] that we can only express by this word."[7] Vaugelas goes on to claim that *sécurité* names "something different than *seureté*, *asseurance*, and *confiance*, though it seems to come close to *confiance*, and that *sécurité* means a sure or assured confidence [*confiance suere ou asseurée*], or even a confidence that one believes to be sure, even when it may not be." For Vaugelas, even though *sûreté* and *sécurité* are modern variants of the single Latin term *securitas*, there is now a semantic nuance that differentiates them

---

[7] Vaugelas, *Remarques*, 43.

enough to warrant the inclusion of both terms. To put it simply, if *sûreté* names a condition of being, *sécurité* denotes a condition of belief. The former is ontological, offering a statement of objective fact, whereas the latter expresses a merely subjective—and therefore potentially false—assumption. According to Vaugelas, the sense of *sécurité* is therefore unique and must not be confused with *sûreté*. The fact of stability that *sûreté* expresses cannot cover the supposition of stability, especially amid the fact of instability.

From the perspective of modern English, we could easily clarify Vaugelas's argument by identifying the relation between *sûreté* and *sécurité* roughly as the difference between the English *safety* and *security*; for indeed, *sûreté* is conventionally and consistently translated into English as *safety*. Derived from the Latin *salvus* (in good health, unharmed), *safety* denotes the concrete fact of being removed from danger, whereas *security* merely denotes the presumption that one is safe, whether this be true or not. This distinction fairly corresponds to the way Vaugelas differentiates *sécurité* and *sûreté*. The difference moreover, is not absent from the history of the French language. Dictionaries attest the archaic *sauveté* (from *salvus*), which was employed from the twelfth to the fifteenth century and which gave us the English *safety*. However, by Vaugelas's seventeenth century, *sauveté* had become obsolete, its meanings almost entirely assumed by *sûreté*. In modern French, *salvus* can still be heard in the verb *sauver* (to save, to rescue) and related terms like *salubre* (healthy), *sauf* (safe), and *salut*, the word for religious "salvation" as well as the common greeting (from the Latin imperative *salve*); yet the condition of being safe is now sufficiently covered by the substantive *sûreté*. Without having recourse to the obsolete *sauveté*, Vaugelas is altogether prescient in insisting on the unique sense of *sécurité*, while many of his contemporaries and near contemporaries refused to acknowledge what they believed to be but a negligible difference. Other modern languages do in fact elide the safety-security distinction altogether: German *Sicherheit*, Italian *sicurezza*, Spanish *seguridad*, and Russian безопасность are all employed to denote both general meanings. These terms' semantic coverage would reinforce the position of Vaugelas's opponents, namely that there is hardly a conceptual distinction between "safety" and "security," or that there is sufficient semantic overlap to sanction the use of a single term.

Although Vaugelas does not press the issue any further, any number of historical conjectures could be made as to why *sécurité* emerged alongside *sûreté* precisely in the middle of the seventeenth century and, perhaps concomitantly, why the archaic *sauveté* was deemed to be no longer useful or adequate. The age, which—as Grimmelshausen's *Simplicissimus* described it in 1669—many believed to be the last, was terrifyingly unstable.[8] One might refer to the deeply fraught religious and political crises that marred Europe's collective mentality: the ravages of the Thirty Years' War, the violent revolts against Spanish hege-

---

[8] Hans Jacob Christoffel von Grimmelshausen, *Simplicissimus Teutsch* (1669), 17.

mony from the Low Countries to Sicily, civil war in England, anarchy in Poland, massive riots in Russia, peasant uprisings in Switzerland. Moreover, one could allude to the ongoing drive toward secularization, especially in the New Science, where the repose of certainty (*sûreté*) came to be regarded as inimical to the spirit of experimentation, where any eschatological notion of salvation (*sauveté*) would simply be considered irrelevant. The popularity of the word *sécurité*, with its inherent ambivalence, would seem to correspond to the general unease that rendered any statement of surety questionable.

Centuries later, in the tense year of 1939, for his inaugural lecture before the Prussian Academy of Sciences in Berlin, the Romance philologist and war veteran Emil Winkler opened his reflections on the word *sécurité* by citing Vaugelas's prediction ("I foresee that one day this word will be of great use . . .") and commenting that this prophecy was "much more fateful [*schicksalsreicher*] than he [Vaugelas] could have guessed."[9] Thus, a scholar faced with the inevitability of fresh war instinctively reverts to the European devastation evoked by the year 1647. In the horrific days of the destruction, poverty, and lawlessness that marked the last phase of the Thirty Years' War, the philologist senses a "fateful" foreshadowing of fresh devastation. It is in times of great insecurity that *security* itself demands urgent and careful consideration.

When we follow Vaugelas's recommendation and turn to classical Latin usage, the differences between "security" and "safety" reveal a political relevance. As already mentioned, in the late Roman Republic, the Latin term that best corresponds to a modern sense of military or political security—that is, protection from external or internal threats to the state, territory, or populace—is the noun *salus* (related to *salvus*); *securitas*, at this time, refers primarily to an internal, emotional state. That is to say, up until Augustus's accession, political-civil safety was neatly distinguished from psychological tranquillity. The term *salus* is derived from the root *sar/*sal "guard" and is therefore related to common words like *servare* (to save, deliver, protect) and *servus* (servant, slave), that is, the one who attends to these tasks. Included among the connotations of *salus* is a sense of wholeness and intactness, which is heard in other related terms such as *salvus* (saved, unharmed) and *sollus* (whole, entire, unbroken [cognate with the Greek *holos*]). What is guarded is specifically a well-defined totality, a unified Roman *populus* as opposed to a dispersed and unconnected *multitudo*. According to Julius Caesar, it is through this ideal of unity that Rome derived its indomitable strength and allowed it to prevail against the Gauls, who were characterized from the very first sentence of the general's account as being "divided into three parts," both tribally and linguistically (*Bellum Gallicum* 1.1).[10]

[9] Emil Winkler, "Sécurité," 2.

[10] Catherine Torigian analyzes the military ramifications of Caesar's opening description of the Gauls (*Gallia est omnis divisa in partes tres*), which is consistently contrasted against Roman integrity. "The Λόγος of Caesar's *Bellum Gallicum*, especially as Revealed in Its First Five Chapters," in *Julius Caesar as Artful Reporter*, 45–60.

Thus, when the individual, territorial or civil wholeness is threatened, the worried concern is precisely denoted as *sollicitudo*, which literally describes a condition where the "whole" (*sollus*) has been "shaken" (*citus*).

The disquieting solicitude that battered Roman spirits through decades of civil wars was ultimately addressed by Caesar, who assumed sole responsibility for healing division and restoring wholeness. Yet, for the statesman Cicero, the dictatorship, which essentially exiled him from the Forum, spelled a fresh concern, namely the breakdown of republican values. Ciceronian *securitas* is consequently first and foremost the "peace of mind" (*tranquillitas animi*) that would neutralize the political threat. Faced with a loss of political power, suffering from the anxiety (*cura*) for the health of the Republic and for his own public role, Cicero turned to moral philosophy, to the private cultivation of *securitas* as the "blessed life" that might sustain the orator in times of profound crisis.[11] The rhetoric of the late essays is consistent: no longer capable of actively contributing to the *salus populi*, Cicero opts to enter the *vita contemplativa* and simply take care of himself (*cura sui*).

Vaugelas's France of 1647—on the cusp of its own civil war with the emergence of the Fronde parlementaire—immediately points to similarities with the last days of the Roman Republic. The distinction between military safety (*sûreté*) and psychological *sécurité*, therefore, would speak well to the varying aspects of mid-seventeenth-century life. Still, Vaugelas's contemporaries were at first unwilling to distinguish safety from security. In the decades that followed Vaugelas's *Remarques*, a significant number of grammarians would continue to weigh in on the matter. In 1651, for example, Scipion Dupleix's grand project to "purify" modern French stressed the fact that the term *sécurité* is simply a variant spelling of *sûreté* and that both words in fact refer to the same concept. Thus, because *sûreté* had already been properly "nationalized" by modern rules of orthography, Dupleix saw no reason whatsoever to muddy the current lexicon with a superfluous term. The lawyer Olivier Patru concurred: *Ce mot [sécurité] à mon avis n'est pas françois* (In my opinion, this word [*sécurité*] is not French).[12] And so, the academic debate continued in face of the ever-increasing popularity of the word.

Toward the century's end, when it was no longer possible to ignore the fact of the word's widespread usage, lexicographers began to deploy Vaugelas's remark and make the subtle but decisive distinction that governs today's usage: *sûreté* is when you believe you are safe and you really are; *sécurité* is when you believe you are safe, but you may in fact not be. In his *Éclaircissement sur le Livre de la vie monastique* (1688), Nicolas Andry accordingly spoke of "deceptive security" (*sécurité trompeuse*) and associated it with a "false peace" (*paix fausse*): "It is no longer a question whether this word [*sécurité*] is good; usage

---

[11] Cicero has his speaker Piso (a Peripatetic) identify *securitas* with the *beata vita* in *De finibus* 5.8.23.

[12] These assessments have been collected in Jeanne Streicher, *Commentaires sur les Remarques de Vaugelas*, 1: 91–92.

has established it so well that anyone having difficulty employing it would not be French. It does not signify the same thing as *seureté* or *asseurance*, it marks only the persuasion that one is in safety [*en seureté*]."[13] Within three decades, then, the word *sécurité* changed its status considerably: at first suspected of being non-French, it now served as a test to show whether a speaker was French enough to use it properly. Andry's remarks were finally confirmed by the Académie in an authoritative statement first published in 1705 and upheld both in the *Encyclopédie* of Diderot and D'Alembert and later in Emile Littré's magisterial dictionary of 1863:

> This word [*sécurité*] signifies an internal confidence, a tranquillity of the mind, well founded or not, in a situation where there could be something to fear, & it is in this sense that it differs from *seureté* which characterizes the state of someone who has nothing to fear.[14]

The distinction could be understood in at least two ways: first, in nearly perfect accordance with republican Latin usage, *sécurité* denotes a more subjective, psychological disposition, whereas *sûreté*, like the Latin *salus*, expresses a more objective, physical condition; second, *sécurité*, now regarded as an apparatus or an institution, addresses the emotional *causes* of fear, whereas *sûreté* deals with the fearful *effects* at hand.[15] As Jean Delumeau remarks: "The evolution of language has therefore pulled the two words derived from *securitas* in two different as well as complementary directions."[16]

Apart from all historical arguments, in adopting a rather fanciful, exceedingly Cratylist method, one could also suggest a purely lettristic basis for this key divergence. Whereas the word *sûreté*, in following the conventions of French orthography, exhibits the smooth disappearance of the intervocalic *c*, the word *sécurité* forces one to articulate the hard palatal consonant that disrupts the expression's easy flow. The hard *c*, of course, is the mark of *cura*—the concern, worry, or anxiety that *securitas* strives to eliminate. With *sûreté* this *cura* is almost entirely elided, surviving merely in the circumflex that notes its disappearance—here, in the judgment of the Académie, you believe you are safe and you really are; however, with *sécurité*, the troubling *cura* continues to impose its debilitating power, as the word performs an interruption at the roof of your mouth and creates a caesura, a slight but worrisome hiatus, which qualifies the pronouncement of safety. The bothersome *cura* is still to be heard, still in force: I believe I am secure, even when I know that I may in fact be in a frightfully dangerous situation. Thus, Antoine Furetière in his *Dictionnaire uni-*

[13] Cited in Streicher, *Commentaires*, 1: 92.
[14] Cited in Streicher, *Commentaires*, 1: 92.
[15] In his *Passions de l'âme* (1690), Descartes practically equates *sécurité* and *assurance* and regards them as a transformation of hope: "When hope is so strong that it chases fear away entirely, it changes its nature and is named *sécurité* or *assurance.*" René Descartes, *Œuvres et lettres*, 775–76.
[16] Jean Delumeau, *Rassurer et protéger: Le sentiment e sécurité dans l'Occident d'autrefois*, 12.

versel (published posthumously, 1690) regards *sécurité* as a particular species of *assurance*: "[*Sécurité*] is *assurance* in peril; the lack of fear. A brave man is intrepid amid danger, he remains calm [*tranquille*], as if he were in complete security [*en pleine sécurité*]. One admires the security of this man who cannot save himself [*qui ne se sauve point*], since he has many enemies and bad business dealings."[17] Security exists, even when salvation is lost.

As philologists, Vaugelas and his associates in the Academy express a concern with the whole of the lexicon. Yet, their holistic care for the language invariably becomes a *souci*—the word for anxious concern derived from the Latin *sollicitudo*—for it responds to discursive instances that unsettle the totality under their watch. While they patiently work as entrusted *servants* of the word, history moves forward. Language continues to change—*altera lingua subit*. The controversy regarding the term *sécurité*, therefore, involves the practice of philology itself, insofar as philology comes across as an enterprise that directly deals with a lexicon that can never be entirely fixed. However, the insecurability of language need not be understood as a cause of frustration. Rather, it could be the very basis for the philologist's resolve to approach every word *cum cura*.

Two Kingdoms

> The way to be safe is never to bee secure.
>
> Francis Quarles, *Enchyridion* (1641)

The ambivalent interpretations of security that course through Roman literature—interpretations that are themselves grounded in the shifting valuations of *cura*—accompanied the term's adoption and usage in seventeenth-century Europe. As argued above, Vaugelas's primary and ultimately decisive argument for the inclusion of *sécurité* into the French lexicon was based on the word's ambiguity, on its capacity to express a disjunction between belief and fact: *sécurité* is the feeling of being safe, well founded or not. To enjoy security while being truly out of harm's way is to benefit from a condition of being carefree; but to proceed securely without acknowledging imminent or already present dangers is to be either heroic or perilously careless.

For Vaugelas's compatriots and for their European neighbors, the divergent values of security, which characterized the emotional life of the individual, could be discerned in the age's transindividual institutions. Specifically, whereas political theory tended to sponsor a positive notion of security, theology gravitated toward a negative assessment. Throughout this century of war and religious strife, citizens would demand public security from their rulers, who came

---

[17] Antoine Furetière, *Dictionnaire universel* (1690), s.v. "securité."

more and more to be idealized as invincible protectors, while they would suspect and defy clerical authorities who promulgated the impossible promise of
spiritual security.[18] Martin Luther had already anticipated and ostensibly influenced this basic seventeenth-century split. In Luther's view, sovereign authorities were instituted by God to maintain justice, peace, and order in the world;
the security they provided, therefore, was to be appreciated as a divinely sanctioned good. In strictly theological matters, however, an individual's inner
sense of security should be disparaged as a sinful disposition, insofar as it
breeded self-confidence and idleness, causing one to forget humility, relax self-
vigilance, and neglect attentive study of scripture.

The divergent valuations of security in Luther's writings reflect the theologian's well-known division of "two kingdoms," which was first expressed in his
treatise *On Temporal Authority* (*Von weltlicher Obrigkeit*, 1523): "We must di-
vide the children of Adam and all mankind into *two classes*, the first belonging
to the kingdom of God, the second to the kingdom of the world."[19] Composed
just two years after his excommunication, the essay grappled with questions of
governmental power and its limitations. Whereas the papacy was intent on exercising authority in both spiritual and secular matters, Luther strove to keep
each realm rigorously separate, assigning to each "kingdom" its own areas of
executive rights and responsibilities. Within the secular sphere of quotidian
existence, the desire for security is legitimate; yet within the spiritual sphere of
religious life, security is damning.

The spiritual realm is primarily concerned with the salvation of a true Christian's soul. It combats evil by means of the Gospel through the workings of the
Holy Spirit and therefore never has recourse to mundane law or physical acts of
violence, which Luther, in an allusion to Paul's Epistle to the Romans 13, sum-
marizes under the heading of "sword." However, because the secular realm is
disorderly, sinful, and occupied by a majority that is non-Christian or only
nominally Christian, worldly sovereignty is compelled and sanctioned by God
to wield the sword so as to create and maintain security on earth.

> If this were not so, men would devour one another, seeing that the whole
> world is evil and that among thousands there is scarcely a single true Chris-
> tian. No one could support wife and child, feed himself, and serve God. The
> world would be reduced to chaos. For this reason God has ordained two
> governments: the spiritual, by which the Holy Spirit produces Christians
> and righteous people under Christ; and the temporal, which restrains the

---

[18] The point is compellingly made by Delumeau, *Rassurer et protéger*, 14.

[19] Martin Luther, *Von weltlicher Uberkeytt, wie weyt man yhr gehorsam schuldig sey*, in *Werke* (Weimarer Ausgabe [WA]), 11: 245–80; 249 [*On Temporal Authority: To What Extent It Should Be Obeyed*, in
Luther's Works, 45: 81–129]. The "two-kingdoms theory" was first proposed by Harald Diem in 1938, *Luthers Lehre von den zwei Reichen*. For further discussion, see Heinrich Bornkamm, *Luther's Doctrine of the
Two Kingdoms in the Context of His Theology*.

un-Christian and wicked so that—no thanks to them—they are obliged to keep still and to maintain an outward peace.[20]

With this pessimistic view of mankind's evil nature, Luther endorses civil authority that restores order and thereby protects the citizenry by means of disciplinary power. Because true Christianity is so rare in the world, the secular sword is necessary for taming human nature. The same sentiment is expressed in a later sermon from 1529:

> It is the function and honor of worldly government to make men out of wild beasts and to prevent men from becoming wild beasts. It protects a man's body so that no one may slay it; it protects a man's wife so that no one may seize and defile her; it protects a man's child, his daughter or son, so that no one may carry them away and steal them; it protects a man's house so that no one may break in and wreck things; it protects a man's fields and cattle and all his goods so that no one may attack, steal, plunder, or damage them. Protection of this sort does not exist among the beasts, and if it were not for worldly government there would be none of it among men either; they would surely cease to be men and become mere beasts.[21]

Fully in the tradition of man's innate wolfishness—*homo homini lupus*—Luther grants justification to a program of public security that was defined by Augustine as *tranquillitas ordinis* and was consistently promulgated throughout the Middle Ages.[22] Prayers for the protection of the Holy Empire, clearly derived from classical Roman formulae, enjoyed a lasting place in church liturgy from Merovingian times if not earlier. For example, in the Sacramentary attributed to fifth-century Pope Gelasius I, we find an *oratio secreta*, beseeching God that he "make the Roman borders secure from every enemy" (*Romanos fines ab omni hoste faciat esse securos*).[23] By consigning the office of public peace-keeping exclusively to secular sovereignty—to the *weltliche Obrigkeit*—that is, by denying the papal throne of its sword, Luther perpetuates a humanist position that perhaps finds its clearest expression in Dante (*De Monarchia*, ca. 1312) and Marsilius of Padua (*Defensor Pacis*, 1324). With his strict division between the two kingdoms, Luther essentially "renders unto Caesar what is Caesar's" and thereby, in his judgment, attends to Paul's admonition (in Luther's translation): *Eyn igliche seele sey der gewallt und uberkeyt unterthan, Denn es ist keyn gewallt on von Gott; die gewallt aber, die allenthalben ist, die ist von Gott verordnet* (Let every soul be subject to power and authority, for there is no power that is not of

---

[20] Luther WA 11: 251.

[21] Luther WA 30.2: 555–56.

[22] Augustine, *De civitate Dei* 19.13.

[23] Migne, *Patrologia Latina*, vol. 74 col. 1217. For discussion, see Werner Conze, "Sicherheit, Schutz," 5: 834.

God; rather the power, which is all around, is ordained by God, Rom. 13:1).[24] The force of this statement is further reinforced by a passage that Luther cites from the First Epistle of Peter. I again translate literally from Luther's rendering: "Subject yourselves to all human order, be it to the king as the noblest or to the ministers who have been sent by him to avenge evil and praise the pious" (1 Peter 2:13–14).[25]

It is therefore in accordance with the divine will that princes work to establish order within their realms, both by controlling internal conflicts and by addressing external threats. Public security, therefore, is ultimately a gift from God:

> God is love: everyone must see and grasp that if only he opens his eyes. For daily all his goods are there before your eyes wherever you look, the sun and moon and the entire heaven full of light, the earth full of foliage, grass, grain and all kinds of growth which has been given to you for nourishment; also one's father and mother, house and yard, peace, protection and security [*Sicherheit*] through the government of worldly authority [*durch weltlicher Oberkeit regiment*], and so forth.[26]

Security is a gift, insofar as it allows the Christian, who necessarily lives in a sinful world, to live without care about the safety of his person and property. This removal of worry "before one's neighbors"—*coram hominibus*—prepares the ground for a more crucial concern, namely the Christian's standing "before God"—*coram Deo*.

Now focusing on the soul's relation to salvation, the positive valuation of security is no longer viable but rather is replaced by clear disdain. When viewed through the perspective of the other, spiritual kingdom, the individual's inner sense of security would only be interpreted as symptomatic of a dangerously sinful pride. The final exhortation of Luther's Ninety-Five Theses tellingly reads: "And thus it is better that they trust to enter into heaven through many tribulations than through the security of peace" (*Ac sic magis per multas tribulationes intrare celum quam per securitatem pacis confidant*).[27] This closing proclamation alludes to a passage from the Acts of the Apostles, where, upon being stoned and left for dead at Lystra, Paul unexpectedly recovers, returns to

---

[24] Cited in Luther, *Von weltlicher Uberkeytt*, WA 11: 247. The translation that Luther prepared for this essay varies slightly from his Bible translation of 1534, which reads *Jedermann sei untertan der Obrigkeit, die Gewalt über ihn hat. Denn es ist keine Obrigkeit ohne von Gott; wo aber Obrigkeit ist, die ist von Gott verordnet* (Let every man be subject to the authority which has power over him. For there is no authority that is not of God; but where there is authority, it is ordained by God). The translation is noteworthy for its elision of the word "soul" and the telling reduction of the plural *exousiai* (authorities) to the singular *Obrigkeit*: Πᾶσα ψυχὴ ἐξουσίαις ὑπερεχούσαις ὑποτασσέσθω. οὐ γὰρ ἔστιν ἐξουσία εἰ μὴ ὑπὸ θεοῦ, αἱ δὲ οὖσαι ὑπὸ θεοῦ τεταγμέναι εἰσίν.

[25] Luther WA 11: 247.

[26] Luther WA 36: 429. The sermon is from 1532.

[27] Luther, *Disputatio pro declaratione virtutis indulgentiarum* (1517), WA 1: 238.

Antioch, and encourages his disciples: "We must go through many hardships to enter the kingdom of God" (Acts 14:22). This explicit, theological denigration of security can be found throughout Luther's writings and must be distinguished from its affirmation in regard to civil order. In moving from one *Reich* to the other, we are able to track a complete revaluation of the concept of *securitas*. "In the presence of men" (*coram hominibus*), security is a good; "in the presence of God" (*coram Deo*), it is decidedly an evil. A Christian could expect to be carefree in this world, but should never be careless concerning the next.

In Luther's assessment, security is sinful because it is connected either to a haughtiness based on being convinced of salvation or to a negligent attitude that fails to give proper attention to the Holy Word. *Nihil est pestilentius securitate* (Nothing is more pestilenial than security), because it expresses assurance in matters, like one's state of grace, where no assurance is granted.[28] In his Second Disputation against the Antinomians, Luther laments: "The security and presumption of these pestilential beasts is so great that they cannot be sufficiently confounded and crushed."[29] And this pride of self-assuredness invariably stems from a lack of hermeneutic *cura* regarding scripture: "Such impiety and security follow when the Word of God is neglected and not studied attentively. These men become atheists, Epicureans, and selfish lovers."[30] As in Cicero, the Latin concept of *securitas* is associated with Epicurean *ataraxia*, which is now, however, entirely disparaged for its godlessness. We have seen how the Stoic Seneca finds fault with Epicurean contentment. For the latter-day theologian and reformer, the removal of fear robs the soul of its one path to true salvation: *securitas enim tollit fidem et timorem Dei* (For security takes away faith and the fear of God).[31] As Bernardino of Siena recognized, fear is theologically expedient insofar as it breeds vigilance. In his explication of Psalm 68, Luther is especially clear: "There is no greater adversity than prosperity, no greater danger than no danger. The reason is because it makes men incautious [*incautos*]."[32] Luther makes allusion to a favorite passage from Paul's First Letter to the Thessalonians:

> While people are saying, "Peace and safety [*pax et securitas*]," destruction will come on them suddenly, as labor pains on a pregnant woman, and they will not escape. But you, brothers and sisters, are not in darkness so that this day should surprise you like a thief. You are all children of the light and children of the day. We do not belong to the night or to the darkness. So then, let us not be like others, who are asleep, but let us be awake and sober. For those who sleep, sleep at night, and those who get drunk, get drunk at

---

[28] Luther, WA 25: 331. See Schrimm-Heins, "Gewißheit und Sicherheit," 1: 207–12.
[29] Luther WA 39.1: 426; cited in Schrimm-Heins, "Gewißheit und Sicherheit," 1: 210.
[30] Luther WA 43: 417; cited in Schrimm-Heins, "Gewißheit und Sicherheit," 1: 210.
[31] Luther WA 39.1: 356.
[32] Luther WA 3: 424.

night. But since we belong to the day, let us be sober, putting on faith and love as a breastplate, and the hope of salvation [*spem salutis*] as a helmet. (1 Thess. 5:3–8)

Securitas as excessive self-confidence (and therefore self-deception) is detrimental to the salvific plan; it obstructs the expression of the "hope of salvation" (*spes salutis*), which can serve as effective armor precisely because it keeps the faithful awake and cautious. In other words, salvation (*salus*) becomes the primary *cura* of one's life, a *cura* that would be fatally relaxed by the privation implicit in *securitas*.

Lutheran warnings against the delusions of worldly security contribute forcefully to the general disposition of the baroque in the following century. Here, negligence and spiritual disregard characterize those too attached to earthly things. Dangerously worry free, they allow themselves to be drawn off the right path, blinded by that which is transient and empty, indifferent to the fact that this life is but a pilgrimage, a perilous exile fraught with evil temptations and vain hopes, an illusory dream, a vale of tears. The seventeenth-century poet Johann Michael Moscherosch typically combined Lutheran piety and German patriotism when he spoke out against the present-day decadence with its corrupt morals. His persistent attacks against what he saw as the effeminizing effects of Gallic civilization won him the sobriquet *Franzosenfresser* (gobbler of the French) for posterity. To remedy the age's tendency to sloth, to awaken his neighbors from the baneful sleep of security or carelessness, he composed a long treatise addressed directly to his children. Its title explicitly responds to the ill effects of removing care: *Insomnis cura parentum* (The Parents' Sleepless Concern, 1643). Throughout, he casts aspersions upon *die sichere Weltkinder* (the careless children of the world) and prays that his own offspring will never be lulled into false comfort:

> Lord Jesus Christ. For the smallest creature of your omnipotence, the ant, you have planted an earnestness and zeal in nature, that they may never become idle, but rather spend their time with diligent work. Pour into my children's hearts a desire to act right, and to be assiduous in all things that are not against you. Grant that they do not surrender themselves to leisure and indolence, nor make themselves unworthy and unfit for all the gifts and mercies that you show to mankind. Rouse up their hearts from the sleep of security [*vom Schlaff der Sicherheit*], so that they may busily and actively accomplish your holy will.[33]

Elsewhere, Moscherosch implores God to protect his children from "security and sacrilege, that they may not grow wild in wickedness" (*Behüte sie vor Sich-*

---

[33] Hans Michael Moscherosch, *Insomnis cura parentum* (1643), 60. The phrase *sichere Weltkinder* is found in Moscherosch's *Gesichte Philanders von Sittewald*, part 2 (1665), 265. For a general discussion, see K. G. Knight, "Johann Michael Moscherosch: An Early Baroque Satirist's View of Life."

erheit und Frevel, daß sie nicht erwilden in der Boßheit).[34] Somewhat audible in the verb *erwilden* (grow wild) is the force of the human *will*, which seduces individuals away from the vocations and duties ordained by God's "holy will." For the sake of the soul's eternal life, one prays that God's grace may keep one's earthly existence on the right path, that sinful drowsiness be held at bay, that one adheres to one's allotted work, like the smallest ant, carried out with pious industry. The father's insomniac care entreats his Lord that his children may never be without care, that, for as long as they live, they may be protected from security.

FUNDAMENTUM INCONCUSSUM

si curis domus anxia . . . (if your house is anxious with cares . . .)

Ausonius, *Ode* 7.2

In the West Frisian municipality of Franeker, the Sjaerdema Castle rested on a broad polder enclosed by a series of three dikes, which guarded the grounds from flooding. Although the castle was entirely demolished in 1727, the series of zeedijks still stand today, commonly known as the *wakende dijk*, the *slapende dijk* and the *dromende dijk*—the "waking dike" nearest the coast, then the "sleeping dike" and the "dreaming dike"—three lines of defense against the sea. For centuries this fortification system has safeguarded both the château and its inhabitants, including most famously René Descartes, who in 1639 composed a first draft of his *Meditationes de Prima Philosophia* here, thrice sheltered from the tides.[35] Far enough from the sea, yet close enough to be constantly aware of its menacing temper, the philosopher found an especially apt environment for seeking certainty and negotiating hyperbolic doubt. At the head of his second *Meditation*, Descartes offers a vivid description of his travails:

> The Meditation of yesterday filled my mind with so many doubts that it is no longer in my power to forget them. And yet I do not see in what manner [*qua ratione*] I can resolve them; and, just as if I had all of a sudden fallen into very deep water [*in profundum gurgitem*], I am so disconcerted [*turbatus*] that I can neither make certain of setting my feet on the bottom, nor can I swim and so support myself on the surface. (2.1)[36]

---

[34] Moscherosch, *Insomnis cura parentum*, 30.

[35] Cf. Richard Watson, *Cogito, Ergo Sum: The Life of René Descartes*, 24–25.

[36] The Latin text of 1641 reads *In tantas dubitationes hesterna meditatione conjectus sum, ut nequeam amplius earum oblivisci, nec videam tamen qua ratione solvendae sint; sed, tanquam in profundum gurgitem ex improviso delapsus, ita turbatus sum, ut nec possim in imo pedem figere, nec enatare ad summum;* and the French version, published in 1647, reads *La Méditation que je fis hier m'a rempli l'esprit de tant de doutes, qu'il n'est plus désormais en ma puissance de les oublier. Et cependant je ne vois pas de quelle façon je les pourrai résoudre; et comme si tout à coup j'étais tombé dans une eau très profonde, je suis tellement sur-*

Feeling his impotence before a deluge of doubts, the perturbed philosopher (*turbatus*) may be seeking security as Cicero defined it, namely as the "tranquillity of the soul" that comes with the removal of "every disturbance": *Vacandum autem omni est animi perturbatione* (There must be freedom from every disturbance of the soul, *Off.* 1.69). In the previous *Meditation*, Descartes claimed that his peaceful solitude should provide the ideal conditions for such an achievement. The original Latin is particularly resonant; I translate very literally:

> *Opportune igitur hodie mentem curis omnibus exsolvi, securum mihi otium procuravi, solus secedo, serio tandem & libere generali huic mearum opinionum eversioni vacabo.* (1.1)

> Today, therefore, having opportunely delivered my mind from all cares, having procured for myself secure leisure, I retire alone, and shall finally have time here, seriously and freely, for the general overthrow of my opinions.

Descartes's brief variation on the theme of *cura* is noteworthy: today is the day when his mind has been rid of "all cares" (*curis omnibus*), a riddance that corresponds to the procurement (*procuravi*) of "secure leisure" (*securum otium*). The accomplishment, moreover, amounts to an unburdening (*vacabo*) that explicitly relates to the Ciceronian prerequisite for security—*vacandum est. Cura* as "anxiety," "doubt" or "fear" has been duly discharged, "taken care of" (*procurare*), and *securitas* is clearly the result. All the same, it is Descartes's concern that removes his concern, which means, of course, that some kind of concern remains in place, like a "waking dike" that keeps the waters at bay but only by keeping the waters in constant sight. By the second *Meditation*, the philosopher plummets into an abyss of doubt, prepared to drown.

The only thing that can save him, the only life preserver of certainty that can keep him afloat in this sea of doubt, is the "thinking thing"—the *res cogitans*—that defines his self in contradistinction to a mere *sense* of self. "After having thought well about it, and having carefully [*soigneusement*] examined everything, one must then conclude and take as constant that the proposition: *I am, I exist*, is necessarily true" (*Med.* 2.3). In the second *Discourse on Method*, Descartes intensifies this careful approach by employing figures of demolition:

> It is true that we have no example of people demolishing all the houses in a town for the sole purpose of rebuilding them in a different way to make the streets more beautiful; but one does see many people knock down their own in order to rebuild them, and that even in some cases they have to do this because the houses are in danger of falling down and the foundations are insecure [*que les fondements n'en sont pas bien fermes*].[37]

---

pris, que je ne puis ni assurer mes pieds dans le fond, ni nager pour me soutenir au-dessus. René Descartes, *Méditations*, in *Œuvres et lettres*, 274.

[37] Descartes, *Discourse on Method and the Meditations*, 36–37 [*Œuvres et lettres*, 134].

No edifice is safe, no structure immune: everything is subject to inspection and condemnation, provocatively, in order to render the thinking mind secure. In the following *Discourse*, he speaks of his long journey of doubt: "My whole plan had for its aim assurance [*m'assurer*] and the rejection of shifting ground [*la terre mouvante*] and sand in order to find rock or clay."[38] Like Poseidon Asphaleios, the exemplary philosopher causes the ground of his mind's representations to quake. Method is figured as seismic activity.

Descartes's establishment of an "unshakeable foundation" (*fundamentum inconcussum*)—the self-possessive *cogito* of free will—is commonly understood as a result of the philosopher's willful isolation, his decided withdrawal from the political and social fray that defined his age. Certitude by any means—authority, sensory knowledge, or reason—may be forever uncertain, but at least there is the security that dispels the single doubt that the doubting subject is indeed a thinking subject. On this basis, Franz-Xaver Kaufmann singles out the Reformation and its philosophical-theological aftermath to support his general thesis, cited above, namely that Reformation marks the crucial moment when "certitude" as an "external stabilization" is replaced by a subject-centered "security" understood limitedly as an "internal stabilization."[39] Like Cicero at Tusculum, Descartes makes his key discovery against the backdrop of an unstable world from which he has fled.

Yet, also like Cicero, the achievement of security in the face of certainty's failure is meaningless without the community in which the *cogito* remains embedded. Timothy Reiss has persuasively demonstrated how Descartes's foundation can be understood only within the thinker's immediate historical context.[40] It is noteworthy that Descartes, in the autobiographical account given in the *Discourse on Method* (1637), frames his great discovery with references to events leading to the outbreak of the Thirty Years' War in 1619:

> I was, at that time, in Germany, whither the wars, which have not yet finished there, had called me, and as I was returning from the coronation of the Emperor to join the army, the onset of winter held me up in quarters in which, finding no company to distract me, and having, fortunately, no cares [*soins*] or passions to disturb me, I spent the whole day shut up in a stove-heated room [*proêle*], where I had complete leisure to meditate on my own thoughts. (*Disc.* 2)[41]

The event that Descartes witnessed was the coronation of Ferdinand of Spain whose militant Catholicism spurred Protestants in Bohemia to offer the crown to Frederick V, the Elector Palatine. The harsh winter that detained Descartes in

---

[38] Descartes, *Discourse on Method*, 50 [*Œuvres et lettres*, 145].

[39] Franz-Xaver Kaufmann, *Sicherheit als soziologisches und sozialpolitisches Problem*, 25.

[40] Timothy Reiss, *Mirages of the Selfe: Patterns of Personhood in Ancient and Early Modern Europe*, 488–518.

[41] Descartes, *Discourse on Method*, 35 (slightly modified) [*Œuvres et lettres*, 132].

Germany is the selfsame season that defined Frederick, known for posterity as the "Winter King," which refers to the brief duration of his Bohemian reign. Such was the turmoil that triggered the Thirty Years' War, which caused Descartes to take refuge and, as his letters repeatedly show, would continue to rage behind the scenes of his philosophical project. Reiss therefore surmises "that during the winter of the *Discourse*, the instability of the sociopolitical situation, in 1637 no less than in 1619–20, at the very beginning of his original thinking, could be seen only as a counter to the stability desired of Method."[42] The maelstrom from which the philosopher sought salvation could therefore serve as a figure for the dogmatic battles among the various confessional factions.

According to the biographical tradition, above all in Adrien Baillet's *Vie de Monsieur Des-Cartes* (1691), the German *proêle* where the philosopher sat out the winter of 1619 was the site of the series of three life-changing dreams. Descartes apparently recorded the dreams, which he purportedly regarded as divine revelation and the source of his novel method. Unfortunately, the only extant account is from Baillet.[43] The first two dreams were terrifying—ghosts, gusts of wind, an inability to walk upright, and a deafening thunderclap—but the final vision was altogether pleasant. Rather than indulge in a full reading, I would simply like to focus on a single detail: midway through this last dream, Descartes comes upon an anthology of poems, which he opens at random; his eyes immediately fall on the line: *Quod vitae sectabor iter?* (What road in life shall I follow?). Reminiscent of the famous sortilegium that catalyzed Augustine's conversion, this scene not only marks a new beginning for the thinker but also heralds a new age of security. The verse opens the second *Eclogue* of Ausonius, the fourth-century Latin poet who was born in ancient Bordeaux (Burdigala):

> *Quod vitae sectabor iter, si plena tumultu*
> *sunt fora, si curis domus anxia, si peregrinos*
> *cura domus sequitur, mercantem si nova semper*
> *damna manent, cessare vetat si turpis egestas*
> *si vexat labor agricolam, mare naufragus horror*
> *infamat*
>
> (*Ecl.* 2.1–6)

> What road in life shall I follow, if the courts are full
> of tumult, if the home is anxious with cares, if care of home
> pursues travelers, if fresh damages always attend
> the merchant, if foul poverty forbids rest
> if toil troubles the farmer, if the horror of shipwreck
> defames the sea

---

[42] Timothy Reiss, "Descartes, the Palatinate, and the Thirty Years War: Political Theory and Political Practice," 113. This article is an earlier version of the chapter revised for *Mirages of the Selfe*, 488–51.

[43] For a full description and analysis, see Alice Browne, "Descartes's Dreams."

The nagging concerns compel the search for the right road. Cares motivate the discovery of a secure, unassailable method. Among the *curae* listed in Ausonius's lament, the threat of shipwreck is perhaps most intense.

In Descartes's day, the sea continued to serve as the site for any number of religious, moral, and legal dilemmas. Needless to say, the conflation of these three major areas of concern reached a boiling point in the seventeenth-century war and would not cool down until the signing of the Peace Treaty between the Holy Roman Emperor and the King of France and Their Respective Allies in October 1648. As this Peace of Westphalia makes clear, the means for establishing security among the European states was a refreshed insistence on *territorial* sovereignty—a reassertion of landed existence that had now been rescued from the stormy tides of horrific conflict. This climate was directly anticipated in the political theories of Jean Bodin, who aimed to shield state sovereignty from confessional clashes, and Hugo Grotius, whose treatise *Mare liberum* (1609) called for preserving the sea as a free space, which could reaffirm the landed property of the nation. Subsequently, an analogous configuration would emerge in the work of Thomas Hobbes, whose Leviathan is specifically understood as a beast from the sea.

Descartes's philosophical quest to secure epistemology with provisional certainty, to excavate and build a *fundamentum inconcussum* upon solid ground, however slight, should be understood within the same political context. Starkly expressed, the presupposition—often quite explicit—of the emerging international system of sovereign states, where each should enjoy authority within its territorial limits, is that the state be regarded as a rational subject, as a *res cogitans*, as a unitary figure set upon the edge of turbulent waters. Upon land, this single entity—be it the individual subject or the sovereign nation—could rest somewhat assured in face of the conflicts that raged beyond the shored-in limits, where opposing religious doctrines or other, aggressive states were poised to crash in and potentially flood the ground. The "antient Security," which in some remote past had presumably been maintained by hierarchical structures of church and empire, would now, following the Great Schism, the fragmentation of principalities, and decades of devastating war, seem achievable only if the sovereign borders retained their definition in a more lateral relationship, if unity held out before roaring plurality. The history of every contemporary walled state, the plotting of every fortified barrier, from Israel to Arizona, is traceable to Westphalia, invariably linked to this threat to sovereign unity.[44]

---

[44] For a sustained critical analysis, see Wendy Brown, *Walled States, Waning Sovereignty*.

Repercussions

SOCIETAS CUM SECURITATE

GOTTFRIED WILHELM LEIBNIZ never shied away from complexities or difficulties. Born just two years before the signing of the Westphalian Peace, he would devote his philosophic and scientific career to harmonizing discordances and unifying disparities, calculating the otherwise incalculable and reconciling the seemingly unreconciliable. In brief, this exemplary optimist was determined to secure what had heretofore been deemed essentially insecurable. As the motto he suggested for Berlin's Society of Sciences demonstrates—*Theoria cum Praxi*—his indefatigable ambition to grapple with every problem, to deal with every enigma, and to reflect on every conundrum was consistently undertaken toward the improvement of human life, be it the stability of a political regime, the safety of the populace, or the health of the individual. From the transcendent perspective of his speculative capacities, Leibniz regarded all the crises that plagued humankind as interrelated: the competing systems and theories among the new scientists, not to mention their collective critiques of Aristotelian-Scholastic authority, were reflected in the confessional disputes that pitted Lutherans against Catholics, Calvinists against Lutherans, and Arminians against Calvinists and therefore perpetuated conflicts between the various towns, states, nations, dioceses, and principalities that composed the central European landscape. The treaties negotiated at Osnabrück and Münster might have quelled the excessive violence, but they hardly put an end to the ecclesiastical, political, and social disorder that would come to characterize the seventeenth century. Ecclesiastical schism and imperial fragmentation across the German states were but components of a general desecurement further intensified by accelerated urbanization, the opening of vast trade routes, and the formation of global empires. Very much a child of this postwar generation, of these exhilarating yet frightening times, Leibniz was destined to address the multifaceted pressures, challenges, and concerns that overburdened his age.[1]

[1] Cf. Maria Rosa Antognazza, *Leibniz: An Intellectual Biography*, 17–24.

Leibniz's vocation was not solely defined by altruism. In an early letter to Antoine Arnauld from 1670, he sincerely expresses his own private motives:

> Among so many distractions, I claim there is hardly anything toward which I have been inclined more ardently over the course of my life, however short, than restoring my security in the future [*quod me securum redderet de futura*], and I confess that this one thing has been by far the greatest cause of my philosophizing; truly, to win a prize not to be condemned—peace of mind [*quietem mentis*].[2]

Despite his staunchly Lutheran upbringing, Leibniz did not exhibit any misgivings concerning "security." Rather than mistrust security as self-deception or spiritual negligence, he seemed to follow in the tracks of his father, a professor of moral philosophy in Leipzig, and instead regard security in the Ciceronian and Senecan sense of "tranquillity," the ideal of bringing the mind to rest—*quies mentis*. However, whereas the Stoic tradition tended to understand *securitas* as an accomplishment, Leibniz here suggests that this prized possession is something lost and to be "restored" (*redderet*)—an enterprise more congruent with the Machiavellian concept of *riddure ai principii*, which aims to cure the state by returning to founding principles. Consequently, in terms of his "philosophizing," Leibniz vastly expanded the scope and aims of Descartes's security project. Whereas Cartesian method was restricted to problems of knowledge or "science," Leibniz employed the same premises—the unity of the human intellect and the truthfulness of God—to remedy inconsistencies in the realms of religion, morality, and politics as well. For Leibniz, Descartes's work marked a valuable contribution to the progress of thought but was, in the end, merely "an antechamber" to true philosophy—"l'antichambre de la Verité."[3] Descartes had discovered the right path but failed to pursue it to the end. Leibniz maintained that all of creation is attributable to a single, indivisible, infallible, universally valid spirit: from a theological perspective, it is God; yet in questions of knowledge, it is Reason; and in matters of action, individual or political, it is Justice. Thus, the universalizing thrust of Leibniz's thinking is of a piece both with his ecumenism and with his moral and political views. The Cartesian who rejects phenomena as false simply because they can be doubted lacks the courage to face conflicts that may arise within any aspect of human experience. Instead, Leibniz refused to be daunted by uncertainty. In this regard, he should be numbered among those seventeenth-century theoreticians of probability like Pierre de Fermat, Blaise Pascal, and Jakob Bernoulli, who strove to develop models of rational judgment and action in the face of grave uncertainty.[4] Moreover, for Leibniz, given the truthfulness of universal spirit and the incontrovertible ne-

---

[2] Gottfried Wilhelm Leibniz, *Sämtliche Schriften und Briefe*, II.1, 172.

[3] See Leibniz's letters to Christian Philipp (December 1679) and, much later, to Nicolas Rémond (January 10, 1714), in *Die philosophische Schriften von G. W. Leibniz*, 4: 282 and 3: 607, respectively.

[4] For a comprehensive, historical analysis of probability in relation to cognitive security, see Rüdiger

cessity of the Real, no problem could ever be considered forever incurable. Reason, Justice, and Truth are to be presupposed, despite the limitations of any individual mind.

Formally trained in jurisprudence, Leibniz developed early on a social theory, the core principle of which was a universal idea of Justice congruent with Reason and Truth. By means of his typically eclectic method, Leibniz garnered three axioms from Roman law, axioms that he understood as the basis for a just society, that is, for a society that aims toward establishing the general good: *neminem laedere* (to harm no one); *suum cuique tribuere* (to grant to each his own); and *honeste vivere* (to live honestly).[5] European peace would result only when every state fully respected these three simple principles of defense, equity, and piety, when particular national wills submitted to and harmonized with the aims of human civilization as a whole. From the perspective of Reason, therefore, perpetual peace was certainly possible, even if it remained highly improbable. For his entire career, Leibniz upheld the verity of his rational principles, while conceding, sadly, their unrealizability among men.

A year before his death, he composed a series of letters to the Abbé de Saint Pierre, member of the Académie Française, whose *Project for Perpetual Peace* (parts 1 and 2 published in Utrecht, 1713) had been submitted to Leibniz for review. The abbé's sincere desire for a European federation, for the reestablishment of a modified *Respublica Christiana*, within which independent sovereigns could coexist harmoniously, resonated forcefully with Leibniz's own vision:

> I read your excellent work with care. . . . Men lack only the will to deliver themselves from an infinity of evils. If five or six persons wanted to, they could end the great schism in the West, and put the Church in good order. A sovereign who really wants to can preserve his state from the plague. . . . A sovereign could also safeguard his state against famine. But, to bring about the end of wars, it would be necessary that another Henry IV, together with some great princes of his time, favor your project. The evil is that it is difficult to suggest it to great princes.[6]

According to the abbé, the security of peace would never be achieved by relying on treaties or some precarious balance of power. Instead, an international congress would be necessary, a supergovernment whose normative directives, reinforced by real military power, would alone be capable of maintaining rational order. "There will never be any sufficient security for the execution of treaties of

---

Campe, *Spiel der Wahrscheinlichkeit: Literatur und Berechnung zwischen Pascal und Kleist*. On Leibniz and his intellectual context, see especially Campe's fourth chapter, 103–25.

[5] These principles are explicitly outlined in Leibniz's preface to the 1700 ("Mantissa") supplement of his *Codex juris gentium diplomaticus*, in *Werke*, 6: 457–59. For further discussion, see Paul Schrecker, "Leibniz's Principles of International Justice."

[6] Letter to the Abbé de Saint Pierre (February 7, 1715), in Leibniz, *Political Writings*, 177.

peace and commerce in Europe, so long as the refuser cannot be constrained by a sufficient force to execute them."[7]

For Leibniz, the solution promised by the kind of federal union that the Abbé de Saint Pierre adumbrated—a governing body, which, as Leibniz indicates, had already been suggested in Henry IV's "Great Design"—was doomed to fail because of the fallibility of man in general. Peace would indeed be secured, if power could be indissolubly bound to Justice, but this was little more than a naïve wish persistently discredited by the vagaries of human history. The wills and desires of Europe's princes would continue to prevent the establishment of harmony and thereby mark the international landscape, as Hobbes would have it, as a state of nature, a savage realm plagued by the war of all against all: a "time wherein men live without other security than what their own strength and their own invention shall furnish them withal"; a time marked by "continual fear and danger of violent death," whereby "the life of man [is] solitary, poor, nasty, brutish, and short."[8] Hobbes understood that each individual would have to transfer his will to a single sovereign in order to institute peace; and Leibniz fully agreed with the essentials of this structure. Yet, in Leibniz's opinion, like Descartes, Hobbes did not go far enough. In allowing independent sovereigns to possess full power within their realms—plentitudo potestatis—Hobbes set the stage for perpetual conflict among the disparate nations. If the abbé was naïve in believing in the marriage of power and Justice, Hobbes was pernicious in promoting positive law, that is, a nationalist, autocratic power indifferent to criteria of universal Justice.

In a draft of a letter to Hobbes, which he never sent, Leibniz indicated where his own views converged and diverged with those of the English philosopher:

[H]aving begun with the study of human nature, you observe that there is, in men just as much as in animals, a certain urge to pursue every immediate object of desire, and that this hope is checked only by the fear which can arise from the fact that the efforts of so many other people are directed at the same object. And, since you assumed that each person has the right to do whatever may seem necessary for the preservation of his own safety [ad incolumitatem tutandam], and as you decided that everyone must be the judge of his own needs, it was easy for you to conclude that in that state of affairs a just war would be waged by all against all. And since that war would involve general slaughter, because of the equality of people's forces (given that the strongest man can be killed by the weakest), the arguments for peace began to be raised at that point. Thus far I have no complaints.[9]

---

[7] Cited in Patrick Riley, "The Abbé de Saint Pierre and Voltaire on Perpetual Peace in Europe," 186–87.

[8] Hobbes, Leviathan, 8.9, 76.

[9] The letter is dated ca. 1674 and can be found in Thomas Hobbes, The Correspondence, 2: 731.

Leibniz explicitly will not raise the objection, often lodged by theologians, that it is better to suffer violence in this world than to forfeit eternal beatitude in the next. He does not question the legitimacy of protecting one's safety, of preserving a certain "freedom from harm" (*incolumitas*). Like Hobbes, Leibniz defines the state as a large society aimed toward security. However, whereas Hobbes regards security as *protection from harm*, Leibniz employs the term to refer to the *maintenance of peace*. That is to say, for Leibniz, peace shields us from the violent designs of others, whereas security is directed at preserving the conditions of this peace. This is precisely the sense that would carry over into the Preamble of the United States Constitution: to "secure the Blessings of Liberty to ourselves and our Posterity."

Leibniz's letter continues: "The next question is, how can that peace, once started, be made firm [*firmetur*]? For if there is no security of peace [*pacis securitas*], the state of war will remain, and each person will retain the right to strike the first blow at his opponent."[10] Leibniz agrees with Hobbes that citizens must purchase their safety with obedience, yet a sovereign can demand absolute obedience only if he is capable of absolutely securing the peace, of setting it down on firm land—a promise that no mortal ruler can make. And because, in regard to human actors, this promise is impossible, a citizen would be well advised to retain some rights, especially against tyranny. "If a tyrant often and indiscriminately vents his rage [*si saepe si indiscriminatim saeviat tyrannis*], I think you will not deny that even on your philosophical principles, people who see danger approaching will have the right to join together in alliances."[11] Tyranny fails to secure the peace, not only because it savagely acts out of self-interest but also because it occasions the withholding of obedience. For without complete obedience, there can be no security. God alone—and His universal State of Truth and Justice, informed by divine Reason—is the sole sovereign who could procure perfect security and who, therefore, deserves perfect obedience. In Leibniz's judgment, absolute security—not merely peace, but the security of peace— is attainable only by way of rational theocracy.

The concluding paragraph of Leibniz's *Monadology* refers to this city of God as a universal and universally just monarchy—a *Rechtsstaat*, which upholds constitutional law and thereby secures the peace, as opposed to the Hobbesian *Machtstaat*, which is governed strictly by means of power.

> Under this perfect government, there will be no good action that is unrewarded, no bad action that goes unpunished, and everything must result in the well-being of the good, that is, of those who are not dissatisfied in this great state, those who trust in providence, after having done their duty, and who love and imitate the author of all good, as they should, finding pleasure

[10] In Hobbes, *Correspondence*, 2: 732.
[11] In Hobbes, *Correspondence*, 2: 732.

in the consideration of his perfections according to the nature of genuinely *pure love*, which takes pleasure in the happiness of the beloved.[12]

It is clear that this vision of ideal Justice refutes a key Hobbesian motive: an individual's pleasure or benefit need not be equated with harming another, with acting wolfishly against a competitor, but rather can entail benevolence. More implicitly, this passage further rejects Hobbes's model of sovereignty, which is grounded exclusively in mechanistic power. As Leibniz consistently argues, God's omnipotence must be understood together with the necessity of his existence. The striking consequence of this collocation of qualities is that power cannot be the dominant attribute of God, for the very reason that the divine Ruler lacks the power to eradicate his necessary existence.[13] By analogy, although every sovereign is by definition powerful, this power cannot be construed as unlimited. Specifically, political power is limited to the task of holding open possibility, that is, of securing the citizens' potential capacity to flourish. In a letter to Pierre de Falaiseau, Leibniz is quite explicit:

> My definition of the State, or of what among the Latins is called the *Republica*, is a great society, the goal of which is common security [*la seureté commune*]. It would be hoped that one could procure for men something more than security, to wit, happiness, and one must apply oneself to that; but at least security is essential, and without it the good ceases. That is why subjects are allowed to take the oath of fidelity to the enemy of their master who has conquered them, their master no longer being able to do anything for their security.[14]

As for the grandest possibility of perfect security and perfect happiness, that rests solely with God as the governor of the universe. The passage from the *Monadology* cited above continues:

> This [pure love] is what causes wise and virtuous persons to work for all that appears to be in conformity with the presumptive or antecedent divine will, and nevertheless, to content themselves with what God brings about by his secret, consequent, or decisive will, since they recognize that if we could understand the order of the universe well enough, we would find that it surpasses all the wishes of the wisest, and that it is impossible to make it better than it is.[15]

Metaphysics intersects with political theory when one considers the contingency of the given world, a contingency that serves to recall that other worlds

---

[12] Leibniz, *The Principles of Philosophy, or, The Monadology* (1714), § 90, in *Discourse on Metaphysics and Other Essays*, 81.

[13] On this point, see Peter Fenves, *Arresting Language: From Leibniz to Benjamin*, 60.

[14] Leibniz to Falaiseau, July 8, 1705, in *Werke* (Klopp, ed.), 9: 143. On the close relationship of *securitas* and *felicitas* in Leibniz's political theories, see Erwin Ruck, *Die Leibniz'sche Staatsidee*, 83–99.

[15] Leibniz, *Monadology* (§ 90), 81.

are possible. Two basic principles inform the *Monadology*: the principle of contradiction for necessary truths ("A cannot be A and non-A at the same time in the same place"); and the principle of sufficient reason for contingent facts ("There is nothing without a reason"). These two fundamental premises compel the wise to search for causes (or sufficient reasons) that would explain the contingent truths of our world, that is to say, the facts that define this world as *one possibility among others*. For Leibniz, this search should ultimately point to the necessary, noncontingent truth of God's existence, to God's necessary possibility as *the only possible possibility*. Leibniz would argue: because existence in fact exists, its nonexistence must be impossible; and because this world is contingent (one possibility among others), then its sufficient reason must derive from something outside itself, it must be secured by something necessary. Leibniz's *Theodicy* (1710) tracks this homeward voyage back onto *terra firma*:

> One must seek the reason for the existence of the world, which is the whole assemblage of *contingent* things, and seek it in the substance which carries with it the reason for its existence, and which in consequence is *necessary* and eternal.[16]

Perfect security obtains in God, who alone exists necessarily. Thanks to his infinite goodness and justice, it is therefore "impossible to make [this world] better than it is." It is crucial to stress the analogy operative in Leibniz's theory of the state: if the security procured by the mortal sovereign secures the possible—the citizens' potential to flourish—then the security that inheres in God's order is the best possible.

VOLTAIRE'S CURIOSITY

Varying views of the world—either as the perpetual object of care exhibited by a perfect, benevolent deity (the world as garden) or as a wonderful mechanism carefully produced by a divine craftsman and then left to operate automatically (the world as clock)—were by the eighteenth century becoming increasingly difficult to validate. The ongoing religious, political, and social conflicts, coupled with the paradigmatically senseless disaster of the Lisbon earthquake in 1755, would suggest that God was not as careful or solicitous as conventionally purported. That God may not be merely *inscrutable* but in fact *careless* invariably jeopardized any prolonged sense of security, for how could care be removed if there was no ultimate agent to remove it? Voltaire's *Candide* (1759) speaks directly to these concerns, both by means of a satirical critique of Leibnizian theory—of "sufficient reason," of "monads," and, not least, of "the best of

---

[16] Leibniz, *Theodicy: Essays on the Goodness of God, the Freedom of Man, and the Origin of Evil*, 127 (emphasis in original).

all possible worlds"—and by elevating each individual to the status of caretaker. The text's famous conclusion—"il faut cultiver notre jardin" (we must cultivate our garden)—redefines human security as the condition of being *without as well as with care*.

Every page of *Candide* demonstrates that the motivating problem of this reassessment was the problem of the origin of evil. Should the all-too-obvious presence of evil in the world be traced back to a theological, metaphysical, or moral cause? That is, should the ills that plague life be attributed to God, nature, or mankind?[17] Leibniz had outlined the metaphysical interpretation in his *Theodicy* by drawing on the other—theological and moral—interpretations. The work's full title, *Essais de théodicée sur la bonté de Dieu, la liberté de l'homme, et l'origine du mal* (Essays of Theodicy on the Goodness of God, the Freedom of Man, and the Origin of Evil), attests to this authorial intention. In brief, Leibniz, with typical conciliatory flair, insists on both divine providence and human freedom and subsequently locates the cause of moral evil or sin in this freedom. In other words, he applies his key principle of sufficient reason to account for the contingent fact of evil in the world, a fact that can, as we have seen, ultimately be secured by the necessary existence of God. Voltaire would accept unequivocally the validity of the principle of sufficient reason: in a review of Leibnizian theory, inspired by Émilie du Châtelet's engagement with the German philosopher in her *Institutions de physique* (Lessons in Physics, 1740), Voltaire endorses the central thesis: "Il n'y a rien sans cause." Yet, although "there is nothing without cause," it cannot be granted that this verity is capable of proving the existence of God:

> Leibniz claimed that there was no phenomenon of nature that was the work of chance or the work of the unmotivated will of the Supreme Being; but that each had a sufficient reason for its existence, whether in the very nature of things or in the perfection of the general order of the universe; this is what he has maintained, but has not proven: he has attempted to give it metaphysical proofs; but it is easy to see that these presume a knowledge of the divine essence which we are unable to have.[18]

Voltaire's critique is straightforward enough: he questions the key move essential for Leibnizian securitization, namely the progression from the principle of sufficient reason (for contingent truths) to the principle of contradiction (for necessary truths). Sufficient reason, therefore, is not sufficient to secure knowledge, to remove concerns—the principle of *sans cause* does not as a matter of course lead to the condition of being *sans souci*.

Nearly two decades later, in *Candide*, Voltaire would subject the entire train of Leibnizian reasoning to sardonic critique with the risible figure of Maître

---

[17] Cf. Ira Wade, *Voltaire and* Candide: *A Study in the Fusion of History, Art, and Philosophy*, 5.

[18] Voltaire, *Expositions du livre des Institutions physiques dans laquelle on examine les idées de Leibnitz* (1740), in *Œuvres complètes*, 23: 129–46, here 130 n. 1.

Pangloss, who is mockingly introduced as the great synthesizer of systems: "Pangloss taught metaphysico-theologico-cosmolonigology."

"It is demonstrably true," he would say, "that things cannot be otherwise: for, everything having been made for a purpose [fin], everything is necessarily for the best purpose. Observe how noses were made to bear spectacles, and so we have spectacles."[19]

In good Leibnizian fashion, the finality implicit in purposiveness marks how contingent phenomena, governed by the principle of sufficient reason, are ultimately grounded or justified by being attached to something necessary (i.e., the necessary existence of God)—a realm ruled not simply by sufficient causes but more securely by the principle of contradiction ("things cannot be otherwise"). The opening chapter of *Candide* exposes both principles to memorable ridicule: when young Cunégonde, the Baron's daughter, strolls through the castle's grounds, she espies Pangloss "giving a lesson in applied physiology to her mother's maid, a very pretty and very receptive little brunette."

As Miss Cunégonde had quite a gift for science, she noted in breathless silence [*sans souffler*] the repeated experiments to which she was witness. She saw clearly the doctor's sufficient reason, the effects and the causes, and returned home all agitated, her thoughts provoked, and filled with desire to be a scientist, musing that she might well be able to be young Candide's sufficient reason, just as he could well be hers.[20]

The primal scene takes mademoiselle's breath away and in its stead injects agitation, a burning *cura* that already renders any *securitas* unlikely. When the Baron discovers his daughter kissing Candide behind a screen, the unwitting young man is "expelled from paradise on earth." The hard fact of sufficient reason precipitates the fall into unmoored contingency.

Candide opens like a fairy tale—"Once upon a time in Westphalia . . ."—and we can already sense that the Westphalian peace of the castle of Baron Thunderten-tronckh will hardly persist. Misadventures and horrific calamities, violence and suffering, will turn the story into a picaresque narrative of philosophy's failings and redefined humanism. On the one hand, the *conte* is a sobering account of shattered dogmas, harsh disillusionment, and shocking cruelty; an admission of God's powerlessness and mankind's godlessness. On the other hand, it is also a demonstration of human resilience, the capacity to survive, and the readiness to attend to the principle of hope. The key, motivating event, depicted early in the text, is the Lisbon earthquake. Immediately upon reaching harbor, after a terrifying storm at sea, Candide and his companions witness how the land itself can become as treacherous as the sea, how tidal waves transmute into

---

[19] Voltaire, *Candide and Other Stories*, 3 (slightly modified) [*Romans et contes*, 138].
[20] *Candide*, 3 [139].

seismic waves: "Whirlwinds of flame and ash covered the streets and public squares: houses disintegrated, roofs were upended upon foundations, and foundations crumbled."[21] As his correspondence makes clear, like many thinkers of his age, Voltaire was gravely affected by the devastation that struck Portugal on All Saints' Day, 1755. Apart from the general panic that spread across Europe, there were intense and prolonged philosophical discussions debating the possible theological, moral, and physical causes of the catastrophe. In brief, the aftershocks quickly shifted from geographical to intellectual areas as well as from metaphorical to empirically concrete registers: Descartes's relatively innocent figure of "the shifting ground"—*la terre mouvante*—became frighteningly real as the old problem of the origin or meaning of evil, with which Leibniz had masterfully grappled, reopened like a gaping abyss along the fault line that coursed beneath the asphalt of human cognition.

For theologians defending Christian orthodoxy or the idea of divine Providence, as well as for scientists depending on the regularity of the natural order, the event that shook the Portuguese capital represented a state of exception that would either uphold or definitively destroy notions of sovereignty. Beliefs in preestablished harmony required recalibration; trust in geological and cartographic measurements underwent serious rethinking. Practically every major European thinker contributed to the discussion.[22] Preachers of every confession, from the Iberian Peninsula to Switzerland and Britain, evoked human sinfulness and divine vengeance; while Newtonians posited planetary, meteorological, and electrical causes. Kant, who would devote no less than three essays on the earthquake, collated the various physical causes proffered by Europe's burgeoning seismologists, carefully reviewed the material, and discouraged any one who would argue against nature's indifference to human suffering.[23] The age of the earth's desecurement that began with Galileo's notorious declaration, *Eppur si muove!* (And yet it moves!), no longer simply applied to our planet's relegated position in the cosmos but now referred to the very ground below our feet.

In this spirit, Voltaire resisted every teleological explanation by composing a long *Poem on the Lisbon Disaster* (1756), which considered the ultimate insufficiencies of abstract explications in the face of the catastrophe's concrete effects on individual lives.[24] As the poem's alternate title indicates, the verses constitute

---

[21] *Candide*, 12 [148].

[22] For an overview with comprehensive analyses, see the articles collected in *The Lisbon Earthquake of 1755: Representations and Reactions*, T. Braun and J. Radner, eds. See also Harald Weinrich, "Literaturgeschichte eines Weltereignisses: Das Erdbeben von Lissabon."

[23] Kant published a series of three essays in 1756, within a year of the disaster: "Von den Ursachen des Erderschütterungen bei Gelegenheit des Unglücks, welches die westliche Länder von Europa gegen des vorigen Jahres betroffen hat"; "Geschichte und Naturbeschreibung der merkwürdigsten Vorfälle des Erdbebens, welche an dem Ende des 1755sten Jahres einen großen Theil der Erde erschüttert hat"; and "Fortgesetzte Betrachtung der seit einiger Zeit wahrgenommenen Erderschütterungen." Kant, *Gesammelte Schriften*, 1: 417–72.

[24] Voltaire, "Poème sur le désastre de Lisbonne, ou examen de cet axiome: tout est bien," *Œuvres complètes* (Moland, ed.), 9: 465–80.

"an examination of the axiom 'All is well'"—an allusion to the concluding line of the First Epistle of Alexander Pope's *Essay on Man* (1733): "One truth is clear, whatever is, is right." During his extended sojourn in England, Voltaire had developed a deep admiration for the poet of Twickenham; and he would continue to praise Pope's genius, despite growing discomfort with the implications of philosophical optimism.[25] In the aftermath of the Lisbon earthquake, this discomfort elevated to outrage:

> *O malheureux mortels ! ô terre déplorable !*
> *O de tous les mortels assemblage effroyable !*
> *D'inutiles douleurs éternel entretien !*
> *Philosophes trompés qui criez: « Tout est bien »*
> *Accourez, contemplez ces ruines affreuses,*
> *Ces débris, ces lambeaux, ces cendres malheureuses,*
> *Ces femmes, ces enfants l'un sur l'autre entassés,*
> *Sous ces marbres rompus ces membres dispersés*

(1–8)

> O unhappy mortals! O deplorable earth!
> O dreadful gathering of all mortals!
> Eternal maintenance of useless pain!
> Mistaken philosophers who cry: "All is well"
> Come, contemplate these frightful ruins,
> This wreckage, these shreds, these unfortunate cinders,
> These women, these children heaped one upon the other,
> These scattered limbs beneath the broken marble

The exasperated apostrophes express a desperation that quickly challenges optimists to behold the devastation, to acknowledge the carnage, to face with honesty this inventory of damage and human pain. With relentless drive, the opening couplet iconically portrays the inevitability of death shared by all: the plural "*mortels*" pronounced directly before the caesura of each alexandrine, framing a tricolon of despondent vocatives—"O mortals . . . O earth . . . O mortals' gathering." The earth, too, is mortal, as though by contamination: fragile, vulnerable, transient. The tone is further sustained by poetic deixis ("*this* wreckage, *these* shreds"), which transforms reflective spectators into participating witnesses. Voltaire is not interested in reporting a story of the recent past; he wants instead to conjure an event that is happening right now, in which everyone is implicated. The old Lucretian stance, secured by distance, gazing upon the shipwreck from above, has thus become impossible.

> *Tranquilles spectateurs, intrépides esprits,*
> *De vos frères mourants contemplant les naufrages,*
> *Vous recherchez en paix les causes des orages :*

[25] Cf. Wade's chapter on "Voltaire and Pope," in *Voltaire and* Candide, 62–83.

Mais du sort ennemi quand vous sentez les coups,
Devenus plus humains, vous pleurez comme nous.

(24–28)

Tranquil spectators, intrepid minds,
Contemplating the shipwreck of your dying brothers,
You seek in peace the causes of the storm:
Yet when you feel the blows of hostile fate,
You become more human, you cry as do we.

Voltaire's rhetorical assault aims to force the researcher to quit the transcendent position that Lucretius described as a source of pleasure, "removed from care" (*cura semota*). When the spectator becomes a participant, when the contemplator finds himself in the midst of hellish danger, when the security of carefree reflection is shattered, care returns and humanizes.

To open the entry on "curiosity" in his *Philosophical Dictionary*, which was begun in 1752 but not completed until 1764, Voltaire cites the proem to the second book of *De rerum natura* before addressing the Roman Epicurean:

Pardon me, Lucretius! I suspect that you are mistaken [*trompez*] here in morality as you are always mistaken in physics. In my opinion, it is curiosity alone that makes people run [*fait courir*] to the shore to see a vessel being overwhelmed in a storm. It has happened to me; and I swear to you that my pleasure, mingled with concern [*inquiétude*] and uneasiness [*malaise*], was not at all the fruit of my reflection; it did not come at all from a secret comparison between my security [*sécurité*] and the danger of these unfortunate men: I was curious and sensitive [*curieux et sensible*].[26]

Lucretius proclaimed that it is "sweet" or "pleasant" (*suave*) "to watch from the shore another man's struggle." Voltaire concedes that this "pleasure" (*plaisir*) exists; yet he regards it as having been grossly misinterpreted. In his opinion, Lucretian imperturbability—*securitas* as *ataraxia*—is morally reprehensible because it renounces the emotions that constitute our humanity. Instead, Voltaire bears witness to his own *curiosité*, which comprises *cura* and thereby rejects any condition that is free from care. Indeed, Voltaire engages the etymological figure when he explicitly contrasts *sécurité* with being *curieux* in the sense of being filled with concern. The resonances with the Lisbon poem are clear: the decision to remain secured in a place distant from the disaster is a mark of Lucretius's mistake—*vous vous trompez*; in contrast, the curious man is "made to run" (*fait courir*) to the water's edge, just as the "mistaken philosophers" (*philosophes trompés*) in the *Poem on the Lisbon Disaster* are commanded to "run" (*accourez*) to the site of human agony. With subtle flourish, the act of running to scene (*accourir, courir*) lightly rhymes with the *cura* that motivates *curiosité*.

---

[26] Voltaire, *Dictionnaire philosophique* (1764), in *Œuvres complètes* (Moland, ed.), 18: 306.

In a later text on "Natural Law and Curiosity" (1768), eventually collected under the *Dialogues et Entretiens philosophiques*, the heartlessness of Lucretian security is again contrasted with a humanly instinctual drive to be curious. To begin, the first interlocutor broaches the pessimistic view generally assigned to Hobbes that man is by nature evil—*homo homini lupus*. As an example, he offers the case of a shipwreck, remarking that men and women "run with secret pleasure [*courent avec un secret plaisir*] to the sea's shore to enjoy the spectacle of a vessel battered by the winds which is breaking apart and being swallowed up by the waves, while the passengers lift their hands to the heavens and fall into the watery abyss."[27] To justify his claim, as we would expect, he cites the proem of book 2 of *De rerum natura*: *Quibus ipse malis careas quia cernere suave est* (because perceiving from what evils you are spared is sweet), which Voltaire translates into a neat alexandrine, *On voit avec plaisir les maux qu'on ne sent pas* (One sees with pleasure the evils that one does not feel). The second interlocutor promptly counters this view:

> Lucretius doesn't know what he's saying, & he is highly prone to do so [*il y est fort sujet*], despite his beautiful descriptions. One runs to such a spectacle out of curiosity. Curiosity is a sentiment natural to mankind; yet there is not one of these spectators who would not make every last effort, if he could, to save [*sauver*] those who are drowning.[28]

Lucretian security is exposed as inhuman and therefore elicits a response fully grounded in the curiosity that characterizes mankind's nature.

Like *sécurité*, the term *curiosité* has had a polyvalent career in French discourse, which likewise reaches back to Latin usage.[29] The nominalized form *curiositas* is very rare in classical texts, employed only once in Cicero's extant works to denote a general desire for knowledge or inquisitiveness.[30] However, Cicero frequently uses the adjective *curiosus* to describe someone who devotes care (*cura*) upon something, one who exhibits diligence or careful thought.[31] At times, the implied need to know can become excessive, at which point *curiosus* is closer to the Greek *polypragmōn*, which generally has the pejorative sense of being meddlesome or prying. Hence, Cicero casts ridicule on those who believe that the gods are "curious": here it would be better to adopt Lucretius's Epicureanism and recognize that the gods are simply not concerned with human affairs.[32] Much later, it is Augustine who considers the moral ramifications of a typically human *curiositas*, which he defines as a lustful desire to see and to know (*concupiscentia oculorum*), a sensually marked longing that was respon-

---

[27] Voltaire, *Dialogues et Entretiens philosophiques: Entre A, B, C, ou l'A, B, C. Quatrième Entretien: "De la loi naturelle & de la curiosité"* (1768), in *Œuvres* (Palissot, ed.), 36: 299.

[28] Voltaire, "De la loi naturelle & de la curiosité," in *Œuvres* (Palissot, ed.), 36: 300.

[29] For a comprehensive analysis of the term's history, see André Labhardt, "*Curiositas*: Notes sur l'histoire d'un mot et d'une notion," and Maria Tasinato, *Sulla curiosità: Apuleio e Agostino*.

[30] Cicero, *Att.* 2, 12.2.

[31] For examples, see Lewis and Short, *OLD*, s.v. "curiosus."

[32] Cicero, *De natura deorum* 1.20.54.

sible for the fall and continues to distract mankind from what should be the true object of knowledge, namely God.[33] When *curiosité* first enters into the French language, it retains the fundamental ambivalence between a state of devoted care and an instance of indiscreet meddling, between noble solicitude and base nosiness.[34]

For Voltaire, to deny curiosity is to deny the care that defines life. He would agree with Lucretius that *cura* is deeply linked to the emotions and passions, but he would reject any security that strives to suppress or eliminate these emotions. Unlike the garden of Epicurus, which initiates a philosophical life by renouncing disturbing concerns, the garden to be cultivated at the end of *Candide* is a garden attained after shipwrecks, earthquakes, and other devastating episodes. Hans Blumenberg, who makes this point, elaborates it further by considering the hermit's wisdom in *Zadig*. For the hermit, the passions "are like the wind that fills the sail of a ship, which, although it sometimes capsizes the ship, is also responsible for its moving at all."[35] In this age of Enlightenment, in this great epoch of experimentation, where the scientist embarks upon journeys to the perilous limits of knowledge, curiosity names that motivating force, which enlivens life, keeping it afloat and maintaining progress, despite the risks involved.[36] As for the spectator upon the shore, curiosity marks the measure of his moral capacity for sympathy. Rather than rejoice in his safety, he is afflicted with disquietude and malaise. The security of remaining unaffected, which is concomitant with the security of optimism, of believing in a harmonious system secured by God's benevolence, is inaccessible to *homo curans*. The temptation to live without care is ultimately vain. The same holds true for the man who cares little about anything, like the aptly named Pococuranté, the Venetian nobleman visited by Candide and Martin. Toward the end of *Candide*, the two young men, who are here explicitly designated as "the curious ones" (*les curieux*), are fascinated by Pococuranté, an oversated malcontent, whose general disaffection leads to neither desperation nor hope but simply boredom, whose only pleasure, as Martin points out, is not having any pleasure at all.[37]

SANS, SOUCI.

By the time Frederick was crowned King of Prussia in 1740, he had already been corresponding with Voltaire for some four years. Although he had vowed to his exceedingly stern father that he would never again try to flee his destiny—the last attempt ended traumatically when, at the age of eighteen, the

[33] See Augustine's discussion in *Confessions* 10.
[34] See Littré, *Dictionnaire*, s.v. "curiosité."
[35] H. Blumenberg, *Shipwreck with Spectator*, 34.
[36] Blumenberg offers a full examination of this rehabilitation of curiosity in the third part of *The Legitimacy of the Modern Age*, 229–453. See also Peter Harrison, "Curiosity, Forbidden Knowledge, and the Reformation of Natural Philosophy in Early Modern England."
[37] See *Candide*, chap. 25, 78–84 [214–19].

crown prince was forced to witness the decapitation of his companion and co-conspirator, Hans Hermann von Katte—Frederick nonetheless continued to nourish his youthful dream of pursuing a philosophical life. In August 1736, the prince first contacted Voltaire to express his sincere admiration and to request the *philosophe's* collected writings. Voltaire responded, highly encouraged that there existed "in the world a prince who thinks like a man, a philosophical prince who will make men happy."[38] The notion of an enlightened despot with an eye on the *beata vita* is already in place, the promise of a ruler who would take care of his subjects, as opposed to reigning over them, inhumanly unconcerned. With a sincere sense of mission, Voltaire would soon receive, edit, and expand upon the Frederick's *Anti-Machiavel* (1738–39), a treatise that describes a benevolent statesman in contrast to the Florentine's cynical *principe*. In letter after letter, Frederick acknowledged the importance of cultivating the arts and sciences, while also emphasizing the need for distance.

> Although my greatest pleasure would be the study and culture of the fine arts, you realize, monsieur, more than anyone, that they demand rest, tranquillity, and mindful contemplation;
>
> *Car loin du bruit et du tumulte,*
> *Apollon s'était retiré*
> *Au haut d'un coteau consacré*
> *Par les neuf Muses à son culte.*
> *Pour courtiser les doctes sœurs,*
> *Il faut du repos, du silence,*
> *Et des travaux en abondance*
> *Avant de goûter leurs faveurs.*
> *Voltaire, votre nom, immortel dans l'histoire,*
> *Est gravé par leurs mains aux fastes de la gloire.*
>
> For far from the noise and the tumult,
> Apollo had retired
> Up on a hilltop consecrated
> By the nine Muses for his worship.
> To court these learned sisters,
> One needs rest and silence,
> And works in abundance
> Before enjoying their favors.
> Voltaire, your name, immortal in history,
> Is engraved by their hands with the splendor of glory.[39]

The prince's octosyllables closely adhere to the ideal of Ciceronian *securitas*, the disposition gained by moving away from worldly concerns. Such a disposition,

---

[38] Voltaire to Frederick of Prussia, August 26, 1736, in *Œuvres complètes* (Moland, ed.), 34: 106.
[39] Frederick of Prussia to Voltaire, January 1737, *Œuvres complètes* (Moland, ed.), 34: 203.

slightly recalibrated so as to accommodate all the arts, would grant the constancy and dignity that would otherwise drown in the tumult of political affairs.

Not very long after his coronation, Frederick began plans for his summer palace in Potsdam. It was to serve as a modern-day Tusculum, a retreat for philosophers, scholars, and artists to gather, free from all worries. Voltaire, who would eventually insist on mankind's mortality, was nonetheless flattered by this bid for immortalization and would soon enough take up rooms at Sanssouci.

The palace's name ostensibly designates this would-be temple to a contemplative life unperturbed by cares, a place "far from the noise and the tumult" of Berlin. Yet, in his book of anecdotes on the life of Frederick the Great, Friedrich Nicolai relates a story that has served as another source for the name of the summer residence. While strolling about the construction site with Voltaire's close friend, the Marquis d'Argens, the king pointed to a crypt at the top of the hill—*le coteau consacré*—and remarked, "When I'm there, I shall be without care [*sans souci*]."[40] Nicolai interprets this statement as an allusion to Lucretius: *Tu quidem ut es leto sopitus, sic eris aevi / quod superest, cunctis privatu doloribus aegris* (Assuredly, as you lie asleep in death, so you will be for time to come, free from every distressing pain, *De rer. nat.* 3.904–5). As in Hyginus's fable, the end of life marks the absence of care. The Epicurean rejection of an afterlife of punishment or reward should release the mind of the fear of death. Is the palace at Potsdam, then, to be understood as a mausoleum, a place to be as carefree as a corpse?

This line of interpretation is not the only one to have been put forward. Other biographers have turned instead to the theatrical troupes of medieval Paris, Les Enfants sans Souci, who used to put on farcical performances during the holidays, poking fun at clergy and nobility. Frederick's sister, Wilhelmine, conjures the mood of this carnivalesque attack on authority, when she mockingly describes her behavior at the funeral of her despised father-in-law: *nous ferons un peu les enfants sanssouci.*[41] "Playing the part of the carefree children" suggests ridiculing paternal figures; and Frederick, who always harbored hatred and fear for his father, could employ the frivolous name while disguising a deep animosity.[42] Potsdam would constitute a haven from the active, military life ordained by the father, a site immured from the detestable concerns and anxieties of leadership: again, a grave, however not for the philosophical son but rather for the loathsome father and everything he represented. The satirical effect would not have been lost on Voltaire.

These more or less straightforward interpretations of the name—the residence as a crypt for the son or for the father—are incapable of reckoning with the highly curious lettering that adorns the palace's principal entrance:

[40] Friedrich Nicolai, *Anekdoten von König Friedrich II von Preussen*, vol. 1 (1788), 203–4.
[41] Letter dated June 14, 1735. Cited in H. D. Kittsteiner, *Das Komma von SANS, SOUCI.*, 14.
[42] Cf. Kittsteiner, *Das Komma*, 14–15.

SANS, SOUCI.

The inserted comma and the final period are sufficiently unconventional to invite a deciphering, especially given Frederick's well-known penchant for creating rebuses with letters and typographic symbols as well as Voltaire's "great appetite" to play along.[43] Certainly the inserted comma above the palace's portal would have caught Voltaire's attention. In an early letter, following Frederick's request to look over his French, Voltaire couched his critique with ingratiation: "It is true that Your Royal Majesty possesses French infinitely better than I know the Latin language; yet there are always some small commas to put in, some dots on the *i*'s, and I'll take care [*je me charge*], if you approve, of the small details."[44] What, then, do the details of this comma and this period signify? What is the strange punctuation—SANS, SOUCI.—attempting to communicate?

H. D. Kittsteiner has collated most of the proffered solutions, in addition to submitting his own. It is noted, for instance, that the seventeenth and eighteenth centuries commonly employed punctuation marks to denote the various religious conventions, a cryptographic device generally implemented by policing agencies for the purpose of identification: colon, "Catholic"; semicolon, "Lutheran"; comma, "Calvinist"; dash, "Jewish"; and period, "Deist." The absence of a mark would simply indicate an atheist. Because the odious father had maintained the Calvinism of the Prussian monarchy, the comma could again signal an erasure of the paternal influence: Sans, Souci—"Without Calvinism (or the Calvinist), (without) Care." One could subsequently read the ending period as a secret admission of the young king's turn to Deism.[45]

Alternatively, and perhaps more scandalously, one could press the etymological sense of the French term for comma, "virgule" (*virgula*, "a little twig") and read it as an allusion to the operation that Frederick purportedly underwent because of a syphilis infection: "Without the little twig, (without) care." Reading the *virgule* could take the name of the residence as an apotropaic mockery of the fear of castration, as a tabernacle of the fetish that would affirm by way of denial. Was the sovereign, therefore, playing the "enfant sans souci" by demeaning paternity *tout court*?

Yet another solution, which could be particularly relevant to aspects of security, was first put forward by Eberhard Cyran, who reads the lettering as an interlingual pun: *Sans Komma Souci = Sans comme à souci* (Without as well as with care).[46] The combination of French and German would be appropriate for Frederick's inclinations. The merits of this reading are reinforced by the resi-

---

[43] I am alluding, of course, to the well-attested anecdote where Frederick devised a rebus to invite Voltaire to Sanssouci: "Venez à ci/sans" ("Come to *sans sous ci*"), to which Voltaire laconically replied, "G a" ("G grand a petit" = "J'ai grand appétit").

[44] Voltaire to Frederick, October 12, 1737 in *Œuvres complètes* (Moland, ed.), 34: 319.

[45] Kittsteiner, *Das Komma*, 27.

[46] Eberhard Cyran, *Sanssouci: Traum aus dem Sand*, 46.

dence's architectural layout. As Kittsteiner points out, the rooms on the left were reserved for the guests who could enjoy a carefree stay, while the rooms on the right belonged to Frederick, who remained burdened by concerns.[47] That is, the quarters marked off by *sans (souci)* would be distinguished from the chambers governed by the *comme à souci*. Hence recognizing the pragmatic conditions of a life without concern: the prerequisite for the guests' secure existence is the presence of a sovereign whose duty is to assume all care. Just as the king's desire for philosophical contemplation required distance "from the noise and the tumult," so his friends' continued security necessitated Frederick's commitment to his royal office. Sanssouci would be an Epicurean grave, a mortifying crypt, were it not for the worries that perpetuate motion.

That Voltaire would come to regard Sanssouci as a devitalizing prison house is evident across his correspondence during his extended stay in Potsdam from the summer of 1750 to the spring of 1753. Inevitably, at least in regard to critical inquiry, a carefree life is philosophically careless. One could readily conclude that Voltaire deliberately set about to desecure his standing with his prince. The dubious speculations with the Jewish financier Abraham Hirschel, his flirtations with Mme Charlotte-Sophie Bentinck, and finally his merciless attack on Frederick's favorite, Pierre Louis Moreau de Maupertuis, head of the newly founded Berlin Academy, all left the *philosophe* on very shaky ground. Later, after Voltaire's escape from Potsdam and after his humiliating arrest in Frankfurt under the watch of Frederick's henchmen, Voltaire would describe his years in Prussia as a devastating shipwreck: "Sailors in port like to talk about their storms, but is there any port in this world? People shipwreck everywhere, even in a small brook."[48] Two years later, while cultivating his garden at Les Délices, he would catch wind of the terrifying news out of Lisbon.

INQUIRIES

> Cura, s.f. (*Myth.*), concern [*l'inquiétude*], goddess who formed
> man, & who since this time has never lost sight of her work.
>
> *Encyclopédie* (1754), s.v. "Cura"

Out of the lonely depths of exile, Ovid berates a close friend who has since abandoned him. With an unmistakable tone of pained humiliation, the poet is unsure how to deal with the insult:

> *Conquerar, an taceam ? ponam sine nomine crimen,*
> *an notum qui sis omnibus esse velim ?*
>
> (*Ex ponto* 4.3.1–2)

---

[47] Kittsteiner, *Das Komma*, 7.
[48] Letters to the Comtesse Lützelburg, September 2, 1753; cited in Blumenberg, *Shipwreck with Spectator*, 37.

> Should I complain or keep silent? Should I make a nameless charge,
> or should I wish to make you known to all?

The opening alternative, whether to indulge in lament or practice restraint, clearly does not refer to writing the poem, which, once begun, has already broken the silence. Instead, it refers to the accusation lodged against the poet's erstwhile companion. The question (*quaestio*) literally involves the act of complaint (*questus*) itself: if the poem should be a proper *questus*, it would need to divulge the name of the accused. The problem is that, by naming, the victim would maintain a relation of care with the perpetrator, who apparently no longer cares about the poet. If he should name the one who injured him, he would place himself in the weaker position, still disturbed by concerns for someone who is ostensibly without concern.

> *ille ego sum qui nunc an vivam, perfide, nescis,*
> *cura tibi de quo quaerere nulla fuit*
>
> (17–18)
>
> I am the man, faithless one, who you don't know if I still live,
> about whom you had no care to inquire

At Rome, the two men were inseparable, enjoying a shared life. Now, following the shift in fortune and the poet's painful banishment, the former ally is scolded for his cold insouciance. The perfidious addressee has broken the trust (*fides*) of friendship by remaining blissfully ignorant, nestled in *securitas*, with no care (*nulla cura*) to upset his comfort. By means of paronomasia, Ovid not only associates his potential lament (*conquerar*) with his addressee's incapacity to inquire (*quaerere*) but further links these verbs to the affect of care (*cura*). He thereby seems to engage an etymological figure that is well attested in the lexicographical tradition, namely one that associates *cura* with the verb of "seeking" and "looking for" (*quaerere*). It is concern that motivates investigation, care that propels the search.

Of course, the semantics of inquiring hardly need the etymological argument, which would at any rate be difficult to support with the methods of modern linguistics. We clearly ask about what we care about. All the same, the literal connection between *quaerere* and *cura* has played a significant role in the history of ideas from Augustine to Heidegger, that is, from the theologian who would have God be the focal point of all concerned questions to the philosopher of existence (*Dasein*) constituted by "care" (*Sorge*). For Heidegger, it is *Sorge* that motivates human *Dasein* to pose the being of existence as the central question for thinking.[49] As we have already seen with Voltaire, the general project of the eighteenth-century Enlightenment is but another variation of con-

---

[49] On Heidegger's exploitation of the *cura-quaerere* theme in specific relation to Augustine, see Theodore Kisiel, *The Genesis of Heidegger's Being and Time*, 201–3. This topic is further discussed below in chapter 14.

necting *cura* and *quaerere*, where the *careful* and *curious* examination of every object of knowledge is carried out against positions *secured* by dogma or authoritative doctrine.

The program is frequently discernible in the writings of David Hume, for example in the text ultimately named *Enquiry concerning Human Understanding* (1748), the very title of which adroitly performs the *cura-quaerere* theme. According to the traditional *figura etymologica*, every *enquiry* is an *enquiry concerning*, a questioning inspired by care. At times, Hume can be quite explicit, for example when he acknowledges the "doubts and errors" that accompany philosophical investigation: "They may even prove useful, by exciting curiosity, and destroying that implicit faith and security, which is the bane of all reasoning and free enquiry."[50] Arguing against baneful security, Hume demands philosophical *accuracy*, encouraging both himself and his readers to "cultivate true metaphysics *with some care*, in order to destroy the false and the adulterate."[51] The target here is that band of "careless reasoners" who irresponsibly proffer metaphysical discourses that promulgate dogmatic solutions and render superstition attractive. For Hume, these peddlers of words may provide security, but they do so by extinguishing the inquiring spirit, paving the way to despair. In his earlier work, the *Treatise of Human Nature* (1739–40), Hume writes:

> There is not, in my opinion, any other natural cause why security diminishes the passions, than because it removes that uncertainty which increases them. The mind, when left to itself, immediately languishes and, in order to preserve its ardor, must be every moment supported by a new flow of passion. For the same reason, despair, though contrary to security, has a like influence.[52]

Certain knowledge—secured by rules of causation—no less than despair puts an end to all questioning. Hume lightly engages the Augustinian-Lutheran interpretation of "pestilential" *securitas* as a state defined by idle negligence and thus reads Stoic *apatheia*, the suppression of the passions, as outright apathy. The Scottish philosopher, who would famously wake Kant from his "dogmatic slumber," insists on the passions that move thinking forward, despite the perils involved. In the conclusion to the *Treatise of Human Nature*, Hume recognizes the risks but refuses to be daunted by them:

> Methinks I am like a man, who, having struck many shoals, and having narrowly escaped shipwreck in passing a small firth, has yet the temerity to put out to sea in the same leaky weather-beaten vessel, and even carries his ambition so far as to think of compassing the globe under these disadvantageous circumstances.[53]

---

[50] David Hume, *Enquiry concerning Human Understanding*, sec. 4.1, 26.
[51] Hume, *Enquiry concerning Human Understanding*, sec. 1, 12 (emphasis added).
[52] Hume, *A Treatise of Human Nature*, 421.
[53] Hume, *A Treatise of Human Nature*, "Conclusion" to book 1, 263.

This "Conclusion" is hardly straightforward and has given rise to conflicting interpretations. In one sense, Hume inscribes himself within the general rehabilitation of curiosity that inaugurated the efflorescence of the new science nourished by empiricism and the promise of experimentation. His path is altogether analogous with the itinerary announced by the frontispiece to Francis Bacon's *Instauratio magna* (1620): a mighty ship passing through the Pillars of Hercules, its sails buffeted by strong winds that drive the craft toward the infinite horizon of the not yet known. In another sense, however, Hume's "leaky weather-beaten vessel" travels on the far side of optimism, proceeding much more cautiously and with much greater suspicion. Experience may persuade us that this vessel is trustworthy, but such trust can at any moment be broken. Probability can be calculated and some measure of credibility may be gained, but no system is airtight. Water continues to seep in, perfidiously. The modest image of Hume's curious journey in an uncertain bark aptly portrays a skeptic who is even skeptical of his skepticism.[54] The care that motivates his inquiries keeps his ambition alive, preventing him from wallowing in lethargic despair, which is but the obverse of secure complacency. In Hume's view, the despondency that results from radical skepticism barely differs from the ease promoted by dogmatism; both can be cured only by unremitting care, by undaunted inquiry.

In yet another sense, as the "Conclusion" continues, it becomes clear that Hume is adumbrating a narrative of isolation that stands in need of correction.[55] Curiosity has brought him to the brink of fearful desperation:

> I am first affrighted and confounded with that forelorn solitude, in which I am placed in my philosophy, and fancy myself some strange uncouth monster, who not being able to mingle and unite in society, has been expelled all human commerce, and left utterly abandoned and disconsolate.[56]

Like Descartes, he is left alone with his questions ("When I turn my eye inward, I find nothing but doubt and ignorance"). Yet, instead of hereby discovering the unshakeable fundament of a transcendent ego, Hume is concerned that introspection will leave him forever lost, perhaps like Ovid, wasting away in exile.[57] In the end, nature alone is capable of saving him:

> [Nature herself] cures me of this philosophical melancholy and delirium, either by relaxing this bent of mind, or by some avocation, and lively impression of my senses, which obliterate all these chimeras. I dine, I play a game of backgammon, I converse, and am merry with my friends; and when after

[54] In his essay "The Skeptic," Hume discusses the excesses of the skeptical position. See Richard Popkin, "David Hume: His Pyrrhonism and His Critique of Pyrrhonism"; and David Fate Norton, *David Hume: Common Sense Moralist, Skeptical Metaphysician.*

[55] See, e.g., John Richetti, *Philosophical Writing: Locke, Berkeley, Hume,* 227–28; and Adam Potkay, *The Passion for Happiness: Samuel Johnson & David Hume,* 55–56.

[56] Hume, *A Treatise of Human Nature,* 264.

[57] Cf. Potkay, *The Passion for Happiness,* 55.

three or four hours' amusement, I would return to these speculations, they appear so cold, and strained, and ridiculous, that I cannot find in my heart to enter into them any further.[58]

As for Voltaire, society is salvific for Hume, insofar as it is the site of mutual concern among friends—the *cura amicorum*—without which, curiosity would be vain.

Informed by care, Hume's method stands to produce a kind of security that can save us from false security, a provisional security that does not devolve into sheer carelessness. It is precisely this provisional security—a security demanding constant concern—that belongs to Hume's vision of political and social life. In his essay "On the Rise and Progress of the Arts and Sciences" (1742), Hume turns to the political preconditions for acquiring knowledge. Again, freedom is essential:

> Here then are the advantages of free states. Though a republic should be barbarous, it necessarily, by an infallible operation, gives rise to *law*, even before mankind have made any considerable advances in the other sciences. From law arises security: From security curiosity: And from curiosity knowledge.[59]

Here, "security" is essentially understood in the Hobbesian sense: a protection "against mutual violence and injustice."[60] It defines what Hume calls "the common life" and must be distinguished from the security promised by dogmatists, insofar as it promotes rather than squashes curiosity.[61] Law is arbitrary and may even be barbarous, but it is the necessary expression of human custom and habit. Like Voltaire, Hume adopts a gardening metaphor: security is the condition of possibility of curiosity, which allows knowledge to flourish; yet, "like some plants, [the arts and sciences] require a fresh soil." The provisionality of the law implies the fragility of the security it produces as well as security's accomplishments: custom may permit some degree of credibility and predictability; it may stave off hopelessness or carelessness; but in the end, it cannot patch over contingency: "[H]owever rich the land may be, and however you may recruit it by art or care, it will never, when once exhausted, produce any thing that is perfect or finished in the kind."[62]

All the same, Hume recognizes the civil benefits of religion, especially when its moral precepts complement the laws of the state. The belief in divine rewards and punishments has a salutary effect among the populace, "and those,

[58] Hume, *A Treatise of Human Nature*, 269.
[59] Hume, "On the Rise and Progress of the Arts and Sciences," in *Essays Moral, Political, and Literary*, 180.
[60] Hume, "On the Rise and Progress," 178.
[61] On the relation between Hume's "mitigated skepticism" and his political theory, see Steven Wulf, "The Skeptical Life in Hume's Political Thought."
[62] Hume, "On the Rise and Progress," 197.

who attempt to disabuse them of such prejudices, may, for aught I know, be good reasoners, but I cannot allow them to be good citizens and politicians; since they free men from one restraint upon their passions, and make the infringement of the laws of society, in one respect, more easy and *secure*."[63] That is to say, the security supplied by the church prevents people from disregarding the law, from committing crimes "securely," or without a care for others.

The few passages selected above sufficiently demonstrate the polysemous nature of "security" in Hume's usage: on the one hand, "security" is akin to despair, insofar as it diminishes the passions that motivate inquiry; on the other hand, "security" is the sociopolitical prerequisite for curiosity and hence knowledge. A devoted student of Hellenistic and Roman philosophy, Hume was well aware of the ambiguous significations of *securitas*. As is often the case, the value of security depends on the quality of the *cura* it implicitly removes. A major element of Hume's descriptive psychology and its normative ramifications is the distinction, fully elaborated by Frances Hutcheson, between calm passions that benefit the mind and violent passions that disturb it.[64] Social security, which checks the violent passions of one's neighbors, is clearly a good, preparing the tranquil ground upon which curiosity and the acquisition of knowledge may flourish: "[V]iolent passion hinders men from seeing distinctly the interest they have in an equitable behavior towards others."[65] Yet cognitive security, which extinguishes the passion for wisdom, virtue, friendship, and so forth, can only be detrimental. Hume therefore departs from traditional Academic and Stoic doctrine in renouncing a model whereby passion is subordinated to reason. Moral life does not consist in the rationalization of emotions. Instead, positive passions work against negative passions to achieve happiness. In this regard, good security is an eradication of damaging concerns by means of beneficial concerns.

> And though a philosopher may live remote from business, the genius of philosophy, if carefully cultivated by several, must gradually diffuse itself throughout the whole society, and bestow a similar correctness on every art and calling. The politician will acquire greater foresight and subtlety, in the subdividing and balancing of power; the lawyer more method and finer principles in his reasonings; and the general more regularly in his discipline, and more caution in his plans and operations.[66]

For Hume, in order to be carefree, one must remain careful.

---

[63] Hume, *Enquiry concerning Human Understanding*, sec. 11, 147 (emphasis added).
[64] For a concise account, see John Immerwahr, "Hume on Tranquilizing the Passions."
[65] Hume, *Treatise on Human Nature*, 537.
[66] Hume, *Enquiry concerning Human Understanding*, sec. 1.5, 10.

Revolution's Chances

THE REST IN PEACE

> To be entombed in peace is to die in the security of good
> conscience.
>
> Jaucourt, *Encyclopédie*, s.v. "Paix (*Critiq. sacrée*)"

MUCH COULD BE MADE of Kant's claustrophilia. As Heinrich Heine reminds us, the philosopher led an "almost abstract life of a confirmed bachelor [*Hagestolz-enleben*] in a quiet, remote little street in Königsberg," the old, East Prussian border town in which Kant was born and where he would contentedly spend his long career, seldom venturing beyond the city walls.[1] The image of the solitary professor has persisted: a creature of habit, neurotically punctual, holding a physical distance from the world-historical events that defined his times—in Heine's characterization, a perpetual *Hagestolz*, a "confirmed bachelor" or "male spinster" who preferred to keep to himself. As usual, Heine's word choice is rich in connotation: the typically eighteenth-century term *Hagestolz* reaches back to the old Germanic *Hag*, which marks off an enclosure (cognate with English *hedge*), and the word *Stolz*, which may evoke a sense of "pride"—and can even summon ideas of the "fool" (*stultus*)—but in fact derives from the Middle High German preterite form of the verb *stellen* (to place, to position), as in "shape" (*Gestalt*) or "institution, establishment" (*Anstalt*). In old Germanic culture, the *Hagestolz* referred to the younger son, who would not inherit the father's estate but instead would be granted a neighboring property bordered by a "hedge."[2] Without inheritance, thanks to the system of primogeniture, this younger son would be less apt to marry, living out a bachelor's life, fenced off from the paternal court. Heine thus links Kant's bachelorhood with his remote quarters, depicted as leading what we might call a "peaceful" (*friedlich*) life apart from the world, that is, one set within a "border fence"—an *Umfriedigung* or *Einfriedigung*, which are precisely the terms that the Grimms' *Dictionary* list as synonyms of *Hag*.

---

[1] Heinrich Heine, *Zur Geschichte der Religion und Philosophie in Deutschland* (2nd ed., 1852), in *Werke*, 4: 123.

[2] Cf. Grimms's *Wörterbuch*, s.v. "Hagestolz."

Many have alluded to the apparently unremarkable life of the philosopher who, despite his Pietist upbringing, saw no reason to maintain a journal or divulge any profound confessions. Kant's biographers generally despair over the fact that their subject had "no biography."[3] Kant seems to contribute to this assessment when he introduces the definitive edition of the first *Critique* with an epigraph from Francis Bacon—*de nobis ipsis silemus: de re autem quae agitur petimus, ut homines eam non opinionem sed opus esse cogitent* (concerning ourselves we are silent: but concerning the matter to be treated I beg men to think of it not as opinion but rather as work).[4] By separating the author from the work at hand, Kant pushes the existential conditions of authorship—the life itself—into concealment and thereby discourages all attempts to interpret the course of thinking by means of biographical anecdote. This gesture of divorcing the life from the opus is indeed an honored philosophical tradition. Martin Heidegger, who would come to have quite good reasons for remaining silent, held true to this hermeneutic principle when he opened his 1924 course on Aristotle with a summary dismissal of personal factors: "Regarding the personality of a philosopher, our only interest is that he was born at a certain time, that he worked, and that he died."[5] On the one hand, this insistence on distinguishing the man from the thought answers to any charge that philosophy is somehow out of touch with the real world, a charge that spans from Aristophanes to Elias Canetti, whose novel *Die Blendung*, which explores the ramifications of having a "head without a world," bore the earlier title *Kant fängt Feuer* (Kant Catches Fire). On the other hand, the bracketing out of biographical detail, the decision to leave the personal life to the side, could be understood as making a more positive, philosophical point. In the first instance, it is concluded that life does not matter, while in the second, it is the very nonrelation between life and work that does matter.

Heine's brief account of Kant tends to support the latter judgment. Concerning the philosopher's peaceful existence, Heine gleefully comments, "It is difficult to describe his life story [*Lebensgeschichte*]. For he had neither life [*Leben*] nor story [*Geschichte*]." The initial implication is that vitality—the measure of liveliness in any life—is determined by the events that punctuate and inform a life. Yet what Heine finds particularly fascinating is the discrepancy between the stillness of Kant's lifeless life and the internal energy concealed within: "Strange contrast between the outer life of the man and his destructive, world-crushing thought!" Cloaked by punctuality and orderliness, Kant's fellow townspeople would hardly be able to surmise the devastating nature of his published work: "Truly, had the citizens of Königsberg sensed the full significance of this thought, they would have felt a more ghastly aversion

---

[3] For references, see Howard Caygill, *A Kant Dictionary*, 7.

[4] Kant, *Kritik der reinen Vernunft* (1787), in *Gesammelte Schriften*, 3: B ii. The epigraph is taken from Bacon's Prefatio to the *Instauratio magna* (1620).

[5] Martin Heidegger, *Basic Concepts of Aristotelian Philosophy*, 4.

for this man than for an executioner, since an executioner executes only human beings."[6] For Heine, himself a political exile and perpetual victim of censorship, Kant is noteworthy above all for the secret he harbored, for the way he shielded his revolutionary thought from arousing suspicion among his neighbors. Kant's singular philosophical intervention thus comes to assume the status of a true "secret" (*Geheimnis*), one that was hedged within the safety of "the home" (*das Heim*).

In this regard, Kant would appear to have violated the very first article he listed in his draft of a *Perpetual Peace* (1795): "No conclusion of peace [*Friedensschluß*] shall be considered valid [*gelten*] as such if it was made with a secret reservation [*mit dem geheimen Vorbehalt*] of the material for a future war."[7] Kant hereby recommends caution concerning the distinction between outer appearance and inner intention—the very distinction that incited Heine's wariness concerning Kant himself. The first article of *Perpetual Peace* serves as a warning to Kant's readers—those approaching any declaration of "perpetual peace," including the present essay, no less than those who contemplate Kant's own tranquil, uneventful life—that there could always be a secret held within, capable of disrupting any settled sense. For a life, however lifeless, is still alive.

As for the treatise *On Perpetual Peace* (*Zum ewigen Frieden*), there is, indeed, much reason for concern. To begin, the idea that Kant would devote an explicitly political piece to something deemed "eternal" (*ewig*) seems to contradict the nature of political processes as well as the philosopher's entire critical enterprise, both of which depend on temporal conditions. For Kant, critical reflection, including any formulation of a political theory, requires that one forgo the presumptive standpoint of eternity.[8] To follow Heine's provocation, we would do well to search for the "secret"—the "secret reservation" (*geheimer Vorbehalt*) that is perhaps lodged within the public announcement of an eternal peace. We might question what is here being "reserved" (*vorbehalten*) or "enclosed" (*eingefriedet*), and how it might qualify or even threaten the "peace" (*Friede*) being outlined.

That a lasting peace was desirable in 1795 is perfectly understandable. The exhilaration and the dread that characterized the revolutionary age—the euphoria and the despair, the doomsday fears and the millenarian hopes—had by then brought many to the brink of exhaustion. The initial hope of rebuilding human society afresh according to Nature, Reason, or Progress with the promise of greater freedom and equality for all had degenerated into nearly endless warfare, radical devastation, and rampant violence. Ambivalence and uncertainty were taking its toll on almost everyone's resilience. Profound irony—soon to be promulgated by Friedrich Schlegel and the Jena Romantics—or bla-

---

[6] Heine, *Zur Geschichte der Religion und Philosophie*, in *Werke* 4: 123.

[7] Immanuel Kant, *Zum ewigen Frieden*, in *Gesammelte Schriften*, 8: 343 ["Perpetual Peace," in *Political Writings*, 93].

[8] Cf. Peter Fenves, *Late Kant: Towards Another Law of the Earth*, 92.

tantly satirical skepticism would seem to be fitting responses to an age that witnessed a merciless Terror carried out beneath the dual banners of "public safety" (*salut publique*) and "public security" (*sûreté publique*).

Thus, in 1795, after the signing of the Treaty of Basel, whereby the Kingdom of Prussia agreed to withdraw from the First Coalition against the French Republic, Kant contributed his own thoughts on the possibility and possible impossibility of lasting peace, not without indicating a satirical aspect.[9]

> *Zum ewigen Frieden* [Toward Eternal Peace]. —Whether this satirical heading on that Dutch innkeeper's sign [*Schild*] upon which a graveyard was painted is valid for *mankind* in general, or particularly for heads of state, who can never have enough of war, or perhaps only for philosophers, who dream that sweet dream, may be set aside [*dahin gestellt sein*]. The author of the present [treatise] stipulates that, since the practical politician places the theoretical one at his feet, looking down on him with great self-satisfaction and regarding him as an academic who, with his ideas devoid of reality, brings no danger to the State which must proceed from principles of experience, and as someone who can always be allowed to hurl his eleven pins [*Kegel*] all at once without the *worldwise* statesman needing to turn around; in case of a conflict with the theoretical politician, the practical one must proceed consistently and not scent danger to the state behind the opinions ventured and openly expressed; —by this *clausula salvatoria* the author will herewith know that he is expressly guarded in the best form against all malicious interpretation.[10]

This carefully drawn preface rests on the incongruity, later highlighted by Heine, between the practical world of politics and the theoretical sphere of political thought. Kant's paratextual paragraph—this *clausula salvatoria*—aims to save or secure the subsequent theorizations from assault. In one sense the statement confirms that the academic's ideas are devoid of reality and incapable of real influence, that they pose no danger to the state and that authorities therefore should leave philosophers in peace. However, in another sense, the "little saving clause" is ironic insofar as its function undermines its premise: if political theory was truly inconsequential in relation to actual politics, if such thought was in fact powerless in comparison to the practical effects of political power, then why would it be in need of confinement? The question is two-pronged. Why would one have to sequester philosophy: in order to protect the philosopher from the world or in order to save the world from philosophy?

---

[9] For an interpretive account of the essay within the historical context, see Otfried Höffe, "Einleitung: Der Friede—ein vernachlässigtes Ideal," in *Immanuel Kant: Zum ewigen Frieden*, Höffe, ed., 5–29.

[10] Kant, *Zum ewigen Frieden*, 343 ["Perpetual Peace," 93]; I have modified the translation considerably, in order to relay greater literalness. Peter Fenves's own translation has been helpful in this regard (*Late Kant*, 93).

The alternatives were not mutually exclusive. Quite explicitly, the French Revolution promoted itself as the culmination of Enlightenment philosophy and ideals. The 1789 *Declaration of the Rights of Man and the Citizen*, which aims to preserve the rights of "liberty, property, security [*sûreté*], and resistance to opposition," was perceived as a palpable threat to governing bodies across the German states intent on maintaining the status quo. The latter feared that the security of the people required the demolition of the social and civil structures that kept their own regimes secure. Anxiety was ubiquitous. One had to remain on guard against spies, conspirators, and assassins. Just two years before writing *Perpetual Peace*, Kant suffered the consequences of this general leeriness when he angered his king, Friedrich Wilhelm II, by publishing arguments against institutionalized religion. The preface above, precisely as a *clausula salvatoria*, can indeed be taken as a device to shield himself from the sovereign's wrath, to secure himself from the Prussian state's security.[11] By arguing that his thinking has no practical consequences, Kant may believe he is sanctioned to toss out the eleven articles that constitute the essay—"to hurl his eleven pins all at once"—without exciting concern from the court.

The *clausula salvatoria* therefore guards the theorist from malicious repercussions by explaining theory's impotence. However, a third alternative is also possible, whereby the preface strives to save philosophy from itself. As the Grimms' *Dictionary* indicates, Kant's phrase "to hurl one's eleven pins" (*seine elf Kegel werfen*) may allude to a popular saying that means "to make the impossible possible."[12] In this sense Kant's "philosophical sketch [*Entwurf*]" hurls (*wirft*) its missiles against the foundational criteria of his own critical project, which famously restricted itself to the possible, leaving the impossible—like the noumenal or the eternal—off to the side, consigned to an inaccessible zone, hidden behind a hedge.

For the philosopher who once intended to demonstrate reason's "secure course" (*sicheren Gang*) by renouncing metaphysical gropings, the promise of an eternal resting place would end up making the possible impossible.[13] The notion of security that informs the entire preface to the 1787 edition of the first *Critique* is characterized by provisionality, by a constant readiness for modification, which is the measure of reason's service to scientific progress. Yet, in 1795, Kant proffers a treaty for *eternal* peace that is signed by no one save himself, suggesting either that the treatise itself is invalid or that it negotiates the terms of a philosophy at war with itself. Both readings might account for the

[11] For a concise account of Kant and his problems with censorship, see Hans Saner, "Die Negativen Bedingungen des Friedens," 46–47.

[12] Grimms's *Wörterbuch*, s.v. "Kegel." This observation is made by Susan Shell, who also cites additional meanings of *Kegel*, including "illegitimate offspring" and "bullet." The latter, as Shell points out, implies that Kant's "sketch" (*Entwurf*) is "less innocuous than the colloquial meaning of the phrase in question would suggest." "Bowling Alone: On the Saving Power of Kant's Perpetual Peace," 167 n. 7.

[13] The term *sicheren Gang* is from the opening sentence of the preface to the 1787 edition of the *Critique of Pure Reason*, in *Gesammelte Schriften*, 3: vii.

fact that Kant places the entire enterprise beneath the "satirical heading on that Dutch innkeeper's sign [*Schild*] upon which a graveyard [*Kirchhof*] was painted"—a sign that is certainly also a "shield," even if it is unclear who is thereby shielded. Kant picked up the joke from Leibniz, whose letter to Grimarest on the Abbé de Saint Pierre's "Project for Perpetual Peace" (1712) recalls the inscription of *Pax perpetua* found in a cemetery—"for the dead do not fight any longer; but the living are of another humor."[14] As Susan Shell comments, "The nub of the innkeeper's satire amounts to this: what men yearn for (permanent deliverance from death at one another's hands) is identical, in the last analysis, to death itself."[15] Peace comprises demobilization and a cessation of action, a decision to abandon the "secure course" of progress and call it a night. Whether this satirical joke is intended for "mankind in general," for "heads of state," or "only for philosophers, who dream the sweet dream" is a question that is best left unanswered. Literally, Kant would like to set the entire matter aside. The thinker who equated security with the progressive, incessant development of reason and freedom could persist only by shunting off the *cura* for everlasting peace.

On the surface the treatise may address the feasibility of an eternal settlement, yet that does not mean that life, which is "of another humor," ceases to fight behind the ordered appearance. The vital resistance to perfectly content satisfaction (*Zufriedenheit*) is the prerequisite for continued progress and improvement. Ever since his critical turn, the "secure course" (*der sichere Gang*) is held by keeping philosophy "on course": "on its way," perpetually "in progress" (*im Gang*). Here, security devotes itself to concerns by never allowing concern to be fully exterminated—hence, the carefulness discernible in Kant's satirical *clausula*. In brief, the promise of peace must retain its promissory force so as to prevent the mass graves that are, sadly, often dug by the wish for complete security, by a complete eradication of the enemy. "It thus follows that a war of extermination, in which both parties and right itself might all be simultaneously annihilated, would allow perpetual peace only on the vast graveyard of the human race."[16] Although political philosophers may find in Kant's treatise a blueprint for national self-determination and international accord, the "conclusion of peace" (*Friedensschluß*) presented here concludes nothing. As Kant's final paragraph suggests, the task "toward perpetual peace" (*zum ewigen Frieden*) is a task that, "as solutions are gradually found, constantly draws nearer to its goal."[17] The hope for arrival is grounded in arrival's ongoing deferment.

---

[14] Leibniz, *Political Writings*, 183. Leibniz had conjured the same image in his preface to the *Codex Juris Gentium Diplomaticus* (1693). For a comprehensive account of Kant's citation from Leibniz, see Georg Cavallar, *Pax Kantiana: Systematisch-historische Untersuchung des Entwurfs* Zum ewigen Frieden *von Immanuel Kant*, 21–22; and Fenves, *Late Kant*, 188–89 n. 1.

[15] Susan Shell, "Cannibals All: The Grave Wit of Kant's Perpetual Peace," 151–52.

[16] Kant, *Zum ewigen Frieden*, 8: 347 ["Perpetual Peace," 96].

[17] Kant, *Zum ewigen Frieden*, 8: 386 ["Perpetual Peace," 130].

OPPORTUNITIES

Although set in a distant time and place, Heinrich von Kleist's story "The Earth-quake in Chile" (1807) can be read as an allegory of the author's own revolu-tionary climate, as an implicit commentary on the epoch's contingencies and ambiguities. Specifically, Kleist plays on what the French Revolution and its immediate aftermath persistently exhibited, namely that disaster could usher in unforeseen chances, that loss could be a prelude to gain and success a harbinger of failure. Kleist's story sets off when sudden tremors interrupt the protagonist, Jeronimo Rugera, from committing suicide in his prison cell. Like a revolution, the quake arrives at a moment of gravest despair, precisely when Jeronimo is poised to hang himself.

> Life seemed detestable to him and he resolved to kill himself by means of a rope left there by chance [*Zufall*]. He was standing ... by a pillar in the wall and fastening the bracket embedded in the pillar's capital, when sud-denly the greater part of the town, with a crash as though the firmament were falling in, sank and buried under its rubble everything that lived and breathed.[18]

A contravening miracle from the outside interrupts the melancholic resolution within. The tightly mortared bricks held in place by the rigid pillars of the law prove to be much more fragile than ever expected. Upon finding a rope to fix his fate, Rugera looks on as the masonry disintegrates. One chance (the discov-ery of the rope) provides the means for escaping life, while a second chance (the earthquake) opens up a means for escaping death.

Rugera's liberation is premised on the annihilation of "everything that lived and breathed" (*alles, was Leben atmete*). The condemned man's unanticipated salvation at the expense of so many lives corresponds to a structural pattern that came to characterize the revolutionary age. Like an earthquake, the world-historical events in France shattered society to the core, causing institutions to crumble, upsetting long-held beliefs, decimating well-established hierarchies of power; and yet, such destructive energy was commonly greeted with rejoicing. One might view this upheaval as the eradication of all values held dear—as the loss of everything that hitherto defined, ordered, and benefited human soci-ety—but one might just as well regard the event as the instauration of new, more humane values, as the accomplishment of freedom from oppression, en-slavement, and injustice. A true *kairos*, marking the end of the past and the beginning of the future, the Revolution served as an occasion for mourning and celebration—as an event both horrifying and exhilarating, damning and liber-

---

[18] Heinrich von Kleist, "Das Erdbeben in Chili," in *Sämtliche Werke und Briefe*, 2: 145–46 ["The Earth-quake in Chile," in *Selected Writings*, 313 (modified)].

ating. Lives came to ruin while countless others flourished. Financial catastrophe coincided with extraordinary windfalls. Old authorities collapsed to make room for new regimes. God, like the king, might have died, but only to clear the ground for a new Panthéon and a new emperor.

Instead of death, Kleist's protagonist discovers an escape from his confinement opened up by the deadly destruction: "[T]he whole structure tilted toward collapsing into the street and was only prevented from doing so utterly because, in its slow fall, it was met by the fall of the building opposite [*gegenüberstehenden*] and made an accidental [*zufällige*] arch with that."[19] In addition to recalling the link between falling and accident (*Zufall*; *ad-cadere*), Kleist's syntax is strikingly iconic, physically demonstrating how the fall of each building against (*gegen*) each other creates an opening for Rugera's flight. The arc that stretches from the definite article (*der*) to its noun (*Fall*) forms the verbal picture that reflects the liberating archway: *und nur der, seinem langsamen Fall begegnende, Fall des gegenüberstehenden Gebäudes*—literally, "and only *the*, its long fall encountering, *fall* of the neighboring building." In this way, one fall folds into another, producing an odd type of securement, an accidental reconfiguration of an accident, one that occurs without subjective agency or calculation, yet all the same, one that constitutes a window of opportunity for the subject capable of converting it to an advantage. In a different but relevant context, Samuel Weber speaks of this kind of spontaneous act as a response "to an event that is sufficiently *singular* to resist subsumption under established rules and procedures."[20] Given the scenario set up by Kleist, we may ask: What theory of security could accommodate the singularity of the event? And what concerns might arise, when the elimination of concern is achieved by unpredictable, irreversible chance?

Kleist, who was languishing in a prison under French watch when this story was sent to the publisher, Johann Friedrich Cotta, knew that he was living in an era of total disruption, a time of happy accidents and incalculable misfortune. For Kleist, security as *asphaleia*—the state where the threat of falling (*sphallein*) is defused—no longer obtains, because everything is falling everywhere, for good or bad, for gain or loss. In his exceptional reading of Kleist's "Earthquake," Werner Hamacher focuses on the text's metaphors of falling, which destruct all teleological claims: "The happy accident [*Zufall*] and the fortunate coincidence [*Zufälligkeit*] of evil accidents do not offer a secure ground upon which solid representations of the world and its relation to a highest Being could be established; on the contrary, they are everywhere exposed to chance [*Zufall*]."[21] Yet, as Kleist's tale reveals, some kind of security is gained not simply despite the lack of a secure ground but precisely because of this groundlessness.

[19] Kleist, "Das Erdbeben in Chili," 146 ["The Earthquake in Chile," 313].

[20] Samuel Weber, *Targets of Opportunity*, 5.

[21] Werner Hamacher, "The Quaking of Presentation: Kleist's 'Earthquake in Chile,'" in *Premises: Essays on Philosophy and Literature from Kant to Celan*, 267.

Jeronimo's beloved Josephe, a young nun condemned to death for her unchastity, also sees her life secured through desecuring circumstances. The earthquake hits at the precise moment of the execution. If the security of the law and the security of the prison walls had held, the lovers would have perished. Yet the opportunities for survival close up almost as soon as they open. Kleist's story ends with the gruesome bludgeoning of the couple by the angry mob that regards the pair as the polluting source of their tribulations. Don Fernando, who implicated himself in the lives of the young couple when he gave his own infant over to Josephe for nursing, pleads with a high-ranking naval officer to imprison the pair "for the security of both of them" (*zu ihrer beiderseitigen Sicherheit*).[22] Whereas Jeronimo's life is at first saved when the secured walls of the prison house fall apart, by the tale's end being sent back to a cell would be the only chance for survival. If the prison initially protected society from the criminal, now, in Kleist's concluding pages, confinement would protect the man from a raving mad society. This slight opportunity, however, is insufficient to preserve them from the mob's violence. A miraculous security occasioned by an unforeseen event can unforeseeably be ripped away. The neutrality of chance renders any securement through chance fatally fragile.

Back in Kleist's own time, along the fault lines of European cities, the asphalt had long been cracking beneath the weight of sublime incomprehensibility. The encounter with the sublime could be quite devastating, yet for Kant, whose importance for Kleist should always be taken into account, the manifestation of the violent power (*Gewalt*) of the sublime was always a unique invitation for the subject to marshal a countering force (*Gegen-Gewalt*), to seize this singular opportunity that would enable reason to step in and exercise control.[23] If sensuous perception fails before the sublime, that failure provides the platform for reason's triumph. The argument is based on Kant's fundamental division of the human subject, which is on the one hand "intelligible" and autonomous, while being on the other hand a "phenomenal" object among all others within the world of deterministic nature. The failure of the sensuous sphere is in fact the failure of the determination that denies the human subject its freedom. When the walls of the understanding collapse, the free, moral postulate of mankind comes to the fore. For Kant, the Revolution was sublime precisely in this sense, because it produced both a defeat and a victory, a dual accomplishment that still must be portrayed with deep ambivalence.

In his last publication, *The Contest of the Faculties* (1798), Kant reflects on the Revolution's ambivalence and thereby contributes to the sense of an analogous rhythm between forfeit and gain, between desecurement and resecurement:

---

[22] Kleist, "Erdbeben," 157 ["Earthquake," 322 (modified)].

[23] Cf. Kant, *The Critique of the Power of Judgment*, §28 (*Kritik der Urtheilskraft*, in *Gesammelte Schriften*, 5: 260). For an extended analysis, see Winfried Menninghaus, "Zwischen Überwältigung und Widerstand: Macht und Gewalt in Longins und Kants Theorien des Erhabenen."

The revolution which we have seen taking place in our own times in a nation of gifted people may succeed or it may fail. It may be so filled with misery and atrocities that no right-thinking man would ever decide to make the same experiment again at such a cost, even if he could hope to carry it out successfully at the second attempt. But I maintain that this revolution has aroused in the hearts and desires of all spectators (who are not themselves caught up in it) a sympathy that borders almost on enthusiasm, although the very utterance of this sympathy was fraught with danger. It cannot therefore have been caused by anything other than a moral disposition within the human race.[24]

Kant thus situates his theoretical intervention between the Revolution's "success" and its "failure," between enthusiastic "sympathy" and sympathy "fraught with danger." Kant's compromising antitheses reflect a tension common among German intellectuals of the day, caught between initial euphoria and subsequent disillusionment. At least up until the royal family's debacle at Varennes, most German thinkers were supportive of the Revolution, insofar as it brought hope that France would establish a more liberal, constitutional monarchy. With the rise of the Jacobin Terror, positions had to be severely recalibrated. The case of Kant is especially complex by the fact that he allowed the ambivalence to remain unresolved—denouncing the Revolution and Jacobin excess while appreciating the events' value as a "historical sign."[25]

The passage above appears in the second essay of the *Contest of the Faculties* collection ("A Renewed Question: 'Is the Human Race Continually Improving?'"), which stages a "contest" between the "higher faculty" of law and the "lower faculty" of philosophy. The question of progress pits law against philosophy and renews thinking by reiterating a persistent task of Kant's critical philosophy—namely, how to distinguish moral concerns from legalism. To begin formulating an answer to this inquiry, Kant clarifies at the outset that he aims to consider "a portion of human history, not a history of the past but rather a history of future times, that is, a predictive history."[26] As Kant goes on to explain, a predictive history—a "universal" history of "progress"—must have its basis in the moral (free, noumenal) sphere, which means that this basis can be knowable only through "an event which has actually occurred." A singular event alone is capable of demonstrating "that man has the quality or power of being the cause [*Ursache*] and (since his actions are supposed to be those of a being endowed with freedom) the *author* [*Urheber*] of his own improvement."[27]

[24] Immanuel Kant, *Der Streit der Fakultäten*, in *Gesammelte Schriften*, 7: 85 [*Political Writings*, 182 (slightly modified)].

[25] For a comprehensive analysis, see Stathis Kouvelakis, *Philosophy and Revolution: From Kant to Marx*, 9–27.

[26] Kant, *Streit der Fakultäten*, 79 [177].

[27] Kant, *Streit der Fakultäten*, 84 [181].

Kant is drawn to the Revolution because it is a phenomenal event that indicates the noumenal, which alone can originate actual progress.[28] Hence, however terrifying or dangerous, however miserable or atrocious, the event of the Revolution manifests mankind's "moral disposition"—a manifestation that cannot fail to engender enthusiasm and sympathy.

From the warm security of his rooms in Königsberg, far from the turmoil, the philosopher could indulge in the spectacle because, thus removed, he is able to recognize the event in relation to the larger scheme of things. Not entirely unlike the Burkean aesthete, he could enjoy the "delightful horror" of the sublime without any fear of being physically harmed, without any threat to self-preservation. However, the main point for Kant is that the Revolution is a "historical sign," that is, a singular event irreducible to any deterministic order, a singularity, moreover, that inspires an enthusiastic sympathy—an affect or even a passion [pathos] that attests to the thinker's concern.[29] Kant may be safe in Prussia, but he is not without care. Far from retreating into apatheia, Kant underscores his sympatheia. This commitment is precisely what distinguishes him from the Lucretian paradigm. The empirical events, which may or may not be justified, which may or may not be legal, in any case summon a deep moral response in the heart of the spectator:

> It is merely the way of thinking of the spectators [Es ist bloß die Denkungsart der Zuschauer], as it reveals itself in public while the drama of great political changes is taking place. . . . Their reaction (because of its universality) proves that mankind as a whole shares a certain character in common, and it also proves (because of its disinterestedness) that man has a moral character, or at least the makings of one. And this does not merely allow us to hope for human improvement, it is already a form of improvement itself, insofar as its influence is strong enough for the present.[30]

When viewed from a distance, encouraged by the universality of ideal history, the insecurity of the Revolution secures a feeling of human morality, regardless of any juridical problems. To be sure, from a strictly legal perspective, Kant could not condone the empirical events unfolding in France. In an essay from 1793, explicitly directed against Hobbes but not without responding to the recent regicide, the philosopher does not equivocate:

> All resistance against the supreme legislative power, the incitement of the subjects to violent expressions of discontent, all defiance which breaks out into rebellion, is the greatest and most punishable crime in a common-

[28] Cf. Robert Lehman, "Finite Stakes: Toward a Kantian Theory of the Event," 62.
[29] The affective implications of sympathy in Kant's essay are fully elaborated by Alenka Zupančič, "Enthusiasm, Anxiety and the Event."
[30] Kant, Streit der Fakultäten, 84 [182 (slightly modified)].

wealth, for it destroys its very foundations. This prohibition is *unconditional* [*unbedingt*].[31]

Although killing the governing body cannot be justified, this very transgression nonetheless serves as the occasion for sympathy. Like an earthquake, the Revolution awakes a feeling of humanity's common lot.

But is this modicum of sympathy sufficient for securing the path of progress? How long could it last before the state reasserted its own security, arguing for the establishment of a perpetual peace and thereby consigning the people to the *Friedhof* of history? Already by the first decade of the nineteenth century, Kantian optimism broadly shifts into Kleistian pessimism, as the conclusion of his "Earthquake in Chili" powerfully attests. The escape from death, saved by an escape to life, only prepares the conditions for an ultimate ghastly fall. Philosophical history may train its careful eyes on the idea of progressive freedom, but the state's institutional machine continues to be oiled by security measures of its own.

THE STATE AND THE NATION

It remains a peculiar and ultimately tragic twist of historical fate that the fervor for universal freedom prepared the blueprint for future totalitarianism, that justifiable reactions to Napoleonic imperialism among the German population would set the stage for violent nationalism. The philosopher perhaps most responsible for these conversions was Johann Gottlieb Fichte, the erstwhile supporter of republican ideals and reputed Jacobin who felt compelled to instigate the latent power of the Prussian monarch. In 1808, faced with the French occupation of Berlin, suffering at first hand the humiliation of defeat, the professor conceived his series of famous speeches aimed to define and subsequently encourage the German people to withstand the foreign incursion. German nationalism with its resolutely anti-French sentiment here finds its roots.[32] Rather than investigate in detail Fichte's fourteen *Reden an die Deutsche Nation* (*Addresses to the German Nation*), I simply want to sketch out the well-known dichotomies that articulate the philosopher's discursive logic throughout— French "civilization" versus Germanic "culture," citizenry versus *das Volk*, state versus the nation—with particular focus on the two distinct species of "security" that herewith emerge.

[31] Kant, "Vom Verhältniß der Theorie zur Praxis im Staatsrecht (Gegen Hobbes)," *Über den Gemeinspruch: Das mag in der Theorie richtig sein, taugt aber nicht für die Praxis*, in *Gesammelte Schriften*, 8: 299 [*Political Writings*, 81(modified)]. Cf. Lehman, "Finite Stakes," 63.

[32] For an extended analysis, see Louis Dumont, "A National Variant, I: German Identity: Herder's *Volk* and Fichte's *Nation*," in *Essays on Individualism: Modern Ideology in Anthropological Perspective*, 113–32; and Etienne Balibar, *Masses, Classes, Ideas: Studies on Politics and Philosophy Before and After Marx*, 61–84.

The Eighth Address opens with the crucial question: *Was ist ein Volk?* (What Is a People?).[33] Although clearly derived from Herder, Fichte's sense of the *Volk* immediately pushes toward a far more political meaning. For him, defining the people depends on a further question: "What is patriotism [*Vaterlandsliebe*], or, as one might express it more correctly, what is the individual's love [*Liebe*] for his nation?"[34] This more specific question affords a better definition of the German *Volk* because, as Fichte soon asserts, the German alone is capable of the love that is patriotism. This capacity is due to the purported fact that the German is "the original man who has not died in an arbitrary association [or constitution]"—*der ursprüngliche, und nicht in einer willkürlichen Satzung erstorbene Mensch.*[35] The arbitrary organization that mortifies humankind is literally one that has been "set up" (*Satzung*), one that Fichte will link to the idea of the "state" and the Roman *civitas* with its connotations of civilization.

Inspired by Tacitus's popular depiction of the ancient Germanic tribes and their stubborn resistance to Rome's civilizing program, Fichte conjures the image of an earnest, honorable, and loyal people who struggled for freedom from Roman imposition. In light of the present emperor from Paris, the philosopher readily becomes the spokesman for a new Arminius who will liberate the populace from French enslavement.[36] Civilization may be attractive insofar as it addresses *physical* human needs like nourishment, shelter, and safety, yet it should be repulsive insofar as it neglects mankind's *spiritual* concerns. In other words, civilization speaks to human finitude, whereas the individual should be inspired to transcend finitude, to contribute to something greater and higher than one's own life. This desire for transcendence should motivate a personal contribution to the nation, which is natural and not arbitrary, organic and not artificial, eternal and not finite.

The state is based on "positive law," "internal peace," and the preservation of "material or sensuous existence" (*sinnliches Dasein*), but the human subject— and here Fichte deploys his idealism against base materialism—is spiritual, noumenal, and morally free, much more than the bare life of sensuousness.[37] Fichte thus claims, "that an original people [*ein ursprüngliches Volk*] requires freedom, that this is the pledge [*Unterpfand*] for its persistence as originary."[38] Here, Fichte relies on the specific sense of security as collateral (*Pfand*): freedom as a security deposit that maintains trust through any number of perils in view of the future refund of salvation. In putting one's freedom on the line, one is pledged to the eternal and natural posterity of the nation, which alone is capable of providing finite lives with infinite survival.

[33] Johann Gottlieb Fichte, *Reden an die Deutsche Nation*, in *Sämmtliche Werke und Nachlass*, 3.2: 377.
[34] Fichte, *Reden an die Deutsche Nation*, 377.
[35] Fichte, *Reden an die Deutsche Nation*, 378.
[36] On the influence of Tacitus's *Germania* in Fichte's addresses, see Christopher Krebs, *A Most Dangerous Book: Tacitus's* Germania *from the Roman Empire to the Third Reich*, 183–86.
[37] Fichte, *Reden an die Deutsche Nation*, 384.
[38] Fichte, *Reden an die Deutsche Nation*, 385.

The continued life of the *Volk* and its nation therefore serves a "higher purpose" than the state's guarantee of "property, personal freedom, life, and well-being."[39] It is divinely ordained, not arbitrarily managed. To conclude his exhortation, Fichte modulates Kant's principal terms:

> From all this it arises that the State, as a mere government of human life in its usual peaceful path [*im gewöhnlichen friedlichen Gange*], is not primary and existing only for itself, but rather is merely the means for the higher purpose of the eternally consistent and continuing development [*ewig gleichmässig fortgehenden Ausbildung*] of what is purely human in this Nation.[40]

In maintaining the security (*Sicherheit*) of bare life, the state is regarded as a biopolitical machine—a cold mechanism or clockwork no longer in need of God. In the place of the mechanical state, Fichte posits the nation, whose purpose exceeds security as safety and protection by allowing transindividual freedom to serve as security (*Pfand*) through adversity for the reward of posterity. For this reason, the antistatist nature of Fichte's bold nationalism is no contradiction. All the same, the nation, too, so portrayed, engages in a biopolitical theory, not as a mechanical regime over life but as a living organism in its own right. Fichte's now notorious promotion of Germanness—the originality and uniqueness of its language and culture, blood and soil—readily assumes the horrific shape of racism, but only with the gradual conflation of state and nation, a conflation that Fichte's addresses certainly do not discourage. It is at this point, that the state's promise of security becomes coupled with the ultimately thanatopolitical drive of a nation pathologically intent on preserving its dangerously self-constructed sense of purity. Around 1800, the defeat at the hands of the Revolutionary Army may be reconfigured as an opportunity, yet this opportunity, like any chance, cannot master its eventual effects. Philosophical history may keep its eyes trained on progress, but that does not mean that it can determine precisely where that progression may lead.

[39] Fichte, *Reden an die Deutsche Nation*, 386.
[40] Fichte, *Reden an die Deutsche Nation*, 391–92.

13

Vital Instabilities

MICHELET BY THE SEA

THROUGHOUT THE 1830s, under the July Monarchy, France's own grand historian Jules Michelet could rest more or less secure in the comfort zone of the political center. The publication of his teleologically driven *Introduction à l'histoire universelle* in 1831 established his reputation as a proponent of liberal policies—of the steady progress of freedom—policies that were essentially in line with the vision of Louis-Philippe's government. That is not to say that Michelet fully represented the royalist position. On the contrary, his anticlerical disposition and staunch republicanism eventually led him to become quite critical of the government, championing the integrity and dignity of the working classes, which he vociferously celebrated in *Le Peuple* (1846), a book that brought him to international attention and helped fuel the romantic fervor that would come to a fatal halt with the catastrophe of 1848. As would be expected, with the rise of Louis-Napoléon, Michelet found himself even further marginalized.

An ardent defender of republican ideals and outspoken opponent of the new president's blatant antiparliamentarism and dictatorial aspirations, Michelet would suffer dearly in the oppressive climate of the burgeoning Second Empire. In the spring of 1851, his courses at the Collège de France were suspended following accusations that he was transforming his lecture hall into a hostile forum against the Bonapartist regime. Then, after the December coup d'état, he lost both his professorship and his beloved position as director of the National Archives when he refused to swear an oath of allegiance to the government. This political assault on Michelet's career should be compared to the treatment of royalists such as Alexis de Tocqueville and Adolphe Thiers, who were incarcerated at Mazas prison, or to the fates of other republicans like Victor Hugo and Michelet's close friend and colleague Edgar Quinet, who were forced into exile.[1] As for Michelet, he would self-impose his own version of partial exile, leaving Paris more and more frequently.

[1] For further historical details, see Robert Gildea, *Children of the Revolution: The French, 1799–1914*, 59–65.

Relieved of all official duties, disillusioned and utterly dejected, the fifty-four-year-old scholar who had spent his life tied to the centralized capital often accompanied his young bride Athénaïs to the far edges of his country's territory, adopting a nomadic life attracted primarily to the sea: to ports on the Mediterranean (Nervi, Hyères, and Toulon); to villages along the English Channel (Granville, Le Havre, Étretat, and Saint-Valéry-en-Caux); and to the Atlantic seaboard (Saint-Georges-de-Didonne).[2] Professionally and spiritually desecured, Michelet headed for the coast.

The fruit of this conversion—of this turn away from the center where history is forged toward the enduring sameness of nature at the periphery—was a series of books, perhaps written in collaboration with his wife, on the beauty and sublimity of the nonhuman world. *L'Oiseau* (1856), *L'Insecte* (1857), *La Mer* (1861), and *La Montagne* (1868) are best understood as naturalist works, belonging to the genre developed by Georges Cuvier, Geoffroy Saint-Hilaire, and Jean-Baptiste Lamarck, though in a much more popular vein. Together, they mark out a fresh path in Michelet's publishing career and further reflect his abandonment of the urban capital, a decided departure from the realm of human history, which had hitherto been the sole object of his scholarly attentions and the basis for his illustrious career and solid reputation. The brilliant narrative accomplishments of historiography—above all, the magisterial, multivolumed *Histoire de France* and the *Histoire de la Révolution*—would now be read in relation to the mainly descriptive pages on nature and wildlife. These two major categories of Michelet's œuvre would henceforth constitute a complementary pair: whereas the historical work investigates the persons, events, and consequences of an ever-changing world, the naturalist essays involve what endures through time, the immutable and unaltering background to the unfolding of human lives.[3] The achievements, circumstances, and tensions of world incidents, which undergo incessant alteration and modification, contrast with nature, which persists in its fascinating permanence or develops so slowly as to be imperceptible to individual consciousness.

It is thus with his back to the historical-political realm that Michelet opens his exemplary study on *The Sea*. Whereas Kant opened his *Perpetual Peace* beneath a satirical sign from Holland, Michelet sets off with an earnest report:

A brave Dutch sailor, a steadfast and cold observer, who spends his life on the sea, frankly says that the first impression that one gets from it is fear. The water, for every terrestrial being, is the unbreathable element, the element of asphyxiation. Fatal, eternal barrier which irreparably separates the two worlds. Let us not be surprised if the enormous mass of water that one calls

---

[2] On Michelet's political disillusionment and subsequent nomadism, see Paule Petitier, "Bords de mer: La pensée de la marge chez Michelet."

[3] For an extended analysis of the relation between Michelet's historiographical and naturalist writings, see Lionel Gossman, "Michelet and Natural History: The Alibi of Nature."

the sea, unknown and dark in its profound density, always appeared dreadful to the human imagination.[4]

The passage is certainly not untypical; and Michelet could validate his universal claims by drawing on millennia of human experience, testimony, and reflections. The sea's immensity has persistently inspired terror and awe in observers who rest where the surging waters break. Beyond, in the monochrome distance, there stretches a vast expanse, untraceable and disorienting. Michelet's inaugurating, fear-provoking view from the shore (*La mer vue du rivage*) stresses the division into "two worlds": the one where human life can be sustained and the other where it cannot. To face the sea is to contemplate demise, including one's own possible absorption into the infinitude of breathlessness.

Although Michelet has quit society, he does not forgo a fellow human's perspective. Rather, he cannily mediates the scene of dread through the figure of the anonymous and ominous sailor who, like the once nameless Odysseus, has repeatedly confronted the wrath of the waves. Having passed most of his days on board a ship, this navigator can attest to the ocean's horrific power. This rhetorical gesture of reaching out to a second person is capable of unleashing a string of cultural, national, and literary connotations. Identified as Dutch, this "steadfast and cold observer" may be linked, for example, to Holland's long involvement in maritime mercantilism, which notoriously risked the high seas for profit, or to the ghostly helmsman of lore—*der fliegende Holländer*—who can never make it to port. Allusions to anecdotes about capsized boats and shipwrecked victims may emerge. Images of legendary beasts and monstrous fictions may force their way into the picture—Scylla and Charybdis, the Kraken, the Aspidochelone, the Leviathan. The workings of the "human imagination" are sufficiently persuasive for keeping one aground. The observer on the beach trusts the judgment of the experienced observer and acknowledges the sea's dreadfulness. Upon the quiet shore, as Daniel Defoe's *Robinson Crusoe* would verify, there is still the possibility of human survival and even of a human collective, even if it consists of only two.

Michelet opens *La mer* by evoking this minimal society, formed by an imagined interlocutor and witness. Their position is secure, not by means of some protective agency or institution, but rather by the sheer fact of being apart from the terrifying sea, which is the source of profound insecurity. In being spared from both real and imagined threats, the sedentary spectator of this opening paragraph drinks in the deceptive stillness of the surface, simultaneously marveling and shuddering at the shimmering plain that extends across the dark, unfathomable abyss. The beach affords a feeling of security that is defined as safety from this boundless realm of dread, from this deadly zone that swallows

[4] Jules Michelet, *La mer*, 3.

the sun every evening, threatening "every terrestrial being" with suffocation and utter disappearance in an unmarked grave.

By starting out with a view from the beach, Michelet seems to engage in an array of other well-known security projects, like the psychological mechanism of the Burkean sublime, where "delight" as the "removal of pain or danger" closely rhymes with the "removal of concern" denoted by *securitas*.[5] Out of harm's way, protected by aesthetic distance, the subject is invited to enjoy the terrible sublimity that nourishes an inclination to sentimentality, melancholy, and romanticism. Well before Burke, as we have seen, Lucretius had presented the paradigmatic tableau of the spectator watching a shipwreck from afar in order to illustrate Epicurean *ataraxia*, the philosophical achievement of impassivity, which allows the sage to carry on with life undisturbed. Failing to find security any longer within the city, Michelet opts for the security of the shore. Here, beside the ebb and flow of nature herself, the attainment of security is simplified. One need only remain on solid ground. By stripping procedure down to this bare necessity, the path to self-preservation is rediscovered and perhaps can ultimately be brought back to the city.

Is Michelet's turn away from the political sphere anything other than a ploy to turn back to the political? Would it be possible to apply the basic lesson learned on the shore to counter the threats posed by French imperialism? Finally, if the political and social spheres remain on the horizon, can the seaside view in fact afford the attainment of *ataraxia*?

The aesthetic delight or philosophical stance that opens Michelet's *La Mer* counts as sought-after compensation for the series of losses suffered under the Second Empire. He would appear to be discouraged by the historical trajectory that degraded the Revolution's concerned liberalism into a blatant concentration on state security, particularly evident in the establishment of the Sûreté générale in 1858, which could be regarded as compromising individual liberty. Disheartened, the author of *La Mer* turns away from mortal vicissitude and instead settles on the emphatically inhuman element of the ocean. The antitheses, which organize the entirety of Michelet's study, illuminate the reasons why a historian would become a naturalist. As a prehistorical zone, the sea is also an origin or maternal source of history—*la mer est la mère*. The prehistorical is the condition of possibility of the historical. Its formidable power is inescapable. Lionel Gossman's reflections on Michelet's naturalist endeavors are particularly evocative in this regard: "History, for Michelet, is ... nothing less than the never-ending struggle against the ancien régime of nature, the process by which

[5] See Edmund Burke, *Philosophical Enquiry into the Origin of Our Ideas of the Sublime and the Beautiful*, 1.4, 33–4. It would be interesting to consider Burke's conception of "delight" and its implicit security in relation to his political conservatism, which essentially turns on the stability of the sublime church and the beautiful aristocracy. On this issue, see Daniel O'Neill, "Burke on Democracy and the Death of Western Civilization."

nature, woman, and the past in their confusing multitude of unstable, constantly varying forms, are progressively transformed from capricious mistresses of human destiny into trained assistants in the creation of a specifically human order."[6]

Accordingly, Michelet's flight from the capital under Napoléon III is less a turn to nature and more a return. A particularly rich text from 1831, inscribed in Michelet's personal journal, directly indicates how nature—the sea in particular—motivated the historiographical project from its inception. The passage records a Sunday spent in the Norman port of Le Havre. As in the description from *La Mer*, Michelet mediates the view from the shore through a second person. Here, it is not a brave, stern Dutchman but rather the fragile figure of his daughter, Adèle:

> [Sunday, August 7]: Toward afternoon, a walk by myself; a swim in the sea. The storm in the distance . . . *tristis usque ad mortem* . . . Like Chryses, I am thinking about my daughter. Infinity, what do you want of me? I feel so small . . . I am deeply moved by having seen my little child pensive in front of the sea, frail child, on whom I have placed my life and whom I shall not be able to protect. Oh! If only my name could surround you with some respect, with some protection after me! It is also for her that I would have wished for glory.[7]

The figure of the frail daughter has been installed between the scholar and the sea. The historian-scholar looks at the girl who gazes upon the water. This configuration, this emotionally fraught mise-en-scène, significantly modifies the Lucretian image of the philosophical spectator. Rather than sage composure or Epicurean *ataraxia*, it is a "sadness unto death" that here attends the viewer's viewer, ostensibly because he is incapable of procuring perfect safety for his beloved child. Like Chryses, Apollo's priest dishonored by haughty Agamemnon, the solicitous father strives to rescue his daughter from sovereign power. Yet, unable to call upon divine wrath, Michelet's only hope would appear to be a grand historical project—a scholarly, glorious monument that might arrive to shield his offspring from danger, to salvage her from the unbreathable element of infinity.

The father's hope is expressed from the profundity of despair: *tristis usque ad mortem*. The line alludes to the Tenebrae Responsorial for Holy Thursday:

> *Tristis est anima mea usque ad mortem:*
> *sustinete hic, et vigilate mecum:*
> *nunc videbitis turbam, quæ circumdabit me:*
> *Vos fugam capietis, et ego vadam immolari pro vobis.*

---

[6] Gossman, "Michelet and Natural History," 309.
[7] Jules Michelet, *Journal*, 1: 83 (ellipses in original).

Sad is my soul unto death:
stay here, and keep watch with me:
soon you will see a crowd of men surround me.
You shall flee, and I will go to be sacrificed for you.

It is not from Epicurus's Garden but from the Garden of Gethsemane—the Garden of the Passion—where Jesus addressed his disciples from the depths of his own imminent suffering. Whereas the Athenian garden strove to eliminate passions (*pathē*), the garden outside Jerusalem insists on cultivating them. Instead of providing security, Jesus commanded vigilance. All the same, this Good Shepherd moved to give up his life in order to promise a truer, eternal security.

Michelet's citation from Christian liturgy suggests a theological context for his meditations by the sea. On Sunday, August 7, 1831, the date of this diary entry, Michelet was presumably present at the morning service where he would have heard the day's reading from the Gospel of Matthew (14:22–33). Could this passage have instigated his reflections that afternoon? Following the miracle of feeding the multitudes on the shores of Lake Gennesaret, Jesus ordered his disciples to depart by boat, while he went off to pray in solitude. As in Michelet's note, the move away from the crowd into solitude is emphasized, as well as the eventual turn to the sea. In the Gospel account we learn that overnight the disciples' boat had drifted far from land and was being battered by strong gusts:

> And in the night's fourth watch [*quarta vigilia noctis*] Jesus came walking toward them on the sea. But when the disciples saw him walking on the sea, they were troubled, saying, "It is a ghost!" And they cried out in fear [*prae timore*]. But immediately Jesus spoke to them and said, "Take heart [*habete fiduciam*], it is I; do not be afraid." (Matthew 14:25–27)

The day before Jesus fed "the multitudes" (*turbas*), but now he finds his own disciples "troubled" (*turbati*). They perceive the spectacle of a man walking upon the uncrossable sea to be a malevolent specter. Jesus, however, readily comforts them: the objects of his vigilance (*vigilia*) remain objects of concern. He stills the hearts of his spiritual children who have placed their trust in him.

The fearfulness of the sea, of course, could not deter Jesus from rescuing his lost but faithful flock. Miraculously he treads upon the unpaved waters. Yet, is such salvation possible for the mortal historian? Michelet continues:

> I am experiencing an abysmal emptiness inside me. Seeing, on the one hand this terrible image of the infinite, and on the other hand my daughter, and this attraction that calls us back into the chasm of nature, I felt the fiber of my individuality rip apart. The general, the universal, the eternal, these are the homeland of man. It is from you that I shall demand relief, my noble

country; you must take the place of God who has escaped us, you must fill the incommensurable abyss that an extinct Christianity has left in us. You owe us the equivalent of the infinite. We all feel individuality perishing in us. May there begin again the feeling of social generality, of human universality of the world! Then maybe we shall rise again toward God.

Faced with God's absence and an "extinct" religion, the careworn scholar is determined to devote his life to rebuilding "the homeland of man" by means of indefatigable labor. His *History of France*, which will eventually number twenty-seven magisterial volumes, will hopefully allow him to secure an otherwise evanescent humanity. Whereas Jesus sacrificed himself for the sake of the church, Michelet will offer his life up for the sake of his *grand œuvre*. Sensing the abyss tearing him apart from within and threatening to swallow up his offspring, he decides to construct a monument as the only means left for salvation. Historiography may even possibly prepare a return to the divinity. Otherwise, the individual will drown into boundlessness, like a young girl overwhelmed by a massive tide. The journal entry closes:

> The sterile sea, Homer says: . . . yes, the infinite has become sterile, ever since God has been in exile from it: sterile, deserted, devastated, we roll about like a pebble on the shore. It rolls and the swell crashes, breaking its points; its individuality perishes, it becomes like everything else. How to make a distinction henceforth? Individuality perishes with the barbarous life, universality perishes with religion. Ah! May this shipwreck be received by the city; the city is our only asylum. And may it transfigure itself in the sky! It is time to leave: the view of this sterile infinity has saddened me to the point of tears.

Decades later, upon being banished from the city, Michelet returns to the sea, which by now has sufficiently shown that all security projects—theological, political, or scholarly—ultimately succumb to the sea's mighty voracity. The drafting of his long *Histoire*, which ably sustained a single, coherent narrative, sought to stabilize humanity and nation alike, to wrest some identifiable form from nature's formlessness. In the end, these massive efforts of preservation proved fatally insufficient.

Whereas Michelet lamented the dreadful boundlessness of the sea and struggled in vain to secure his and his nation's identity, Friedrich Nietzsche celebrated beside the watery abyss, gaily dancing at God's funeral and at the Self's wake. Although Nietzsche would concede the existence of some instinct of self-preservation, he would view it as one of any number of consequences to a more profound instinct: the notorious "will to power." This will lies deeper than the individual self and is an expression of life itself: namely, life's will to expand, to explode any and all determinations, any and all fixed forms, even or especially when life destroys itself in the process. "The wish to preserve oneself is the symptom of a condition of distress, of a limitation of the really fundamental instinct of life, which aims at the expansion of power, and wishing for that [*in diesem Willen*], frequently risks and even sacrifices self-preservation."[8] For Michelet, the self's perishing was a cause for alarm and also a formidable challenge: a heroic effort to shore up the individual against time and circumstance, against the natural current. For Nietzsche, the self's perishing is also a challenge, but in no way a reason for fright. Instead, it is the sign of the greatest achievement: the self's own overcoming. If Michelet imagines himself in the role of Homer's Chryses, the priest of Apollo, Nietzsche will eventually place all his offerings upon the altar of Dionysus. For Nietzsche, who regarded monumental history as a burden, the desire to remove all concern is debilitating, a desire born of weakness and fear, and therefore a cause of paralysis, which traps life itself into a stable form, secure but lifeless.

Nietzsche: Più Lento

> Only by forgetting this primitive world of metaphor can one live with any repose, security, and consistency.
>
> Friedrich Nietzsche, *On Truth and Lies*
> *in an Extra-Moral Sense*

Nietzsche, who resolutely and joyously occupied interstitial zones of irresolvability, frequently trained his nondisciplinary eye on the benefits of philological slowness, for example in the 1886 preface to *Morgenröthe (Daybreak)*, which I partially cited in my introduction:

> For precisely this reason philology is today more necessary than ever, precisely in this way it attracts us and enchants [*bezaubert*] us most strongly, amidst an age of "work," that is to say, of haste, of indecent and perspiring alacrity, which is intent on "getting everything done" at once, even every book, old and new: —philology itself will not "get everything done" so lightly: it teaches how to read *well* [*gut lesen*], that is, slowly, profoundly, considerately and cautiously [*rück- und vorsichtig*], with ulterior motives [*Hintergedanken*], with doors ajar, with delicate fingers and eyes.[9]

The caution recommended here is aimed toward protesting against those societal pressures that foster hasty productivity and the careless consumerism it serves. In an age driven by utilitarian goals, philology "enchants" (*bezaubert*), introducing a certain "magic" (*Zauber*) that turns our heads in other perhaps irrational directions. Philology thereby nourishes Nietzsche's abhorrence of stabilization. In a note jotted down a year before this preface, Nietzsche con-

[8] Friedrich Nietzsche, *The Gay Science* (§349), 291–92 [*KSA* 3: 585].
[9] Friedrich Nietzsche, *Morgenröte*, *KSA* 3: 17 (emphasis in original) [*Daybreak*, 5 (modified)].

fesses his "deep aversion to relax once and for all in some totalizing view of the world; the magic [*Zauber*] of the opposed way of thinking."[10] In brief, philology's enchantment consists in raising urgent questions and thereby forestalling complacency. In keeping doors ajar, philology holds open what would otherwise be foreclosed. Explicitly neither a discipline nor a science but an "art" (*Kunst*), philology dismisses routine methods of ready-made knowledge and received ideas, delving instead more deeply, casting its gaze backward and forward, "considerately and cautiously" (*rück- und vorsichtig*) with hindsight and foresight. This Epimethean and Promethean movement, incessantly back and forth, motivates the meticulous care devoted to each and every word encountered. Under the aegis of instrumental rationalism and the work it inspires, slowness may be regarded as an idleness that reflects indifference or unconcern; yet philology magically revaluates such inertia as a "good": with Nietzsche's emphasis, "it teaches how to read *well* [gut *lesen*]."

With this key revaluation, Nietzsche enlists philology to serve as a critique of perfect security. A lack of concern characterizes the frenetic pace of the present age, whose "indecent and perspiring alacrity" aims to put all worry to rest and enter into the tomb of perpetual peace. In contrast, philology rejects insouciance. It is beset with hyperbolic cares, informed by a disposition that leads to an altogether different, desecuring activity. Nietzsche's entire genealogical project is motivated by nineteenth-century developments in historical semantics, a subfield of philology that attended to shifts in morphology, phonology, and etymology across history. Rather than grant that language is capable of establishing a sound and reliable system of reference, this kind of philological work proceeded by treating all linguistic operations with skepticism.[11] At the head of the preface, Nietzsche specifies this work—a work that does not "get everything done"—as "subterranean" (*Unterirdischen*), a technique that "drills, mines, and undermines [*Bohrenden, Grabenden, Untergrabenden*]."[12] It slows down the process of reading and burrows deep below the surface of the everyday sense of words. It disrupts easy communication and distrusts accomplishment; and this is precisely why philological work has everything to do with questions of security:

> I undertook something which could not have been done by everyone: I went down into the depths; I tunneled to the foundation [*Grund*]; I started to investigate and discover an old *faith* which for millennia we philosophers used to build upon the most secure of all foundations [*auf dem sichersten Grunde*]—again and again, even though every previous building collapsed.[13]

---

[10] The note is from Nietzsche's *Nachlaß* (1885–86), *KSA* 12: 142.

[11] On the relation between nineteenth-century comparative philology and Nietzsche's approach to genealogy, see Simone Roggenbuck, "Die genealogische Idee in der vergleichenden Sprachwissenschaft des 19. Jahrhunderts: Stufen, Stammbäume, Wellen." For further discussion, see Geoffrey Harpham, "Roots, Races, and the Return to Philology."

[12] Nietzsche, *Morgenröte, KSA* 3: 11 [*Daybreak*, 1 (modified)].

[13] Nietzsche, *Morgenröte, KSA* 3: 12 [*Daybreak*, 1–2 (modified)].

Security here comprises the sure ground upon which philosophy used to carry on, unimpeded by thwarting fears or burdensome distress. Metaphysics thus attempted to minimize risks to the point where one could build projects with calm certainty and assurance. Philosophical method long depended on laying down "firm foundations," as in the following description given by Leibniz:

> If one builds a house in a sandy place, one must continue digging until one meets solid rock or firm foundations; if one wants to unravel a tangled thread one must look for the beginning of the thread; if the greatest weights are to be moved, Archimedes demanded only a stable place. In the same way, if one is to establish the elements of human knowledge some fixed point is required, on which we can safely rest and from which we can set out without fear.[14]

Nietzsche's philological philosophy digs deeply as well, but even more radically, insofar as the ground it unearths is shown to be hardly firm or stable at all. His tireless mining projects invariably undermine every principle, producing genealogies that are tantamount to an earthquake shattering all composure. Whereas the exploration described by Leibniz is motivated by a desire for safety and freedom from fear, Nietzsche shows himself to be undaunted by terror, fully cognizant of his vulnerability, and ready to acknowledge the fragility of any interpretation.

Within the larger context of *Daybreak*, as elsewhere across Nietzsche's writings, the ground desired by metaphysicians is understood as morality, as the clear distinction between good and evil; and it is precisely this distinction that turns out to be not as secure as conventionally surmised. A slow, profound, and cautious excavation of our moral systems reveals that this "old faith" secures nothing. It aims to demonstrate why every philosophical project erected upon such systems inevitably falls to pieces. In contrast to Leibniz, for Nietzsche every "ground" is insufficient. His patient, critical archaeology problematizes any approach that operates on presumed moral clarity and purportedly unquestionable values—in a word, on hasty reading. The philologist thus keeps doors open, not only to fresh questions and unexpected associations but also to invasions and assaults from without. Philology cannot "get everything done" because the system is never airtight. Hence, the philologist proceeds with "ulterior motives"—*Hintergedanken*—literally, thoughts behind the thoughts that would otherwise support easy, routine, worry-free consumption. Philology's deceleration is infectious (but not sickly): in slowing down, it slows us down, makes us uneasy, wary, insecure.

In this respect, Nietzsche is a great psychologist, an adventurous pioneer of hidden depths. This psychological practice, and its concomitant perspectivism, is fully abetted by the slow-motion method of philology: "All psychology begins with idleness."[15] And when the good, patient reader pauses to mine the soul,

---

[14] Leibniz, *Philosophical Writings*, 93.
[15] Nietzsche, *Twilight of the Idols*, 156 [*KSA* 6: 59].

there emerges the realization that any attempt to settle or determine meaning is a gesture toward preservation that has an altogether weakening effect. The will to security, to put life's concerns to rest, contradicts a more fundamental will to power, a will that is deeply tied to physiological motives:

> Every philosophy that ranks peace above war, every ethic with a negative definition of happiness, every metaphysics and physics that knows some *finale*, some final state of some sort, every predominantly aesthetic or religious craving for some Apart, Beyond, Outside, Above, permits the question whether it was not sickness that inspired the philosopher. . . . Often I have asked myself whether, taking a large view, philosophy has not been merely an interpretation of the body and a *misunderstanding of the body*.[16]

Finalization can never be secured because the body is a site of unceasing conflict: pacification, asceticism, and idealism ignore the primacy of life; they hurry the mind on to escape the messy and frightening realm of existence by promising a freedom from all troubles, but existence cannot be thus evaded without serious consequences. In Nietzsche's view—and arguably for Kant—the afterlife of eternal tranquillity, desirelessness, and the realm of ideal forms are but euphemisms for death.

On this basis, Roberto Esposito credits Nietzsche for discovering the implications of the problem of autoimmunity. The problem stems from institutions that, although intended to safeguard life, end up severely and fatally restricting life. As Nietzsche consistently claims, philosophy has "misunderstood the body" insofar as it has failed to comprehend the conflictual nature of bodily instincts and drives. According to Nietzsche, it was this physiological conflict that first prompted civilization to employ prophylactic measures in the form of institutions, but such immunizing practices—as Hobbes himself recognized—could only shelter life by protecting life from itself. Esposito writes: "The thesis [Nietzsche] advances is that such a logic cures illness in a self-contradictory form because it produces a greater illness than the one it wanted to prevent. . . . The stability and the duration that immunitary programs assure wind up inhibiting that innovative development that they need to stimulate. Impeding the possible dissolution of the organism, they also stop its growth, condemning it to stasis and impoverishment."[17] Fortification becomes immurement, whereby the malnourished soul ultimately perishes. Undaunted by fear yet fearful of the total eradication of fear, Nietzsche rejects the comforting, anesthetized state of security for the painful yet vital affirmation of life.

> Only great pain, the long, slow pain that takes its time—on which we are burned, as it were, with green wood—compels us philosophers to descend

---

[16] Nietzsche, *The Gay Science* (preface to the second edition), 34–35 (emphasis in original) [*KSA* 3: 348].

[17] Esposito, *Bios*, 91.

into our ultimate depths and to put aside all trust, everything good-natured, everything that would interpose a veil, that is mild, that is medium—things in which formerly we may have found our humanity.[18]

The philosopher's body serves as a source for a new perspective, provided one takes one's time, a perspective gained by slow pain and painfully slow reading, a perspective driven by active, often inscrutable forces that strive to break from abstractions, norms, and conventions. As Pierre Klossowski tersely comments, for Nietzsche "the act of thinking became identical with suffering, and suffering with thinking."[19] Rather than live securely—which is hardly a life at all— Nietzsche notoriously encourages us to "live dangerously": "Build your cities on the slopes of Vesuvius! Send your ships into uncharted seas! Live at war with your peers and yourselves!"[20] Prepared to quit the safety of the shore, Nietzsche, like Machiavelli before him, willfully plunges into the unbounded:

> And now, after we have been on our way in this manner, we argonauts of the ideal, with more daring perhaps than is prudent, and have suffered shipwreck and damage often enough, but are to repeat it, healthier than one likes to permit us, dangerously healthy, ever again healthy—it will seem to us as if, as a reward, we now confronted an as yet undiscovered country whose boundaries nobody has surveyed yet, something beyond all the lands and nooks of the ideal so far, a world so overrich in what is beautiful, strange, questionable, terrible and divine that our curiosity as well as our craving to possess it has got beside itself—alas, now nothing will sate us any more![21]

To Michelet's beached sadness-- *tristis usque ad mortem*—Nietzsche responds with a *gaya scienza* that laughs away all determinations. He maintains this indeterminacy precisely by reading and encouraging others to read with care, *cum cura*. If we approach Nietzsche as good, slow, and careful readers, we would then appreciate the difficulty, if not the utter impossibility, of securing the meaning of any text, including Nietzsche's own. Nothing is safe; nothing immune. Across his late writings, Nietzsche consistently struggles to alert his readers against taking his words as dogma. He drives us to recoil from resting in orthodoxy. As he reminds us in the pages of *Ecce Homo*, his Zarathustra should not be regarded or admired as a prophet or a preacher, as someone who "demands belief"—

> You repay a teacher badly by remaining a pupil. And why don't you want to pluck at my wreath? You are devoted [*verehrt*] to me: but what if your devotion [*Verehrung*] subsides someday? Beware not to be killed by a statue! You

---

[18] Nietzsche, *The Gay Science* (preface to the second edition), 36 [*KSA* 3: 350].
[19] Pierre Klossowski, *Nietzsche and the Vicious Circle*, 23.
[20] Nietzsche, *The Gay Science* (§ 283), 228 [*KSA* 3: 526].
[21] Nietzsche, *The Gay Science* (§ 382), 346 [*KSA* 3: 636].

say you believe in Zarathustra? But who cares about Zarathustra! You are my believers, but who cares about believers![22]

These lines deserve to be read in conjunction with the passage from the *Daybreak* preface cited above. The philological reader, the one who has learned to "read well," must not be a bad reader who desires nothing other than the security of unequivocal knowledge or truth. Philology is worthy of devotion, but this devotion should be used as an instrument to ward off the fatal effects of devotion itself. It instills distrust, which translates into caution, and thereby saves us from the lethal security of petrified authority: "Beware not to be killed by a statue!"

What Nietzsche is decidedly not doing is replacing one secured system with another. His method does not clear the field for a new, more solid securement, but instead continuously plows away. To allude to another image from the *Daybreak* preface, we could say that Nietzsche, too, is like the "scorpion, that stabs its sting into its own body."[23] Faced with this kind of writer, who elsewhere describes himself as a "question mark" or as "dynamite," our only option as readers is to celebrate with him the death of the "old god" of certainty. Reading *cum cura philologica*, we may abandon the secure land of certitude and thereby enter upon the infinite realm of unforeseeable potential. Again, the sea is never too distant:

> At long last the horizon appears free to us again, even if it should not be bright; at long last our ships may venture out again, venture out to face any danger; all the daring of the lover of knowledge is permitted again; the sea, *our* sea, lies open again; perhaps there has never yet been such an "open sea."[24]

Once the moral ground upon which our terrestrial philosophies are based is exposed as weak, fragile, and insecure, we are encouraged to flee *terra firma* for the seas of endless possibility. Nietzsche radicalizes the gesture by going "further," cutting the lines for good and adventurously freeing thought from any methodological mooring. The point is to end the securing of life and instead enliven security:

> *In the horizon of the infinite*—We have left the land and have embarked. We have the bridges behind us—even more, we have destroyed the land behind us. Now, little ship, look out before you! Beside you lies the ocean; true, it does not always roar, and at times it lies spread out like silk and gold and dreams of goodness. But hours will come when you will realize that it is infinite and that there is nothing more fearful than infinity. Oh, the poor bird

---

[22] Nietzsche, *Ecce Homo*, 73 (modified) [*KSA* 6: 260–61]. Nietzsche is here citing from his own *Also sprach Zarathustra*, sec. 1.3.

[23] Nietzsche, *Morgenröte*, *KSA* 3: 13 [*Daybreak*, 2 (modified)].

[24] Nietzsche, *The Gay Science* (§ 343), 280 (emphasis in original) [*KSA* 3: 574].

that felt free and now strikes the walls of this cage! Woe, when you feel homesick for the land as if it had offered more *freedom*—and there is no longer any "land."[25]

MYTH, LIFE, AND ANTHROPOLOGY

Nietzsche clearly was not a theologian. However, this did not prevent him on occasion to speak theologically.

> Theologically speaking—one should listen, for I seldom speak as a theologian—it was God himself who at the end of his day's work lay down as a serpent beneath the Tree of Knowledge: this was how he recuperated from being God. . . . He had made everything too beautiful. . . . The devil is merely God's idleness on every seventh day.[26]

As often with Nietzsche, the blatant rhetorical devices—here, the parenthetical apostrophe, the authoritative persona, the pregnant ellipses—produce an ironic tone without undercutting a serious intent. A further aspect of irony comes to the fore when we realize that, although he claims to be speaking theologically, *als Theologe*, he in fact is interpreting scripture as a mythologist, *als Mythologe*. Whereas dogma, as the central object of the theologian's concern, is grounded in the rigor of the letter, in the *infallibility* of the text, myth is subject to infinite variation, desecured from any source so as to speak to fresh circumstances. That is to say, while a theological approach strives to restitute or restore an original meaning bound to the written word, mythic retelling aims to achieve a revaluation. Hence, Nietzsche emphasizes the oral nature of his intervention: *man höre zu* (one should listen). In contrast, there is the opening of the Gospel of Luke, which stresses the written quality of the evangelium, legitimized by its closeness to the source: "It seemed fitting for me as well, having investigated everything carefully [*akribōs*] from the beginning, to write [*grapsai*] for you, most excellent Theophilus, so that you may know the certainty [*asphaleian*] about the things you have been taught."[27] This "certainty" or "security" (*asphaleia*), which Luther renders as "certain ground or reason" (*gewissen Grund*), is precisely what Nietzsche's mythic re-citation attempts to unsettle.

Like most revolutionary gestures, Nietzsche's biblical variation is not without connections to the past. Identifying Eden's serpent as the Old Testament God, equating the world's creator as the principle of evil, is of course the core premise of the Gnostic myth, which consistently distinguishes the tyrannical Demiurge of this world from the Heavenly Father of salvation from the next world. If Nietzsche were indeed speaking theologically, without irony, this dis-

[25] Nietzsche, *Gay Science* (§ 124), 180–81 [*KSA* 3: 480].
[26] Nietzsche, *Ecce Homo*, 135 [*KSA* 6: 351] (ellipsis in original).
[27] Luke 1:3 (*New American Standard Bible*).

tinction would exhaust the meaning of his elliptical sketch. Yet, his desecurement of scripture works much further by providing a statement on the value of insecurity itself. The passage appears in *Ecce Homo* (1888), in the section providing brief reviews of his previous publications ("Why I Write Such Good Books"). These rehearsals alone attest Nietzsche's willingness to subject his own writings to mythic variation, a measure against the tendency, which he always feared, that his texts would turn into dogma, that his word would become the Word. Specifically, Nietzsche's evocation of the scene in Paradise concludes the two concise paragraphs devoted to *Beyond Good and Evil* (1886), which he describes as "a critique of modernity" combined with more affirmative indications of modernity's potential to overcome itself. He goes on to contrast this book's proximal attention to the present age with *Zarathustra*, which was composed on the basis of great "distance." This shift in focus from the far to the near is concomitant with a conversion from *Zarathustra*'s goodwill to the latter's "avowed hardness and cruelty," which is subsequently described as a "recuperation" (*Erholung*): "Who in the end can guess *what* type of recuperation is needed after a squandering of goodness like Zarathustra?"[28] Thus, the portrayal of how God "recuperated" (*erholte sich*) from being God mirrors Nietzsche's own renewal after the benevolent expenditure that is *Zarathustra*. The concluding desecurement of the scriptural tradition—identifying God as the serpent— is an allegory of the way *Beyond Good and Evil* desecures the previous work.

Paradise was made too beautifully. The stable completeness of his "day's work" was satisfying to the point of utter satiety. And as Nietzsche the self-claimed psychologist recognized, stability and permanence are the conditions for torpor and boredom—in a word, lifelessness. A world created without any room for improvement is a world without any future, without any historical potential, and therefore hardly a world at all. Faced with this eventlessness, God metamorphoses into the serpent that will lure creation into time—a transformation that effects a healing "revival" (*Erholung*).

If Nietzsche seldom speaks theologically, it is because the orientation of his mode of thinking was always decidedly anthropological. Although offered as an account of God's recuperation, the passage ultimately speaks to the lot of mankind. What the ellipses "leave out" (*elleipein*) are the ramifications for human life, which myths always invite their readers to supply. In Paradise, the benevolent God provided for every need; took care of every desire; and consigned the first humans, like Candide in Eldorado or perhaps Nietzsche in Silvaplana, to absolute and therefore listless security. The transformation into the seducing serpent would then be God's most caring act: to make sure that the carefree existence in Eden would not render mankind careless.

Well before Nietzsche's lonely death in 1900, the aftershocks of his prose began to be felt across the intellectual landscape of Europe. In his last writings,

---

[28] Nietzsche, *Ecce Homo*, 135 [*KSA* 6: 351].

the thinker of the mythic opposition between Apollo and Dionysus sensed that he himself was already becoming a myth or perhaps dogma, that his life, which was one thing, was being conflated with his books, which were another.[29] From the 1890s on, hagiographical accounts, composed as the philosopher lay dumb-struck and bedridden under his sister's watch in Weimar, competed with more serious and somewhat more sober engagement. Nietzsche's critique of security as perfect stability, expressed by an affirmation of life and a discrediting of metaphysics, motivated a variety of discourses that would come to characterize an entire epoch. Nietzsche himself indicated that he was to be born posthu-mously, and, in the wake of his ultimate demise, there was no lack of thinkers, writers, and poets eager to celebrate his birth. Indeed, his books exerted a strong appeal on a generation disabused of cultural and political institutions, which more and more came across as utterly exhausted. Reform movements, fueled by a desire for rejuvenation, found their confirmation in multiple modes of thinking from *Lebensphilosophie* (philosophy of life) and vitalism to irratio-nalism and expressionism—each taking many of their purported cues from select readings of Nietzsche's texts. Here was a vociferous spokesman for the sizable opposition to the bourgeois values of peace, prosperity, and security, which were now regarded as anemic fantasies carried over from the Enlighten-ment—feeble glorifications of the individual subject incapable of recognizing his own fragility.

At the turn of the century, politicians like Franz Mehring, leader of the Ger-man Democratic Socialist Party (SPD), read Nietzsche as paving the way for the workers' movement, while more aristocratically (and esoterically) inclined sorts pored over the Dionysian scripture for apocalyptic clues heralding the complete annihilation of conventional, philistine values. In Munich, the charis-matic poet Stefan George and his associates of the so-called Cosmic Circle (Der Kosmikerkreis), including the life-philosopher Ludwig Klages and self-proclaimed Gnostic Alfred Schuler, promulgated the image of Nietzsche as mo-dernity's last prophet. Belonging to this general trend was Ernst Bertram's rhap-sodic biography, *Nietzsche: Versuch einer Mythologie*, published in the utterly desecured year of 1918. Bertram's "Attempt at a Mythology" appeared in George's series *Blätter für die Kunst* and was consequently linked to the high priest of poetry and his own circle. Despite this clear affiliation to the George-Kreis, Bertram's portrayal bore only a superficial similarity to the circle's her-metic mission, presenting Nietzsche in a far more nuanced fashion, specifically as a thinker essentially incapable of supporting any ideological position, in-cluding the one blatantly proffered by the dazzling rhetoric of George and his devoted disciples.[30] Nonetheless, throughout the Weimar Republic, Bertram's extremely popular book nourished the right-wing appropriation of Nietzsche

---

[29] Nietzsche, *Ecce Homo*, 99–100 [*KSA* 6: 298].

[30] Cf. Robert Norton's introduction to his translation of Ernst Bertram's biography: *Nietzsche: Attempt at a Mythology*, xvi–xvii.

and the project of remythicization that he purportedly instigated, eventually leading, under the warped direction of Alfred Baeumler, to the well-known exploitation of Nietzsche by the Nazis. Needless to say, the shameless refashioning of Nietzsche as the poetic philosopher of the Will to Power and the philosophical poet of the Germanic *Volk* speak more to Baeumler's own political aspirations than to Nietzsche's own mode of thought, which would have been repelled by such blatant dogmatization.

To be sure, Nietzsche was not altogether innocent of encouraging quasi-theological interpretations. As we have seen, his own reading of *Beyond Good and Evil* prompted him to adopt a theological voice, as though in anticipation of what his reception might look like. Yet, Nietzsche was more inclined to knock idols over than raise them up. Thus, the theological persona, punctuated by ellipses, is assumed in order to express the mainly anthropological concerns that course through his work. In other words, with Nietzsche, the idea of transcendence no longer applies to some theological realm but rather, more dynamically, to mankind's own capacity to move beyond or further, to step past natural and conventional limits, toward "self-overcoming" and continual "enhancement"[31]—an immanent transcendence that falls to mankind's own responsibility, a call for creative reorientation in this world and a rejection of any escape route to another, including the transindividual phantasm of the *Volk*. Nietzsche's frequent debasements of all nationalist rhetoric—a perpetual sore spot for Nazi ideologues—would alone be enough to wring his books from the fascists' grasp.[32]

Dogmatic interpretations of Nietzsche willfully fail to understand the significance of the philosopher's critique of security, which is always lodged to instigate the enhancement and intensification of time-bound life. To redirect a well-known phrase from Hannah Arendt, the banality of fascist evil would have to be distinguished from the "evil" exhibited by the divine serpent conjured in Nietzsche's recasting of Eden, a figure that pulls God and mankind into history, pulling them forward, mortalizing them—an "evil" that goes beyond the good and evil of any secured and restraining moral system. Fascist ideology locates the drive for vital expansion in the nation itself and therefore arms itself against anything that would impede this "life." The state must be immunized against whatever threatens, parasitically, the national health. Yet, the two primary instruments of fascist biopolitics—eugenics and extermination—demonstrate the ideology's contradictions and its horrifying consequences: at once promoting and destroying lives. Biopolitics not only becomes a euphemism for thanatopolitics but also deludes itself into believing that the life of the nation can be preserved by eliminating whatever is judged to be inimical to this life. It turns to dogma in order to achieve stability; and it is here that it lethally perverts

---

[31] See, e.g., Nietzsche, *Beyond Good and Evil*, §257, 201–2 [*KSA* 5: 205–6].

[32] On Nietzsche's complex views on nationalist trends in the political context of his day, see Christian Emden, *Friedrich Nietzsche and the Politics of History*, especially 79–128.

Nietzsche, who would insist that stability is the surest path to debilitation. Whereas the Nazis notoriously rallied against "degenerate art" (*Entartete Kunst*), Nietzsche regarded "degeneration" (*Entartung*) itself as an agent of "ennoblement"—health is accomplished by means of inoculation, not quarantine.[33] In Nietzsche's view, the French Revolution had nothing to do with the moral progress of humanity, and still less with the teleological drive of the Spirit, but rather with the simple fact that the aristocracy surrendered its prerogatives and settled into the complacent role of being "a mere *function* of the monarchy."[34]

For Nietzsche, the thesis of self-overcoming entails that any measure of self-preservation must be provisional, lest it become a means of devitalizing self-paralysis. The provisionality of preservation wards off complacency, lethargy, and therefore vulnerability. Life is the perpetual striving to avoid being no longer. One may relate this tendency to the capacity for immanent transcendence, to the human potential to detach from the experiential world to which mankind nevertheless belongs. This freedom from natural restrictions is what Max Scheler defined as man's "world-openness" (*Weltoffenheit*), a capacity for emancipation from instinctual drives and environmental circumstances. For Scheler, this fundamentally human condition is at once a source of transcendent possibility and pure anxiety. In *Die Stellung des Menschen im Kosmos* (*Man's Place in Nature*, 1928), Scheler unfolds a "philosophical anthropology" that considers the various travails of modernity—isolation, mechanization, social disintegration, and so forth—as a fundamental lack of orientation, of man not knowing his "position in the cosmos."[35] Yet this problem of localization becomes the source for human ingenuity, the very precondition for human creativity.

Helmuth Plessner, in *Die Stufen des Organischen und der Mensch* (*The Stages of the Organic and Man*), also published in 1928, lends further emphasis to mankind's natural deficiency and the opportunities it affords by insisting on humanity's "eccentricity"—a term borrowed from Friedrich Hölderlin in his criticism of Hegel. Whereas all other animals are "centrically" equipped with instincts, eccentricity compels humans to develop compensatory means for orientation in their lifeworld. As with Nietzsche, man is encouraged to enhance life, to become a creative artist, to live aesthetically by means of the images, metaphors and extramoral lies that alone justify existence—an "aestheticodicy" for the future. In the wake of God's death, mankind is called upon to create its world, rather than be a passive subject to its givenness.

Scheler's and Plessner's philosophical anthropology, as it developed during the Weimar Republic, was clearly a response to the catastrophic destabilization attributable to the First World War. More than ever, theological and

---

[33] Nietzsche, "Ennoblement through Degeneration," *Human, All Too Human*, § 224 [*KSA* 2: 187–89]. On this subject and its relation to biopolitical regimes, see Esposito, *Bios*, 103–5.

[34] Nietzsche, *Beyond Good and Evil*, § 258, 202 [*KSA* 5: 206] (emphasis in original).

[35] Max Scheler, *Die Stellung des Menschen im Kosmos* (1928).

cosmological-scientific interpretations demonstrated their inadequacy to produce meaning. Philosophical anthropology offered fresh solutions, yet resisted normative assessments that might establish fixed truths of some universal, human essence. Instead, it focused on the universal conditions that rendered every established position both *necessary* and *provisional*. Constancy is an attribute of the functions of human activity but not its contents. Specifically, for Plessner, philosophical critique or skepsis is a vital mode of *Entsicherung*—a *descuring* that vividly removes the "safety catch" (*Sicherung*) of false authority and dogmatic, reifying patterns of thought.[36] Although Plessner sets his sights on these secured positions in order to the clear the ground for a more secure security, he stresses that any stabilization that ignores its provisionality is doomed to debilitate the very life it aimed to save.

On this point, philosophical anthropology overlaps significantly with the intentions of psychoanalytic theory. Psychoanalysis employs a host of methods designed to defuse defense mechanisms, topple resistances, unwork repression, or interpret sublimations, all of which can be defined as mental devices developed to shield the ego from the redoubtable force of unconscious drives. Freud's *Civilization and Its Discontents*, in particular the fifth chapter ("The Restriction of Sexuality and Aggression in Favor of Security"), is a sustained study of the grand security projects he collectively identifies as culture. Yet, as in Plessner, a psychoanalytic *cure* must instigate a desecurement of these defense mechanisms in the hope of introducing a sounder, healthier disposition. Thus, Freud engages the Plautine-Hobbesian line of human cruelty—*homo homini lupus* (man is a wolf to man)—in order to laud the benefits of a secure state, understood individually and collectively, while at the same time acknowledging it as a source of failed gratification.[37]

As the philosophical anthropology of the day recognized, it is precisely this failure that Nietzsche strove to circumvent. Arnold Gehlen, who explicitly built upon the work of Scheler and Plessner, developed his own anthropological theory on the basis of a definition that he found among Nietzsche's posthumous writings, namely that man is "a not yet determined animal" (*ein noch nicht festgestelltes Tier*).[38] For Gehlen, too, human institutions are security projects aimed to remedy or compensate for mankind's essential lack of instinctual capabilities. To corroborate Nietzsche's definition, Gehlen repeatedly refers to Herder's characterization of mankind as a "deficient creature" (*Mängelwesen*), who is by nature incapable of dealing with the "flood of stimulation" that flows from within consciousness and without. "Man has what could . . . be termed a dangerous lack of true instincts and needs an unusually long period of protection

---

[36] Helmut Plessner, "Die Aufgabe der Philosophischen Anthropologie" (1937), in Plessner, *Conditio humana*, 33–51; see esp. 46–47.

[37] Sigmund Freud, *Civilization and Its Discontents*, 69.

[38] Arnold Gehlen, *Der Mensch, seine Natur und seine Stellung in der Welt* (1940) [*Man, His Nature and Place in the World*, 4, see also 24–25].

and care [*Sorge*] during his infancy and childhood."[39] Instinctually destitute, face to face with unforeseen contingencies, man seeks "relief" (*Entlastung*) in the form of "institutions," a general term that Gehlen uses to refer to habitual patterns of cognition and behavior.[40] In brief, institutions assume the role of man's caretaker, organizing experience, guiding affects, and thereby providing assurance: "[T]he world is reduced to the familiar things we know. This is a process of relief: the field of surprises is transformed through action into an accessible, manageable world in which impressions and outcomes can be anticipated."[41] Ultimately, then, the degree of security that human being enjoys is proportionate to its rational capacity for calculation and anticipation, in a word, for presentifying the future.

THE WORK OF MYTH, THE WORK ON MYTH

> The text is a moral object: it is the written in so far as the written participates in the social contract. It subjects us, and demands that we observe and respect it, but in return it marks language with an inestimable attribute which it does not possess in its essence: security.
>
> Roland Barthes, *Theory of the Text* (1973)

It could be argued that the pitfalls of failing to adapt to sudden change would equally apply to relying too much on rational assessments of probability. Although correct anticipation is crucial for circumventing imminent danger, calculation, which is always formulated on the basis of prior experience, and the kind of knowledge thereby instituted can also mislead or impede successful choices for action. Expectations may not only be thwarted; they may also be blinding. Hans Blumenberg, who repeatedly acknowledged his debt to philosophical anthropology, refers to this problem, explicitly in relation to Gehlen, as "the absolutism of institutions."[42] For Blumenberg, the basic premise of Gehlen's theory is sound: given man's "world-openness," he is exposed to experiences that he is biologically unequipped to handle and therefore must act in order to secure his existence.[43] Security is gained by achieving distance from reality, by arriving at self-determination. Yet, as Blumenberg would point out, this very distance, this obstacle installed between the subject of experience and

[39] Gehlen, *Man*, 33.
[40] Gehlen, *Man*, 79.
[41] Gehlen, *Man*, 119.
[42] Hans Blumenberg, "Anthropologische Annäherung an die Aktualität der Rhetorik" (1971), in *Ästhetische und metaphorologische Schriften*, 415 ["An Anthropological Approach to the Contemporary Significance of Rhetoric," 439]. On Blumenberg's relation to Scheler, Plessner, and Gehlen, see Vida Pavesich, "Hans Blumenberg's Philosophical Anthropology: After Heidegger and Cassirer."
[43] Cf. Gehlen, *Man*, 30.

its environment, also limits engagement with the world. Mankind survives by forming concepts (*Begriffe*); human being copes with experiential trials by reducing their immediacy, by conceptually grasping (*begreifen*) the world; but such measures of comprehension can never be complete, and rationalizations can never be perfectly adequate. Instead, they stand in need of continued modification, reforming, and reworking.

Accordingly, when Blumenberg comes to paraphrase Gehlen's main postulate, he turns to the field of "rhetoric," where truth has always been subordinate to efficacy, and assigns the mediating role to metaphors as opposed to concepts.

> Man's deficiency in specific dispositions for reactive behavior vis-à-vis reality—that is, his poverty of instincts—is the starting point for the central anthropological question as to how this creature is able to exist in spite of his lack of fixed biological dispositions. The answer can be reduced to the formula: by not dealing with this reality directly. The human relation to reality is indirect, circumstantial, delayed, selective, and above all: "metaphorical."[44]

The distinction that Blumenberg draws is between an act that attempts to comprehend something and one that strives to comprehend something *through* something else. The perils of reification or stagnation implicit in the former are evaded by the greater adaptability and flexibility of the latter.

Reflections on security projects that are viable (and not paralyzing) inform Blumenberg's analyses in *Work on Myth* (1979), a text that brings the concerns of philosophical anthropology into even closer connection with Nietzsche's thinking.[45] For Blumenberg, the study of myth does not entail an investigation into the links between ritual practices and stories of the gods, or, in the manner of Ernst Cassirer, a determination of innate "symbolic forms" that human beings implement to organize reality, or even an evaluative consideration of myth as a preliterate, prescientific worldview that is subsequently rendered obsolete. In contrast to all of these established methods, Blumenberg's *Work on Myth* focuses on myth's function, on its point of departure, on its role in human experience.

Like rhetoric and metaphors, and even like Gehlen's institutions and concepts, myth provides distance from what Blumenberg now calls the "absolutism of reality." The absolutism of reality names a situation deep in humanity's past, where "man came close to not having control of the conditions of his existence and, what is more important, believed that he simply lacked control of them."[46] This state, which Blumenberg in fact characterizes as a Hobbesian "state of nature," is not posited as a verifiable occurrence in archaic prehistory but rather as

---

[44] Blumenberg, "Anthropologische Annäherung," 415 [439].

[45] On Blumenberg's relation to philosophical anthropology, see Franz Josef Wetz, "The Phenomenological Anthropology of Hans Blumenberg," and Wayne Hudson, "After Blumenberg: Historicism and Philosophical Anthropology."

[46] Hans Blumenberg, *Work on Myth*, 3–4.

a limit concept that allows the determination of myth's function in human life. Following the typical plot of evolutionary anthropology, Blumenberg rehearses the story of the development of man's bipedal stance and his move from the protected zone of the forest into the exposed realm of the open savanna. This relocation occasions not only a "sudden lack of adaptation" but also a new "capacity for foresight."[47] Merely reactive flight before a present object of fear is no longer sufficient for the innumerable unknown and invisible threats that now assail human being; anticipation must be developed and become more prognostic. Possible situations need to be conjured before they emerge; stories have to be told, plotted out in advance. Hence, Blumenberg arrives at the basic function of myth: to reduce the absolutism of reality, to reduce anxiety, to make life somewhat more livable. Myths therefore express the human concern to mitigate concerns, to create some manner of security.

Faced with the absolutism of reality—that is, the absolute contingency of the overpowering world of experience—myth converts objectless anxiety into a nameable fear; it depletes power by giving it a designation, by turning it into something that can be addressed and perhaps even influenced. Myth transforms the open horizon of undefined danger into a system—ultimately, into a pantheon—of forces that can be negotiated. With myth "the world ceases to contain as many monsters"; "the world becomes 'friendlier'"; "it approaches what the man who listens to myth needs: to be at home in the world."[48] This, then, is the "work of myth," which should not be starkly distinguished from reason, insofar as both—*mythos* and *logos*—respond to the same general problem of absolute contingency. Yet, although similar in function, the approaches of myth and reason differ considerably. Whereas reason offers to give explanations that are indifferent to the historical and cultural value of the object studied, myth is concerned more with "significance" (*Bedeutsamkeit*)—a term, which Blumenberg adopts from Wilhelm Dilthey, that does not neglect involvement in time, in what Heidegger would call the "worldhood" of the world. Significance, in other words, is related to human finitude.

If the "work of myth" achieves an originary depontentiation of the absolutism of reality, mankind is poised to continue a "work on myth" that reflects shifting demands across epochs and cultures. An "absolutism of images" can never be achieved that is not pathological, as in the omnipotence of thoughts that Freud attributed to narcissism. The human subject can never become sovereign, mastering reality without any remainder. Here, Blumenberg touches on the well-known mechanism of self-defeat implicit in the "dialectic of Enlightenment" diagnosed by Horkheimer and Adorno. Finitude instead causes humans to undergo perpetual oscillation between moments of control and lapses into helplessness, between satisfactory answers and newly emergent inquiries.

---

[47] Blumenberg, *Work on Myth*, 4.
[48] Blumenberg, *Work on Myth*, 113.

In Blumenberg's grander scheme, myth is therefore aligned with rhetoric and metaphor—approaches to experience that are paradoxically grounded in groundlessness: in a "principle of insufficient reason."[49] "[Myth] draws its vitality from the frivolous assumption that the world's capacity for explanation and the need to give rational grounds for behavior in it are not what matters."[50] Blumenberg's *principum rationis insufficientis* is not merely a parodic reversal of Leibnizian epistemology but also a reminder that every securitization is liable to be desecured, that every position produced by the work of myth ultimately requires the work on myth, a strategy of "reoccupation" that grapples with fresh concerns. "The myth that is varied and transformed by its receptions" takes into account "the historical situations and needs that were affected by the myth and were disposed to 'work' on it."[51] The title of Blumenberg's later essay, *Shipwreck with Spectator: Paradigm of a Metaphor of Existence*, is telling: whereas metaphysics struggled to ascertain a "ground of existence" (*Daseinsgrund*), the work on myth investigates a "metaphor of existence" (*Daseinsmetapher*).[52]

Nietzsche's resistance to dogma—which is connected with his concern that his own writings may be read dogmatically—is a testament to his mythical mode of thought. Whereas dogma assertively and authoritatively requires submission to a truth that is universally valid, myth is nourished by variability, by a careful attention to differentiation. Unlike dogma, myth does not exclude heretics; it does not insist on the rigorous fixity of scripture. As Nietzsche famously remarked, truth is purely rhetorical, nothing but "a mobile army of metaphors, metonyms and anthropomorphisms."[53] Even when he "speaks theologically," Nietzsche is simply reoccupying a dogmatic position that effectively undercuts the dogmatic intent. Where the Enlightenment disparages myth as an instrument of deception, wielded by the priestly caste, Nietzsche enlists deception itself into an aesthetic program. In Blumenberg's assessment, "Nietzsche . . . wants to force a revaluation of the term *lie*, so as to strike at the moralism of the duty of truthfulness by henceforth allowing talk of the 'beauty and gracefulness of the lie.' What used to be called the trickery of priests has become a sort of

---

[49] Blumenberg, "Anthropologische Annäherung," 422. The "principle of insufficient reason" is further connected to metaphor's irreducibility to conceptualization. On this point, see Blumenberg's essay, "Prospect for a Theory of Nonconeptuality," in *Shipwreck with Spectator*, 81–102.

[50] Blumenberg, *Work on Myth*, 234.

[51] Blumenberg, *Work on Myth*, 174.

[52] Cf. David Adams, "Metaphors for Mankind: The Development of Hans Blumenberg's Metaphorology," 162. For a full account of method and scope, see Blumenberg's seminal essay, "Paradigmem zu einer Metaphorologie" (1960) [*Paradigms for a Metaphorology*]. See also the essays collected in *Metaphorologie: Zur Praxis von Theorie*, Anselm Haverkamp and Dirk Mende, eds.

[53] Nietzsche, "On Truth and Lying in a Non-Moral Sense," in *The Birth of Tragedy and Other Writings*, 146 ["Ueber Wahrheit und Lüge im aussermoralischen Sinne," *KSA* 1: 880]. On the central role of metaphor in Nietzsche's philosophical project, see Sarah Kofman, *Nietzsche and Metaphor*; and the various essays collected in *Nietzsche oder "Die Sprache ist Rhetorik,"* J. Kopperschmidt and H. Schanze, eds.

artistic activity."[54] For Blumenberg, ecclesiastical authority is inherited from a justifiable anthropological need: "To know on whom to depend is always a source of security in one's conduct, a source that is not without advantage for life, and the systems of which can hardly be less old than man himself, if we have to proceed from the assumption that his origin was in a loss of biological security."[55] Yet, when such systems become rigid and fail to attend to the full power of life's circumstantiality, this *security* itself stands to be revaluated. Insofar as it neglects to speak to new concerns, security, despite its name, no longer removes care.

In contrast, the security projects that stem from mankind's creative capacities are a testament to human "care" (*Sorge*). "For care [*Sorge*] is the 'nature' of a creature that cannot preserve itself as nature and hence is 'by nature' worried about itself [*in Sorge um sich*]."[56] Here, Blumenberg clearly incorporates the double sense of *cura* as "attentive concern" and "anxious worry"—in Greek: as *epimeleia* and *merimna*. Both aspects of care contribute to mankind's existence in the world: the troubled encounter with the absolutism of reality and the careful cultivation of technologies and techniques designed to deal with this overpowering reality. Together, as Oliver Müller argues, both sides of *Sorge* define Blumenberg's sense of *humanitas*. "It comes down to how man can arrange himself as man with the world."[57] For this reason, Blumenberg's work does not generally corroborate the demonization of technology that was particularly strong in the postwar period. Müller usefully shows how, already in his early essays, Blumenberg lauds technology as a compensation for human deficiency: "Man is imperiled, metaphysically displaced, however 'technological' determination affords a first instance toward the stabilization of human existence; mankind's reality has become 'feasible' [*machbar*], it no longer confronts in a solely threatening way."[58] For Blumenberg, technology provides a security that alleviates concern, but only by allowing concern to remain operative. Neither immortal like the gods nor instinctually equipped like other animals, mankind resorts to technology as an expression of its unrelenting care.

[54] Blumenberg, *Work on Myth*, 241. For a critical analysis on the relationship between Blumenberg and Nietzsche, see Robert Pippin, "Modern Mythic Meaning: Blumenberg contra Nietzsche."
[55] Blumenberg, *Work on Myth*, 169.
[56] Hans Blumenberg, *Das Lachen der Thrakerin*, 153.
[57] Oliver Müller, *Sorge um die Vernunft: Hans Blumenbergs phänomenologische Anthropologie*, 332. Müller's work provides a systematic investigation into Blumenberg's entire output by focusing on the key notion of *Sorge*.
[58] Müller, *Sorge um die Vernunft*, 75.

The Sorrow of Thinking

SORGE

FOR MARTIN HEIDEGGER, the resilient thinker of Being that reveals itself in withdrawal, notions of security should be treated with utmost caution. If human being is a manifestation of Being—Being as Time, self-disclosing and self-concealing—then any project designed to contain Being or evade its destabilizing call would be a failure in thinking. Hence, Heidegger's impatience with anthropological explanations:

> Anthropology is that interpretation of mankind that fundamentally already knows what man is and thus can never ask who he should be. For with this question it must admit itself to be shaken and overcome. How should this be expected of anthropology, where it specifically has to achieve only the retroactive assurance of the subject's self-assurance [*die nachträgliche Sicherung der Selbstsicherung des Subiectum*].[1]

Heidegger's rejection of anthropology and the consequent critique of securement underlie "The Question concerning Technology" (1955). Here, the problem is this: How can one interrogate technology and its modes of securing without dismissing the necessary engagement with technology's essence? The distinction is crucial: "Technology is not equivalent to the essence of technology." Freedom and a lack of freedom are the criteria. Whereas it is possible "to prepare a free relationship" to the essence of technology, "we remain unfree and chained to technology."[2] Technology enchains when it performs an instrumental function, when it masters over nature or convinces its operators that nature is masterable. And it is in this sense that technology secures.

Accordingly, in grappling with the problem of a "politics of security," Michael Dillon turns to Heidegger's contributions to thinking through technology's challenge:

> The danger of technology is precisely . . . that it will secure security—secure "man" the subject as just another object in the process of securing all other

---

[1] Martin Heidegger, *Holzwege*, 103.
[2] Heidegger, *The Question concerning Technology*, 3–4.

things as objects—secure so effectively that it will secure us from ever even knowing that we have been so secured. And yet this very process of securing, [Heidegger] believes, is actually what may also alert us to its own danger; because human being is even more challenged technologically than the nature which it, in its turn, technologically suborns.[3]

Dillon discerns in Heidegger's thinking a dialectic of security, whereby the subject of technology stands to become subjected to technology. In this regard, the securement of the subject as a fixed point of origin is shown to harbor an inauthenticating menace, one that throws into question any approach that neglects mankind's finitude. As Heidegger consistently proclaims, one cannot intentionally seek to understand and thereby control Being; rather, Being seeks out the thinker. Nonetheless, the thinker also assists in Being's disclosure by responding to Being's call. What Heidegger names the "piety of thought" (die Frömmigkeit des Denkens) is this active-passive relation to Being: answering the call of Being so as to promote its disclosure in human language.

Although technology would seem to be far removed from the piety of thinking, Being, which today reveals and conceals itself in technology, demands sincere involvement.[4] Constituted by Being, the essence of technology names yet another challenge by means of which human being becomes a challenge to itself. By pursuing the question concerning technology, thinking expedites Being's disclosure, a "bringing-forth" (Hervor-bringen) out of concealment into unconcealment. In the Technology essay, Heidegger focuses on the term Entbergen, a word that literally means "to dig up," conjuring quasi-romantic scenes of mining.[5] The verb bergen means "to rescue," "to harbor," and therefore also "to secure in hiding." Thus, the "unconcealment" that is truth (alētheia) is a kind of "de-securing" (Ent-bergen): letting something burst forth from its fixed or secured hiding into revelation.

While Heidegger views security as impeding thought's piety, it is elsewhere clear that some idea of security may contribute to authentic concern. In other words, Heidegger appears to inherit the dynamic ambivalence associated with the word's complex semantic career. On the one hand, there is the cold distance of Lucretian security, which describes the theoretical position that objectifies all experience in a resolutely scientific, calculating, and ultimately nonphilosophical (unthinking) manner. For Heidegger, this metaphysical standpoint dubiously consigns the subject to a position out of the world to which he nonetheless belongs. On the other hand, the "paths of thinking" (Denkwege) seem to be lined with the courageous asphalt that paves the way and prevents a fall into inauthenticity. In his lectures on Parmenides, held during the politically fraught and morally questionable years of 1942–43, Heidegger stresses the

---

[3] Dillon, Politics of Security, 134–35.
[4] Martin Heidegger, The Question concerning Technology, 3–5.
[5] Heidegger, The Question concerning Technology, 11.

meaning of the Greek verb *sphallein* as causing to fall or totter and consequently links it to the Latin cognates *fallere* and *falsum*. For Heidegger, these words of falling and falsehood overthrow what would otherwise endure in unconcealed presence. In this way, *asphaleia* becomes a close synonym of his preferred word for "truth" as *Unverborgenheit* (unconcealedness): *alētheia*. Thus, *alētheia* vividly relates to the meaning of *asphaleia* found in Archilochus, namely the resolve to engage with experience in the thick of experience, neither falling down nor allowing the surrounding world to fall down into technological scientificity. Implicitly, Heidegger betrays his preference for Greek over Latin terms: whereas *securitas* barricades thinking, *asphaleia* opens onto further paths. "Τὸ ἀσφαλές is never the 'certain' and the 'secure' in the modern sense of *certitudo*."[6]

The distinction between Greek *asphaleia*, which contributes to thinking, and Latin *securitas* and *certitudo*, which impede it, represents a consistent pattern in Heidegger's well-known history of the "forgetting of Being." Here, *securitas* becomes the hallmark of the metaphysical, unworldly position that has always been the target of Heidegger's program of destruction. As early as his lectures on the *Phenomenology of Religious Life*, held in the Winter Semester of 1920–21, Heidegger distinguishes the determinate, objectified nature of scientific concepts from philosophical concepts, which remain "vacillating, vague, manifold and fluctuating," marked by a fundamental openness that keeps thinking on a path of "uncertainty" or "insecurity"—*Unsicherheit*.[7] The principal intention of Heidegger's approach is "to keep awake philosophy's need to be ever turning upon preliminary questions" and thereby turn the "insecurity" of philosophical concepts into a "virtue."[8] In these lectures, the first step is to unwork the various Platonist and Neoplatonist "securing tendencies" (*Sicherungstendenzen*), which evade or eradicate the temporality of existence. For Heidegger, the development of Platonism essentially constitutes a metaphysical project *against* historical time. Upon reviewing this transcendentalizing trend, Heidegger considers a second step, closer to his own contemporary intellectual context, namely to recognize the risks implicit in recent efforts by theorists like Oswald Spengler, whose project of cultural relativism aims to circumvent the demands of time by securing life *with* history, that is, by turning history into a series of objectified worldviews. Neither of these tendencies, and not even the Hegelian sublation of both, is sufficient for dealing with the world to which one necessarily belongs. For the young Heidegger, still fresh from the catastrophe of the Great War, all of these approaches neglect to address the disturbance that lies at the core of factic human existence. "That which is disturbed [*beunruhigt*], the reality of life, the human existence in its concern about its own security [*in seiner Bekümmerung um seine eigene Sicherung*], is not taken in itself; rather it

[6] Martin Heidegger, *Parmenides*, 39.
[7] Martin Heidegger, *Phänomenologie des religiösen Lebens*, 3 [*The Phenomenology of Religious Life*, 3].
[8] Heidegger, *Phänomenologie des religiösen Lebens*, 4 [*The Phenomenology of Religious Life*, 4].

is regarded as object and as object it is placed within the historical objective reality. The worry is not answered, but rather is immediately objectified."⁹

Philosophy must keep worried concern (Bekümmerung) awake. It must face up to the disturbance. As a privation of concern, securitas is a philosophical dead end. Hence, in the immediately following semester, Heidegger focuses his reading of the tenth book of Augustine's Confessions, which meditates on the concept of cura. In his explication, it quickly becomes clear that Heidegger finds in Augustinian cura a pre-Cartesian mode of inquiry that does not avoid the facticity of life. Heidegger suggests that, if we should purge Augustine of his Neoplatonic tendencies, we would gain the opportunity to prevent phenomenology, including Husserl's, from falling into falsifying projects keen on securing the cogito.¹⁰ With Augustine, phenomenology stands to discover a radically new assessment of human existence, one that urgently attends to the facticity of life riveted to historical time.

A key passage for Heidegger is one in which Augustine addresses God in confusion:

> When I shall have adhered to you with the whole of myself, I shall never have pain and toil, and my entire life will be full of you. You lift up the person whom you fill; but for the present, because I am not full of you, I am a burden to myself [oneri mihi sum]. There is a struggle between joys over which I should be weeping and regrets at matters over which I ought to be rejoicing, and which side may have the victory I do not know. There is a struggle between my regrets at my evil past and my memories of good joys, and which side may have the victory I do not know. (Conf. 10.2.39)¹¹

Although Augustine does not explicitly refer to cura in this passage, Heidegger identifies this internal contention as a clear expression of the "concern" (Bekümmerung) that characterizes factic life, a life that is remote from God and has therefore become an onus for the living subject. Epistemological doubt characterizes a general insecurity, yet precisely by recognizing the burden of the self, the subject comes to be concerned for security in God. Upon making this interpretive move, which is further supported by passages from Augustine's De doctrina christiana and the Commentaries on the Psalms, Heidegger is able to apply Augustine's series of reflections to construct an entire theory of care that will subsequently ground his reshaping of phenomenological inquiry. In brief, cura names for Heidegger the motivating force that compels human life in one of two directions: either toward the "delight" (delectatio) that defines self-possession in God; or toward the "temptation" (tentatio) that works against this goal by submerging the self back into the world. If cura leads to delight, the

⁹ Heidegger, Phänomenologie des religiösen Lebens, 51[The Phenomenology of Religious Life, 34].
¹⁰ Cf. Chad Engelland, "Augustinian Elements in Heidegger's Philosophical Anthropology: A Study of the Early Lecture Course on Augustine," 263.
¹¹ Augustine, Confessions, 202.

result is "continence" (*continentia*), a coming to rest in the One that is God; but if *cura* leads to temptation, the result is "dispersal" (*defluxus*) into the multiplicity of worldly experience.[12] According to Heidegger, it is Augustine's indebtedness to Neoplatonic models that causes him to impose an axiological judgment that privileges transcendent continence over immanent dispersion. The primary philosophical problem with this kind of evaluation is that it gives priority to a condition of security, insofar as Augustine himself explicitly defines delight as "the end of concern" (*finis curae*). For Heidegger, security of this nature presupposes a path that inauthentically circumvents the difficulties and troubles of life. Heidegger thus writes in an Archilochian key: "What is precisely crucial is to have a radical confrontation constantly with the factic, and not to flee."[13] In order to secure the path of thinking, it is necessary to linger with the insecurity that constitutes being in the world.

All the same, remaining insecurely in the world, resisting the tug of transcendental stability, is no guarantee of authentic questioning. Parallel to the existential *cura* that deals unflinchingly with the difficulty of Dasein is the *cura vana*, the "empty concern" that Augustine evokes in regard to the three Johannine temptations: "fleshly desire," "curiosity," and "worldly ambition." When Heidegger brackets out Platonic-theological axiology, this empty concern comes to serve as the mark of merely "bustling activity" (*Geschäftigkeit*). In contrast, the *cura* linked to the burden of life is much more fruitful for thought, insofar as it stages a test. Whereas for Augustine *tentatio* can be understood only as the *temptation* that pulls the self into *defluxus*, into the dispersal that signals distance from God, for Heidegger *tentatio* is also a *trial* that incessantly challenges the thinker and thereby maintains the openness of true (disclosive) questioning. Augustine cites the book of Job (7:1): *Et nemo securus esse debet in ista vita, quae tota tentatio nominatur*, which Heidegger transposes to a secular key: "No one should be secure in this life, which is called a total trial." "That is," as Heidegger continues, "inasmuch as *tentatio* is there, life, the *ista vita*, has to be experienced in this way—understanding the self in this in its full facticity of experience."[14]

Despite the tendentiousness of Heidegger's reading—the term *cura* hardly occurs with such emphasis in the tenth book of the *Confessions*—other passages from Augustine's works, not cited in Heidegger's course, confirm the generally negative sense of the term *securitas*. For example, in his commentary on the First Epistle of John, Augustine elaborates how Christ cleanses us from sin by remarking, "Christ . . . takes from you an evil security, and puts in a useful fear."[15] Likewise, in his treatise on *Holy Virginity*, Augustine refers to those who

---

[12] For a comprehensive analysis, see Kisiel, *The Genesis of Heidegger's Being and Time*, 192–217. See also Thomas Flynn, "*Angst* and Care in the Early Heidegger: The Ontic/Ontologic Aporia."

[13] Heidegger, *Phänomenologie des religiösen Lebens*, 265 [*The Phenomenology of Religious Life*, 199].

[14] Heidegger, *Phänomenologie des religiösen Lebens*, 217 [*The Phenomenology of Religious Life*, 161].

[15] *Christus . . . tollit tibi malam securitatem, viserit utilem timorem.* Augustine, *Homily on the First Epistle of John* §7.

sin out of "deadly security" (*cum mortifera securitate*).[16] As we have seen, it is this Augustinian critique of security that sparks Luther's outspoken suspicions. Nonetheless, the positive connotations of *securitas*—specifically as the certitude of God's grace—is not entirely absent from Augustine's texts. In the *Confessions* (2.6.13), as well, Augustine has occasion to celebrate the "reliable security" (*firma securitas*) that is indeed available, albeit only with God .

After Augustine, any unease before the equivocacity of *securitas* is duly addressed and rectified in the Christian tradition. Gregory the Great, for instance, stresses how the church should exploit the fear of being unsure as a service to the faithful who may thereby remain urgently concerned for their salvation. As Gregory proclaims, "Security is accustomed to being the mother of negligence"[17] (*Moralia* 24.11.62). For Heidegger, it is precisely this negative tradition of *securitas*—as "the mother of negligence"—that persists from Scholasticism straight to the Reformation and plays a crucial role in restoring phenomenological inquiry.

In the years that follow his lectures on Augustine, beginning with the seminar on Aristotle in 1922 and culminating with the publication of his magnum opus, *Sein und Zeit*, in 1927, *cura*, now reconfigured as *Sorge*, emerges as the key notion that characterizes the constitution of human Dasein. Like English "care" (< Gothic *kara* [grief, trouble]), *Sorge* belongs initially to a semantic field expressing worry, unrest, and apprehension, and is directly cognate with English "sorrow." Related terms in contemporary German cover an important range of meanings, including the nouns *Fürsorge* (aid, welfare), *Besorgnis* (anxiety, worriedness), and *Vorsorge* (precaution, prevention), and the verbal phrases *etwas besorgen* (to attend to something, to take care of something) and *jemanden versorgen* (to provide for someone, to look after someone). For Heidegger, given its aspect of relationality, the term *Sorge* exhibits a function analogous to the one that "intentionality" plays in Husserl's method.[18] The careful attendance to the facticity of existence prevents thinking from evading the conditions of "this very life," *ista vita*. In Heidegger's fundamental reversal, *cura* counters everything that would have us fall away from our fallenness. Throughout *Being and Time*, the attraction of tranquillity is tantamount to inauthenticity, insofar as it causes us to neglect the fallen condition of our existence. As Heidegger explains, this *Verfallenheit* is decidedly not a "'fall' from a purer and higher 'primal state' [*Urstand*]" but rather the state of the only life we have.[19] His critique of security, therefore, is always specifically a critique of *securitas* as the "removal of care," which he implicitly distinguishes from *asphaleia* as the "prevention of falling" or, more specifically, as the "prevention of falling from our

---

[16] Augustine, *De sancta virginitate* 50.

[17] *Mater negligentiae solet esse securitas* (*Moralia* 24.11.62).

[18] For a comprehensive analysis of the link between Heidegger's *Sorge* and Husserl's "intentionality," see Aldo Masullo, "'Sorge': Heideggers Verwandlung von Husserls Intentionalitätsstruktur."

[19] Martin Heidegger, *Sein und Zeit*, §38, 176.

fallenness." Evading our constitution in time begins with the translation from Greek to Latin.

When Heidegger read Hyginus's Cura fable aloud to his students in Marburg in 1925, he characterized the text as a "naïve interpretation" of human existence (*Dasein*), as a fitting illustration of Dasein's self-interpretation within the horizon of temporality.[20] As Heidegger informs us, he happened upon Hyginus's myth in Konrad Burdach's lead article for the very first number of the *Deutsche Vierteljahrsschrift für Literaturwissenschaft und Geistesgeschichte* entitled "Faust und die Sorge" (1923).[21] Here, Burdach traces a literary tradition instigated in the eighteenth century by Johann Gottfried Herder and later exploited by Goethe for the conclusion of his *Faust*. As Burdach argues, the personification of "care" (*Sorge*) that Goethe introduces in the final pages of his life work is indebted to Herder's short piece "Das Kind der Sorge" (The Child of Care), a recasting of the Hyginian fable and first published among other "paramythic poems" in the 1787 collection, *Zerstreute Blätter* (Scattered Leaves). In the history of Heidegger's project, it is noteworthy that the Hyginus fable constitutes the very first literary text that the philosopher submits to analysis.

Scholars generally agree that it was Burdach's article that motivated Heidegger's decision to change his translation of *cura* from *Bekümmerung* to *Sorge*, and henceforth name *Sorge* as the constitutive being of time-bound Dasein. The role of the Hyginus fable in *Being and Time*, where it is again cited *in toto*, should not be underestimated. For Heidegger this "pre-ontological document" demonstrates how, given the temporality of care, human Dasein can never enjoy pure self-presence. The origin is fractured. A temporal gap always intrudes, preventing immediacy. For Heidegger Hyginus's text forcefully expresses how "care" (*Sorge*) comprises the "Being of Dasein"—"*the* kind of Being which dominates [man's] *temporal mode in the world*."[22] Even a merely ontic or psychologically descriptive interpretation of *Sorge* can serve Heidegger's ontological interests, insofar as "care" comprises relationality (human being cares for something or someone) and temporality (human being cares for the evanescent). Thus, the reading in *Being and Time* almost effortlessly moves from "ontic generalizations" to a rigorous "existential-ontological interpretation."[23] This latter interpretation is based entirely on the ambivalent meanings of *cura* that were highlighted in Burdach's article, namely between "anxious exertion" (*ängstliche Bemühung*) and "carefulness" (*Sorgfalt*) or "devotedness" (*Hingabe*). What appears as ambivalence on the ontic level proves to be a crucial insight on the level of the ontological: "In the 'double meaning' of 'care,' what we have in

---

[20] The Marburg lectures from the 1925 summer semester have been published as *History of the Concept of Time: Prolegomena* [*Prolegomena zur Geschichte des Zeitbegriffs*].

[21] Konrad Burdach, "Faust und die Sorge."

[22] Martin Heidegger, *Being and Time*, 243 (emphasis in original; translation slightly modified) [*Sein und Zeit*, 198–99].

[23] Heidegger, *Being and Time*, 243 [*Sein und Zeit*, 199]. On the shift from an ontic or philosophical anthropological interpretation to fundamental ontology, see Graeme Nicholson, "The Constitution of Our Being."

view is a *single* basic state in its essentially twofold structure of thrown projection."[24] This single, twofold structure implies that security, in removing anxious cares, also obliterates devoted concern.

With care, the security and comfort of one's everyday surroundings begins to wither, just as time evanesces from one moment to the next. With care, a general feeling of being at home yields to uncanniness. As George Steiner comments, "It is as if we had been caught, all of a sudden, in the interstices of the busy mesh of being, and stood face to face with the ontological, with the *Daseinsfrage* [question of Being]."[25] Caring is thus linked to the freedom that projects beyond inauthenticity and thoughtless subjectivity. Because care is always a caring-for, human being anxiously and devotedly stands free for whatever comes.[26] Again, Steiner's gloss is helpful, despite its orientation from Jean-Paul Sartre: "The careless man and the uncaring are not free. It is *Sorge* that makes human existence meaningful, that makes a man's life signify. To be-in-the-world in any real, existentially possessed guise, is to care, to be *besorgt* [careful]."[27] Implicitly, with security, we evade the very temporality that constitutes human being. With Heidegger, Steiner reformulates the founding Cartesian premise: "I care, therefore I am."[28]

Returning to Hyginus, we recall how Blumenberg spotted an erasure of paternal resemblance in the fable. In Heidegger's thinking, however, it is not paternity that is being eradicated. Rather, Cura's parentage is shown to be a birth into time and thus a birth into radical insecurity. For Heidegger, Saturn's judgment is therefore truly an *Urteil*, a decision that maintains and exacerbates what Friedrich Hölderlin called the "primal split" or *Urtheilung*: the converged divergence of corporeal sensibility and spiritual rationality that orients how human existence comes to take place.[29] Care alone holds the polarities together, like a bridge that crosses an otherwise uncrossable river. As a result, any substantial, permanent, transcendent subject—like the one Descartes dreamed of against radical doubt—is shown not to rest on an "unshakeable foundation" (the *fundamentum inconcussum* of the *Meditations*) but rather upon the soft humus into which it inevitably sinks.

Always Found, Never Sought

By entering into a pact with Mephistopheles, Faust believed that he would embark upon a life untroubled by concern. In the first part of Goethe's tragedy,

[24] Heidegger, *Being and Time*, 243 [*Sein und Zeit*, 199].

[25] George Steiner, *Martin Heidegger*, 99–100.

[26] In a different context Kierkegaard also emphasizes the futurity of "anxious care" (*bekymring*) in his reflections on Matthew 6:24–34 ("Consider the lilies of the field . . ."): Søren Kierkegaard, *The Anxieties of the Heathen*, in *Christian Discourses*, 12–93.

[27] Steiner, *Martin Heidegger*, 101.

[28] Steiner, *Martin Heidegger*, 101.

[29] Friedrich Hölderlin, "Judgment and Being," in *Essays and Letters on Theory*, 37–38 ["Urtheil und Seyn," in *Sämtliche Werke*, 4: 216–17].

during the jolly scene in Auerbach's Tavern, the devil reassures his protégé that those under his watch have nothing to worry about: *So lang' der Wirt nur weiter borgt, / Sind sie vergnügt und unbesorgt* (As long as the landlord continues to lend, / they are cheery and unconcerned, *Faust I*, 2166–67). That is to say, they are removed from care because the "landlord" is taking care of everything. As the German proverb recalls, *Borgen macht Sorgen*—literally, "lending brings trouble" or, in Polonius's unforgettable formulation, "Neither a borrower nor a lender be" (*Hamlet* 1.3.75). And, indeed, thanks to Mephistopheles's inexhaustible line of credit, across dozens of adventures and thousands of lines, Goethe's protagonist is able to strive continuously and securely without any effort, anxiety, or concern. Yet, at the tragedy's conclusion, care finally appears, personfied as *Sorge*, who forces an encounter with the hero. Soon thereafter, Faust will be dead.

Burdach's 1923 article "Faust und die Sorge" is one of the first attempts to come to terms with this final scene. Important articles on the significance of *Sorge* followed, each offering key interpretive insights, yet none of them integrated their reading of *cura* into what I understand to be absolutely crucial, namely the semantic field of *securitas*.[30] A reconsideration of the conclusion of *Faust* should demonstrate to what extent Goethe's tragedy is implicated in the moral philosophical themes and metaphorical figures linked to the history of security.

Before *Sorge* takes to the stage, we find Faust perched upon a high pinnacle, complaining to Mephistopheles of the waters' recalcitrance to human design:

> *Mein Auge war aufs hohe Meer gezogen;*
> *Es schwoll empor, sich in sich selbst zu türmen,*
> *Dann ließ es nach und schüttete die Wogen,*
> *Des flachen Ufers Breite zu bestürmen.*
> *Und das verdroß mich; wie der Übermut*
> *Den freien Geist, der alle Rechte schätzt,*
> *Durch leidenschaftlich aufgeregtes Blut*
> *Ins Mißbehagen des Gefühls versetzt.*
>
> (Faust II, 4.10198–205)

> My eye was drawn to the high sea;
> It swelled, towering itself upon itself,
> Then ebbed and shook the waves,
> Storming the flat shore's expanse.
> And that annoyed me; as its presumption
> Shifts the free spirit, which cherishes all rights,

---

[30] Important contributions include: Max Kommerell, "Faust und die Sorge"; Paul Stöcklein, "Fausts Kampf mit der Sorge"; Hans Jaeger, "The Problem of Faust's Salvation"; and, more recently, Warren Thomas Reich, "Sorge in Goethes Faust: Goethe als Moralist" and Ellis Dye, "Sorge in Heidegger and in Goethe's *Faust*."

Into a state of uneasy feeling
Through passionately agitated blood.

In contrast to Lucretius's unperturbed sage, Faust feels his blood roil before the surging surf. The turbulent waters directly correspond to his perturbed soul. Finding no comfort in the cool, spectatorial distance, he is stirred to action. He decides to quit the *templa serena* and enter upon a grand project: to harness the sea's energy and thereby develop an artificial landscape wrested from the sterile waters, to render its purposelessness purposeful.[31] As such, Faust's intentions align perfectly with Heidegger's discussion in the "Technology" essay, where one of the first examples is a hydroelectric plant in the Rhine.[32] In *Faust*, the conquest of the mighty sea will represent a final accomplishment in a life not lacking in achievement.

The sight of the stormy sea instigates Faust, who formerly approached all tasks and challenges with a carefree disposition. The scene essentially brings the hero back to the unsettling disposition that he used to suffer prior to signing the devilish pact. At that time, in a passing comment to his assistant Wagner, Faust confided: *Die Sorge nistet gleich im tiefen Herzen, / Dort wirket sie geheime Schmerzen* (Care nests deep right in the heart, / There she works her secret pain, *Faust I*, 644–45). What Mephistopheles would offer is literally *securitas*, which should remove from Faust's soul all the *curae* that would disturb and inhibit striving. Now, toward the tragedy's end, there are ample signs that those once banished cares are returning. To crown his project of domesticating the sea through canals and dikes, Faust plans to construct a tall watchtower, from which he could survey his work. Yet another obstacle remains: precisely on the spot where the tower should be built, there is a humble hut occupied by the aging couple, Baucis and Philemon, who stubbornly refuse to move. Mephistopheles, the great enabler, expeditiously has the hut burned to the ground. The couple drops dead from fear. Faust is devastated (11370–73).

Alone on his balcony, Faust watches as four "gray women" emerge from the smoke and ash. They slowly approach his abode. Like the "Fear and Threats" that scale the walls of the master's tower in Horace (*Odes* 3.1.37–38), these ominous crones appear to have come directly out of Vergil's Orcus (*Aen.* 6.273–77): *Mangel, Schuld, Sorge*, and *Not*—Want, Debt, Care, and Need. Yet, because the wealthy man can never know want, debt, or need, it is Care alone who is capable of penetrating the domestic fortress. She easily passes through the palace's security system, "creeping through the keyhole" (11391), and then addresses the old man who stands powerless before her:

Würde mich kein Ohr vernehmen,
Müßt' es doch im Herzen dröhnen;

---

[31] For a probing account of this final phase of Faust's striving, see Marshall Berman, *All That Is Solid Melts into Air*, 60–71.

[32] Heidegger, "The Question concerning Technology," 5.

In verwandelter Gestalt
Üb' ich grimmige Gewalt.
Auf den Pfaden, auf der Welle,
Ewig ängstlicher Geselle,
Stets gefunden, nie gesucht,
So geschmeichelt wie verflucht. –
Hast du die Sorge nie gekannt?

(*Faust II*, 5. 11424–32)

Would there be no ear to hear me,
The heart would still throb;
In transformed shape
I exert grim power.
Upon the path, upon the waves,
An eternally anxious companion,
Always found, never sought,
Flattered as well as cursed. —
Have you never known Care?

Faust may have believed that he proceeded through life without a care, yet this "anxious companion" was in fact never too far off. His carefree attitude was but an exercise in carelessness, a failure to notice the throbbing concerns that were nonetheless present. *Sorge* gives Faust a lesson in humanity: *Wen ich einmal mir besitze, / Dem ist alle Welt nichts nütze* (Whomever I once possess, / For him nothing in the whole world is of use [11453–54]). The remark closely glosses Saturn's judgment as reported by Hyginus: *quamdiu vixerit, Cura eum possideat* (As long as he should live, let Cura possess him). Care "possesses" (*possidet, besitzt*) the man, not only by exercising power over him but also by taking her "seat" (*sedes, Sitz*) at the core of his being. In brief, *Sorge* humanizes Faust.

Before leaving, *Sorge* blinds Faust—and in earlier manuscripts robs him of hearing as well. The next morning, deprived of his senses, he goes out to survey the construction site and realizes his striving has at last come to an end. The draining of swamps and the digging of canals, the forging of irrigation lines and the construction of mills—all proceed at a heated pace. The work barely conceals its violence, and yet is no longer without care. The dream is to "open a space for many millions to live, *not securely*, but free for action" (*Eröffn' ich Räume vielen Millionen, / Nicht sicher zwar, doch tätig-frei zu wohnen* [11563–64; emphasis added]). As Marshall Berman notes, "[Faust] expands the horizon of his being from private to public life, from intimacy to activism, from communion to organization. He pits all his powers against nature and society; he strives to change not only his own life but everyone else's as well."[33] The world that Faust incessantly tried to secure through knowledge, power, and industry

---

[33] Berman, *All That Is Solid*, 61.

is now irradiated by a Care that he never knew but was always there. Immediately following Faust's blinding, the hero wanders outside and pronounces the fateful line that, according to the Mephistophelean pact, must mark the end of his ceaseless striving: *Verweile doch, du bist so schön!* (But stay a while, you are so fair! [11582]). At this point the once restless soul sinks to the ground and dies. He will be redeemed in heaven, arguably not despite his long record of criminal acts but rather because in the end he rediscovered care.[34]

The characterization of *Sorge* in Goethe's tragedy clearly contributes to the function of Care in Heidegger's work. In *Being and Time*, Heidegger abandons Augustinian care as *Bekümmerung* (and Kierkegaard's analogous notion of *bekymring*), insofar as this word is tainted by its inscription in Platonic-Christian axiology and eschatology; and instead opts for Faustian *Sorge*, which does not seem to suffer from any such ideology. Yet Heidegger is so intent on demonstrating that *cura* constitutes human being that he neglects to hear an Augustinian echo in Faust's declaration. Heidegger's earlier lectures on Augustine's *Confessions* focus exclusively on *cura*, which Heidegger suspects of having been misguided by Neoplatonic "security tendencies." What is altogether surprising, however, is that Heidegger does not comment on the subsequent eleventh book, which contains Augustine's famous discussion of time. Here, as is well known, Augustine grapples with the difficult concept of time and tentatively concludes that the only way to understand God's relation to the world is through the rigorous distinction between our human realm of constant transience and the changeless, absolutely timeless sphere of the divine. Augustine's conclusion could be written off as yet another Neoplatonic gesture, were it not for the fact that he describes the decidedly mortal recognition of timelessness in terms that are highly reminiscent of Heideggerean *asphaleia*, of a resolute standing in place, of not falling down:

> Who will lay hold upon [their heart] and hold it still that it may stand a little while [*paululum*], and a little while may grasp the splendor of eternity which stands forever, and may compare it with time whose moments never stand, and may see that it is not comparable? (*Conf.* 11.11)

The anaphoric usage of the verb "stand" (*stare*) is striking as well as the object of God's love, the heart of man, which should recall the *thymos* of the Archilochus fragment. Within the larger context of this passage in the *Confessions*, it is clear that the "heart" (*cor*) is a metaphor for the *cura* that strives toward security in the oneness of God. Augustine may be alluding to Varro's popular etymology, cited previously, where the noun *cura* is derived from the syntagm *cor urat*—*cura* is "what burns the heart" (*De ling. lat.* 6.46). The point is that, for Augustine, the "end of care"—the *finis curae*—is in fact better understood as

---

[34] See Jaeger, "The Problem of Faust's Salvation," 56; and Warren Reich's elaboration in "Sorge in Goethes Faust," 155.

asphaleia as opposed to *securitas*. *Asphaleia* does not renounce or flee from the mortal condition but rather "stands" within this very condition, within human facticity. In Augustine, the heart is encouraged by God to stand "a little while." Similarly, Faust is compelled to proclaim, *Verweile doch, du bist so schön!* With his cognitive senses completely damaged by Care, the hero stands a little while and brings his incessant activity to an end. His end does not imply the eradication of care—*securitas*—but rather the irradiation of the world by means of care. Blind and deaf, Faust stands a little while (*paululum*) before that which stands forever. In sinking to the ground, at last touched by care, Faust does not fall up and out of the world—Neoplatonically—but rather falls onto the ground of time itself.

Fear and Trembling

> Poseidon sat at his desk and calculated. Administering all the
> waters gave him endless work. He could have had some assistants,
> but since he took his job very seriously, he calculated everything
> through one more time and so any assistance helped him little.
>
> Franz Kafka, "Poseidon"

> Franz Kafka could have written a novel: *The Enemy*.
>
> Carl Schmitt, *Glossarium*

The ambivalence of security constitutes a turbulent undercurrent beneath the political theorizations of Carl Schmitt. On the surface, Schmitt's much discussed notions of sovereignty, the exception, and decisionism reflect a committed belief in the primacy of state safety classically expressed in the Ciceronian formula *salus populi suprema lex*—"The safety of the people is the highest law." Nonetheless, Schmitt at times challenges this prioritization of security, whose privative force, in his view, tends to become manifest in the way the private sphere dangerously impinges upon state policy. This tension cannot be explained entirely by the distinction, mentioned above, between *safety* and *security*, between *salus* and *securitas*; nor is it simply because political theorists from Hobbes onward frequently employed both terms interchangeably. Rather, a brief consideration of Schmitt's reflections would reveal a much more complex affair, something that emerges when political theory and philology collide.

After the moral and existential catastrophe of 1945, the security problem and its attendant questions were only further exacerbated. Having served two years in American internment for his former involvement with the Nazi party, banned forever from teaching by occupying authorities bent on reeducation, with his library confiscated and his prospects in ruins, the renowned exegete of political theology abandoned the security zone of his devastated capital for the relative tranquillity of his childhood home, where he had recourse to little else but sardonic wit. In a note published posthumously in the collection entitled *Glossarium*, Schmitt, who had once considered a career in philology, adopts the role of lexicographer:

> 3.8.48. *Französisch: sécurité; deutsch (bisher): Gemütlichkeit. Die verinner-lichte, ins Interieur verlegte, zugleich aber doch säkularisierte Gnadengewißheit, das Ende von Furcht und Zittern bei einer guten Tasse Kaffee und einer Pfeife würzigen Tabaks. Wiedererscheinen gut verschleierter Wollust, nachdem Luther und die Herrenhuter so hart gegen die Sicherheit als eigentliche Wollust getobt hatten. Wo ist nun deine Wollust? fragt der Prophet den aus seiner Sicherheit herausgeworfenen Jämmerling. Wo ist nun dein Zittern? frage ich die-sen zum Milliardär gewordenen Quäker.*[35]

> August 3, 1948. French: *sécurité*; German (until now): *Gemütlichkeit*. The internalized, interiorized, but at the same time secularized certainty of grace [*Gnadengewißheit*], the end of fear and trembling at a nice cup of coffee and a pipe of spiced tobacco. The reappearance of well-veiled lust [*Wollust*], after Luther and the Moravians had raged so sternly against security as actual lust. "Where now is your lust?" the prophet asks the weakling expelled from his security. "Where now is your trembling?" I ask this Quaker turned billionaire.

With typical conciseness and inimitable élan, Schmitt informs his critique of bourgeois security with a historical sense of the key term's shifting lexical career. This brief exercise in semantics is motivated by a rapid accumulation of synonyms—*security* or *Sicherheit* as "cozy comfort" (*Gemütlichkeit*), as the "certainty of grace" (*Gnadengewißheit*), as the "end of fear and trembling," and finally as "actual lust" (*eigentliche Wollust*). In addition to all the political, social, and cultural anthropological ramifications of these lines, Schmitt's passage should be read at least initially as exposing the signifying diversity of the head word.

These lines, penned at the height of the Nuremberg Trials, can certainly be read as a somewhat weak attempt at self-justification: Was it not Schmitt's commitment to lived experience that compelled him to flirt—quite insecurely—with the Nazi regime, so as to report on it from a privileged perspective? Is it not important for all to see that he never was a stay-at-home, a ridiculous *deutscher Michel* in sleeping gown and nightcap, who cowardly avoided real confrontation? His musings may further reflect recent reconfigurations of international political discourse performed in an American mode. In particular, his lines may have been spurred by the signing of the U.S. National Security Act

---

[35] Carl Schmitt, *Glossarium: Aufzeichnungen der Jahre 1947–1951*, 185.

of 1947, the landmark piece of legislation that established both the National Security Council and the Central Intelligence Agency. In line with Michel Foucault's analyses, this act represented an explicit and decisive shift from an older model of *defense*, based on territorial protection, to an idea of *security*, one adopted from earlier, Depression-era discourse—immediately linked to Roosevelt and his "Freedom from fear" campaign—and now applied to consolidate military objectives with social, cultural, and economic concerns.[36] By rechristening defense objectives as security measures, authorities reshaped policy, purportedly in response to new problems emerging within the global landscape in the wake of the Second World War. *Security*, it was argued, was the single concept that could adequately address the unprecedented variety of problems soon to be associated with the Cold War.

Schmitt's dictionary-like entry exhibits an approach that is philological to the extent that it is open to the vast network of mythical, linguistic, and cultural valences and traditions that have motivated the term's usage across history. It is attuned to the shifting semantic course that has granted *security* a nearly inexhaustible versatility, while consigning the word to often-frustrating vagueness. It is important to stress that Schmitt's misgivings about an excessive privileging of the idea of security are lodged from the political right. The target is clearly the self-assured man who presumes to be safely ensconced within his domestic space, nestled within the *oikos* where he can wallow in his own private interests and remain impervious to any noise without. Schmitt repudiates this creature of economics and devout worshiper of a secularized, monetized divinity. He scorns the artificial paradise that is conjured under the influence of sanctioned substances, the caffeine and tobacco that provide just the right dose of stimulation so as to prevent complete torpor. Tucked up within this quiet shelter, the bourgeois claustrophile can indulge in "sensuality" or "sexual ecstasy," that is, in the *Wollust* that also names, within the Christian tradition, the mortal sin of *luxuria* or "lust." For this decadent man of pleasure, "security" denotes specifically the enclosed *Gemütlichkeit* that emboldens the individual subject and paves the way to licentiousness. Schmitt's attack on the liberal is therefore also aimed at the libertine. It describes the state of comfort that enables people to participate in illicit, devilish acts without worrying about the moral judgments of others, for this luxury is emphatically "well veiled"—*gut verschleiert*—immune from external accusations, invulnerable, untouchable, *secure*: at least "until now."

The antibourgeois sentiment is as familiar as it is dated. From a historical perspective, Schmitt's formulation properly belongs to a particular critique of rationalization that is attributable to thinkers responding to and reacting against the perceived political failures of the Weimar Republic. Examples of this kind of vitriol against liberal complacency and the absence of moral values may

---

[36] See Bill McSweeny, *Security, Identity and Interests: A Sociology of International Relations*, 20–21.

be found in a broad variety of German interwar writings across the entire political map. Generally speaking, the terms of such observations stem from the way Max Weber articulated the problem of modernity in 1905, namely, in *The Protestant Ethic and the Spirit of Capitalism*. The satirical edge of Schmitt's gloss on the word *sécurité* may owe a stylistic debt to Flaubert's *Dictionnaire des idées reçues*, but the theoretical content is almost wholly Weberian. The moments along the historical trajectory that Weber pursues—from the subjective, inward turn of the Reformation through secularization and disenchantment to the famous construction of modernity's "iron cage"—all have nearly exact analogues in Schmitt's concise entry. And it is precisely with the evocation of "internalization," "the secularized certainty of grace," "Luther," "Herrnhut," and the "Quaker" that Schmitt reveals his affinity with a lexicon very much tied to Weber's analyses.

In *The Protestant Ethic*, for example, Weber closely anticipates Schmitt's remarks by associating *Gemütlichkeit* and "security" with Quaker philosophy:

> The concept of "comfort" [*Gemütlichkeit*] embraces the range of ethically permissible uses of wealth, and it is no coincidence that the development of the style of life defined by that concept has been observed earliest and most clearly in the most consistent representatives of this whole philosophy, the Quakers. Their ideal was the cleanliness and security of the comfortable middle-class home, in contrast to the glitter and dazzle of Cavalier pomp, which, resting on shaky economic foundation, preferred shabby elegance to sober simplicity.[37]

A comparison of this passage with Schmitt's text shows how the latter adopts the former's terminology and then reconfigures it to new ends. Specifically, Schmitt regards the history of secularization as a gradual process of "neutralization," which amounts to a "depoliticization," insofar as his "concept of the political" famously rests on the primary distinction between friend and enemy.[38] Where Weber sees an ascetic, religiously motivated Quaker, Schmitt sees a self-styled "Friend" who objects to all conflict and therefore remains insistently apolitical, not out of some moral conviction but rather for the sake of profit. The "Quaker turned billionaire" is the capitalist at work in a secularized, godless, and therefore valueless world—someone who no longer suffers from pious fear, a Quaker who has forgotten how to quake: "Where now is your trembling?"

Schmitt consistently disdains the person who is thus carefree, one who does not take sides, who has chosen not to choose. As Derrida stresses, for Schmitt, "the political itself, the being-political of the political, arises in its possibility with the figure of the enemy."[39] Self-immured, this Friend has refused to be an Other, and without otherness, there can be neither society nor politics. In the privacy of his home, which is thought to be cordoned off from all community, this individualist believes that he can exist as a non-Other. Security as coziness is purchased with the negation of alterity.

As mentioned, Schmitt is not alone in questioning the bourgeois ideals of prosperity, peace, and security. Such a critique is broadly recognizable among Weimar discourses on both the right and the left, from Georg Lukács's theory of reification to Ernst Jünger's poetics of danger, from Walter Benjamin's critique of violence to Heidegger's *Destruktion* of metaphysics.[40] For example, Benjamin was fascinated with and highly critical of this image of the bourgeois warmly secured in his castle. For the *Arcades Project*, he opened a fresh dossier devoted to "The Interior" of nineteenth-century private residences and its furnishings, which revealed traces of medieval fortifications (*Konvolut* I). Benjamin cites the observations of the Weimar art historian Adolf Behne, who points out the many analogies that link an armoire, with its elaborate drawers and shelving, to the fortress surrounded by ramparts, outwork, and moats. In the diagonal arrangement of the furniture and objets d'art, Behne is reminded of feudal military strategy.[41] For Behne, an analysis of interior design should reveal "the unconscious retention of a posture of struggle and defense":

> Just as the knight, suspecting an attack, positions himself cross-wise to guard both left and right, so the peace-loving burgher, several centuries later, orders his art objects in such a way that each one, if only by standing out from all the rest, has a wall and moat surrounding it. He is thus truly a *Spießbürger*, a militant philistine.[42]

A German cultural historian would have no trouble connecting the nineteenth-century, norm-abiding philistine (*Spießbürger*) back to the medieval townsman who conventionally defended himself with a "pike" (*Spieß*). The observation corroborates Schmitt's theory. The enlightened bourgeois gentleman, who thinks he follows the march to perpetual peace, does not need to worry about political antagonisms. Yet he has forgotten that he already sits, however comfortably, in the midst of conflict.

Regardless of the vast differences in their commitments and priorities, both Benjamin and Schmitt share deep suspicions of antipolitical claims. Like Schmitt, Benjamin too discerns a fundamental "nihilism" in "the innermost core of bourgeois *Gemütlichkeit*" and comments: "From the cavern, one does not like to stir."[43] Yet Benjamin, especially at the time when he is gathering documenta-

[39] Jacques Derrida, *The Politics of Friendship*, 84.
[40] For an account of Weber's formative role in the intellectual life of Weimar, see Lawrence Scaff, *Fleeing the Iron Cage: Culture, Politics, and Modernity in the Thought of Max Weber*.
[41] Benjamin cites from Adolf Behne, *Neues Wohnen—Neues Bauen* (Leipzig, 1927), 61–62. See Benjamin, *The Arcades Project*, 212.
[42] From Behne *Neues Wohnen—Neues Bauen* (1927, 45–48; cited in Benjamin, *The Arcades Project*, 215.
[43] Benjamin, *The Arcades Project*, 216.

tion for the *Passagen-Werk*, is not willing to renounce altogether the possibility of progress, even if it could only be expressed in a melancholic mode. To this end, still within the "Interior" *Konvolut*, Benjamin turns to Marx's early writings on historical materialism, where he discovers the following: "Humanity is regressing to the state of cave-dweller . . . [but] it is regressing in an estranged, malignant form. The savage in his cave . . . feels . . . at home there. . . . But the basement apartment of the poor man is a hostile dwelling."[44] Because the *Spießbürger* is too content in his security to contribute to social justice, Benjamin, with Marx, turns his attention to the worker.

Schmitt would just as well leave the bourgeois to suffocate in his coziness, but his authoritarianism could never allow support for a revolution that is purely social—and therefore not political—in its intent. For Schmitt, the activism that brews just below the surface of the proletariat's despair aims toward another evasion of the political that is just as detrimental as the pacifist complacency of the bourgeoisie. In order to correct the problems of security as *Gemütlichkeit*—problems that, in Schmitt's opinion, lead to overrationalism, constitutionalism, and bureaucratization—it is necessary to interrogate the legitimacy of liberal individualism itself. That is to say, it is necessary to insist on the primacy of the *state* in contradistinction to the *individual*, no matter if it is the bourgeois in his commodious cavern or the sweaty factory man in his sunless flat. Instead of a Marxist inspired social revolution, Schmitt would propose a conservative revolution, one that upholds the feudal structures of God and Sovereign.[45]

Despite the vast, unbridgeable distances between their ideological commitments and philosophical premises, every one of these thinkers, Schmitt included, betrays to greater or lesser degree an adherence to a certain vitalist, Nietzschean tradition as articulated by Weber, one that protests the gross quantification of human life and the bureaucratization of human relations, in brief, one that resists the reduction of experience to technological calculability. With slight modification, they would all agree with Weber's assessment of the times as being enslaved to the "mighty cosmos of the modern economic order," which is a mechanism of its own making.[46]

Carl Schmitt, who attended Weber's seminal "vocation" lectures in Munich and also participated in Weber's course on "Universal Social and Economic History" (1919–20), explicitly employed the sociologist's terms to forge his own theoretical position in *Political Romanticism* (1919), where German romantic

---

[44] Karl Marx, *Der historische Materialismus: Die Frühschriften* (Leipzig, 1932); cited in Benjamin, *The Arcades Project*, 223.

[45] For an extended discussion that delineates Schmitt's political theory in relation to his contemporaries, see Richard Wolin, "Carl Schmitt: The Conservative Revolutionary Habitus and the Aesthetics of Horror."

[46] Weber, *The Protestant Ethic and the Spirit of Capitalism*, 120. As Weber goes on to describe, "Today this mighty cosmos determines, with overwhelming coercion, the style of life *not only* of those directly involved in business but of every individual who is born into this mechanism, and may well continue to do so until the day that the last ton of fossil fuel has been consumed" (120–21; emphasis in original).

writers are characterized as self-absorbed, passive, and dangerously apoliti-cal.[47] In a word, they represent a resignation from what Weber refers to as a "politics of responsibility." Rather than view romanticism as an irrational anti-dote to a hyperrationalized world, Schmitt regards the movement's aestheticiz-ing, reality-negating program to be the perfect and necessary complement to the technological-economic order, part and parcel of the selfsame "machine." For Schmitt, both the technological manipulation of nature and its subjectively detached aestheticization are direct consequences of rationalization and secu-larization. Hardly opposed to the "spirit of capitalism," romanticism is its pro-found ally.[48]

CRITIQUE OF COMPLACENCY

Frequently in the analyses of the times scattered across his writings from the 1920s and 1930s, Schmitt casts aspersions on the Enlightenment principles that aim to neutralize political conflict so as to ensure the benefits that proceed from well-established norms. He repeatedly faults a society that feebly operates within a sphere believed to be thoroughly calculable and without risk. "Until now," this cozy situation has been the staid accomplishment of the nonpolitical German. "Until now," the incurious bourgeois could cultivate his nonchalance with little consequence. However, by 1945, every German had been thrown into a state of deep insecurity. Schmitt, too, would regard himself as a victim. Despite his insistence that he had always been a severe critic of the party, he paid dearly under the American de-Nazification program.[49] Upon his release in 1947, he headed directly to Plettenberg in the Sauerland, to the house where he was born and raised. In a gesture that betrayed deep-seated pride and a ten-dency to see himself as a persecuted victim, unjustly accused and grossly mis-understood, he named his home "San Casciano," a reference to the country residence where Machiavelli found refuge after the fall of the Florentine Repub-lic. Delusions of grandeur notwithstanding, during his first years of exile, Schmitt wrote nothing that could compare to Machiavelli's *Prince* or the *Dis-courses on Livy*. Instead, the sole literary artifacts stemming from this period

[47] On Weber's influence in Schmitt's early work, see John P. McCormick, *Carl Schmitt's Critique of Liberalism: Against Politics as Technology*, 31–82.

[48] In the 1924 preface to *Political Romanticism*, Schmitt writes: "It is only in an individualistically dis-integrated society that the aesthetically productive subject could shift the intellectual center into itself, only in a bourgeois world that isolates the individual in the domain of the intellectual, makes the indi-vidual its own point of reference, and imposes upon it the entire burden that otherwise was hierarchically distributed among different functions in a social order. In this society, it is left to the private individual to be his own priest" (20).

[49] Although he had joined the NSDAP in 1933, he pointed out that, on the basis of his Catholic views, he had been publicly vilified in 1936 by the SS in the notorious pages of the *Schwarzes Korps* and was subsequently removed from his chairmanship of the Nazi League of German Jurists. On Schmitt's involve-ment in the Nazi Party and his postwar exile, see Heinrich Meier, "The Philosopher as Enemy."

are his prison notebooks tellingly published as *Ex captivitate salus*; and the papers retrieved from the state archive of North Rhine–Westphalia that compose the *Glossarium*.

A heterogeneous collection of political commentary and social observation, a mixture of brilliantly free associations and often painful self-reflection, the *Glossarium* not only reinforces and complements Schmitt's major theoretical positions but also provides rare insights into his personal disposition, viewpoints, and tastes, often with shocking sincerity and not a little self-pity. Excerpts from his correspondence are mingled with meditations on literary texts; his views concerning the philosophical tradition, including meditations, hitherto unavailable, on the thought of Heidegger, are indispensable for situating the jurist's place within his broader historical context.[50] Above all, as already suggested, the *Glossarium* is an exercise in philology.

In this regard, Schmitt's gloss on *sécurité* is exemplary. Its flashes of insight attract the reader, who, like an Etruscan *fulgurator*, is invited to locate their significance by referring to Schmitt's published corpus, where arguments are more fully elaborated. What the *Glossarium* entry presents in shorthand can be transliterated hermeneutically so as to yield more explicit sense. It should be borne in mind that Schmitt dubiously sketches out his merciless critique from within the protected burrow of the maternal home. On what basis, we may then ask, can the security of the writer deride the security of his enemy? In what way does the walled-in burgher differ from the withdrawn legal scholar? To what extent is his characterization of the secured, comfortable, lustful, and quakeless Quaker an exercise in self-portraiture?

Schmitt's entry differs from his earlier political theory insofar as it introduces a moral aspect that his generally antiliberal position would otherwise reject. Strictly speaking, according to Schmitt's consistent view, morality, together with aesthetic and economic principles, corrupts the stark independence of "the concept of the political." As he points out, each domain of human thought entails its own governing criteria; each sphere articulates its specific terms. For morality, it is the distinction between good and evil; in aesthetics, between beautiful and ugly; and in economics, between profitable and unprofitable. In contrast to these endeavors, the political is based solely on the distinction between friend and enemy.[51] Rather than explaining further the signifi-

[50] As Heinrich Meier states, "[The *Glossarium*] contains sufficient material to give new nourishment to the heated debate between Schmitt's morally indignant critics and his apologetic admirers for years to come." Meier, "The Philosopher as Enemy," 328–29.

[51] "The political enemy need not be morally evil or aesthetically ugly; he need not appear as an economic competitor, and it may even be advantageous to engage with him in business transactions. But he is, nevertheless, the other, the stranger; and it is sufficient for his nature that he is, in a specially intense way, existentially something different and alien, so that in the extreme case conflicts with him are possible. These can neither be decided by a previously determined general norm nor by the judgment of a disinterested and therefore neutral third party." Carl Schmitt, *The Concept of the Political*, 25–27 [*Der Begriff des Politischen* (1932), 26–27].

282 • Chapter 14

cance and implications of Schmitt's concept of the political, it is sufficient here to register a curious slippage in the *Glossarium* passage. Despite his serious misgivings regarding the depoliticizing trends due to ethical compromises, Schmitt clearly passes a moral, that is, nonpolitical judgment on the bourgeois lifestyle. The nestled plushness of the curtained den, sealed off from outside view, encourages the nameless gentleman to luxuriate in his every desire, to gratify every lust, without caring about allegations of immorality. However, what is noteworthy in Schmitt's brief gloss is the subtle shift in translative decisions: the passage moves almost imperceptibly from a conventional critique of bourgeois complacency (security as coziness) to a less expected, moralist assault on bourgeois lasciviousness (security as insouciance). Schmitt's opening, *political* critique of the bourgeois's apolitical position yields to a *nonpolitical* critique of bourgeois immorality. How does this happen?

We have already seen that, judging from its initial usage in Cicero, the word *securitas* has more to do with the domain of moral psychology than with the political sphere of public or territorial defense. To be *securus* means to have one's mind free from agitation, to stand psychologically upon solid, unassailable asphalt. If a notion of defense is to be included among Cicero's connotations, it should be limited to an idea of protection against matters that would upset this balance, matters generally stemming from the political sphere. The fortification erected by these security projects therefore names the bulwark of tranquil selfhood, the Stoics' "inner citadel" that makes the soul invulnerable and steadfast in character. It would be a mistake, however, to ignore the concrete political implications of this image. As discussed above, in *De officiis*, the public aspect of private *securitas* is perfectly evident.

Moreover, Schmitt's passing reference to the "certainty of grace" (*Gnadenge-wißheit*) refers to the Augustinian-Lutheran doctrine that certitude implies the inability of the Christian subject to be perfectly sure of his or her salvation. Thus, when Schmitt evokes how "Luther and the Moravians had raged so sternly against security as actual lust," he is alluding to the way Luther commonly contrasted *securitas* with the "fear of God" (*timor Dei*) that checks our pride and saves us from divine wrath.[52] In the *Glossarium* passage, Schmitt's turn of phrase, which is aimed at a "weakling" (*Jämmerling*), identifies security as the "actual sensuality" (*eigentliche Wollust*) that causes one to ignore one's spirituality, to fail to attend Paul's famous command to the Philippians, namely that they "should work out [their] salvation with fear and trembling" (*cum metu et tremore vestram salutem operamini*, Philippians 2:12). As Kierkegaard would stress, insofar as security eradicates *cura*, it removes the very anxiety that motivates the salvific program.

Schmitt retains this notion of *securitas* that is grounded in eradication. With self-perpetuating if not mad logic, the concern for security is always a concern

---

[52] See sections 7 and 11 of the Heidelberg Disputation (1518), WA 1: 358–59.

for being without concern. In glossing *sécurité* alternately as *Gemütlichkeit* and *Gewissheit*, Schmitt augments and complicates this basic sense of removal. On the one hand, the privation implicit in bourgeois coziness is manifested in the snug privacy of someone who entertains no relation to the outside. It names the deceptive dream of the unpolitical man, who dangerously appeals to a moral as opposed to a political standard of freedom. On the other hand, dubiously blessed by secularized grace, this stereotype relaxing in his easy chair is accused of relishing the pleasures of self-satisfaction with the *secure*—"carefree"—disposition of someone immune from moral law. This coincidence of the nonmoral and the moral underwrites Schmitt's vacillating characterization. Having turned his home into a safe house, into a haven of inaction, the bourgeois employs moral arguments to keep state intervention at bay. Yet this same pleasure-seeking individual abandons the moral sphere, insofar as he fears and trembles at nothing. The moral ambivalence that is ascribed to the complacent liberal further reflects Schmitt's own ambivalence regarding the meaning of security. How could the security outlined by classical political theory be saved from becoming antipolitical carelessness? How might a politics of responsibility be salvaged from the snares of irresponsibility, negligence, and insouciance?

While still incarcerated under American watch, locked within the discomfort of his cell, Schmitt persistently reflected on the themes of captivity and salvation, on the ravages of secularization and political neutralization. In this spirit, he would turn again and again to his favorite authors, to Jean Bodin and Thomas Hobbes, who continued to serve as a source of greatest concern— "They kept my thinking awake and drove it forward, even as the positivism of my time oppressed me, and a blind need for security [*ein blindes Sekuritäts-bedürfnis*] wanted to paralyze me."[53] This line, which appears in Schmitt's first postwar publication, *Ex captivitate salus*, speaks of a paralysis that differs from both the paralysis of fear, illustrated, say, in Lorenzetti's fresco series, and the paralysis of security, as described by political theorists. That Schmitt resorts to a rare form of the key term—*Sekurität* as opposed to *Sicherheit*—may point to a philological impulse that infringes on the author's political theoretical expertise. It is as if Schmitt were reverting to his first academic plans, while still a young man, to pursue a degree in classical philology, before accepting the advice of his family and choosing jurisprudence. The paralysis evoked here, I would contend, is nothing less than the outcome of a dynamic encounter between political theory and philology.

[53] *Sie haben mein Denken wachgehalten und vorwärtsgetrieben, als der Positivismus meiner Jahrgänge mich bedrückte und ein blindes Sekuritätsbedürfnis mich lähmen wollte.* Carl Schmitt, *Ex captivitate salus*, 64.

15

Surveillance, Conspiracy, and the Nanny State

ANOTHER LIFE

WITHOUT CARE NO ONE can be secure. This is true for security as well as for safety. Yet, the requirement of care does not mean that the concern must fall solely to the one to be secured. Because threats—particlarly those that jeopardize life itself—can often overwhelm the wherewithal of a single subject, it is common to appeal to institutions and agencies that are better equipped and therefore in a more advantageous position to take care of individuals. The secured subject relinquishes the responsibility of care by submitting to a higher authority, by obeying the will of a collective, or simply by trusting technology. A sovereign state, which occupies a privileged place above the populace, can arguably foresee and identify threats better than others. The structure that defines this relation between the one securing and the one secured differs little from that which allows gadgets, devices, and sensors to catch what human senses might miss. In both cases, individual care is relegated to persons or machines that are designed, technologically or ideologically, for *accuracy*.

The provision of security, then, is not only an act of care but also an expression of power. And power is always something that stands to be abused. Agencies of twentieth-century totalitarian regimes—for example, the East German Republic's Stasi (Ministerium für Staatssicherheit)—consistently and explicitly claimed to maintain security by inculcating insecurity among the masses. The perverse logic is that fear alone sustains the need for security, which consequently legitimizes the state's existence.[1] This logic has at least two alternative results. On the one hand, the care for the individual citizen has simply been converted to the care for the state. Here, security is a dehumanizing project that shifts all concern to a realm well beyond the human. On the other hand and with no slight irony, precisely by promulgating fear among the populace, such projects also inadvertently humanize. Stripped of personal security—deprived of the privation of concern—the subjects of these regimes are left with nothing more and nothing greater than the capacity to care.

---

[1] On this point, see Crépon, *La culture de la peur: 1. Démocratie, identité, sécurité*, 49.

The dynamics between security and human care comes to the fore in Florian Henckel von Donnersmarck's internationally acclaimed film *Das Leben der Anderen* (*The Lives of Others*, 2006). The story begins in 1984, a clear Orwellian index, and deeply engages with the techniques of power and ideologies of legitimization commonly associated with the East German government. In brief, what the film persistently demonstrates is how transindividual, transhuman security procedures carried out in the name of the state are undermined when human concerns or insecurities come into consideration. The plot centers on Gerd Wiesler (Ulrich Mühe), an interrogations expert, committed socialist, and frighteningly effective Stasi officer. He has been assigned by his superior to monitor the day-to-day life of the renowned playwright Georg Dreyman (Sebastian Koch); and he initially performs this task with his usual discipline and clinically applied methods. At the film's beginning we observe Wiesler as little more than a cog in the machine, a ruthless analyst with a keen sense for mendacity and prevarication, an efficient, self-effacing master of wiretapping, surveillance, and enhanced observation.

Expressionless, Wiesler sits absolutely still, a paradigm of patience, attention, and vigilance, living up to his weasalish name. Equipped with headphones and a characterless sports jacket buttoned to the neck, this balding man almost perfectly blends into the cold, drab grey of the radio transmitters that surround him. The flesh of the face, although somewhat ashen, provides the only hint of color. The technological gear, which replicates Wiesler's motionlessness, further compromises this already diminished depiction of the human subject. The electronic components—the sound meters, the knobs, the switches and faders—seem to have transformed the figure into yet another instrument of technology, as if the human form were but a prosthetic extension of the system. This technologization of the human is underscored by the bureaucratic, numerical moniker—HGW XX/7—that chillingly supplants Wiesler's proper name. Especially when compared to those under surveillance, HGW XX/7 is an inhuman utensil, completely divorced from human community.

The chiaroscuro of the film's original poster emphasizes this point. Engulfed in darkness and shadow, Wiesler's personhood fails to receive the light that illuminates Dreyman and his girlfriend Christa-Maria Sieland (Martina Gedeck). The armor of his tightly buttoned jacket contrasts with the opened shirt collar of his victim wrapped in amorous embrace. HGW's red fingerprint demonstrates how the agent is nothing outside the system that has inscribed him. Life—human life—belongs to others. As Eva Horn comments, "HGW's loneliness, the fact that he, unlike his victims, has no life, reduces him to a mere listening device, sitting in the attic of the house at his listening post with headphones. He is a medium—and nothing but a medium."[2] Yet, while Wiesler

[2] Eva Horn, "Media of Conspiracy: Love and Surveillance in Fritz Lang and Florian Henckel von Donnersmarck," 140.

listens to what is taking place in Dreyman's apartment, we the viewers are also observing Wiesler. HGW may be a mere medium for the state's security initiatives, but for us he is a man who has been or is still in the process of being medialized. The portrayal decisively complicates our anxiety about invasive security methods by turning to the fragile individuality of the security officer himself. The mechanizing, dehumanizing effects visible in the shot signal a loss that the film diligently strives to restitute. Throughout, the oscillating focus from the victimized object of surveillance to the dehumanized agent illustrates how security projects potentially entail deprivations for all involved, how both the object and subject of security stand to lose something vital.

The restitution begins as soon as Wiesler learns that Dreyman is being observed not because he is suspected of being a "subversive" but rather because the East German minister of culture is infatuated with and lusts after Sieland, who is living in the playwright's home. The surveillance order, therefore, was not issued on the basis of concern for the regime's security but instead on the basis of a wholly personal, sexually charged *cura*. Hardly a dangerous enemy of the state, Dreyman turns out to be an unsuspecting victim of conspiracy. As in a Roman tragedy, Dreyman is regarded by the state's functionaries as an obstacle to be overcome, a rival who must be eliminated in order for the statesman to secure the object of his lascivious desire.

The emergence of an all-too-human concern fatally disrupts the routinized procedures of the Stasi officer and essentially *demechanizes* Wiesler, who is suddenly and irreversibly recalled to his humanity.[3] He slowly but decisively becomes emotionally attached to Dreyman and Sieland, fascinated by the couple's movements, their conversations, their intimacy. Wiesler's increasing fondness eventually redefines the objective of his security enterprise. No longer acting as a political instrument for the state, Wiesler begins to protect the private lives of Dreyman and Sieland. He takes the risk to meet Sieland personally, whose own insecurity has led her to prostitute herself out of fear that she would otherwise ruin her acting career, first by sleeping with Bruno Hempf (Thomas Thieme), the repulsive minister of culture, and later by becoming an "unofficial informant" (an *Inoffizieller Mitarbeiter*, or IM) for the state. Wiesler meanwhile is shown to be less and less enthralled to the system that he once upheld so vigorously. Posing as a fan, Wiesler suggests to Sieland that her talent requires no patron. In appreciation and with a rare moment of sincerity, she thanks the stranger and tells him that he is "a good person" (*ein guter Mensch*). Subsequently, back at his listening post, Wiesler is pleased to hear her swear to Dreyman that she will no longer keep her sordid appointments with Hempf. It is as

---

[3] It is precisely this humanization of the Stasi officer that many German critics, mindful of the horrors of the East German regime, found especially questionable; and this has been a fairly common critique among German scholars working on the film. For a brief overview, see Cheryl Dueck, "The Humanization of the Stasi in *Das Leben der Anderen*."

a man—as a good *Mensch*—that Wiesler is able to touch the lives of the others and thereby begin to live himself.

The state that cares only for itself can never provide security for anyone or for anything other than itself. Its security program exclusively removes the concerns that threaten its own legitimacy and power. Its effects, therefore, are to spread insecurity among the populace. Sieland, too, must secure her own career by desecuring others. HGW opts out of this program altogether by becoming a man, by becoming Gerd Wiesler, who ultimately learns to care for other humans and thereby provide them with safety. Dreyman, who is known to be a devoted communist, believes at first that he has nothing to fear. His own disillusionment, which parallels Wiesler's, occurs during his birthday party with friends. This event broaches the uncomfortable issue of blacklisting artists and writers. Dreyman's colleague, the theater director Albert Jerska (Volkmar Kleinert), who has suffered dearly from being blacklisted, hands over his birthday present to Dreyman: a piano score of an etude entitled "Sonata for the Good Man" (*Sonate vom guten Menschen*). Wiesler is thereby brought into even closer proximity with his surveillance subject, because both have now been identified by the same human quality. Wiesler's concern for Dreyman is therefore in a sense concern for himself. Days later, when Dreyman learns that Jerska has hanged himself, his anger and frustration impel him to write an article on suicide rates in East Germany, figures that are tightly suppressed by the state, again as a security measure. The plan is to publish the piece anonymously in the West German periodical *Der Spiegel*. Upon being baptized as a good man by the distraught Jerska, Dreyman could regard his birthday as a rebirth into humanity. At the piano, he plays through Jerska's sonata, a rehearsal for the ode that he will compose on a typewriter's keyboard and present as a memorial to his dead friend.

To be human is to be mortal, to be prey to contingencies beyond one's control. And Dreyman correspondingly takes necessary precautions before setting himself to work on the dangerous article. Fully aware that every typewriter in East Germany is registered with the state, he will write the piece on a miniature model that had been smuggled in from the West and is hidden beneath the floorboards. Furthermore, to confirm that his apartment is not bugged, he and his friends devise a ruse, pretending to be engaged in a smuggling plot. In other words, Dreyman stages a fake conspiracy in order to conspire securely against the state that has conspired against him. Wiesler refrains from contacting the authorities, which attests to his sympathy as well as convinces Dreyman (falsely) that he is not under watch. The playwright can proceed with his subversive writing relatively without concern, thanks of course to his unknown but effective protector. Wiesler is still a security agent, yet now an altogether "good" one, one who in fact provides security rather than promulgate insecurity and collective paranoia on behalf of a brutally inhuman regime.

The apathy that ideally characterizes all instruments of mediation is over-come by increasing passion. Wiesler's official reports are no longer *accurate* because his *cura* is now directed far from state matters. The disrupting emer-gence of strong, impassioned sentiment marks the replacement of political cal-culability by classical aesthetic feeling. Wiesler picks up a volume of Brecht's poetry that he discovers on Dreyman's desk and closely reads it through. The poem that is singled out in the film is Brecht's well-known lyric "Erinnerung an die Marie A.," which dates from 1920 but was first published in the *Hauspostille* collection of 1927. The camera closes in on Wiesler's face as he reads the text, yet in voiceover, it is Dreyman who is heard enunciating the lines:

> *Und fragst du mich, was mit der Liebe sei?*
> *So sag ich dir: Ich kann mich nicht erinnern.*
> *Und doch, gewiß, ich weiß schon, was du meinst*
> *Doch ihr Gesicht, das weiß ich wirklich nimmer*
> *Ich weiß nur mehr: Ich küsste es dereinst.*

> And should you ask me, what's become of love?
> I'll tell you: I cannot remember.
> And yet, certainly, I do know what you mean
> But her face, I really know no longer
> I only know now: I kissed it once.

In addition to reinforcing the sympathetic relationship between Dreyman and Wiesler, between perpetrator and victim, the poem evokes the themes of tran-sience, fleeting desire, and failed memory that define the human condition. The rapid alternation between knowing and not knowing is reflected in the repeti-tion of forms of *wissen* (to know): *gewiß, ich weiß* schon . . . das *weiß* ich wirk-lich nimmer / Ich *weiß* nur mehr. The desire for certainty—*Gewißheit*, a con-cept closely linked to security—is both motivated and frustrated by the erstwhile lover's concern. Moreover, these lines from Brecht's "breviary" (*Haus-postille*) decidedly diverge from the conventional image of Brecht as someone who is politically engaged, ironic, and cynical. In the utterly private scene of Wiesler's reading, the poetry serves to depoliticize art and is made to speak instead to transcendent and universal values, values that would appear to con-tradict the historical materialist vision associated with Brecht.[4] To be sure, the sympathetic relationship between Dreyman and Wiesler—that is, between a type of "actor" and "spectator"—militates against Brecht's entire concept of epic theater, based as it is on breaking the illusion that would foster such identifica-tions. These refunctionalizations of Brecht are fairly evident in the persistent references to "the good person" (*der gute Mensch*)—in Sieland's remark to

[4] On this point, see Mary Beth Stein, "Stasi with a Human Face? Ambiguity in *Das Leben der Anderen*," 575; and Gary Schmidt, "Between Authors and Agents: Gender and Affirmative Culture in *Das Leben der Anderen*," 243–44.

Wiesler and in Jerska's piano etude, *Sonate vom guten Menschen*, which at the film's end will serve as the title of Dreyman's memoir dedicated to agent "HGW XX/7." These clear allusions to *Der gute Mensch von Sezuan* both reinforce and disprove the lesson of Brecht's parable: on the one hand, as both Shen Te and Wiesler come to realize, in order to remain good, one must adopt masks and be willing to dissemble in a society that will ultimately abuse moral integrity; on the other hand, and contrary to Brecht's argument, it is only in the post-*Wende* sphere of capitalist liberalism that such goodness can in fact flourish.

In *Das Leben der Anderen*, humanization is consistently linked to a liberal view that poses as an apolitical position. Statements from the director corroborate this claim. In an interview with John Esther, Donnersmarck explains, "I really don't believe there is such a thing as politics. It's all about individuals. . . . So I tried to focus on individual psychology in the film. Rather than tell a political story, I show how people make the politics and how that affects people." The director continues by recommending that one should "strike a balance between principle and feeling . . . between Vladimir Lenin and John Lennon."[5] Metaphors of balancing commonly surface in discussions of public security, especially where the provision of safety measures is linked to a necessary sacrifice of certain civil liberties. One does not have to conjure an entirely Orwellian scenario to find how security's promise to eliminate fear or provide stability may encroach upon, compromise, or severely limit human freedom. Indeed, suspicions about exchanging liberty for security course through world history and are perhaps most popularly expressed in the overquoted line long attributed to Benjamin Franklin: "Those who would give up essential liberty to purchase a little temporary safety, deserve neither liberty nor safety."[6] As we might expect, this intimation reaches back to classical Roman literature, for example in Livy's account of the early Republic or in Horace's lyric reflections on the dynamics of life within the burgeoning Empire.

Throughout this long history, the *cura* about existential threats, which state security claims to provide, is supplanted by a *cura* about the limitations and trade-offs required for the former. In *Das Leben der Anderen* both species of *cura* characterize the human condition and hence a humanitarian ideal. For Seneca, the "absence of concern" denoted by *securitas* should be understood in relation to the "absence of disturbing passions" denoted by Stoic *apatheia*. Although it would be difficult—but not altogether impossible—to interpret Donnersmarck's film within a purely Stoic context, it does appear to be sufficiently

[5] John Esther, "Between Principle and Feeling: An Interview with Florian Henckel von Donnersmarck," 40.

[6] This sentence first occurs as a quote from a message to the governor from the Pennsylvania Assembly in Richard Jackson's *An Historical Review of the Constitution and Government of Pennsylvania*, which was published in London by Franklin in 1759, p. 289. It was also used as the motto for the book's title page. A later variant, also set in quotation marks, is found among Franklin's notes for an address to the Pennsylvania Assembly in February 1775, published in *Memoirs of the Life and Writings of Benjamin Franklin*, 1: 517.

clear that the concerns exhibited by the story's individuals (Wiesler, Dreyman, Sieland, among others) are designated by the passions or *pathē* that characterize what the filmmaker regards to be human. In the interview cited above, it is the impassioned music of John Lennon (and perhaps also his deeply personal forays into political activism) that represents the basic, universal human feelings that must be summoned to balance against the rigorous, political program of Vladimir Lenin. Donnersmarck seems to regard this Manichaean struggle between musical sentiment and ideological tenacity as central to the film's conception. In another interview, he divulges that it was the old story about Lenin's love for Beethoven's *Appassionata* piano sonata, first related by Maxim Gorky, that supplied the initial inspiration for the screenplay. According to Gorky, Lenin confessed, "I don't want to listen to it because it makes me want to stroke people's heads, and I have to smash those heads to bring the revolution to them." Donnersmarck adds: "I suddenly had this image in my mind of a person sitting in a depressing room with earphones on his head and listening into what he supposes is the enemy of the state and the enemy of his ideas, and what he is really hearing is beautiful music that touches him."[7]

However, the optimism expressed here is qualified by the fact that at the film's end, the two protagonists, Dreyman and Wiesler, fail to come into personal contact, even though the Wall has come down, even though the Stasi has been dissolved and the files are now a matter of public record. Nonetheless, the distance maintained between the two figures can also be regarded as the constitutive gap that is prerequisite for care. After the mechanism of State Security has been broken apart, the bonds of humanity are once again reinforced by the *cura* that joins us by keeping us separate. In Germany, the controversy sparked by this film essentially turned on the complaint that a Stasi officer was not depicted with sufficient cruelty. This presumed failure arguably robbed today's audience from a particular pleasure, namely to compare our present society with the recent past and thereby conclude that we are not as bad as people back then. In contrast, Donnersmarck appears to lodge a serious warning: we better hold on to our humanity, lest it disappears entirely into the warm bath of complacency.

SECURITY BY NUMBERS

In 2006, the same year that saw the release of *Das Leben der Anderen*, the Körber Stiftung of Hamburg invited twelve young photography artists to submit work that would address the institute's selected theme, entitled *Balanceakt: Sicherheit* (Balancing Act: Security). The resulting show, held in Hamburg's Deichtorhallen, aimed to demonstrate, according to curator Ingo Taubhorn,

---

[7] Alan Riding, "Behind the Berlin Wall, Listening to Life."

how security had become "one of the burning themes of the present, where world-political developments and serious changes in the life of every individual question the state of this basic human need."[8] Whereas Donnersmarck would stress *cura* as a universal characteristic of humanity and therefore as a vital component in protests against the state's security projects, Taubhorn recalls that the desire for security, too, is no less universally human. That is not to say that Taubhorn neglects the historical configurations and reconfigurations of this "basic human need," since it now calls for an urgent reassessment in light of current developments in international relations and in societal experience. Taubhorn shares aesthetic presuppositions with Donnersmarck, yet with the opposite emphasis: art should reveal how history has modified and continues to modify the meaning of humanity, but it is the longing for security that here defines what it means to be human.

As with Donnersmarck, the show at the Körber Stiftung also specifies the tension between security and individuality as a "balancing act," which immediately conjures the same liberal viewpoint discernible in the filmmaker's work.[9] However, while Donnersmarck appears to take the liberalist position as natural—that is, as something both apolitical and ahistorical—the conception of the Körber exhibition, precisely by naming security as fundamental to humanity, directly challenges the givenness of this perspective.

A further challenge, which addresses both positions, would consist in pressing the ramifications of the balancing metaphor itself. Here, three distinct but overlapping problems may be raised: *quantification, consequence,* and *abuse.* First, the metaphor of balancing implies that both security and liberty are being evaluated as goods that can be measured into quantifiable units. As in the Franklin quote mentioned previously, both security and liberty may be understood as commodities that can be "purchased." In contemporary discourse, we speak of being "more secure" or "less secure." We learn that security is being "increased," "reduced," or "enhanced." In other words, through quantification, a citizen may be asked or even be willing to sacrifice *a certain amount* of liberty in order to obtain *a certain amount more* of security, especially when an imminent, grave threat outweighs whatever equilibrium has formerly been conceived as normal. Yet, is it possible to submit experiential risks and protections to a quantifiable analysis? How can it ever be determined that the curtailment

---

[8] Ingo Taubhorn, "Ein Forum junger Fotografie," 8.
[9] In addition to evoking the "balancing act" that typically accompanies discourses on security and liberty, the exhibition's title further alludes to a recent genre of popular studies for coping with everyday concerns; for example, Maria Rerrich's *Balanceakt Familie* (1994), which teaches how to adapt to new lifestyles while raising children in today's world; and Gerhard Schaefer's *Balanceakt Gesundheit* (1998), which promotes the ideal of moderation for healthy living in an increasingly stressful environment. In discussing practical issues that used to fall squarely within the domain of moral philosophy, these books are not unrelated to the topic of security, which, since ancient Rome, has consistently been a subject for moralists.

292 • Chapter 15

of a certain liberty would necessarily lead to a decrease in a specific risk? What would be the basis for such an exact trade-off?[10]

Second, there is the issue of what moral philosophers disparage as "consequentialism": If liberty is understood as a fundamental right—that is, as something that should be impervious to special consequences—how can any event, however catastrophic, be used as an argument to diminish that right? What criteria could justify the infringement of rights accorded to innocent citizens?[11] Conversely, if security is taken as a basic human need, why should an individual's demand for freedom ever be considered as legitimate? In balancing security and liberty we appear to subject both notions to consequences that seriously undercut claims that would establish either one as inalienable.

Finally, and particularly close to Donnersmarck's concerns, given the political case that the sacrifice of liberty for security entails the enhancement of state power, what might protect citizens from an abuse of that power? It is in response to this last problem that theorists speak of an autoimmunitary logic, whereby the freedom secured by institutions threatens to be extinguished by those very procedures. The securing of liberty, based upon the eradication of threats to that freedom, can be shown to be a strategy that destroys the liberty it was designed to safeguard. Here, immunization turns against its own immune subjects. In Roberto Esposito's terms, the cure "produces a greater illness than the one it wanted to prevent."[12] Fear is paralyzing, but security, too, may paralyze.

Among the entries selected for the 2006 Körber exhibition, the series by the German-Australian photographer Boris Eldagsen is especially attuned to this list of security-liberty problems. Eldagsen's presentation is entitled "Sicherheit nach Zahlen—Safety by Numbers" and therefore already explicitly addresses the issue of quantification. Before analyzing Eldagsen's contribution, it would be helpful to learn how the project was conceived. In an interview with *Die Zeit*, he traces its inspiration to his recent move from Berlin to Melbourne:

> Three years ago when I came to Australia, I wanted to know: What new dangers are in store for me? What do I do in a country where there are snakes, crocodiles, sharks, and poisonous spiders? The Australians laughed at me. They learn all that by kindergarten. For that reason I began to collect for myself safety tips [*Sicherheitshinweise*], which I found in tourist brochures, newspapers, posters and state notices. In the process I quickly noticed that these tips are, in part, entirely absurd [*teilweise völlig absurd*].[13]

---

[10] These questions form the basis of Jeremy Waldron's discussion in "Security and Liberty: The Image of Balance."

[11] For an excellent overview, see the essays included in *Consequentialism and Its Critics*, S. Scheffler, ed.

[12] Esposito, *Bios*, 91.

[13] "Erst Angst machen, dann beruhigen," *Die Zeit*, July 7, 2007. All subsequent citations are from this interview.

The artist, who laughably infantilized himself by wanting to acquire what every native kindergartner already knows, readily discovered how the local government hovers over society like a worrisome parent and thereby reduces its citizens to a condition bordering on puerility. The satirical potential of the material required no artistic modification: "In the cafés, one is not only warned that the coffee is hot, but also urged to place a paper coaster beneath the coffee cup, so that the cup can not slip off the table." Needless to say, the insecurity that the Australian government instills in this fashion is in no way comparable to the terror promulgated by the Stasi. All the same, Eldagsen's startling combination of partiality and entirety (*teilweise völlig*) suggests that although a portion of these security protocols is unquestionably absurd, a portion of them is not. How, then, can one strike a balance between what is valid and what is not or between the expedient and the useless? How can one insure that security concerns do not cause psychological or moral imbalances? Too much anxiety about imminent threats and disruptions would be stultifying, yet to be entirely unheedful of potential risks could be perilous. What are the criteria for drawing the limits between prudence and recklessness?

Over a three-year period (2003–6), Eldagsen amassed 750 specific warnings, which he then numbered and classified under nine general rubrics, which range from security in the home and the city to precautions for the outback and the sea, from information on recommended procedures during emergencies and natural disasters to advice on avoiding danger while driving and traveling.[14] Under the first category, "Safer Living in your Home," he lists published statements dealing with all aspects of domestic experience, from the "House Number" ("1. Your house number should be clearly visible from the street. Avoid the temptation to use Roman numerals or fancy lettering that may be hard to read") to the "Bedroom" ("41. Never *smoke* in bed"). Advice on securing the home moves from choosing the ideal height for the front fence—one that will not obscure the entrance and thereby provide cover for burglars—to marking valuables, planning evacuation, and understanding how to deal with an intrusion: "81. Don't confront the intruder, but *switch on the lights* and make a lot of noise moving about."

As Eldagsen traveled the country, collecting all manners of safety advice, he photographed typical scenes from Australian life. The pictures were subsequently enlarged and inscribed with tiny numbers in white that refer back to his compiled compendium of warnings, instructions, and suggestions—a "Safety Bible" that would accompany the exhibition. To illustrate, I have chosen a moderately long shot image of a tidal pool on a beach in Sydney (Fig. 15.1). Because the photos were taken with the still photo function of a mini digital video camera, with each file no larger than one megabyte, the blown up image

[14] The complete set of entries is found in Boris Eldagsen, *Sicherheit nach Zahlen*, available on the artist's Web site: http://archiv.eldagsen.com/photography2.htm.

Figure 15.1. Boris Eldagsen, "Strandbad, Sydney," *Sicherheit nach Zahlen*. Körber Stiftung, Hamburg (2006). Courtesy of the artist (www.eldagsen.com).

was considerably blurry. From a distance, the minuscule numbers are hardly visible, yet upon closer viewing, they gradually become more readable as the image itself becomes less distinct. In Eldagsen's words, the tiny numbers appear "like little flies on the windshield of perception."[15] For the sake of brevity, I will focus merely on the two major clusters of numerical codes that punctuate the scene from the beach in Sydney: one surrounding the couple facing each other by the pool at the bottom of the frame slightly to the right; and the other encompassing a figure swimming in the ocean in the background center.

The white-printed numbers puncture the scene saturated in blue and compel the viewer to become a reader, to abandon the quasi synchrony of the photographic field for the diachronic linearity of the messages. Each number is an invitation to attend to a text beyond that of the picture's frame. Apprised of the nature of Eldagsen's project, one may arguably suffer some presentiment of danger in this move from image to text, or at least anticipate a parody of danger. That is to say, one does not expect this quiet, ordinary scene to remain as innocuous as it first appears. So numbered, the picture resembles an illustration from some technical manual, as if the quotidian has now become an area that commands concern or requires careful attention.

[15] Eldagsen, personal correspondence, September 29, 2011.

When we turn to the texts, we discover that the severity of the different threats varies. For example, the number attached to the young man knee-deep in the pool (557) simply encourages swimming lessons; while the reference for the figure draped in a large towel (560) reminds us, again like children, to "empty all buckets and paddle pools after playing." These two directives, located under the rubric "Sicherheits-Tipps für Wasser" (Water Safety Tips), barely rise above the ridiculous. In contrast, the string of numbers that is situated between the two figures tells a much different story. In their iconic positioning alone, which neatly forms a vertical barrier, the three numbers already suggest that the present encounter may be one in dire need of protection. And indeed, the references go on to redefine this casual meeting on a summer day into a scene of possible sexual predation and entrapment:

175. Use your own transport to meet him there. Consider paying your own way.

174. If you have a *date*, don't give out too much personal info if you don't know him too well.

146. Girls and boys should carry *condoms*, using them for all forms of sexual activity. Say no to sex to avoid unwanted sex. You need to be clear and firm in saying no. Remove yourself from any uncomfortable situation.

Unlike the previous two "tips," these advisory messages fall under different headings—"Sicherheit in der Stadt" (Safety in the City) and "Sicherheit für Kinder" (Safety for Children).[16] A single frame of reference proves insufficient for protecting oneself at the water's edge. Multiple narratives of varying degrees of urgency must be considered in order to reduce all risks to a minimum. Just as the inscribed numbers goad us to shift from the immediacy of the scene, where we well might imagine ourselves on the beach, to the mediated realm of advice and cautionary messages, far from the sand and sun, so does this series of warnings impel us even further: no longer simply concerned with threats specific to the shore, we now are asked to consider more general menaces that could, in fact, emerge anywhere.

The heterogeneous narratives that Eldagsen musters, which range from dispensable or self-evident information to valid admonitions, ostensibly belong to every security project, insofar as they develop scenarios intended to arouse suspicion, commend vigilance, and prescribe appropriate strategies of defense. To be secure requires the capacity to envision as many specific threats as possible. One's imaginative faculty—the *Einbildungskraft*—must be fully engaged; it must be capable of picturing what could happen, of internally producing an image (*Bild*), regardless of likelihood. In order to be safe, one must have re-

---

[16] For his English version, Eldagsen uses the phrase "Safe City" and "Safer Living for your Kids," respectively.

course to the imagination, one must be able to foresee all potential (not yet actual) events—a delusional enterprise, since the event *qua* event is unforeseeable. It is precisely this reasoning that motivated the now famous judgment proclaimed by the United States' 9/11 Commission Report, namely that the governmental intelligence agencies in charge of predicting attacks were to blame for a "failure of the imagination." Hence, there have been scattered reports that, since 2002, the U.S. Department of Homeland Security has repeatedly invited science-fiction writers in order to discuss potential plots and thereby rectify this particular deficiency. In comparison, Eldagsen's numerical codes render it quite simple to "connect the dots."

The ironic and at times cynical impulse of Eldagsen's work reveals the fundamental and fairly self-evident ambiguity at the heart of every security project. On the one hand, the move from synchronic image to linear narrative operates on the same desire that induces awareness. I can be secure only when I know what dangers may lie in store, only when I entertain the temporal dimension of possible events. On the other hand, the accretion of fictional scenarios contributes to my sense of unease or, in fact, my insecurity. A tranquil afternoon at the beach has turned perilous. It requires no profound psychological insight to recognize that security measures may instill as much fear as they are meant to assuage. A situation of heightened security, in whatever form, stands to be unnerving insofar as it calls to mind the lurking dangers and the potential losses that continue to pose a threat. It serves as a reminder that there are significant risks that may at any point impinge upon our existence or upset our calculations.

This disquieting consequence for the subject of security is unavoidable. Modes of protection invariably conjure what is being warded off. In order to feel secure, we bear in mind the menace that is defused, the attack that is averted. We acknowledge the reality or at least the possibility of the perils from which we are being guarded—a reality that is poised to dispel our very sense of safety. Feeling secure means feeling secure-from and therefore involves the recognition of our insecurity, our vulnerability. Unless we are afraid, there is no possibility of enjoying our freedom from fear. The subject of security is necessarily the subject of apprehension. We feel secure only because we can be frightened.

The second cluster of numbers in Eldagsen's *Strandbad* image, the ones enveloping the swimmer at sea, corroborates and further exacerbates this inevitable problem:

613. *Don't swim* in areas known to be inhabited by sharks.

587. If you are seized with a *cramp* or in trouble in the water: stay calm; float on your back; and wave one arm for help.

594. Never swim directly after a *meal*.

593. Do not enter the water under the influence of *alcohol or drugs*.

For the hypervigilant, the mere thought of plunging into the cold water would constitute the gravest of decisions. Even if one's stomach was safely empty, even if one has abstained at this early hour in the day from drinking, from taking illicit drugs or abusing pharmaceuticals, the ocean remains potentially infested with carnivorous fish. What Eldagsen shows is that hypervigilance can only result in insecurity. He is therefore not unaware of the political ramifications of the safety campaigns that he detects in all aspects of Australian life. In the *Zeit* interview, he explicitly speaks of the consequences:

> The government first makes people anxious, in order to reassure them with the words: Have a good time, we'll worry about everything [*Lasst es euch gut gehen, wir kümmern uns um alles*]. But as the people move further and further away from their own responsibility, they acquire a taste for this role of being helpless and would like to be more and more protected.

By issuing endless warnings, the state apparatus perpetuates the Hobbesian contract that purchases security with individual freedom. Moreover, Eldagsen's plotted numbers parody the quantification of life that is the hallmark of bio-power. Numerization is always the instrument of choice for administrative control, which endeavors to intervene in every sphere of individual experience— hence the emphasis on Wiesler's code name, HGW XX/7, throughout *Das Leben der Anderen*. Yet these numerical markers of authority's presence, no matter how restrictive, may also offer a sense of comfort and assurance that, once introduced, are difficult to renounce.

The enterprise of numerization, ascribable to state bureaucracy, reduces singularity to an abstract code and thereby threatens to subordinate individuals to a general system. Numerization is the first step toward exchangeability. Tellingly, Eldagsen's first entry in his "Safety by Numbers" collection deals with house numbers, which effectively reflect the order imposed by official agencies. The vast majority of the images relayed in Eldagsen's photo-essay points to such processes of dehumanizing quantification. However, not every warning that Eldagsen cites promotes complacency or immobility. At times, albeit rarely, the "nanny state" (as Eldagsen's Australian friends characterize their country) expects you to unbuckle yourself and leap into live action. In these special cases, the general advice to avoid or ward off danger is replaced by proactive instructions. To return to the coast off Sydney, we follow other references suggesting that, for the observer, staying on the shore would hardly offer relief. The numbers to the left of the swimmer raise the possibility of a much different kind of trouble:

> 629. *Capsized boat*: If you capsize, first try to flip and bale out. If you are unable to right the boat, don't attempt to swim to shore.

> 591. If you see someone in trouble in the water, *get help* quickly.

> 631. *Man overboard*: Fast action and constant observation is the priority. If a buoyancy aid—a lifebuoy or life line—is available, throw it while the person

is in range. In a powered craft, you can turn quickly—get one member of the crew to watch the person in the water throughout the rescue. . . . Be aware of the risk of injuring the person in the water while attempting the rescue, especially in rough weather. Getting someone aboard any boat can be hard—in smaller boats try sliding the person in over the side without swamping the boat—alternatively, hang a loop of rope over the stern as a foothold.

In the scenarios imagined here, the perspective abruptly shifts from the swimmer to the spectator—"Fast action and constant observation is the priority." If we align the subjective position with the camera, we see how the scene's interpretation moves from a sympathetic identification with the distraught individual at sea to a reconsideration of one's own role as bystander. If I thought I could save myself from drowning or from being the victim of a shark attack by remaining on land, I must now respond to another and ostensibly more urgent situation: I have been summoned, like Wiesler in Donnersmarck's film, to save the life of another. I occupy the place of the potential rescuer; I have been called to perform. Seeing another at risk, I must surrender my security. The dizzying logic is clear: no longer mortified, I place my life at risk and thereby remain alive, secure in the insecurity that defines my humanity.

As Kafka had already suggested, it is one's mortality that ultimately may save one's life.

On the Main

We were now on the main sea, abandoned to the winds and
billows, without any other means of security than the care of the
pilot, whom it was always in our power to choose, among great
numbers that offered their direction and assistance.

Mary Wollstonecraft, "An Allegory,"
The Female Reader (1789)

THE POWER OF HOPE PERSISTS, even or especially for those who have abandoned themselves to life's contingencies. Unmoored, adrift, at prey to the elements, even the solitary voyager is not alone. Face to face with the precarious-
ness of the illimitable void, some relation is established. Yet this relationship,
thus installed, can neither be fixed nor come to rest. Any tranquilizing *opposition* between internal subject and external object—a distinction that might
have been valid upon the firmness of the shore and may yet be accomplished
upon return—is lost at sea, flooded over, yielding instead to the dynamic *difference* that characterizes being in the world. "Abandoned to the winds and billows," the subject of experience, who is hardly a subject in the strict sense, must
forgo the drive to objectify, manipulate or master. All the same, this renuncia-
tion does not exclude fullest engagement, nor does it reflect an attitude of indifference. Even within this general condition of desecurement, a modicum of
security remains possible, thanks to a certain capacity to care.

Without care there can be no thought of security. In Wollstonecraft's "allegory," the will to security is explicitly reflected in the care taken to choose one's
caregiver. However the vessel and its helmsman may be conceived—the ship of
state and its governor, the church's nave and its pastor, the community and its
participants, the fragile barque and the individual it bears, and so forth—passengers who brave the tumultuous waves may be unable to steer the course
definitively but are still capable of resisting complete resignation. "The power to
choose" has not been eradicated; and the care implicit in this choice is echoed
by "the care of the pilot." For the act of guiding—be it assigned to an external
agency or institution, to a collective or an individual's own consciousness—
strives to bring the craft into safe harbor. Piloting is *believed* to be in response

to specific concerns. Constituted by the darkness and the openness of the future, this faith has little to do with cognition. It is rather motivated and sustained by the care devoted to selecting the agent or means of caring.

These modalities of care do not make the voyage any less perilous. Nothing or no one can fully eliminate the threat of eventual shipwreck. Yet those who take security for granted are exposed to an even graver danger. In denying the fortuitousness of what may happen, in dismissing the inscrutability of the event, the position of the caring pilot may be usurped by the tyrant who feeds upon his subjects' indifference, encouraged and licensed by collective insouciance. This tyrant may be none other than a projection of the passenger who relentlessly grasps onto the weak plank of subjective control—a strategy designed for mastery but in fact destined to sink the victim into the whirlpool of faithlessness and despair.

Rather than offer salvation from the contingencies of experience, philology affirms an adherence to contingency's unavoidability. It saves life, but only humbly, that is, by maintaining the finitude that constitutes humanity, by attending to the historical limits of vocabulary, syntax, and usage, less interested in making a successful transit into authoritative meaning and more committed to the unprotected process of crossing itself, from one language to the next, from one context to the next. Philology decelerates, halting consolidation into concepts of power, concepts that work to avoid the unavoidable. Any regime that attempts to secure legitimacy and meaning, any subject that strives to secure perfect stability and substance, invariably neglects these limits and thereby becomes all the more limiting through exercises in neurotic, asphyxiating protectionism. In contrast, through its careful, sensitive attendance to the vagaries of human expression, limited and limitless, philology persistently raises fresh questions on concept formation and consequently opens new avenues for consideration, interpretation, and critique. As long as we live, we live *cum cura*. Endowed with the gift of language, we retain the power to choose.

Works Cited

Adams, David, "Metaphors for Mankind: The Development of Hans Blumenberg's Met-aphorology," *Journal of the History of Ideas* 52 (1991), 152–66.

Agamben, Giorgio, "Security and Terror," C. Emcke, trans., *Theory and Event* 5:4 (2002), n.p.

——, *State of Exception*, Kevin Attell, trans., Chicago: University of Chicago Press, 2005.

Allen, J. H., and Greenough, J. B., *New Latin Grammar for Schools and Colleges, Founded on Comparative Grammar*, Boston: Ginn, 1903.

Althusser, Louis, *Machiavelli and Us*, F. Matheron, ed., London: Verso, 1999.

Anderson, William S., "Horace *Carm.* 1.14: What Kind of Ship?" *Classical Philology* 61 (1966), 84–98.

Antognazza, Maria Rosa, *Leibniz: An Intellectual Biography*, Cambridge: Cambridge University Press, 2009.

Apter, Emily, *The Translation Zone: A New Comparative Literature*, Princeton: Princeton University Press, 2006.

Arendt, Hannah, *The Human Condition* (1958), Chicago: University of Chicago Press, 1998.

——, *The Portable Hannah Arendt*, Peter Baehr, ed., New York: Penguin, 2003.

Aristotle, *The Ethics of Aristotle*, J.A.K. Thomson, trans., New York: Penguin, 1955.

Arlacchi, Pino, *L'inganno e la paura: Il mito del caos globale*, Milan: Il Saggiatore, 2009.

Arnim, H. von, ed., *Stoicorum Veterum Fragmenta*, 3 vols., Leipzig: Teubner, 1903–24.

Arquilla, John, and Ronfeldt, David, *Networks and Netwars: The Future of Terror, Crime, and Militancy*, Santa Monica: RAND, 2001.

Atkins, E. M., "'Domina et Regina Virtutum': Justice and *Societas* in *De Officiis*," *Phrone-sis* 35 (1990), 258–89.

Augustine, *Confessions*, H. Chadwick, trans., Oxford: Oxford University Press, 1992.

Ayres-Bennett, Wendy, *Vaugelas and the Development of the French Language*, London: Modern Humanities Research Association, 1987.

Balibar, Etienne, *Masses, Classes, Ideas: Studies on Politics and Philosophy Before and After Marx*, J. Swenson, trans., New York: Routledge, 1994.

Bartlett, Robert, "An Introduction to Hesiod's *Works and Days*," *Review of Politics* 68 (2006), 177–205.

Baudrillard, Jean, *Symbolic Exchange and Death*, Iain Hamilton Grant, trans., London: Sage, 1993.

Baxandall, Michael, *Painting and Experience in Fifteenth-Century Italy*, Oxford: Oxford University Press, 1972.

Benardete, Seth, *The Bow and the Lyre: A Platonic Reading of the* Odyssey, Lanham: Rowman & Littlefield, 1997.

Benjamin, Walter, *Gesammelte Schriften*, 4 vols., R. Tiedemann and H. Schweppen-häuser, eds., Frankfurt am Main: Surhkamp, 1980.

———, *Selected Writings*, vol. 2 *(1927–1934)*, M. Jennings, ed., Cambridge, MA: Harvard University Press, 1999.

———, *The Arcades Project*, H. Eiland and K. McLaughlin, trans., Cambridge, MA: Harvard University Press, 1999.

Benveniste, Emile, *Problèmes de linguistique générale*, vol. 1, Paris: Gallimard, 1966.

Bergren, Ann, *The Etymology and Usage of* πεῖραρ *in Early Greek Poetry*, New York: American Philological Association, 1975.

Berki, R. N., *Security and Society: Reflections on Law, Order and Politics*, New York: St. Martin's Press, 1986.

Berlin, Isaiah, *Four Essays on Liberty*, Oxford: Oxford University Press, 1969.

Berman, Marshall, *All That Is Solid Melts into Air* (1982), 2nd ed., New York: Verso, 2010.

Bertram, Ernst, *Nietzsche: Attempt at a Mythology*, R. E. Norton, trans., Urbana: University of Illinois Press, 2009.

Bernardino of Siena, *Le prediche volgari*, 5 vols., C. Cannarozzi, ed., Florence: Liberia editrice fiorentina, 1940–58.

Blum, Elisabeth, *Schöne neue Stadt: Wie der Sicherheitswahn die urbane Welt diszipliniert*, Basel: Birkhäuser, 2003.

Blumenberg, Hans, *The Legitimacy of the Modern Age*, R. Wallace, trans., Cambridge, MA: MIT Press, 1983.

———, *Work on Myth*, R. Wallace, trans., Cambridge, MA: MIT Press, 1985.

———, *Die Sorge geht über den Fluß*, Frankfurt am Main: Suhrkamp, 1987.

———, *Das Lachen der Thrakerin: Eine Urgeschichte der Theorie*, Frankfurt am Main: Suhrkamp, 1987.

———, "An Anthropological Approach to the Contemporary Significance of Rhetoric," R. M. Wallace, trans., in *After Philosophy: End or Transformation?* K. Baynes, J. Bohman, and T. McCarthy, eds., Cambridge, MA: MIT Press, 1987, 429–58.

———, *Shipwreck with Spectator: Paradigm of a Metaphor of Existence*, S. Rendall, trans., Cambridge, MA: MIT Press, 1997.

———, *Ästhetische und metaphorische Schriften*, A. Haverkamp, ed., Frankfurt am Main: Suhrkamp, 2001.

———, *Care Crosses the River*, Paul Fleming, trans., Stanford: Stanford University Press, 2010.

———, *Paradigms for a Metaphorology*, Robert Savage, trans., Ithaca: Cornell University Press, 2010. ["Paradigmen zu einer Metaphorologie," *Archiv für Begriffsgeschichte* 6 (1960), 7–142.]

Blundell, Mary Whitlock, "Parental Nature and Stoic Οἰκείωσις," *Ancient Philosophy* 10 (1990), 221–42.

Boisacq, Emile, *Dictionnaire étymologique de la langue grecque*, Heidelberg: Winter, 1950.

Bolzoni, Lina, *The Web of Images: Vernacular Preaching from Its Origins to St Bernardino da Siena*, C. Preston and L. Chien, trans., Aldershot: Ashgate, 2004.

Booth, Ken, "Security and Emancipation," *Review of International Studies* 17 (1991), 313–26.

Booth, Ken, and Wheeler, Nicholas, *The Security Dilemma: Fear, Cooperation and Trust in World Politics*, New York: Palgrave Macmillan, 2008.

Bornkamm, Heinrich, *Luther's Doctrine of the Two Kingdoms in the Context of His Theology*, Philadelphia: Fortress, 1966.

Bossy, John, *Christianity in the West, 1400-1700*, Oxford: Oxford University Press, 1985.

Bowsky, William, "The Medieval Commune and Internal Violence: Police Power and Public Safety in Siena, 1287-1355," *American Historical Review* 73 (1967), 1-17.

Branca, Vittore, ed., *Merchant Writers of the Italian Renaissance*, M. Baca, trans., New York: Marsilio, 1999.

Braun, Theodore, and Radner, John, eds., *The Lisbon Earthquake of 1755: Representations and Reactions*, Studies in Voltaire and the Eighteenth Century, Oxford: Oxford University Press, 2005.

Brown, Wendy, *Walled States, Waning Sovereignty*, New York: Zone, 2010.

Browne, Alice, "Descartes's Dreams," *Journal of the Warburg and Courtauld Institutes* 40 (1977), 256-73.

Burchell, Graham, Gordon, Colin, and Miller, Peter, eds., *The Foucault Effect: Studies in Governmentality*, Chicago: University of Chicago Press, 1991.

Burdach, Konrad, "Faust und die Sorge," *Deutsche Vierteljahrsschrift für Literaturwissenschaft und Geistesgeschichte* 1 (1923), 1-60.

Burgess, J. Peter, *The Ethical Subject of Security: Geopolitical Reason and the Threat against Europe*, New York: Routledge, 2011.

Burke, Anthony, *Beyond Security, Ethics and Violence: War against the Other*, New York: Routledge, 2007.

Burke, Edmund, *Philosophical Enquiry into the Origin of Our Ideas of the Sublime and the Beautiful*, A. Phillips, ed., New York: Oxford University Press, 2009.

Burkert, Walter, *Greek Religion*, J. Raffan, trans., Cambridge, MA: Harvard University Press, 1985.

Burton, Robert, *The Anatomy of Melancholy*, Holbrook Jackson, ed., New York: New York Review Books, 2001.

Butler, Judith, *Precarious Life: The Powers of Mourning and Violence*, New York: Verso, 2004.

Buzan, Barry, Waever, Ole, and de Wilde, Jaap, eds., *Security: A New Framework for Analysis*, Boulder: Lynne Rienner, 1998.

Bynum, Caroline Walker, *Jesus as Mother: Studies in the Spirituality of the High Middle Ages*, Berkeley: University of California Press, 1982.

Campe, Rüdiger, *Spiel der Wahrscheinlichkeit: Literatur und Berechnung zwischen Pascal und Kleist*, Göttingen: Wallstein, 2002.

C.A.S.E. Collective, "Critical Approaches to Security in Europe: A Networked Manifesto," *Security Dialogue* 37 (2006), 443-87.

Cavallar, Georg, *Pax Kantiana: Systematisch-historische Untersuchung des Entwurfs* Zum ewigen Frieden *von Immanuel Kant*, Vienna: Böhlau, 1992.

Caygill, Howard, *A Kant Dictionary*, Oxford: Blackwell, 1995.

Chandler, David, and Hynek, Nik, *Critical Perspectives on Human Security: Rethinking Emancipation and Power in International Relations*, New York: Routledge, 2010.

Chantraine, Pierre, *Dictionnaire étymologique de la langue grecque*, 4 vols., Paris: Klincksieck, 1968.

Clines, J. A., "The Image of God in Man," *Tyndale Bulletin* 19 (1967), 53-103.

Cobianchi, Roberto, "Fashioning the Imagery of a Franciscan Observant Preacher: Early Renaissance Portraiture of Bernardino da Siena in Northern Italy," *I Tatti Studies: Essays in the Renaissance* 12 (2009), 55-83.

Considine, P., "Some Homeric Terms for Anger," *Acta Classica* 9 (1966), 15-25.

———, "The Etymology of μῆνις," in *Studies in Honour of T.B.L. Webster*, 2 vols., Bristol: Bristol Classical Press, 1986, 1: 53–64.

Conze, Werner, "Sicherheit, Schutz," in *Geschichtliche Grundbegriffe: Historisches Lexikon zur politisch-sozialen Sprache in Deutschland*, 8 vols., O. Brunner, W. Conze and R. Koselleck, eds., Stuttgart: Klett, 1972–97, 5: 831–62.

Crépon, Marc, *La culture de la peur: 1. Démocratie, identité, sécurité*, Paris: Galilée, 2008.

Cyran, Eberhard, *Sanssouci: Traum aus dem Sand* (1977), Berlin: Arani, 1991.

Darnstädt, Thomas, *Der globale Polizeistaat: Terrorangst, Sicherheitswahn und das Ende unserer Freiheiten*, Munich: Deutsche Verlagsanstalt, 2009.

Debby, Nirit Ben-Aryeh, "War and Peace: The Description of Ambrogio Lorenzetti's Frescoes in Saint Bernardino's 1425 Siena Sermons," *Renaissance Studies* 15 (2001), 272–86.

de Grazia, Sebastian, *Machiavelli in Hell*, Princeton: Princeton University Press, 1989.

Deleuze, Gilles, and Guattari, Félix, *A Thousand Plateaus: Capitalism and Schizophrenia*, B. Massumi, trans., Minneapolis: University of Minnesota Press, 1987.

Delumeau, Jean, *Rassurer et protéger: Le sentiment e sécurité dans l'Occident d'autrefois*, Paris: Fayard, 1989.

de Man, Paul, *The Resistance to Theory*, Minneapolis: University of Minnesota Press, 1986.

Der Derian, James, "The Value of Security: Hobbes, Marx, Nietzsche, and Baudrillard," in *On Security*, R. D. Lipschutz, ed., New York: Columbia University Press, 1995, 24–45.

Derrida, Jacques, *Acts of Religion*, G. Anidjar, ed., New York: Routledge, 2002.

———, *Rogues: Two Essays on Reason*, P.-A. Brault and M. Naas, trans., Stanford: Stanford University Press, 2005.

———, *The Politics of Friendship*, G. Collins, trans., London: Verso, 2005.

Descartes, René, *Œuvres et lettres* (Bibliothèque de la Pléiade), A. Bridoux, ed., Paris: Gallimard, 1953.

———, *Discourse on Method and the Meditations*, F. E. Sutcliffe, trans., New York: Penguin, 1968.

Detienne, Marcel, and Vernant, Jean-Pierre, *Les ruses de l'intelligence: La mètis des Grecs*, Paris: Flammarion, 1974.

———, eds., *The Cuisine of Sacrifice among the Greeks*, P. Wissing, trans., Chicago: University of Chicago Press, 1989.

Diekstra, F.N.N., "Confessor and Penitent: Robert de Sorbon and the *Cura Animarum*," *Medieval Studies* 71 (2009), 157–96.

Diem, Harald, *Luthers Lehre von den zwei Reichen*, Munich: Kaiser, 1938.

Dillon, Michael, *Politics of Security: Towards a Political Philosophy of Continental Thought*, London: Routledge, 1996.

———, "Lethal Freedom: Divine Violence and the Machiavellian Moment," *Theory and Event* 11 (2008).

Dillon, Michael, and Neal, Andrew, eds., *Foucault on Politics, Security and War*, New York: Palgrave Macmillan, 2011.

Dougherty, Carol, *The Raft of Odysseus: The Ethnographic Imagination of Homer's Odyssey*, Oxford: Oxford University Press, 2001.

Dueck, Cheryl, "The Humanization of the Stasi in *Das Leben der Anderen*," *German Studies Review* 31 (2008), 599–609.

Dumont, Louis, *Essays on Individualism: Modern Ideology in Anthropological Perspective*, Chicago: University of Chicago Press, 1986.

Dyck, Andrew, *A Commentary on Cicero's De officiis*, Ann Arbor: University of Michigan Press, 1996.

Dye, Ellis, "Sorge in Heidegger and in Goethe's *Faust*," *Goethe Yearbook* 16 (2009), 208–18.

Eire, Carlos, *War Against Idols: The Reformation of Worship from Erasmus to Calvin*, Cambridge: Cambridge University Press, 1986.

Ellington, Donna S., "Impassioned Mother or Passive Icon: The Virgin's Role in Late Medieval and Early Modern Passion Sermons," *Renaissance Quarterly* 48 (1995), 227–61.

Emden, Christian, *Friedrich Nietzsche and the Politics of History*, Cambridge: Cambridge University Press, 2008.

Engberg-Pedersen, Troels, "Discovering the Good: *Oikeiōsis* and *Kathēkonta* in Stoic Ethics," in *The Norms of Nature: Studies in Hellenistic Ethics*, M. Schofield and G. Striker, eds., Cambridge: Cambridge University Press, 1986: 145–83.

———, *The Stoic Theory of Oikeiōsis: Moral Development and Social Interaction in Early Stoic Philosophy*, Aarhus: Aarhus University Press, 1990.

Engelland, Chad, "Augustinian Elements in Heidegger's Philosophical Anthropology: A Study of the Early Lecture Course on Augustine," *Proceedings of the American Catholic Philosophical Association* 78 (2005), 263–75.

Ensler, Eve, *Insecure at Last: A Political Memoir*, New York: Villard, 2006.

Ernout, Alfred, and Meillet, Antoine, *Dictionnaire étymologique de la langue latine*, Paris: Klincksieck, 1979.

Esther, John, "Between Principle and Feeling: An Interview with Florian Henckel von Donnersmarck," *Cineaste* 32 (2007), 40–42.

Esposito, Roberto, *Communitas: Origine e destino della comunità*, Turin: Einaudi, 1998.

———, *Bios: Biopolitica e filosofia*, Turin: Einaudi, 2004.

———, *Bios: Biopolitics and Philosophy*, T. Campbell, trans., Minneapolis: University of Minnesota Press, 2008.

———, *Communitas: The Origin and Destiny of Community*, T. Campbell, trans., Stanford: Stanford University Press, 2010.

———, *Immunitas: The Protection and Negation of Life*, Z. Hanafi, trans., Cambridge: Polity, 2011.

Evrigenis, Ioannis, *Fear of Enemies and Collective Action*, Cambridge: Cambridge University Press, 2008.

Ewald, François, "Norms, Discipline and the Law," *Representations* 30 (1990), 138–61.

Febvre, Lucien, and Martin, Henri-Jean, *L'apparition du livre*, Paris: Michel, 1958.

———, *The Coming of the Book: The Impact of Printing, 1450–1800*, David Gerard, trans., London: Verso, 1984.

Feldges-Henning, Uta, "The Pictorial Programme of the Sala della Pace: A New Interpretation," *Journal of the Warburg and Courtauld Institutes* 35 (1972), 145–62.

Fenves, Peter, *Arresting Language: From Leibniz to Benjamin*, Stanford: Stanford University Press, 2001.

———, *Late Kant: Towards Another Law of the Earth*, New York: Routledge, 2003.

Fichte, Johann Gottlieb, *Sämmtliche Werke und Nachlass*, 8 vols., I. H. Fichte, ed., Berlin: Veit, 1845–46; reprint: Berlin: De Gruyter, 1965.

Flynn, Thomas, "*Angst* and Care in the Early Heidegger: The Ontic/Ontologic Aporia," *International Studies in Philosophy* 12 (1980), 61–76.

Foucault, Michel, *The Care of the Self: The History of Sexuality*, vol. 3, R. Hurley, trans., New York: Vintage, 1988.

——, *The Order of Things: An Archaeology of the Human Sciences*, New York: Vintage, 1994.

——, *"Society Must Be Defended": Lectures at the Collège de France, 1975–1976*, D. Macey, trans., New York: Picador, 2003.

——, *The Hermeneutics of the Subject: Lectures at the Collège de France, 1981–1982*, G. Burchell, trans., New York: Picador, 2005.

——, *Security, Territory, Population: Lectures at the Collège de France, 1977–1978*, trans. G. Burchell, New York: Palgrave Macmillan, 2007.

Fränkel, Hermann, *Early Greek Poetry and Philosophy*, M. Hadas and J. Willis, trans., New York: Harcourt Brace Jovanovich, 1975.

Franklin, Benjamin, *Memoirs of the Life and Writings of Benjamin Franklin*, 6 vols., London: Colburn, 1818–19.

Frei, Daniel, *Sicherheit: Grundfragen der Weltpolitik*, Stuttgart: Kohlhammer, 1977.

Freud, Sigmund, *Gesammelte Werke*, 18 vols., Frankfurt am Main: Fischer, 1999.

——, *The Future of an Illusion*, J. Strachey, trans., New York: Norton, 1961.

——, *Civilization and Its Discontents*, J. Strachey, trans., New York: Norton, 1961.

Fricke, Hans, *Politische Justiz: Sozialabbau, Sicherheitswahn und Krieg*, Berlin: Verlag am Park, 2008.

Fromm, Erich, *The Dogma of Christ*, New York: Routledge, 2004.

Furetière, Antoine, *Dictionnaire universel*, Paris: La Haye, 1690; facsimile reprint: Paris: Champion, 1978.

Galinsky, Karl, "The Anger of Aeneas," *American Journal of Philology* 109 (1988), 321–48.

Gehlen, Arnold, *Man, His Nature and Place in the World*, C. McMillan and K. Pillemer, trans., New York: Columbia University Press, 1988.

Gianotti, Gian Franco, *Per una poetica pindarica*, Turin: Paravia, 1975.

Gildea, Robert, *Children of the Revolution: The French, 1799–1914*, Cambridge, MA: Harvard University Press, 2008.

Gildenhard, Ingo, *Creative Eloquence: The Construction of Reality in Cicero's Speeches*, Oxford: Oxford University Press, 2011.

Gill, Christopher, *The Structured Self in Hellenistic and Roman Thought*, Oxford: Oxford University Press, 2006.

Gilligan, Carol, *In a Different Voice: Psychological Theory and Women's Development*, Cambridge, MA: Harvard University Press, 1982.

Godefroy, Frédéric, *Dictionnaire de l'ancienne langue française et tous ses dialectes du IX au XV siècle* (1902), New York: Kraus, 1961.

Gossman, Lionel, "Michelet and Natural History: The Alibi of Nature," *Proceedings of the American Philosophical Society* 145 (2001), 283–333.

Graver, Margaret, *Stoicism and Emotion*, Chicago: University of Chicago Press, 2007.

Greenstein, Jack, "The Vision of Peace: Meaning and Representation in Ambrogio Lorenzetti's *Sala della Pace* Cityscapes," *Art History* 11 (1988), 492–510.

Grimm, Jacob, and Grimm, Wilhelm, *Deutsches Wörterbuch*, 33 vols., Munich: Deutscher Taschenbuch, 1984.

Grimmelshausen, Hans Jacob Christoffel von, *Simplicissimus Teutsch* (1669), D. Breuer, ed., Frankfurt am Main: Deutscher Klassiker, 1989.

Hägglund, Martin, *Radical Atheism: Derrida and the Time of Life*, Stanford: Stanford University Press, 2008.

Hahn, Jürgen, *The Origins of the Baroque Concept of Peregrinatio*, North Carolina Studies in the Romance Languages and Literatures 131, Chapel Hill: University of North Carolina Press, 1973.

Hamacher, Werner, *Premises: Essays on Philosophy and Literature from Kant to Celan*, P. Fenves, trans., Cambridge, MA: Harvard University Press, 1996.

———, *Für die Philologie*, Frankfurt am Main: Roughradio, 2009.

Hansen, William, "Odysseus' Last Journey," *Quaderni Urbinati di Cultura Classica* 24 (1977), 27–48.

Harpham, Geoffrey, "Roots, Races, and the Return to Philology," *Representations* 106 (2009), 34–62.

Harris, William, *Restraining Rage: The Ideology of Anger Control in Classical Antiquity*, Cambridge, MA: Harvard University Press, 2001.

Harrison, Peter, "Curiosity, Forbidden Knowledge, and the Reformation of Natural Philosophy in Early Modern England," *Isis* 92 (2001), 265–90.

Harrison, Robert Pogue, *Gardens: An Essay on the Human Condition*, Chicago: University of Chicago Press, 2008.

Hauser, Manfred, *Der römische Begriff Cura*, Winterthur: Keller, 1954.

Hauser, R., "Acedia," in *Historisches Wörterbuch der Philosophie*, 13 vols., Joachim Ritter and Rudolf Eisler, eds., Basel: Schwabe, 1971–2007, 3: 73–74.

Haverkamp, Anselm, and Mende, Dirk, eds., *Metaphorologie: Zur Praxis von Theorie*, Frankfurt am Main: Suhrkamp, 2009.

Heidegger, Martin, *Sein und Zeit* (1927), Tübingen: Niemeyer, 1993.

———, *Holzwege*, Frankfurt am Main: Klosterman, 1950.

———, *Being and Time*, J. Macquarrie and E. Robinson, trans., New York: Harper & Row, 1962.

———, *The Question concerning Technology*, W. Lovitt, trans., New York: Harper & Row, 1977.

———, *Prolegomena zur Geschichte des Zeitbegriffs*, Petra Jaeger, ed., Frankfurt am Main: Klostermann, 1979.

———, *Parmenides*, A. Schuwer and R. Rojcewicz, trans., Bloomington: Indiana University Press, 1992.

———, *History of the Concept of Time: Prolegomena*, Theodore Kisiel, trans., Bloomington: Indiana University Press, 1992.

———, *Phänomenologie des religiösen Lebens*, Frankfurt am Main: Klostermann, 1995.

———, *The Phenomenology of Religious Life*, M. Fritsch and J. A. Gosetti-Ferencei, trans., Bloomington: Indiana University Press, 2004.

———, *Basic Concepts of Aristotelian Philosophy*, R. D. Metcalf and M. B. Tanzer, trans., Bloomington: Indiana University Press, 2009.

Heine, Heinrich, *Werke*, 4 vols., Helmut Schanze, ed., Frankfurt am Main: Insel, 1968.

Hesiod, *Works and Days*, Martin West, ed., Oxford: Clarendon Press, 1978.

———, *Theogony, Works and Days, Testimonia*, 2 vols., Glenn Most, ed., Cambridge, MA: Harvard University Press, 2006.

Held, Virginia, *The Ethics of Care: Personal, Political, Global*, Oxford: Oxford University Press, 2006.

Herz, John, "Idealist Internationalism and the Security Dilemma," *World Politics* 2 (1950), 157–80.

Hilton, Paul, *Security Metaphors: Cold War Discourse from Containment to Common House*, New York: Peter Lang, 1996.

Hippocrates, vol. 2, W.H.S. Jones, trans., Cambridge, MA: Harvard University Press, 1959.

Hobbes, Thomas, *The Metaphysical System of Hobbes*, M. Calkins, ed., Chicago: Open Court, 1913.

———, *Leviathan, with Selected Variants from the Latin Edition of 1668*, E. Curley, ed., Indianapolis: Hackett, 1994.

———, *The Correspondence*, 2 vols., N. Malcom, ed., Oxford: Clarendon Press, 1994.

———, *On the Citizen*, R. Tuck and M. Silverthorne, eds., Cambridge: Cambridge University Press, 1998.

Höffe, Otfried, ed., *Immanuel Kant: Zum ewigen Frieden*, Berlin: Akademie, 1995.

Hölderlin, Friedrich, *Sämtliche Werke* (Große Stuttgarter Ausgabe), 8 vols., F. Beißner, ed., Stuttgart: Kohlhammer, 1943–85.

———, *Essays and Letters on Theory*, T. Pfau, ed., Albany: State University of New York Press, 1988.

Holmberg, John, ed., *Das Moralium Dogma Philosophorum des Guillaume de Conches, Lateinisch, Altfranzösisch, und Mittelniederfränkisch*, Uppsala: Almquist & Wiksells, 1929.

Hölscher, Uvo, Review of G. S. Kirk, *Songs of Homer*, *Gnomon* 39 (1967), 433–44.

Horkheimer, Max, and Adorno, Theodor, *Dialectic of Enlightenment* (1944), J. Cumming, trans., New York: Continuum, 1997.

Horn, Eva, "Media of Conspiracy: Love and Surveillance in Fritz Lang and Florian Henckel von Donnersmarck," *New German Critique* 103 (2008), 127–44.

Hubbard, Thomas, *The Pindaric Mind: A Study of Logical Structure in Early Greek Poetry*, London: Brill, 1985.

Hudson, Wayne, "After Blumenberg: Historicism and Philosophical Anthropology," *History of the Human Sciences* 6 (1993), 109–16.

Hume, David, *Enquires concerning Human Understanding and concerning the Principles of Morals*, L. A. Selby-Bigge and P. H. Nidditch, eds., Oxford: Clarendon, 1975.

———, *A Treatise of Human Nature*, L. A. Selby-Bigge and P. H. Nidditch, eds., Oxford: Clarendon, 1978.

———, *Essays, Moral, Political, and Literary*, Eugene Miller, ed., Indianapolis: Liberty Classics, 1987.

Huysmans, Jef, "International Politics of Insecurity: Normativity, Inwardness and the Exception," *Security Dialogue* 37 (2006), 11–29.

Hyginus, *Fabulae*, H. J. Rose, ed., Leiden: Sythoff, 1934.

———, *Fabulae*, P. K. Marhsall, ed., Leipzig: Teubner, 2002.

Iacometti, F., and Lisini, A., eds., *Cronache Senesi*, Bologna: Zanichelli, 1931–39.

Immerwahr, John, "Hume on Tranquilizing the Passions," *Hume Studies* 18 (1992), 293–314.

Instinsky, Hans Ulrich, *Sicherheit als politisches Problem des römischen Kaisertums*, Baden-Baden: Verlag für Kunst und Wissenschaft, 1952.

Inwood, Brad, *Ethics and Human Action in Early Stoicism*, Oxford: Clarendon Press, 1985.

Jaeger, Hans, "The Problem of Faust's Salvation," in Jaeger, *Essays on German Literature 1935–1962,* Bloomington: Indiana University Press, 41–98.

Jelinek, Elfriede, *Die Klavierspielerin,* Reinbek bei Hamburg: Rowohlt, 1983.

——, *The Piano Teacher,* J. Neugroschel, trans., New York: Grove Press, 2009.

Johnson, Barbara, "Philology: What Is at Stake?" *Comparative Literature Studies* 27 (1990), 26–30.

Kafka, Franz, *Gesammelte Werke,* 12 vols., H. G. Koch, ed., Frankfurt am Main: Fischer, 2002.

——, *Briefe, 1902–1924,* Max Brod, ed., Frankfurt am Main: Fischer, 1958.

——, *The Complete Stories,* N. N. Glatzer, ed., New York: Norton, 1983.

——, *The Office Writings,* S. Corngold, J. Greenberg, and B. Wagner, eds., Princeton: Princeton University Press, 2009.

Kamerbeek, J. C., "Archilochea," *Mnemosyne* 14 (1961), 1–15.

Kant, Immanuel, *Gesammelte Schriften* (Akademie Ausgabe), 23 vols., Berlin: Reimer/de Gruyter, 1900–.

——, *Political Writings,* H. S. Reiss, ed., Cambridge: Cambridge University Press, 1991.

——, *The Metaphysics of Morals,* M. Gregor, trans., Cambridge: Cambridge University Press, 1996.

——, *Critique of Pure Reason,* Paul Guyer and Allen Wood, trans., Cambridge: Cambridge University Press, 1997.

Kantorowicz, Ernst H., "ΣΥΝΘΡΟΝΟΣ ΔΙΚΗΙ," *American Journal of Archaeology* 57 (1953), 65–70.

——, *The King's Two Bodies: A Study in Mediaeval Political Theology* (1957), Princeton: Princeton University Press, 1997.

Kaufmann, Franz-Xaver, *Sicherheit als soziologisches und sozialpolitisches Problem,* Stuttgart: Enke, 1970.

Kempers, Bram, "Gesetz und Kunst: Ambrogio Lorenzettis Fresken im Palazzo Pubblico in Siena," in *Malerei und Stadtkultur in der Dantezeit: Die Argumentation der Bilder,* H. Belting and D. Blume, eds., Munich: Hirmer, 1989: 71–84.

Kierkegaard, Søren, *Christian Discourses,* W. Lowrie, trans., Princeton: Princeton University Press, 1971.

Kirk, G. S., Raven, J. E., and Schofield, M., eds., *The Presocratic Philosophers,* 2nd ed., Cambridge: Cambridge University Press, 1983.

Kisiel, Theodore, *The Genesis of Heidegger's Being and Time,* Berkeley: University of California Press, 1993.

Kittsteiner, H. D., *Das Komma von SANS, SOUCI.,* Heidelberg: Manutius, 2001.

Kleist, Heinrich von, *Sämtliche Werke und Briefe,* 2 vols., Helmut Sembdner, ed., Munich: Deutscher Taschenbuch Verlag, 2001.

——, *Selected Writings,* David Constantine, trans., Indianapolis: Hackett, 2004.

Klossowski, Pierre, *Nietzsche and the Vicious Circle,* trans. D. W. Smith, Chicago: University of Chicago Press, 1997.

Knight, K. G., "Johann Michael Moscherosch: An Early Baroque Satirist's View of Life," *Modern Language Review* 49 (1954), 29–45.

Knorr, Ortwin, "Horace's Ship Ode (*Odes* 1.14) in Context: A Metaphorical Love-Triangle," *Transactions of the American Philological Association* 136 (2006), 149–69.

Kofman, Sarah, *Nietzsche and Metaphor,* D. Large, trans., Stanford: Stanford University Press, 1993.

Kohut, Heinz, *The Search for the Self: Selected Writings, 1950–1981*, 4 vols., P. H. Ornstein, ed., New York: International Universities Press, 1991.

Kommerell, Max, "Faust und die Sorge," *Goethe-Kalender* 32 (1939), 89–130.

Kopperschmidt, Josef, and Schanze, Helmut, eds., *Nietzsche oder "Die Sprache ist Rhetorik,"* Munich: Fink, 1994.

Kosta, Barbara, "Inscribing Erika: Mother-Daughter Bond/age in Elfriede Jelinek's *Die Klavierspielerin*," *Monatshefte* 86 (1994), 218–34.

Kouvelakis, Stathis, *Philosophy and Revolution: From Kant to Marx*, G. M. Goshgarian, trans., London: Verso, 2003.

Krause, Keith, and Williams, Michael, "Broadening the Agenda of Security Studies: Politics and Methods," *Mershon International Studies Review* 40 (1996), 229–54.

———, eds., *Critical Security Studies: Cases and Concepts*, Minneapolis: University of Minnesota Press, 1997.

Krebs, Christopher, *A Most Dangerous Book: Tacitus's* Germania *from the Roman Empire to the Third Reich*, New York: Norton, 2011.

Kurke, Leslie, *The Traffic in Praise: Pindar and the Poetics of Social Economy*, Ithaca: Cornell University Press, 1991.

Labhardt, André, "*Curiositas*: Notes sur l'histoire d'un mot et d'une notion," *Museum Helveticum* 17 (1960), 206–24.

Lehman, Robert, "Finite Stakes: Toward a Kantian Theory of the Event," *diacritics* 39 (2009), 61–74.

Leibniz, Gottfried Wilhelm, *Werke*, 11 vols., O. Klopp, ed., Hanover: Klindworth, 1864.

———, *Die philosophische Schriften von G. W. Leibniz*, 7 vols., C. I. Gerhardt, ed., Berlin: Weidmann, 1875–90.

———, *Sämtliche Schriften und Briefe*, Akademie der Wissenschaften, ed., Berlin: Akademie Verlag, 1923–.

———, *Philosophical Writings*, G.H.R. Parkinson, ed., London: Everyman, 1973.

———, *Theodicy: Essays on the Goodness of God, the Freedom of Man, and the Origin of Evil*, E. M. Huggard, trans., Chicago: Open Court, 1985.

———, *Political Writings*, P. Riley, ed., Cambridge: Cambridge University Press, 1988.

———, *Discourse on Metaphysics and Other Essays*, D. Garber and R. Ariew, trans., Indianapolis: Hackett, 1991.

Leisner, Andrea, *Zwischen Weltflucht und Herstellungswahn: Bildungstheoretische Studien zur Ambivalenz des Sicherheitsdenkens von der Antike bis zur Gegenwart*, Würzburg: Königshausen & Neumann, 2002.

Lesky, Albin, *Thalatta: Der Weg der Griechen zum Meer*, Vienna: Rohrer, 1947.

Levine, Michael, *Writing through Repression: Literature, Censorship, Psychoanalysis*, Baltimore: Johns Hopkins University Press, 1994.

Lévy, Carlos, *Cicero Academicus: Recherches sur les Académiques et sur la philosophie cicéronienne*, Rome: Ecole française de Rome, 1992.

Littré, Emile, *Dictionnaire de la langue française*, Paris: Hachette, 1884.

Locke, John, *Two Treatises of Government*, Peter Laslett, ed., Cambridge: Cambridge University Press, 1988.

Long, A. A., *From Epicurus to Epictetus: Studies in Hellenistic and Roman Philosophy*, Oxford: Clarendon Press, 2006.

Long, A. A., and Sedley, D. N., eds., *The Hellenistic Philosophers*, 2 vols., Cambridge: Cambridge University Press, 1987.

Lucretius, *De rerum natura*, 3 vols., Cyril Bailey, ed., Oxford: Clarendon Press, 1947.

Luther, Martin, *Werke* (Weimarer Ausgabe), 120 vols., Weimar: Böhlau, 2000.
——, *Luther's Works* (American Edition), 75 vols., J. Pellikan and H. Lehmann, eds., Philadelphia: Fortress, 1955–76.
Machiavelli, Niccolò, *The Prince and the Discourses*, C. Detmold, trans., New York: Modern Library, 1950.
Macrobius, *Saturnalia*, 2 vols., J. Willis, ed., Leipzig: Teubner, 1963.
Malherbe, François de, *Œuvres*, 5 vols., M. L. Lalanne, ed., Paris: Hachette, 1862.
Malkin, Irad, "Postcolonial Concepts and Ancient Greek Colonization," *Modern Language Quarterly* 65 (2004), 341–64.
Masullo, Aldo, "'Sorge': Heideggers Verwandlung von Husserls Intentionalitätsstruktur," in C. Jamme and O. Pöggler, eds., *Phänomenologie im Widerstreit: Zum 50. Todestag Edmund Husserls*, Frankfurt am Main: Suhrkamp, 1989: 234–54.
McCormick, John P., *Carl Schmitt's Critique of Liberalism: Against Politics as Technology*, Cambridge: Cambridge University Press, 1997.
McNeill, John T., *History of the Cure of Souls*, New York: Harper Collins, 1977.
McSweeny, Bill, *Security, Identity and Interests: A Sociology of International Relations*, Cambridge: Cambridge University Press, 1999.
Meier, Heinrich, "The Philosopher as Enemy: On Carl Schmitt's *Glossarium*," M. Brainard, trans., *Graduate Faculty Philosophy Journal, New School for Social Research* 17 (1994), 328–29.
Mendell, Charles, "Horace I.14," *Classical Philology* 33 (1938), 145–56.
Menninghaus, Winfried, "Zwischen Überwältigung und Widerstand: Macht und Gewalt in Longins und Kants Theorien des Erhabenen," *Poetica* 23 (1991), 1–19.
Michelet, Jules, *Journal*, vol. 1: *1828–1848*, P. Viallaneix, ed., Paris: Gallimard, 1959.
——, *La mer*, J. Borie, ed., Paris: Gallimard, 1983.
Migne, J.-P., ed., *Patrologiae cursus completus (Series Latina)*, Paris, 1879–90.
Monahan, Torin, *Surveillance in the Time of Insecurity*, New Brunswick, NJ: Rutgers University Press, 2010.
Moscherosch, Hans Michael, *Insomnis cura parentum* (1643), L. Pariser, ed., Halle: Niemeyer, 1893.
——, *Gesichte Philanders von Sittewald*, part 2 (1665), F. Bobertag, ed., Berlin: Spemann, 1883.
Muellner, Leonard, *The Anger of Achilles: Mēnis in Greek Epic*, Ithaca: Cornell University Press, 1996.
Müller, Herta, *Immer derselbe Schnee und immer derselbe Onkel*, Munich: Hanser, 2011.
Müller, Oliver, *Sorge um die Vernunft: Hans Blumenbergs phänomenologische Anthropologie*, Paderborn: Mentis, 2005.
Nagy, Gregory, "Hesiod," in *Ancient Greek Authors*, T. J. Luce, ed., New York, 1982.
——, *Pindar's Homer: The Lyric Possession of an Epic Past*, Baltimore: Johns Hopkins University Press, 1990.
——, *Greek Mythology and Poetics*, Ithaca: Cornell University Press, 1990.
Neocleous, Mark, *Critique of Security*, Montreal-Kingston: McGill-Queen's University Press, 2008.
Newman, Robert, "Rediscovering the *De Remediis Fortuitorum*," *American Journal of Philology* 109 (1988), 92–107.
Nicholson, Graeme, "The Constitution of Our Being," *American Philosophical Quarterly* 36 (1999), 165–87.
Nickel, Rainer, ed., *Archilochos: Gedichte*, Düsseldorf: Artemis & Winkler, 2003.

Nicolai, Friedrich, *Anekdoten von König Freidrich II von Preussen*, vol. 1, Berlin: Stettin, 1788.

Nietzsche, Friedrich, *Sämtliche Werke, Kritische Studienausgabe*, 15 vols., G. Colli and M. Montinari, eds., Munich: Deutscher Taschenbuch, 1988.

———, *Beyond Good and Evil: Prelude to a Philosophy of the Future*, W. Kaufmann, trans., New York: Vintage, 1966.

———, *The Gay Science*, W. Kaufmann, trans., New York: Vintage, 1974.

———, *Human, All Too Human: A Book for Free Spirits*, R. J. Hollingdale, trans., Cambridge: Cambridge University Press, 1986.

———, *Daybreak: Thoughts on the Prejudices of Morality*, R. J. Hollingdale, trans., Cambridge: Cambridge University Press, 1997.

———, *The Birth of Tragedy and Other Writings*, R. Speirs, trans., Cambridge: Cambridge University Press, 1999.

———, *The Anti-Christ, Ecce Homo, Twilight of the Idols*, J. Norman, trans., Cambridge: Cambridge University Press, 2005.

Norman, Diana, "Pisa, Siena, and the Maremma: A Neglected Aspect of Ambrogio Lorenzetti's Paintings in the Sala dei Nove," *Renaissance Studies* 11 (1997), 310–42.

———, *Siena and the Virgin: Art and Politics in a Late Medieval City State*, New Haven: Yale University Press, 1999.

Norton, David Fate, *David Hume: Common Sense Moralist, Skeptical Metaphysician*, Princeton: Princeton University Press, 1982.

Nussbaum, Martha, *The Therapy of Desire: Theory and Practice in Hellenistic Ethics* (1994), Princeton: Princeton University Press, 2009.

O'Neill, Daniel, "Burke on Democracy and the Death of Western Civilization," *Polity* 36 (2004), 201–25.

Panofsky, Erwin, *Studies in Iconology: Humanistic Themes in the Renaissance*, Oxford: Oxford University Press, 1939.

Paris, Roland, "Human Security: Paradigm Shift or Hot Air?" *International Security* 26 (2001), 87–102.

Pascal, Blaise. *Œuvres complètes*, Louis Lafuma, ed., Paris: Seuil, 1963.

———, *Pensées*, A. J. Krailsheimer, trans., New York: Penguin, 1966.

Pavesich, Vida, "Hans Blumenberg's Philosophical Anthropology: After Heidegger and Cassirer," *Journal of the History of Philosophy* 46 (2008), 421–48.

Pellisson, Paul, and Abbé d'Olivet, *Histoire de l'Académie Française*, 2 vols. (1653/1700), Charles-Louis Livet, ed., Paris: Didier, 1858.

Perrot, Michelle, Foucault, Michel, and Aguilhon, Maurice, eds., *L'impossible prison: Recherches sur le système pénitentiaire au XIXe siècle*, Paris: Seuil, 1980.

Petitier, Paule, "Bords de mer: La pensée de la marge chez Michelet," *Tangence* 57 (1998), 96–110.

Pfeifer, Wolfgang, ed., *Etymologisches Wörterbuch des Deutschen*, Munich: DTV, 1995.

Pippin, Robert, "Modern Mythic Meaning: Blumenberg contra Nietzsche," *History of the Human Sciences* 6 (1993), 37–56.

Plessner, Helmut, *Conditio humana*, G. Dux, O. Marquard, and E. Ströker, eds., Frankfurt am Main: Suhrkamp, 1983.

Pocock, J.G.A., *The Machiavellian Moment: Florentine Political Thought and the Atlantic Republican Tradition* (1975), Princeton: Princeton University Press, 2003.

Pohlenz, Max, *Antikes Führertum: Cicero De Officiis und das Lebensideal des Panaitios*, Leipzig: Teubner, 1934.

———, *Die Stoa: Geschichte einer geistigen Bewegung*, 2 vols., Göttingen: Vandenhoeck & Ruprecht, 1970–72.

Polzer, Joseph, "Ambrogio Lorenzetti's 'Peace and War' Murals Revisited," *Artibus et Historiae* 23 (2002), 63–105.

Popkin, Richard, "David Hume: His Pyrrhonism and His Critique of Pyrrhonism" (1951), in *Hume: A Collection of Critical Essays*, V. C. Chappell, ed., Garden City, NY: Doubleday, 1966.

Potkay, Adam, *The Passion for Happiness: Samuel Johnson & David Hume*, Ithaca: Cornell University Press, 2000.

Purves, Alex, "Unmarked Space: Odysseus and the Inland Journey," *Arethusa* 39 (2006), 1–20.

Race, William, *Style and Rhetoric in Pindar's Odes*, Atlanta: Scholars Press, 1990.

Reich, Warren Thomas, "Sorge in Goethes Faust: Goethe als Moralist," in *Erzählen und Moral: Narrativität im Spannungsfeld von Ethik und Ästhetik*, Tübingen: Attempo, 2000, 143–65.

Reik, Theodor, *Dogma and Compulsion: Psychoanalytic Studies of Religion and Myths*, B. Miall, trans., New York: International Universities Press, 1951.

Reiss, Timothy, "Descartes, the Palatinate, and the Thirty Years War: Political Theory and Political Practice," *Yale French Studies* 80 (1991), 108–45.

———, *Mirages of the Selfe: Patterns of Personhood in Ancient and Early Modern Europe*, Stanford: Stanford University Press, 2003.

Reydams-Schils, Gretchen, *The Roman Stoics: Self, Responsibility, and Affection*, Chicago: University of Chicago Press, 2005.

Richetti, John, *Philosophical Writing: Locke, Berkeley, Hume*, Cambridge, MA: Harvard University Press, 1983.

Riding, Alan, "Behind the Berlin Wall, Listening to Life," *New York Times*, January 7, 2007.

Riley, Patrick, "The Abbé de Saint Pierre and Voltaire on Perpetual Peace in Europe," *World Affairs* 137 (1974–74), 186–94.

Roggenbuck, Simone, "Die genealogische Idee in der vergleichenden Sprachwissenschaft des 19. Jahrhunderts: Stufen, Stammbäume, Wellen," in *Generation: Zur Genealogie des Konzepts—Konzepte von Genealogie*, S. Weigel, O. Parnes, U. Vedder, and S. Willer, eds., Munich: Fink, 2005, 289–314.

Romm, James, *The Edges of the Earth in Ancient Thought: Geography, Exploration and Fiction*, Princeton: Princeton University Press, 1992.

Rosen, Ralph, "Poetry and Sailing in Hesiod's 'Works and Days,'" *Classical Antiquity* 9 (1990), 99–113.

Rosenzweig, Franz, *The Star of Redemption*, W. Hallo, trans., South Bend, IN: University of Notre Dame Press, 1971.

Rowley, George, *Ambrogio Lorenzetti*, 2 vols., Princeton: Princeton University Press, 1958.

Rubenstein, Nicolai, "Political Ideas in Sienese Art: The Frescoes by Ambrogio Lorenzetti and Taddeo di Bartolo in the Palazzo Pubblico," *Journal of the Warburg and Courtauld Institutes* 21 (1958), 179–207.

Ruck, Erwin, *Die Leibniz'sche Staatsidee*, Tübingen: Mohr, 1909; reprint: Darmstadt: Scientia Verlag Aalen, 1987.

Rudhardt, Jean, *Le thème de l'eau primordiale dans la mythologie grecque*, Bern: Francke, 1971.

Said, Edward, *Humanism and Democratic Criticism*, New York: Columbia University Press, 2004.

Saner, Hans, "Die Negativen Bedingungen des Friedens," in *Immanuel Kant: Zum ewigen Frieden*, Otfried Höffe, ed., Berlin: Akademie, 1995, 43–67.

Saussure, Ferdinand de, *Course in General Linguistics*, W. Baskin, trans., New York: Philosophical Library, 1959.

Scaff, Lawrence, *Fleeing the Iron Cage: Culture, Politics, and Modernity in the Thought of Max Weber*, Berkeley: University of California Press, 1989.

Scheffler, S., ed., *Consequentialism and Its Critics*, Oxford: Oxford University Press, 1988.

Scheler, Max, *Die Stellung des Menschen im Kosmos* (1928), Bonn: Bouvier, 1988.

——, *Man's Place in Nature*, Hans Meyerhoff, trans., New York: Noonday Press, 1961.

Schenk, Gerrit Jasper, "*Human Security* in the Renaissance? Securitas, Infrastructure, Collective Goods, and Natural Hazards in Tuscany and the Upper Rhine Valley," in *The Production of Human Security in Premodern and Contemporary History*, C. Zwierlein, R. Graf, and M. Ressel, eds., special issue of *Historical Social Research / Historische Sozialforschung* 35 (2010), 209–33.

Schestag, Thomas, "Philology, Knowledge," N. F. Schott, trans., *Telos* 140 (2007), 28–44.

Schevill, Ferdinand, *Siena: The History of a Mediaeval Commune*, New York: Scribner, 1909.

Schmidt, Gary, "Between Authors and Agents: Gender and Affirmative Culture in *Das Leben der Anderen*," *German Quarterly* 82 (2009), 231–49.

Schmitt, Carl, *Der Begriff des Politischen* (1932), Berlin: Duncker & Humblot, 1963.

——, *Ex captivitate salus* (1950), Berlin: Duncker & Humblot, 2002.

——, *Political Romanticism*, G. Oakes, trans., Cambridge, MA: MIT Press, 1986.

——, *Glossarium: Aufzeichnungen der Jahre 1947–1951*, E. Freiherr von Medem, ed., Berlin: Duncker & Humblot, 1991.

——, *The Concept of the Political*, M. Konzett and J. McCormick, trans., Chicago: University of Chicago Press, 1996.

Schneier, Bruce, *Beyond Fear: Thinking Sensibly about Security in an Uncertain World*, New York: Copernicus, 2003.

Schofield, Malcom, *Saving the City: Philosopher Kings and Other Classical Paradigms*, New York: Routledge, 1999.

Schrecker, Paul, "Leibniz's Principles of International Justice," *Journal of the History of Ideas* 7 (1946), 484–98.

Schrimm-Heins, Andrea, "Gewißheit und Sicherheit: Geschichte und Bedeutungswandel der Begriffe certitudo und securitas," *Archiv für Begriffsgeschichte* 34 (1991), 123–213 and 138–39.

Sevenhuijsen, Selma, *Citizenship and the Ethics of Care*, L. Savage, trans., New York: Routledge, 1998.

Shell, Susan Meld, "Bowling Alone: On the Saving Power of Kant's Perpetual Peace," *Idealistic Studies* 26 (1996), 153–73.

——, "Cannibals All: The Grave Wit of Kant's Perpetual Peace," in *Violence, Identity, and Self-Determination*, Samuel Weber and Hent de Vries, eds., Stanford: Stanford University Press, 1997, 150–61.

Simpson, J. A., and Weiner, E.S.C., eds. *The Oxford English Dictionary*, 20 vols., Oxford: Clarendon Press, 1989.

Skinner, Quentin, "Ambrogio Lorenzetti: The Artist as Political Philosopher," *Proceedings of the British Academy* 72 (1986), 1–56.

——, "Ambrogio Lorenzetti's Buon Governo Frescoes: Two Old Questions, Two New Answers," *Journal of the Warburg and Courtauld Institutes* 62 (1999), 1–28.

Snell, Bruno, *The Discovery of the Mind in Greek Philosophy and Literature*, T. G. Rosenmeyer, trans., New York: Dover, 1982.

Snyder, Verne, "Kafka's 'Burrow': A Speculative Analysis," *Twentieth Century Literature* 27 (1981), 113–26.

Soja, Edward W., "The Socio-Spatial Dialectic," *Annals of the Association of American Geographers* 70 (1980), 207–25.

Sorabji, Richard, *Emotion and Peace of Mind: From Stoic Agitation to Christian Temptation*, Oxford: Oxford University Press, 2000.

Starn, Randolph, "The Republican Regime of the 'Room of Peace' in Siena, 1338–1340," *Representations* 18 (1987), 1–32.

Stein, Mary Beth, "Stasi with a Human Face? Ambiguity in *Das Leben der Anderen*," *German Studies Review* 31 (2008), 567–79.

Steiner, George, *Martin Heidegger*, 2nd ed.: Chicago: University of Chicago Press, 1987.

Stöcklein, Paul, "Fausts Kampf mit der Sorge," *Dichtung und Volkstum* 44 (1944), 52–78.

Streicher, Jeanne, *Commentaires sur les Remarques de Vaugelas*, 2 vols., Paris: Droz, 1936.

Stubblebine, James, "French Gothic Elements in Simone Martini's *Maestà*," *Gesta* 29 (1990), 139–52.

Szondi, Peter, *Schriften*, 2 vols., J. Bollack et al., eds., Frankfurt am Main: Suhrkamp, 1978.

——, *On Textual Understanding and Other Essays*, H. Mendelsohn, trans., Minneapolis: University of Minnesota Press, 1986.

Tasinato, Maria, *Sulla curiosità: Apuleio e Agostino*, Parma: Pratiche, 1994.

Taubhorn, Ingo, "Ein Forum junger Fotografie," in *Balanceakt Sicherheit*, Ingo Taubhorn, ed., Hamburg: Körber Stiftung, 2007, 8–9.

Theunissen, Michael, *Pindar: Menschenlos und Wende der Zeit*, Munich: Beck, 2000.

Thomas, Keith, *Religion and the Decline of Magic*, New York: Scribner, 1971.

Torigian, Catherine, "The Λόγος of Caesar's *Bellum Gallicum*, especially as Revealed in Its First Five Chapters," in *Julius Caesar as Artful Reporter*, K. Welch and A. Powell, eds., London: Duckworth, 1998, 45–60.

Trojanow, Ilija, and Zeh, Juli, *Angriff auf die Freiheit: Sicherheitswahn, Überwachungsstaat und der Abbau bürgerlicher Rechte*, Munich: Hanser, 2009.

Tronto, Joan, *Moral Boundaries: A Political Argument for an Ethic of Care*, New York: Routledge, 1993.

Turnquist, Gary, "The Pillars of Hercules Revisited," *Bulletin of the American Schools of Oriental Research* 216 (1974), 13–15.

Tuve, Rosemond, "Notes on the Virtues and Vices," *Journal of the Warburg and Courtauld Institutes* 26 (1963), 264–303.

Vaugelas, Claude Favre de, *Remarques sur la langue françoise vtiles à ceux qui veulent bien parler et bien escrire*, Paris, 1647 ; facsimile reprint, J. Streicher, ed., Paris, 1934.

——, *Remarques sur la langue françoise*, Zygmunt Marzys ed., Geneva: Droz, 2009.

Vico, Giambattista, *La scienza nuova*, Paolo Rossi, ed., Milan: Rizzoli, 1977.

——, *New Science*, D. Marsh, trans., New York: Penguin, 1999.

Voltaire, Œuvres, C. Palissot de Montenoy, ed., Basel, 1792.
——, Œuvres complètes, 52 vols., L. Moland, ed., Paris: Garnier, 1877–85.
——, Romans et contes, J. Lupin, ed., Paris: Gallimard, 1972.
——, Candide and Other Stories, R. Pearson, trans., Oxford: Oxford World Classics, 1998.
Wade, Ira, Voltaire and Candide: A Study in the Fusion of History, Art, and Philosophy, Princeton: Princeton University Press, 1959.
Waever, Ole, "Securitization and Desecuritization," in On Security, R. Lipschutz, ed., New York: Columbia University Press, 1995, 46–86.
Walde, Alois, Lateinisches etymologisches Wörterbuch, Heidelberg: Winter, 1910.
Waldron, Jeremy, "Security and Liberty: The Image of Balance," Journal of Political Philosophy 11 (2003), 191–210.
Walker, Robert, "Polis, Cosmopolis, Politics," Alternatives 28 (2003), 267–86.
Watson, Richard, Cogito, Ergo Sum: The Life of René Descartes, Boston: Godine, 2002.
Weber, Max, The Protestant Ethic and the Spirit of Capitalism, P. Baehr and G. C. Wells, trans., New York: Penguin, 2002.
Weber, Samuel, Targets of Opportunity: On the Militarization of Thinking, New York: Fordham University Press, 2005.
Weinrich, Harald, "Literaturgeschichte eines Weltereignisses: Das Erdbeben von Lissabon," in Weinrich, Literatur für Leser, Stuttgart: Kohlhammer, 1971, 64–76.
Weinstock, Stefan, "Pax and the 'Ara Pacis,'" Journal of Roman Studies 50 (1960), 44–58.
Weldes, J., Laffey, M., Gusterson, H., and Duvall, R., eds. Cultures of Insecurity: States, Communities, and the Production of Danger, Minneapolis: University of Minnesota Press, 1999.
West, Martin, ed., Iambi et elegi Graeci ante Alexandrum cantati, vol. 1, Oxford: Oxford University Press, 1989.
Wetz, Franz Josef, "The Phenomenological Anthropology of Hans Blumenberg," Iris 1 (2009), 389–414.
White, Nicholas, "The Basis of Stoic Ethics," Harvard Studies in Classical Philology 83 (1979), 143–78.
Wiegand, Hermann, "Franz Kafka's 'The Burrow' ('Der Bau'): An Analytical Essay," PMLA 7 (1972), 152–66.
Wieseler, Friedrich, "Poseidon Asphaleios," Nachrichten von der Königlichen Gesellschaft der Wissenschaften und der G. A. Universität zu Göttingen 7 (1874), 153–60.
Williams, John, "The Authorship of the Moralium Dogma Philosophorum," Speculum 6 (1931), 392–411.
Winkler, Emil, "Sécurité," Abhandlungen der Preußischen Akademie der Wissenschaften (Philosophisch-historische Klasse) 10 (1939), 2–20.
Winnicott, Donald, Playing and Reality, New York: Basic Books, 1971.
Wolin, Richard, "Carl Schmitt: The Conservative Revolutionary Habitus and the Aesthetics of Horror," Political Theory 20 (1992), 424–47.
Wulf, Steven, "The Skeptical Life in Hume's Political Thought," Polity 33 (2000), 77–99.
Wyn Jones, Richard, Security, Strategy, and Critical Theory, Boulder: Lynne Rienner, 1999.
Žižek, Slavoj, The Indivisible Remainder (1996), London: Verso, 2007.
Zupančič, Alenka, "Enthusiasm, Anxiety and the Event," Parallax 11 (2005), 31–45.

Index

akēdia (*acedia*), 12, 60–63
Adorno, Theodor, 16, 44–45, 259
Agamben, Giorgio, 38, 176–77
Alcibiades, 55
Althusser, Louis, 180
ameleia, 12, 118
Amelēs (river), 12
Anaximander, 89
Andry, Nicholas, 188
apatheia, 12, 51–54, 59, 62, 121, 147, 150, 220, 234, 289
Appian, *Civil Wars*, 108
Apter, Emily, 21
Apuleius, 76
Aquinas, Thomas, *Summa Theologica*, 147n8, 153n18, 158
Archilochus, 105–8, 145, 264, 273
Archippus, 102
Arendt, Hannah, 40, 159, 178, 254
Aristotle, 147, 150, 158, 225, 267; *Eudemian Ethics*, 148; *Nichomachean Ethics*, 125, 148–49, 153n18; *Politics*, 105; *Rhetoric*, 85
Arminius, 236
Arnauld, Antoine, 202
Arquilla, John, 37
askēsis, 12, 46, 248
asphaleia, 12, 58–60, 64, 105–8, 113, 131, 147, 231, 251, 264, 267, 273–74
ataraxia, 12, 51–53, 59, 63, 81, 102, 104, 130, 179, 194, 212, 241, 242
Augustine, 199, 219; *Commentaries on the Psalms*, 265; *Confessions*, 62–63, 213–14, 265–67, 273–74; *De Civitate Dei*, 63, 192; *De doctrina christiana*, 265; *De sancta virginitate*, 266–67; *Homily on the First Epistle of John*, 266
Augustus (Octavian), 59, 108, 117, 129n27, 132, 187
Ausonius, *Eclogues,* 196, 198–200
autoimmunity, 36–41, 44–45, 248

Bacon, Francis, 225; *Instauratio magna,* 221
Bacon, Roger, *Opus maius,* 146

Baillet, Adrien, 199
Bataille, Georges, 39n31
Baudelaire, Charles, 60
Baudrillard, Jean, 29–30
Baeumler, Alfred, 254
Beethoven, Ludwig van, 290
Behne, Adolf, 278
Benjamin, Walter, "Franz Kafka," 27, 40, 46; *Passagen-Werk* [*Arcades Project*], 278–79
Bentham, Jeremy, 160
Bentinck, Charlotte-Sophie, 218
Benveniste, Émile, 86–87
Bergk, Theodor, 107
Berman, Marshall, 272
Bernard of Clairvaux, 151, 161, 162, 167
Bernardino of Siena, Saint, 168–74, 194
Bernoulli, Jakob, 202
Bertram, Ernst, *Nietzsche: Versuch einer Mythologie,* 253
Bible
—Genesis: *1:26,* 69; *2:19–20,* 73; *5:3,* 70; *6:14,* 60
—Ezekiel *34:11–16,* 79
—Job *7:1,* 266
—Matthew: *6:24–34,* 269n26; *14:22–33,* 243; *18:12–14,* 80; *25:35,* 151
—Luke *1:3,* 251
—John: *10:11–18,* 79; *10:27–30,* 79–80
—Acts of the Apostles *14:22,* 193–94
—Philippians *2:12,* 282
—1 Thessalonians *5:3–8,* 194–95
—1 Peter *2:13–14,* 193
—1 John, 266
—Revelation: *13:1,* 170; *21:1,* 168, 170
Bigo, Didier, 43
biopolitics, 44, 45, 81, 177, 254
biopower, 42, 45, 177, 297
Blumenberg, Hans: "An Anthropological Approach to the Contemporary Signifi-cance of Rhetoric," 257–58, 260; *Das Lachen der Thrakerin,* 261; *Die Sorge geht über den Fluß* [*Care Crosses the River*], 70–71, 72, 269; *Shipwreck with Spectator,* 101–2, 104, 214, 260; *Work on Myth,* 258–61

Bodin, Jean, 200, 283
Booth, Ken, 9, 14
Brecht, Bertolt, *Der gute Mensch von Sezuan*, 289; "Erinnerung an die Marie A.," 288
Burdach, Konrad, 268, 270
Burke, Anthony, 8
Burke, Edmund, *Philosophical Enquiry into the Origin of Our Ideas of the Sublime and the Beautiful*, 234, 241
Burton, Robert, *The Anatomy of Melancholy*, 63
Bush, George W., 33
Butler, Judith, 33–34
Buzan, Barry, 15
Bynum, Caroline Walker, 160–61

Caesar, Julius, 114; *Bellum Gallicum*, 187–88
Canetti, Elias, *Die Blendung*, 225
care, etymology of, 78, 267
Carneades, 175
Cassirer, Ernst, 258
Cato the Younger, 123
Chapman, George, *Eastward Hoe*, 64
Châtelet, Émilie du, *Institutions de physique*, 208
Chrysippus, 56n10, 117, 124, 175
Cicero, 51, 56, 58, 59, 65, 157, 173, 185, 188, 194, 198, 202, 215, 274, 282; *De amicitia*, 61–62; *De finibus*, 55–56, 115, 127; *De inventione*, 158; *De legibus*, 59; *De natura deorum*, 213; *De officiis*, 51–52, 55, 114–24, 125–26, 127, 130, 146, 147, 149–50, 174–76, 197, 281; *De oratore*, 122; *Letters to Atticus*, 102, 114, 213; *Philippics*, 119, 176; *Pro Murena*, 123; *Tusculanae Disputationes*, 53, 115, 121, 123–24
Cleanthes, 56n10, 117
Columella, *De re rustica*, 75
Copenhagen School (Security Studies), 14n10, 15
Cotta, Johann Friedrich, 231
Crassus, 114
Cratippus, 117, 119, 126
Crépon, Marc, 67, 284n1
critical security theory, 15–16
cura, 9–12, 25, 27, 46, 51, 52, 54, 58, 60–62, 65, 74–80, 82, 85, 103–4, 106, 114, 120–21, 127–33, 161–62, 188–90, 194–95, 197, 199–200, 209, 212–14, 218–20, 222–23, 229, 249–50, 261, 265–67, 271, 273, 282,

286, 289–90, 291, 300; Cura, personification of, 3–6, 68–73, 76, 130, 132, 161, 268–69, 272; *cura animarum* [care of souls], 78, 81; *cura sui* [care of the self], 43, 54, 56–57, 72, 81, 185, 188
Cuvier, Georges, 239
Cyran, Eberhard, 217

Damascius, 89
Dante Alighieri, *De monarchia*, 192
d'Argens, Marquis, 216
Defoe, Daniel, *Robinson Crusoe*, 240
Deleuze, Gilles, 91–92
Delumeau, Jean, 189
de Man, Paul, 22
Democritus, 12, 55, 102, 127
Der Derian, James, 16, 18–20
De remediis fortuitorum. See *Moralium Dogma Philosophorum*
Derrida, Jacques, 38–39, 277
Descartes, René, 54, 199, 200, 202, 210, 221; *Discourse on Method*, 197–98; *Meditations*, 196–97, 269; *Passions de l'âme*, 189n15
de Wilde, Jaap, 15
Dillon, Michael, 16–17, 19–20, 180–81, 262–63
Dilthey, Wilhelm, 259
Diogenes Laertius, 84, 118, 122, 125, 176
Domitian, 58
Donnersmarck, Florian Henckel von, *Das Leben der Anderen* [*The Lives of Others*], 285–92, 298
Duccio di Buoninsegna, 163–64
Dupleix, Scipion, 188

Edict of Caracalla, 151, 166
Eldagsen, Boris, 292–98
Enfants sans Souci, Les, 216
Ensler, Eve, 28
Epicureanism, 12, 46, 53, 60, 63, 82, 102–5, 184, 194, 212–13, 216, 218, 241–42
Epicurus, 46, 81–82, 102, 214, 243; *Letter to Menoeceus*, 53; *Principle Doctrines*, 60; *Vatican Sayings*, 60
epimeleia, 12, 46, 54, 261; Epimeleia (personification), 22
Epimetheus, 21, 246
Esposito, Roberto, 39–40, 45, 163n44, 177, 248

Esther, John, 289
ethics of care, 32–34
euthymia, 12, 55–58, 127

Falaiseau, Pierre de, 206
Fermat, Pierre de, 202
Fichte, Johann Gottlieb, *Addresses to the German Nation*, 235–37
First Council of Nicaea, 166
Flaubert, Gustave, 277
Foucault, Michel, 41–45, 54, 57n11, 72, 80–81, 87–88, 160, 276
Fourth Lateran Council, 78–79
Franciscan Observants, 172
Fränkel, Hermann, 108
Franklin, Benjamin, 289, 291
Frederick II, Holy Roman Emperor, 163
Frederick V, Elector Palatine, 198–99
Frederick the Great, 216–18; *Anti-Machiavel*, 215
Freud, Sigmund, 37, 70, 259; *Civilization and Its Discontents*, 256; *The Future of an Illusion*, 164–65
Fromm, Erich, *The Dogma of Christ*, 165–67
Front Islamique du Salut (Algeria), 38
Furetière, Antoine, 189–90

Galileo Galilei, 210
Galinsky, Karl, 123
Gedeck, Martina, 285
Gehlen, Arnold, 257–58
Gelasius I, Pope, 192
Geneva Convention, 38
George, Stefan, 253
Gilgamesh, Epic of, 91
Gill, Christopher, 115n2, 125n20, 126
Gilligan, Carol, 32–33
Goethe, Johann Wolfgang, *Faust*, 131, 268, 269–73; *Pandora*, 22
Gorky, Maxim, 290
Gossman, Lionel, 239n3, 241–42
governmentality, 43, 80
Gregory the Great, Pope, 63, 172; *Moralia*, 267
Grimarest, Jean-Léonor Le Gallois de, 229
Grimmelshausen, Hans Jacob Christoffel von, *Simplicissimus Teutsch*, 186
Grotius, Hugo, 200

Guantánamo Bay, 38
Guattari, Félix, 91–92

Hamacher, Werner, 23–24, 231
Hecaton of Rhodes, 174–76
Hegel, Georg Wilhelm Friedrich, 255, 264
Heidegger, Martin, 17–18, 219, 225, 259, 278, 281; *Holzwege*, 262; *Parmenides*, 263–64; *Phenomenology of Religious Life*, 264–67, 273; "The Question concerning Technology," 262–63, 271; *Sein und Zeit* [*Being and Time*], 72, 268–69, 273
Heine, Heinrich, 224–26
Henry IV, King of France, 203, 204
Herder, Johann Gottfried, 236, 256; "Das Kind der Sorge," 268
Herodotus, 60, 87, 108
Hesiod, *Theogony*, 89–90, 94, 99; *Works and Days*, 95–101, 112, 113, 130
Hirschel, Abraham, 218
Hobbes, Thomas, 14, 40, 46, 59, 64–65, 69, 145, 159–60, 200, 204–6, 213, 222, 234, 248, 256, 258, 274, 283, 297; *De cive*, 67; *Leviathan*, 65–67, 200
Hölderlin, Friedrich, 255, 269
Homer, 55, 125, 147, 244; *Iliad*, 107–8, 124, 245; *Odyssey*, 60, 70, 84, 94, 109–13
Horace, 133, 289; *Odes 1.1*, 131; *1.3*, 85; *1.14*, 128–29; *1.26*, 131; *3.1*, 130–32, 271; *3.30*, 47, 132
Horkheimer, Max, 16, 44–45, 259
Horn, Eva, 285
Hugo, Victor, 238
human security, 13, 14, 208
Hume, David, *Enquiry concerning Human Understanding*, 280–21, 223; *Essays, Moral, Political, and Literary*, 160, 222; *Treatise of Human Nature*, 220–23
Husserl, Edmund, 265, 267
Hutcheson, Frances, 223
Hyginus, 132; *Fabulae*, 3–6, 68–74, 104, 216, 268–69, 272

Jelinek, Elfriede, *Die Klavierspielerin* [*The Piano Teacher*], 30–31, 40
Jerome, Saint, 63
Johnson, Barbara, 23
Jonson, Ben, *Eastward Hoe*, 64
Jünger, Ernst, 278

Kafka, Franz, 40, 298; *Der Bau* ["The Burrow"], 25–28, 29, 30, 41, 46, 47; *Hungerkünstler* ["Hunger Artist"], 46; *In der Strafkolonie* ["In the Penal Colony"], 30, 31; "Jubilee Report for the Workmen's Accident Insurance Institute," 26; Letter to Max Brod, 46–47; "Poseidon," 274
Kant, Immanuel, 33, 210, 220, 224, 237, 248; *The Contest of the Faculties*, 232–35; *Critique of the Power of Judgment*, 232; *Critique of Pure Reason*, 91–92, 225, 228; *Metaphysics of Morals*, 176–77; *On Perpetual Peace*, 226–29, 235, 239; "What Is Enlightenment?" 23–24
Kaufmann, Franz-Xaver, 137, 198
kēdos, 12, 63, 78, 97
KGB, 31, 67
Kierkegaard, Søren, 269n26, 273, 282
Kittsteiner, H. D., 217
Klages, Ludwig, 253
Kleinert, Volkmar, 287
Kleist, Heinrich von, *Das Erdbeben in Chili* ["The Earthquake in Chile"], 230–32, 235
Klossowski, Pierre, 249
Koch, Sebastian, 285
Kohut, Heinz, 30–31
Kosmikerkreis, der [Cosmic Circle], 253

Lactantius, *De ira*, 124
Lamarck, Jean-Baptiste, 239
Leibniz, Gottfried Wilhelm, 201–7, 210, 229, 247, 260; *Monadology*, 205–6; *Theodicy*, 205–9; Letters to: Abbé de Saint Pierre, 203–4; Antoine Arnauld, 202; Pierre de Falaiseau, 206; Thomas Hobbes, 204–5
Lenin, Vladimir, 289–90
Lennon, John, 289–90
Lesky, Albin, 85–86, 89n14
lēthē, 12
Levine, Michael, 47n50
Lévy, Carlos, 126
Littré, Émile, 189
Livy, 178
Locke, John, 14, 160
Lorenzetti, Ambrogio, 138–46, 150–64, 168–74, 283
Lucari, Buonaguida, 163
Lucretius, *De rerum natura*, 60, 101–4, 106, 114, 211–13, 234, 242, 263
Lukács, Georg, 278

Luther, Martin, 64–65, 190–96, 201, 202, 217, 220, 251, 267, 275, 277, 282; *Von weltlicher Obrigkeit* ["On Temporal Authority"], 191–93

Machiavelli, Niccolò, 44, 160, 202, 249, 280; *Discourses of Livy*, 178–81, 280; *The Prince*, 178, 280
Macrobius, *Commentary on the Dream of Scipio*, 146–47, 149; *Saturnalia*, 109n48
Malherbe, François de, 183–85
Manfred of Sicily, 163
Marcus Aurelius, 116
Mark Antony, 115, 117, 129n27, 176
Marsilius of Padua, *Defensor Pacis*, 192
Marston, John, *Eastward Hoe*, 64
Martial, *Epigrams*, 182
Martini, Simone, 163–64
Marx, Karl, 29, 279
Maupertuis, Pierre Louis Moreau de, 218
Mehring, Franz, 253
meletē, 12, 75
Melville, Herman, 91
mercanti scrittori (merchant writers), 173
Michelet, Jules, 238–45, 249; *Histoire de France*, 229, 244; *Histoire de la Révolution*, 239; *La mer*, 239–42; *Le people*, 238
Mill, John Stuart, 14
Ministry for State Security [The Stasi] (German Democratic Republic), 31, 67, 284–86, 288, 290, 293
Monahan, Torin, 35
Montauri, Paolo di Tommaso, 163
Moralium Dogma Philosophorum, 146–47, 149–52
Moscherosch, Michael, *Insomnis cura parentum*, 195–96
Mühe, Ulrich, 285
Müller, Herta, "Jedes Wort weiß etwas vom Teufelskreis" [Every Word Knows Something about the Vicious Circle], 31–32, 41, 42
Müller, Oliver, 261

Nagy, Gregory, 88n12, 100n30, 112n54, 113
Napoléon III (Louis-Napoléon Bonaparte), 238, 242
Neocleous, Mark, 15
Nero, 58

Nerva, 58–59
Nietzsche, Friedrich, 16–17, 18, 245–46, 253, 279; *Die fröhliche Wissenschaft* [*The Gay Science*], 17, 245, 248–51; *Ecce Homo*, 249–52; *Götzen-Dämmerung* [*Twilight of the Idols*], 19–20; *Jenseits von Gut und Böse* [*Beyond Good and Evil*], 252, 254–55; *Menschliches, Allzumenschliches* [*Human, All Too Human*], 46, 253; *Morgenröte* [*Daybreak*], 12–13, 21–22, 245–47; *Ueber Wahrheit und Lüge im aussermoralischen Sinne* ["On Truth and Lying in a Non-Moral Sense"], 245, 260
Nissen, Adolph, *Das Iustitium*, 176
Nussbaum, Martha, 46

orexis, 46
Orwell, George, 160, 285, 289
Ovid, 221; *Ars amatoria*, 75, 132; *Ex ponto*, 132, 218–19; *Medicamina facei feminae*, 75; *Metamorphoses*, 69, 132–33; *Tristia*, 132–33

Panaetius of Rhodes, 117, 119
Patru, Olivier, 188
Pascal, Blaise, 36, 202
Pastior, Oskar, 32
pastoral care, 43, 79–81
Pausanias, 93, 108, 110
pax, 137, 153–57, 164, 194, 229
Peace of Westphalia, 200, 201, 209
Petrarch, *De remediis utriusque fortunae*, 146
philosophical anthropology, 3, 255–58
Pindar: *Olympian 1*, 84; *Olympian 2*, 71n9; *Olympian 3*, 88–89
Pittacus of Mytilene, 84
Plato, 55, 59, 123, 124, 125–26, 147, 264, 266, 273; *Alcibiades*, 55; *Laches*, 148; *Republic*, 12, 55, 56–57, 126–27, 148; *Symposium*, 94; *Timaeus*, 55–56
Plautus, *Asinaria*, 66, 256
Plessner, Helmuth, 255–56, 257n42; *Die Stufen des Organischen und der Mensch* [The Stages of the Organic and Man], 255
Plutarch, *De Iside et Osiride*, 71n9
Polybius, 180
Pompeius, Sextus, 108–9
Pompey (Gnaeus Pompeius Magnus), 114
Pope, Alexander, *Essay on Man*, 211

Priscian, 69
Prometheus, 21, 22, 27, 69, 72, 96n25, 246
Propertius, 75n14

Quarles, Francis, *Enchyridion*, 190
Quinet, Edgar, 238
Quintilian, *Institutio oratoria*, 61, 63, 74, 75, 128–29

RAND Corporation, 37
Reiss, Timothy, 198–99
Ronfeldt, David, 37
Roosevelt, Franklin Delano, 276
Rousseau, Jean-Jacques, 90
Rubenstein, Nicolai, 153

Said, Edward, 21
Saint-Hilaire, Geoffroy, 239
Saint Pierre, Abbé de, *Project for Perpetual Peace*, 203–4, 229
salus, 51, 59, 65, 127, 137, 187, 188, 189, 195, 274, 281, 283
Sartre, Jean-Paul, 269
Saussure, Ferdinand de, 14
Schadewaldt, Wolfgang, 107
Scheler, Max, *Die Stellung des Menschen im Kosmos* [*Man's Place in Nature*], 255–56, 257n42
Schevill, Ferdinand, 165
Schlegel, Friedrich, 226
Schmitt, Carl, 42, 274; *The Concept of the Political*, 281n51, 282; *Ex captivitate salus*, 283; *Glossarium*, 275–83; *Land and Sea*, 86; *Political Romanticism*, 279, 280n48
Schneier, Bruce, 9
Schuler, Alfred, 253
Scipio Aemilianus, 117
Securitate (Romania), 31
securitization, 13, 15–16, 20, 64, 67, 160, 208, 260
security paradox, 9
Seneca, Lucius Annaeus, 56, 116, 124, 146–47, 150, 194, 202, 289; *De beneficiis*, 61, 146, 184–85; *De clementia*, 59; *De otio*, 150n13; *Epistles*, 53–55, 72, 185; *Natural Questions*, 109n47
Shakespeare, William: *Hamlet*, 270; *Macbeth*, 64

Shell, Susan, 228n12, 229
Sicherheitswahn [Security Madness], 34–35
Socrates, 55, 56, 94, 126–27, 148–49
Soja, Edward, 90
Solon, 99
Sophocles: Antigone, 60, 85; Oedipus at
    Colonus, 89n13; Oedipus Tyrannus
    [Oedipus the King], 17, 57–58, 59, 60
Sorge, 27, 46, 78, 131, 219, 257, 261, 262–74
Sorabji, Richard, 126
Spengler, Oswald, 264
Sphaerus, 117
Steiner, George, 269
Stoicism, 12, 46, 53, 55, 56–59, 61, 72, 115,
    116–19, 121–26, 133, 147. 150, 174–76,
    184–85, 194, 202, 220, 223, 282, 289
Strabo, Geography, 87, 108
Szondi, Peter, 22

Tacitus, 235; Agricola, 58–59; Germania, 236
Taubhorn, Ingo, 290–91
Terence, Phormio, 76
Thieme, Thomas, 286
Thiers, Adolphe, 238
Thucydides, 59, 64, 109
thymos, 55–57, 106, 121–22, 124–27, 148, 273
Tibullus, 75
Tocqueville, Alexis de, 238
Trajan, 58–59

Varro, De lingua latina, 74, 76, 273
Vaugelas, Claude Favre de, 182–90
Velleius Paterculus, Historiae Romanae, 58
Vergil, 85; Aeneid, 75, 77, 92, 170, 271
Vettori, Francesco, 179
Vico, Giambattista, La scienza nuova, 158
Villani, Giovanni, 173
Vincent of Beauvais, Speculum historiale, 146
Voiture, Vincent, 182
Voltaire, Candide, 207–14, 215–18, 219, 222,
    252; "Natural Law and Curiosity," 213–14;
    Philosophical Dictionary, 212; Poem on the
    Lisbon Disaster, 210–12; Zadig, 214

Waever, Ole, 15
Weber, Max, 29; The Protestant Ethic and the
    Spirit of Capitalism, 277–80
Weber, Samuel, 37–38, 231
West, Martin, 106
Wilhelmine, Princess of Prussia, 216
William of Conches, 146
Winkler, Emil, 187
Winnicott, Donald, 8–9
Wollstonecraft, Mary, "An Allegory," 299–300

Zeno of Citium, 56n10, 117–19, 123, 175, 179
Žižek, Slavoj, 24
Zola, Émile, Germinal, 17

Writing Outside the Nation by Azade Seyhan

The Literary Channel: The Inter-National Invention of the Novel edited by Margaret Cohen and Carolyn Dever

Ambassadors of Culture: The Transamerican Origins of Latino Writing by Kirsten Silva Gruesz

Experimental Nations: Or, the Invention of the Maghreb by Réda Bensmaïa

What Is World Literature? by David Damrosch

The Portable Bunyan: A Transnational History of "The Pilgrim's Progress" by Isabel Hofmeyr

We the People of Europe? Reflections on Transnational Citizenship by Étienne Balibar

Nation, Language, and the Ethics of Translation edited by Sandra Bermann and Michael Wood

Utopian Generations: The Political Horizon of Twentieth-Century Literature by Nicholas Brown

Guru English: South Asian Religion in a Cosmopolitan Language by Srinivas Aravamudan

Poetry of the Revolution: Marx, Manifestos, and the Avant-Gardes by Martin Puchner

The Translation Zone: A New Comparative Literature by Emily Apter

In Spite of Partition: Jews, Arabs, and the Limits of Separatist Imagination by Gil Z. Hochberg

The Princeton Sourcebook in Comparative Literature: From the European Enlightenment to the Global Present edited by David Damrosch, Natalie Melas, and Mbongiseni Buthelezi

The Spread of Novels: Translation and Prose Fiction in the Eighteenth Century by Mary Helen McMurran

The Event of Postcolonial Shame by Timothy Bewes

The Novel and the Sea by Margaret Cohen

Hamlet's Arab Journey: Shakespeare's Prince and Nasser's Ghost by Margaret Litvin

Archives of Authority by Andrew N. Rubin

Security: Politics, Humanity, and the Philology of Care by John T. Hamilton

GPSR Authorized Representative: Easy Access System Europe - Mustamäe tee
50, 10621 Tallinn, Estonia, gpsr.requests@easproject.com